Doctor Who
and Philosophy

Popular Culture and Philosophy®
Series Editor: George A. Reisch

For full details of all Popular Culture and Philosophy® books, visit www.opencourtbooks.com.

Popular Culture and Philosophy®

Doctor Who and Philosophy

Bigger on the Inside

Edited by
COURTLAND LEWIS
and
PAULA SMITHKA

OPEN COURT
Chicago and La Salle, Illinois

Volume 55 in the series, Popular Culture and Philosophy®, edited by George A. Reisch

To order books from Open Court, call toll-free 1-800-815-2280, or visit our website at www.opencourtbooks.com.

Open Court Publishing Company is a division of Carus Publishing Company.

Back cover illustration, courtesy of Tara Wheeler, http://wittylittleknitter.com

Library of Congress Cataloging-in-Publication Data

Doctor Who and philosophy : bigger on the inside / edited by Courtland Lewis and Paula Smithka.
     p. cm. — (Popular culture and philosophy ; v. 55)
   Includes bibliographical references and index.
   ISBN 978-0-8126-9688-2 (trade paper : alk. paper)
   1. Doctor Who (Television program : 1963-1989) I. Lewis, Courtland, 1977- II. Smithka, Paula J.
   PN1992.77.D6273D62 2010
   791.45'72—dc22

                                      2010038619

Contents

EPISODE 3:

It's a Different Morality; Get Used to It, or Go Home!

The Ethics of Doctor Who

EPISODE 4:

Human Beings, You're Amazing; Apart From that, You're Completely Mad

What the Doctor Teaches Us about Existence

EPISODE 5:

Brilliant! Fantastic! Molto Bene!

Aesthetics in Doctor Who

EPISODE 6:
Lots of Planets Have a North!
Human and Time Lord Culture   337

We've Been Abducted by the Doctor, and We Love It!

The End of Time and the Beginning of Time

On November 22nd 1963 President John F. Kennedy was assassinated in Dallas, closing an important chapter of American history and culture. The very next day, across the pond, *Doctor Who* premiered in Britain, opening a new chapter of British culture and history that would eventually conquer the entire world.

On November 23rd 1963 a time-traveling alien with a blue police box for a ship, called a TARDIS (what could *that* mean?), and a strange generic name—the Doctor, burst onto the small screen. The premiere of *Doctor Who* was, unsurprisingly, overshadowed by Kennedy's assassination and the airing itself was hampered by several power outages. But when "The Daleks" (1963) aired a few weeks later, *Doctor Who* captured the hearts and imaginations of viewers in a way that began the show's journey toward becoming a global phenomenon. The Daleks (what a brilliant invention by Terry Nation and Raymond Cusick!) *required* humans to take up arms against the blind rage and ignorance of those aliens. No human wanted to be EX-TER-MIN-ATED; thus we joined the Doctor in the fight against the Daleks and began our voyage with the Doctor through all of space and time that has lasted nearly fifty years, which, thanks to the new series, promises to continue for another fifty, or so we hope!

Who's the Doctor

When we meet the Doctor (whichever incarnation), we get hooked—*Doctor Who* is like jelly babies for the eyes. When did you become the Doctor's companion on the TARDIS? If it was during the mid-1960s, the show was in black and white and the Doctor was a cantankerous grandfather who had the uncanny ability to tap his chin, look up, and figure his way out of the toughest of jams, even when these jams included Daleks and Cybermen (William Hartnell, 1963–1966). In the late 1960s, he still battled Daleks and Cybermen, but he had Yeti and Ice Warriors, was younger, more childish, played the recorder, and couldn't help but give off the persona of a cosmic hobo (Patrick Troughton, 1966–1969).

It'd be a mistake to leave out the human Doctor who called himself "Dr. Who." "Dr. Who" appeared in two 1960s British movies with several abductees coming on board (Peter Cushing, 1965 and 1966).

If you came aboard in the early 1970s, the show was mostly in color and the Doctor was a brilliant alien scientist marooned on Earth who made do with his new and improved sonic screwdriver, a broken-down TARDIS, and some very impressive karate moves to defeat enemies like the Master, Sea Devils, and Sontarans (Jon Pertwee, 1970–1974).

From the mid-1970s to early 1980s the Doctor welcomed you on board with his charm and apparent omniscience, his long flowing scarf and fedora, jelly babies, and an irresistible smile, which he made effective use of to defeat his old nemeses and new foes, like Zygons and the Black Guardian (Tom Baker, 1974–1981).

If you began in the 1980s you still had the scarf and teeth for a little bit, but you were soon treated to a Doctor who enjoyed cricket, was a little naive in his kindness, managed to get his sonic screwdriver destroyed, and wore a piece of celery on his lapel. Even with all of this, he still had all the charm required to beat the Master, Daleks, and Cybermen on numerous occasions (Peter Davison, 1981–1984).

If your Doctor had cats instead of celery, and a patchwork suit, then you joined in the mid-1980s; a time when the Doctor was fighting new enemies like the Rani (Colin Baker, 1984–1986). The 1980s ended with the Doctor returning to his role as a father-figure, fighting the vilest, and on some occasions the sweetest, of villains in his always fashionable, question mark-covered, sweater-vest (Sylvester McCoy, 1987–1989, 1996).

The appearance of the Doctor was sparse in the 1990s, but if you were lucky enough, you were treated to a half-human Doctor, who was in the mood for love and saved the world from the Y2K disaster that almost happened—thanks (Paul McGann, 1996)!

In the new millennium, we were all treated to a regenerated Doctor as a rather cantankerous young man, who was more like a sailor in his leather jacket than spaceman. Nevertheless, when he told us to "run for your life," we ran (Christopher Eccleston, 2005).

After only a year, the leather jacket was replaced with a suit, glasses, and Chuck Taylors (what some of you might call 'Trainers'). But we also had some of the most exciting adventures ever with this Doctor: Cybermen, Sontarans, Vashta Nerada, Weeping Angels, and, of course, the Master (David Tennant, 2005–2010). (Notice: they keep getting younger!)

Finally, at least for now, if you've just begun watching, then you've been treated to the youngest Doctor ever, who wears a bowtie, has a new sonic screwdriver, is like a lonely Star-Whale, defeats a new race of Daleks, and battles a new batch of Weeping Angels (Matt Smith, 2010–?). The truth is, it really doesn't matter what the Doctor's sense of style was (is), what sort of really cool gadgets he had (has), what his TARDIS looked like on the inside, which companions he toted (totes) around time and space, or which of the scariest monsters imaginable he fought (will fight) at the time, we fell in love with the Doctor.

Who's with Who

Like his companions, we met the Doctor at different times on his journeys, but like Ian and Barbara, we were abducted. Recall, in "An Unearthly Child" (1963) the Doctor, portrayed by William Hartnell, abducts two overly-curious school teachers, Ian and Barbara. Of course, this abduction is Ian's and Barbara's own fault. They're the nosey ones; they followed the Doctor's granddaughter Susan to the junkyard where the TARDIS was hidden; they're the ones that forced their way onto the TARDIS; they got abducted, they deserved it—the Doctor obliges their curiosity, sweeps them across time and space, and after the initial shock of time travel, they loved the fact that they'd been abducted!

Not all companions have been physically abducted, but even the ones who "willingly" join the Doctor have their hearts and minds abducted by the wonder and majesty of what lies beyond the blue box. It's an honor for the Doctor to ask you to join him. It's a sign that he thinks you're capable of considering the abstract, being adventurous, daring, as well as understanding and compassionate towards strange aliens. For viewers, we are his companions, for we see ourselves as Jamie McCrimmon and Ace, rebellious kids who find a father and a friend in the Doctor; Dr. Elizabeth "Liz" Shaw, the competent scientist who equaled the Doctor's intelligence; Sarah Jane Smith, the curious reporter who found the Doctor and his lifestyle irresistible; K-9, the lovable robot dog who never let the Doctor down; Romana, the Doctor's friend and equal; Adric, the outsider who's liked by no one (even most fans), but is loved and respected by the Doctor; and more recently, Rose Tyler, the woman all viewer-companions would like to be, for she's loved by the Doctor; the determined Martha Jones, and the feisty, take no guff from anyone, office temp, Donna Noble, and now, the clever Amy Pond.

Just like the inquiring Ian and Barbara, *Doctor Who* piques our curiosity, our interest, and especially our sense of adventure, and before we know it, we've been abducted. We're swept away in the TARDIS (well, the TARDIS on TV), and we love it!

One of the most rewarding aspects of editing this collection is getting to know our fellow abductees and learn about their philosophical adventures with the Doctor. We hope all of our new reader-companions will enjoy this philosophical journey as much as we have. As you will see, this book is a lot like the TARDIS: it's much bigger on the inside, and once you enter, we think you'll find yourself unable to leave. And if you do leave, like Tegan, Sarah Jane Smith, and Rose, you'll find yourself returning to learn and experience more of both *Doctor Who* and Philosophy.

Next Week on *Doctor Who*, the Doctor Battles Philosophy!

The sense of excitement, joy, wonder, and love that are part of one's *Doctor Who*–experience are the same features that motivate and inspire people to study philosophy and lead a life of reflection and inquiry. This book demonstrates the extent to which *Doctor Who* is philosophical: the themes, ideas, and lessons that infuse so very many of the episodes. This book will challenge our new reader-companions to reflect on one's own personal identity, science, logic, reality, value, friendships, enemies, existence, beauty, and culture. It's this engagement that's the hallmark of both Philosophy and *Doctor Who*. It's no surprise, then, that *Doctor Who* is able to continually abduct new viewer-companions, while at the same time keeping older abductees satisfied, because the search for truth, quest for knowledge, and the love of wisdom is an ongoing and engaging enterprise. From the very beginning, the Doctor set his two hearts on the philosopher's task, and it's now your chance to take a philosophical journey with us, other abductees, and the Doctor in the TARDIS.

On Board the TARDIS

Just as the classic series of *Doctor Who* was separated into episodes, we've created a six-part series that tells the story of *Doctor Who and Philosophy*. Episode 1 examines the many insights the Doctor provides into the problem of personal identity. How do I know I'm the same person over time? Philosophy offers several explanations and many of these explanations are hotly contested. The Doctor's ability to regenerate presents a particularly thorny problem for philosophers. How do we know the Doctor is still *the Doctor* after such radical change? How can he visit his past and future selves? Patrick Stokes, Greg Littmann, David Kyle Johnson, and Richard Hanley offer four distinct explanations for what the Doctor teaches his viewer-companions about personal identity, which will have readers wondering whether they truly know who the Doctor is, and probably questioning who they are too!

Episode 2 takes reader-companions into some of the most fascinating components of our collection: the science, logic, and other really cool stuff of *Doctor Who*. The episode begins with Peter Worley, Philip Goff, and William Eaton, respectively, discussing the nature of time—it's all wibbly-wobbly; the possibility of time travel and the effects that time travelers might or might not be able to cause, like stopping the pyramids from being built; and the possibility of closed causal chains or time loops. These chapters will take you into some possible worlds of mind-bending fun.

Greg Littmann's chapter asks the question, "What's the 'logical' way to live?" Or, "How would an entirely logical creature behave?" You'll meet the Cybermen and Daleks here; so have your sonic screwdrivers ready. From logic, we move to philosophy of biology, where Bonnie Green and Chris Willmott raise the question regarding the ontological status of a species. What this means is that we don't really know *what* a species is: an individual, a kind, a concept. That's okay, biologists don't know either. You'll find some Dalek genetic experimentation and engineering in this chapter, too. Keep those sonic screwdrivers ready!

Paula Smithka's chapter looks at the problem of unobservables or theoretical entities in science and philosophy of science. Since the evidence of our senses, even if indirect, is required to justify claims regarding the existence of unobservables, like quarks or the Vashta Nerada—to be is to be perceived—there's a real problem with the Weeping Angels. For them, to be is *not* to be perceived. The last chapter in this episode raises the question whether science can be done without mathematics. The Carrionites seemed to manage it, what about we humans?

The story of *Doctor Who* and Philosophy takes an intriguing turn in Episode 3, from the world of science to the world of ethics. "It's a different morality; get used to it or go home!" This episode addresses the Doctor's own approach to morality and ethical behavior in Kevin S. Decker's and Laura Geuy Akers's chapters. Does the Doctor have a consistent set of morals or are his ethics a little wibbly-wobbly? Davros ("Journey's End," 2008) accuses the Doctor of "fashioning" his companions into weapons. So, is *that* a moral thing to do?

The Doctor's a feminist! J.J. Sylvia explores the extent to which the Doctor's morality is consistent with feminist ethics of caring. Donna Marie Smith's chapter addresses "Why the Doctor and Rose Tyler Kant Be Together." This chapter is about the relationship which morally improves both of the Doctor and Rose's characters and behaviors, as well as the extent of personal sacrifice which the Doctor makes, winding up alone, again.

Ed Webb and Mark Wardecker ask the question all *Doctor Who* viewer-companions have asked: Should the Daleks be ex-ter-min-ated? Yes! Well, maybe not . . . is there morality in genocide of any species, even a dangerous one? But the Daleks (and the Cybermen) are speciesist! Appealing to Peter Singer's work on animal rights, Sarah Honeychurch and Niall Barr contend that the Daleks (and Cybermen) will never defeat humans because our emotions are important for formulating our moral codes. Just because *they're* speiciesists, doesn't mean humans have to be.

The final chapter in this episode is Courtland Lewis's apologetic for the Cybermen. He contends they're not really *evil*, even though they do bad things to humans. What?! They want to "upgrade" humans. But maybe they're offering us a better life, or so they think; we won't have to suffer *much*. Hey! Don't be speciesist!

Now that all the ethical questions are settled, we take an existentialist turn in Episode 4—we're challenged to consider our own human existence. Even though the Doctor is an alien, he teaches us a lot about what it means to be human. He loves humans because we're "amazing," and of course, we're "totally mad." Michael Hand and Paul Dawson's chapters address the issue of the importance of bodily identity, death, and regeneration—for the Doctor, not humans. But does the Doctor actually die when he regenerates? He did say, "I was dead too long this time" ("Doctor Who: The TV Movie," 1996). The idea of death causes humans cosmic angst; but it's part of our human condition. That's why we love the Doctor— he does what we can't—regenerate. We forget our cosmic angst for a little while when we watch *Doctor Who*. Oh, and there's a bit of reviewing some aspects of personal identity in these two chapters. So, if you didn't get the whole story in Episode 1, you've a second chance. You never know when you might need to convince the Daleks that you're not the person they want to exterminate.

Ruth Deller's chapter, "What the World Needs is . . . A Doctor" intricately and skillfully exposes religious imagery in *Doctor Who*. The Doctor and Jesus Christ—a connection! They play parallel roles. The Daleks and Cybermen didn't notice, but according to Deller, the "Right-wing Christian lobby group *Christian Voice*" took notice because "they protested against the scene in "Voyage of the Damned" where the Doctor ascended, flanked by robot angels on either side, claiming it portrayed him as a Messiah."

Adam Riggio draws upon Friedrich Nietzsche and Gilles Deleuze to explore the nihilism of the Master, the quest for meaning and value which, ultimately, the Master doesn't expect to find; and the Doctor's resentment, desire for revenge, particularly against the Daleks, but recognizes this "Master" side of himself and is able to overcome it and create meaning and value. Continuing with the "dark side" of human reality, using the work of the "quintessential pessimist philosopher," Arthur Schopenhauer, Ken Curry argues that Will is energy or force. This force is mysterious because we don't understand what drives it. He further contends that this Will is the Master side in all of us, just as the Master and the Doctor are aspects of each other: the Doctor says, "In many ways we have the same mind" ("Logopolis," 1981). The Master's mind is in many ways the same as all of our minds. That's pretty scary. In the "dark," we get either the Master or Vashta Nerada! Maybe we should heed the Doctor's warning: "Stay in the light!" ("Silence in the Library," 2008).

Paula Smithka's "Sympathy for the Master," is a bit of an apologetic for the "quintessential bad guy," as Ken Curry describes the

Master. What is it with the editors of this volume? Lewis asks us to consider the Cybermen as beings who act altruistically in their desire to upgrade humans and members of other species. Now, Smithka contends the Master is a victim. They're mad; simply stark-raving mad! Probably, but we ask our reader-companions to look a little deeper into our anti-heroes. The Master is the tool of "the cunning of reason," as Georg Hegel would say; a tool of the historical progression. Actually, it's the surviving Time Lords (that were supposed to have been destroyed by the Daleks!) that make him their pawn in their grand plan of "Return." Hey, what would you do if you heard drums in your head since you were a child?

Roman Altshuler addresses Davros's claim that the Doctor is "the destroyer of worlds" ("Journey's End," 2008). Altshuler forces reader-companions to consider some of the most difficult and sometimes, terrible, decisions the Doctor has made. It's an investigation into the Doctor's "soul," so to speak, in the sense that some of his decisions are, to say the least, morally questionable. Altshuler contends that the Doctor's compassion is a bit sketchy at times. The companions help temper the Doctor's bad wolf by enhancing his compassion. The Doctor gives the aggressor a choice which demonstrates his "authentic concern" for others. Some bad actions . . . but right motives.

Episode 5 deals with aesthetics (beauty) and contains one of Rassilon's crown jewels, Michelle Saint's and Peter A. French's essay "Blink: Monsters, Horror and the Carroll Thesis." In their essay, Saint and French shed new light on our understanding of fear and horror, and show why *Doctor Who* fans are correct in their assessment that "Blink" (2007) is one of the scariest *Doctor Who* episodes ever, even though the monsters, the Weeping Angels, are "beautiful" statues. They also point to the irony that, even though the Weeping Angels may be the scariest creatures, it's not because they do actual violence against their victims—they don't kill their victims, unlike most monsters. Instead, they rip their victims from their present life paths and send them into the past where they live out their lives along a new pathway. Talk about upending one's life plans! But we just can't *not* blink; at least not for long. This is what, in part, makes the Weeping Angels so scary—they prey on what we can't control.

Clive Cazeaux shows reader-companions why and how the Daleks are beautiful, taking us on an aesthetic journey that shows us how beauty and monstrosity can coexist. Of course, we may be trying to notice that beauty peering from the shelter of behind the couch! Gregory Kalyniuk ends the episode with an intriguing suggestion that the writings of G.W. Leibniz serve as a foundation for brilliant science fiction. Kalyniuk weaves analogies between Leibniz's God and the Time Lords arguing that just as God actualizes the "best of all possible worlds" and establishes harmony in that world, so the Time Lords attempt to maintain order in the universe, even though upon entering the Matrix one only has confused ideas. Further Leibnizian motifs can be seen throughout *Doctor Who*—monads (they're windowless, you know) are the basis for the TARDIS, and there's a *calculus ratiocinator* of the Matrix. But you'll just have to read the chapter to achieve some Dalek-type enlightenment on this subject matter.

In our final Episode, we take a step back and look at *Doctor Who* and human culture. Robin Bunce and Deborah Pless, respectively, begin Episode 6 by philosophically examining the cultural underpinnings of *Doctor Who*. Bunce explains how human evil served as the catalyst for Terry Nation's creation of the evil Daleks. The Cold War with the threat of nuclear annihilation and the Cuban Missile Crisis set the climate of fear, where people are at the mercy of those in power. The Daleks become the ultimate enemy of the Doctor and humans, threatening, like nuclear bombs, to ex-ter-min-ate all life. It's Us versus Them; but what's so scary about Them is that they reflect Us. Pless examines how the turmoil of the twentieth century, particularly in the aftermath of World War II that culminated in Britain's decline in world power, led toward decolonization and a new era of British politics and multiculturalism. Like the Doctor, who abhors some of the actions of his Time Lord ancestors, but espouses his identity as a Time Lord, Britons could reject the imperial past but espouse British identity. *Doctor Who* provided a cultural icon and role model for British society.

Alexander Bertland takes on the battle waged between science and myth. He contends that cultures typically take science to be the dominant force in this battle, but Bertland shows us that myth has an important social and cultural role to play. What's more, he provides significant examples from *Doctor Who* that call for a balance between the two, rather than the domination of one over the other. Episode 6 ends with Courtland Lewis's chapter on *Doctor Who*'s role in promoting the enterprise of philosophy, which teaches humans to seek truth, challenge themselves, reflect on their lives and relationships with others, and to make the world a better place.

The book ends with a wonderful collection of quotes from the Doctor and other notable figures from *Doctor Who*. This portion stands alone as something fans will enjoy reading over and over again, and fans will find themselves considering new and different ways of interpreting and understanding the Doctor's words of wisdom. And just in case reader-companions need to refresh their memories of episodes and companions in order to get prepared for their local *Doctor Who* trivia night, we've included a time-travel guide and list of companions.

Allons-y!

Since *Doctor Who and Philosophy* is engaged in demonstrating and explaining the various philosophical features of the longest running science fiction show in history, not every episode or idea can be covered in one volume, but you might be surprised by the number that are. Each Doctor is discussed and an impressive number of TV episodes, books, comics, and audios found their way into the volume. We think our reader-companions will be delighted by the wealth of references to some of the most famous of episodes— "The Genesis of the Daleks" (1975) and "Blink"—to some more obscure ones, like "The Happiness Patrol" (1988) and "The Trial of a Time Lord" (1986). However, we wish to warn our reader-companions that the desire for jelly babies and watching (and re-watching) *Doctor Who* episodes may become (even more) addictive. Join us now in exploring the philosophical world of *Doctor Who*—a place that may cause you to think, reflect, and wonder about things that you may have never considered before. Take care, be careful, don't be afraid to venture into new places and meet new people with all the joy and wonder that the Doctor does, and don't forget your jelly babies!—Allons-y!

Oh, one more thing, our disclaimers: the editors of this volume are not responsible for sugar shock brought about by overconsumption of jelly babies or injuries incurred by tripping over impossibly long scarves, misuse of sonic screwdrivers, or faulty experimental Transmat devices; nor are we responsible for loss of employment due to an insatiable appetite for *Doctor Who* episodes.

Now, Allons-y!

COURTLAND AND PAULA

EPISODE 1

I'm the Doctor. Who?

Personal Identity and the Doctor

1

Just as I Was Getting to Know Me

PATRICK STOKES

Poisoned by spectrox toxæmia, having selflessly used the last of the antidote to save his companion, our hero collapses on the floor and says his goodbyes. "I might regenerate, I don't know . . . feels *different* this time . . ." He begins to hallucinate: visions of his former companions, both living and dead, urge him to fight for life, while his arch-enemy, the Master, gloatingly orders him to die. Then a strange flash of light, and an instant later a vastly different figure, wearing the same clothes but now a couple of sizes too tight, sits bolt upright and surveys his new body. His perplexed companion manages a confused "Doctor?" To which he haughtily replies: "You were expecting someone else?" And we all breathe a sigh of relief that the Doctor has survived yet another brush with death and lives on to fight another day ("The Caves of Androzani," 1984).

Or does he? And just *who* lives on? And what counts as "living on," exactly?

As we know, in the *Doctor Who* universe, a major quirk of Time Lord biology is the capacity to regenerate: to acquire, in times of major physiological trauma, a new body. This can occur up to twelve times, giving each Time Lord a total of thirteen different bodies. Of course, a main character who can simply get a completely new body in times of mortal peril does tend to deflate the dramatic tension somewhat. To compensate, all manner of elaborate plot-points have been built in to keep us guessing each time, such as the mysterious "Watcher" who assists Four's transition into Five in "Logopolis" (1981), to the "Zero Room" that Five needed to recover in immediately afterwards ("Castrovalva," 1982), to Six's post-regenerative derangement ("The Twin Dilemma," 1984).

For most people, the idea of a greatly-extended lifespan with bodily regeneration thrown in has something irresistible about it. To the elderly, the sick and the just plain hung-over alike, the idea of getting a totally new body sounds like a pretty sweet deal: complete physical renewal, restored energy and vigor, and, if you're particularly lucky, the looks of David Tennant (assuming you're male—though admittedly the non-canonical "The Curse of Fatal Death," 1999 suggests that mightn't be mandatory). But philosophers are notoriously unpleasant people, and confronted with something as cool as regeneration, we immediately start asking a whole bunch of annoying questions. So here goes: when the Doctor regenerates, *who* wakes up, exactly?

That sounds like a perfectly stupid question with an obvious answer: the Doctor. He simply undergoes a physiological change, albeit a very big, very dramatic one; sort of like an ultra-accelerated, radical form of puberty, complete with the changing voice and temporary awkwardness. But consider what's happening in a typical regeneration: a bodily organism, on the verge of dying (or, as in the 1996 *Doctor Who* movie, already dead for several hours), undergoes a complete physical transformation. It's never made exactly clear whether the atoms in his body are replaced, but for the sake of conforming with known physical laws wherever possible, let's assume they aren't. So, some or all of the matter within his body is re-arranged and as a result, the person who wakes up from the regeneration process has a very different appearance and character from his predecessor. His tastes and dress sense alter considerably each time, and his disposition towards the people around him also swings wildly between compassion, amiability, arrogance, and downright manipulativeness. There can even be physiological problems, such as the Fifth Doctor's gas allergy ("The Caves of Androzani") that seem specific to the "new" incarnation.

The question is, what features of the situation we've just described *count as survival*? What allows us to say that the person or self (call it what you will) who undergoes the regeneration is the *same* as the person who wakes up afterwards? Why can't we rather say that the pre-regeneration Doctor ceases to exist and is replaced by *another person* who shares the bulk of the previous person's memories and concerns? Looked at that way, regeneration isn't survival at all, but actually a form of death. Yet, Time Lords themselves clearly don't think of it as death—witness the Master's decision in "Last of the Time Lords" (2007) to die rather than regenerate, or the

Fifth Doctor's "Is this death?" quoted above. These questions belong to a problem that's been raging, on this planet at least, for hundreds of years: the infamous Problem of Personal Identity, which William James once described as "the most puzzling puzzle with which psychology has to deal."[1]

The Most Puzzling Puzzle

Since John Locke's *Essay Concerning Human Understanding* (1690), the puzzle of personal identity has driven more people to the point of insanity than staring into the Untempered Schism. Before Locke, the default assumption in Christendom was that the soul was the bearer of identity, though resurrection was still seen as a bodily process of some sort. With Descartes (1641), the soul found philosophical expression as the *res cogitans*, the thinking substance that I find myself to be, and which controls my organic body. Locke, however, claimed that the identity of the *self* was distinct from both the identity of the organism *and* that of the thinking substance (if it exists). Locke argued that the one person could have multiple successive thinking substances and yet still be the same person; on the other hand, if I somehow had Socrates's soul, I still wouldn't necessarily be Socrates. To be the same *self*—and this was a really radical thing to say at the time—it is neither necessary nor sufficient to have the same *soul*.

Yet, Locke went on to claim that if selves aren't *souls*, they aren't *bodies* either. If a cobbler and a prince somehow swap minds in their sleep, we'd say that the prince wakes up in the cobbler's body and vice versa, not that the prince wakes up with the mind of a cobbler.[2] What Locke saw is that when we're confronted with imaginary situations where mind and body come apart like this, our intuition is that *personal* identity follows the psychological facts rather the physical ones. Drawing on this intuition, modern-day neo-Lockeans have claimed that some form of psychological continuity across time is what constitutes selfhood. To be the same self across time is to have some sort of psychological "relatedness" hold between "person-stages" across time.

If we buy that, then it seems there's simply no question about regeneration: the person left immediately after a Time Lord

---

[1] William James, *The Principles of Psychology*, p. 330.
[2] *An Essay Concerning Human Understanding*, p. 340.

regenerates is the same person who was there beforehand. Admittedly, he's very different: his height, build, and apparent physical age alter each time. But as we've seen, the differences go deeper than that: the Doctor's psychological disposition, temperament, and tastes all seem to change radically. Indeed, the Doctor's various "incarnations" have such alarmingly different personalities that when confronted with each other, they each treat each other with barely-disguised contempt. Derek Parfit's example of the young socialist who imagines with horror the conservative he knows he'll one day become,[3] or the example of a repentant criminal looking back on his former life, mirrors the Doctor's reaction upon meeting his other incarnations. The Doctor seems so emotionally alienated from the past selves he remembers being that he feels as if he's *not* them on some level. "I'm definitely not the man I was" declares a relieved Five after meeting three of his previous incarnations in "The Five Doctors" (1983, an episode I'll be discussing a lot from here on), the flippant tone barely hiding his distance from the past selves he encounters.

Self and Memory

Given these enormous changes in temperament and personality, *what sort* of psychological connections might hold between pre- and post-regeneration Doctors that would make them the same person? Locke himself isn't actually much help here; he simply spoke of "sameness of consciousness" across time:

> For as far as any intelligent Being can repeat the *Idea* of any past Action with the same Consciousness it has of it at first, and with the same Consciousness it has of any present Action; so far is it the same *personal Self*. For it is by the Consciousness it has of its present Thoughts and Actions, that it is *Self* to it *Self* now, and so will be the same *Self*, as far as the same Consciousness can extend to Actions past, or to come . . . (*An Essay Concerning Human Understanding*, p. 336)

Locke's Enlightenment successors, at least, all thought they knew what he was talking about here: memory. Insofar as I can (genuinely)

---

[3] In Parfit's example, the young man actually takes steps to frustrate that future self's interests—in effect, treating his future self as a different person altogether. *Reasons and Persons*, p. 327.

remember the events in a person's life, I *am* that person. And what's really amazing is that in "The Five Doctors," the Doctor himself endorses this "Memory Criterion" view of personal identity. As a mysterious figure, later revealed (spoiler alert!) to be Lord High President Borusa, kidnaps Doctors One through Four from their respective eras, the Fifth Doctor experiences a painful "cosmic angst." He puts this down to the "loss" of his past: "I'm being diminished, whittled away piece by piece. A man is the sum of his memories, you know, a Time Lord even more so." Leaving aside the question of why this "cosmic angst" only strikes at one particular moment, it seems the Doctor is siding with Locke on this one. The Doctor *is* his past selves because he *remembers* being them; as he can recall "their" experiences, he and "they" are connected across time by memory, in a way that counts as their being the same person.

Yet even the Memory Criterion—the sonic screwdriver of neo-Lockean identity theorists—won't get us out of this one. In episodes like "The Three Doctors" (1973), "The Five Doctors," and "The Two Doctors" (1985) the Doctor interacts with former and future selves who apparently have completely forgotten the dramatic events they are now living through for the second, third, and fifth time (the Fourth Doctor gets stuck).

You'd think after finding yourself in the Death Zone four times you'd at least remember that Borusa turns out to be the bad guy. And this opens up the Doctor's "sum of his memories" theory to a serious objection first raised against Locke by the eighteenth-century philosophers Thomas Reid and Joseph Butler. Identity is normally understood, according to classical logic, as a one-to-one relationship: either *a* and *b* are the same person, or they aren't. There's no in-between. But, says Reid, imagine that a young boy is thrashed for stealing some fruit from an orchard. Years later, he has become a gallant soldier, and captures a flag in battle. Later still, as an old man, he attains the rank of General. Now, the gallant soldier remembers being thrashed as a boy, and the aged General remembers capturing the flag as a young man—but the General no longer remembers the childhood thrashing. But if memory confers identity, that means that the boy is the same person as the soldier, the soldier is the same person as the general, but the general isn't the same person as the boy.[4] And logically, that's an intolerable vio-

---

[4] *Essays on the Intellectual and Active Powers of Man*, p. 397.

lation of the "principle of transitivity": if $a = b$ and $b = c$, then a must equal c, and here it doesn't.

"The Five Doctors" takes this problem and amplifies it. Despite his normally quite decent personal memory (after all, he remembers things that happened hundreds of years ago), the Doctor apparently doesn't remember at least the events of this episode from one incarnation to the next. Here it's not even a question of transitivity: there's just no continuity of memory between these people. Still, perhaps all this can be explained away; maybe meeting your previous selves somehow wipes parts of your memory. And besides, all modern philosophers who have defended the Memory Criterion view of personal identity have had to try to account for the fact that it seems our identity isn't destroyed every time we forget where we left our car keys.

Meeting Yourself

But identity, as traditionally understood, presents other problems in the multi-Doctor episodes. There's a pretty good philosophical reason why the First Law of Time prohibits meeting one's former and future selves: when this occurs, we are faced with multiple, independently-acting selves, who nevertheless all claim to be the *same* person. And that violates the standard picture of *numerical* identity as a logical relation, whereby one object can't be in two places at once and still be the same object.

When multiple Doctors converge within a single point in time, we have a particularly elaborate version of what Parfit christened a *Branch-Line Case* (*Reasons and Persons*, pp. 199–201). Parfit's idea is this: suppose we have a process for teleporting you from, let's say, Gallifrey to Skaro. You step into the teleporter on Gallifrey and it records every single bit of information about you: your complete physical makeup, the state and position of every neuron in your brain, everything. Then it disintegrates you. At exactly that moment, the information is beamed to Skaro, where another machine uses it to create a perfect replica of you out of organic materials. Because your brain has been perfectly recreated, the person who steps out onto the surface of Skaro (presumably being blasted by Daleks moments later, thus teaching that person a valuable lesson about not visiting nuclear wastelands populated entirely by murderous cyborgs) will have all the Gallifrey-person's memories, up to and including the memory of stepping into the teleporter booth and pressing the "go" button.

How do we describe this case? Have you been teleported from Gallifrey to Skaro, or have you *died* and been replaced by a perfect replica on Skaro? Have you *survived*? Would this be as *good* as survival, slightly worse, or much worse? Well, now Parfit adds a new twist: suppose that the machine on Gallifrey gives you a few minutes before it disintegrates you, while on Skaro "you" have already been assembled. On Gallifrey you even get to talk to your replica on Skaro via video intercom: you find yourself speaking to someone who looks exactly like you, has all your memories, concerns, quirks, loves, hates, projects and commitments. Yet you're able to hold a conversation with this person ("Look out for Daleks!") just as if they're *another* person. In this case, the soon-to-be-disintegrated person on Gallifrey constitutes a "Branch Line" of the self.

And you can see now why the multi-Doctor episodes provide an example of a Branch Line Case. The Doctor's incarnations interact with each other in the same way as in the Gallifrey-Skaro case. Even in "The Five Doctors" when they attempt to unite their minds to overcome Borusa's mind control over the Fifth Doctor, they seem to do so as multiple agents working co-operatively, not as a single agent. Unlike the Branch Line case, though, the different selves are quite dissimilar. What they share is most of their memories, their projects, and commitments (saving the universe from evil, defeating enemies such as the Master and the Cybermen, and so forth), and a name. Are these facts enough to make them all the same person?

Deep Further Facts?

For Parfit, facts like this are all there really is to it; if I know the degrees to which a person's memory and character have persisted across time, well, that's all there is to know. There's no underlying "deep further fact" (like, say, a soul) that confers identity in the logical sense (p. 309). Each of us is simply more or less psychologically related to selves that existed in the past or will exist in the future—and that means there's nothing particularly special about those past and future selves being "me" or not. Accordingly, says Parfit, personal identity isn't what matters in survival.

Teleportation might not count as the survival of the *same* person, but it doesn't seem exactly like (or exactly as bad as) death, either (p. 215). And it's quite possible that regeneration might be preferable to death, even if the pre- and post-regeneration Doctors aren't strictly numerically identical in the logical sense. So long as there's *someone* with a reasonably good degree of psychological continuity with the previous person, someone to pilot the TARDIS and deal with the occasional Sontaran, then we needn't trouble ourselves with unanswerable questions about whether they're the same *self* or not. But is that intuitively satisfying? Doesn't it still seem important that he's the *same* person before and after regeneration?

If we still want to ask questions about whether there's one, ten, or millions of Doctors (according to some theories, we actually have a vast series of selves that each only last for a matter of seconds),[5] we might turn to Robert Nozick's *Closest Continuer* theory. On this theory, to be identical with some former person is just to be the *Closest Continuer* of that former person. This has a certain plausibility to it: the pre- and post-regeneration Doctors are the same person if, and only if, the properties of the post-regeneration Doctor "stem from, grow out of, are causally dependent on" the pre-regeneration Doctor's properties, and there's no other person that stands in a closer (or as close) relationship to the pre-regeneration Doctor.[6] But again, there's clearly no "deep" fact about identity here either.

In "The Trial of a Timelord" (1986), the nefarious prosecutor known as the Valeyard turns out to be both a distillation of the Doctor's own dark side and one of his potential future incarnations ("somewhere between your twelfth and thirteenth regeneration," whatever that might mean), scheming to get control of the Doctor's remaining regenerations and thus become actualized. Closest Continuer theory would have to say that had he succeeded, the Valeyard *would be* the Doctor, as his closest surviving continuer, whereas if he'd failed, he *wouldn't* be. And many philosophers find that unsatisfying, because it means that personal identity depends upon completely external factors that might have nothing to do with the Doctor at all: had the Valeyard slipped in the shower and died on the morning when he otherwise would certainly have killed the Doctor, that would make it true that he had *never been* the Doctor.

---

[5] Galen Strawson, "The Self," p. 359.
[6] Robert Nozick, p. 37.

Person-Stages, Animals, and Narratives

Or we could try the *Four Dimensionalist* approach. According to this theory, what we might call "person-stages" exist at particular times, but *persons* only exist *across* time, as the sum of all the person stages.[7] So the relation between person-stages and the person that they're a part of is sort of like the relation between the British Monarch, who in a sense never dies (because there's always someone we can point to and say, "that's the British Monarch"), and the various people who've held that title, all but one of whom are now dead. So if we're Four Dimensionalists, the Doctor's various incarnations can be viewed as person-stages that together make up one *person*, namely, the Doctor. This looks promising, especially as it fits in with our habit of speaking of different "Doctors," while still insisting they're all one person. But there's the problem: if person-stages are walking, talking, thinking, acting things, things that can talk about themselves and think for themselves, then that implies that when someone acts, there are *two* actors present: a person-stage *and* a person. Hence we'd have to say that the Seventh Doctor *and* the Doctor defeat the gods of Ragnarok ("The Greatest Show in the Galaxy," 1988–89), or that both the Fourth Doctor *and* the Doctor simultaneously offer you a jelly baby. And this raises far more problems than it solves. After all, if someone said, "I just met *both* the American President *and* Barack Obama," at a time when Barack Obama is still the American President, you'd think they were either speaking metaphorically or were confused as to who the current President is.

So what's left? We could reject neo-Lockeanism altogether and try *Animalism*, a currently popular theory that a self simply is an animal rather than something that goes along with that animal. Hence I *just am* this particular human animal, and the Doctor *just is* this particular Gallifreyan animal. There are several problems with Animalism, not least the lack of agreement as to just what Animalism claims, exactly, but it's far from clear how an Animalist could account for the huge disruptions in organic continuity between Doctors—not to mention Romana's apparent ability to adopt a body from another species altogether, as seen in "Destiny of the Daleks" (1979).

---

[7] Raymond Martin and John Barresi, "Introduction" in *Personal Identity*, p. 4.

Alternatively we could drop the strict logical understanding of identity and instead buy into another popular theory, the *Narrative Identity* thesis. Again, this theory comes in several flavors, offered by thinkers as diverse as Alasdair MacIntyre, Daniel Dennett, and Paul Ricoeur. What Narrative theorists broadly have in common is the claim that selves are (or at least are like) stories: just as the plot unifies all the events in an episode of *Doctor Who* into a single comprehensible story, so, they claim, a *narrative* shapes a set of physical, biological, psychological and social facts, spread out across time, into the coherent story *of* a particular self. What *I am* is the lead character in one, or more accurately a great many, stories; my "self" is the "center of narrative gravity" where these various stories intersect.

But again, the multi-Doctor episodes present huge challenges for these theories. What sort of narrative can I tell about myself when I can meet and interact with my former person-stages as if they're separate "actors" in "my" story, or when former person-stages can apparently be taken out of my time-line ("The Five Doctors") or threatened with a non-existence that causes me to fade away ("The Two Doctors")? It's one thing to be the main character in my own story and a bit player in someone else's, but how can I be a bit player in my *own* story?

A Dead End?

And so we seem to have come to a halt, even though I clearly haven't answered the question about whether the Doctor pre- and post-regeneration is the same person. It seems we want to say he's the same person—we *care* that the *same person* survives rather than just that there always be *a* Doctor—but we haven't found any theory that can account for even normal human identity, let alone the special features created by regeneration. But the very fact that after trying to disenchant personal identity in the way we have, we still care about the question "Is he still the Doctor?" seems to tell us something. The poisoned Fifth Doctor clearly sees two options before him: death or regeneration. Whatever we might tell him about the objective lack of continuity between him and his successor surely can't stop this subjective concern for his future self *as* himself. And perhaps that's where the answer lies: maybe the Doctor is *the* Doctor because each incarnation looks upon the others with concern and passion as *being itself*. Perhaps identity isn't a matter of objective continuity—of psychology, physiology, narrative, or whatever—but of some form of *subjective* attitude, whereby my past and future selves are me because I somehow acknowledge or appropriate them as such. In other words, maybe what makes the Doctor *the* Doctor is that he continually takes "ownership" of or responsibility for the vastly different bodies and personalities that constitute the career of "*the Doctor*," even when they occasionally meet and interact as separate agents. What such a form of subjective appropriation might involve, however, isn't entirely clear, and there isn't space here to try to flesh it out.

So, all I've really done here is raised a lot of difficult questions, proposed some possible answers, shown why none of them seems to work, and then gestured vaguely towards where the answer might lie with a frustrating lack of clarity and precision. As I said, philosophers are thoroughly unpleasant people. Still, looking at the paradoxical, mind-bogglingingly "puzzling puzzle" that Locke got us into centuries ago, it's hard not to think that the Doctor would approve of the confusion.[8]

---

[8] This chapter was made possible by a postdoctoral fellowship from the Danish Research Council for the Humanities.

2

Who Is the Doctor?
For That Matter, Who
Are You?

GREG LITTMANN

In 1966, William Hartnell, the first actor to play the Doctor, retired from the role. At the conclusion of "The Tenth Planet" the Doctor declared "this old body is getting a bit thin" and lay on the TARDIS floor. His features melted away and his face, body and personality changed forever, a process that was to become known as "regeneration."

The man who stood up looked and sounded like actor Patrick Troughton, but claimed to be the Doctor. What had happened? Had the Doctor been replaced by someone else or had he just changed form? Companions Ben and Polly weren't at all sure at the time, but for almost fifty years now, viewers have been asked to accept that what look like eleven different men are really all the same person: the Doctor. But what makes him the same person when so much about him is different each time? In other words, what makes the Doctor *the* Doctor rather than someone else?

You might think that tough questions about personal identity are not liable to arise outside of science fiction. However, philosophers have been arguing for many centuries about what constitutes personal identity (that is, about what makes you *you*) and are still arguing about it passionately to this day.

The fact that something happens in *Doctor Who* doesn't mean that it could happen in real life. No sane person would argue that time travel must be possible because they saw the TARDIS do it on television, or that matter must be able to appear out of nowhere because a normal-sized man turned into a huge scorpion-monster in "The Lazarus Experiment" (2007). However, thinking about imaginary situations can help us realize that there are gaps and

15

inconsistencies in our theories. For example, we might have a theory that it's always wrong to break a promise, but this theory has trouble standing in the face of the hypothetical question, "What if you had promised someone that you would go out vandalizing cars with them?"

Fans of Tom Baker will recall that the Doctor uses just such a hypothetical to decide in "Genesis of the Daleks" (1975) that it would be immoral to wipe the Daleks out. As he stands ready to destroy them, he asks whether, if shown a child and told that it would grow up to be a "ruthless dictator who would destroy millions of lives," it would be moral to kill that child. He concludes that it wouldn't be and thus that it wouldn't be moral to wipe out the Daleks. The fact that nobody is really offering the Doctor a child to kill is beside the point—the hypothetical shows that the Doctor has a contradiction in his beliefs and he changes his views accordingly. Similarly, what we are going to be doing by examining the issue of personal identity through the lens of *Doctor Who* is not to treat the show as if it were real, but to mine it for hypothetical situations against which we can test the comprehensiveness and consistency of our theories about personal identity.

Are You Your Body?

So, back to the question at hand: what constitutes personal identity? That is, what makes you *you*, what makes the Doctor *the Doctor*, and what makes anybody else themselves? One natural theory is that personal identity is constituted by bodily identity—that to be the same person is to have the same body. We certainly do use sameness of bodies to identify people. When you meet your friend in the street and say "Hello" you identify this person as your friend by the fact that the body you see looks just like the body your friend has always had.

So far, so good. But if being the same person is a matter of having the same body, what constitutes having the same body? It can't be a matter of having a body with exactly the same form, for at least two reasons. Firstly, we can track sameness of body through bodily changes. Viewers of *Doctor Who* are very familiar with such changes.

- **Most obviously, the Doctor's body alters its size and shape every time he regenerates.**

- Similarly, the William Hartnell Doctor's body is turned invisible in "The Celestial Toymaker" (1966),

- the Patrick Troughton Doctor's companion Jamie has his body first turned into cardboard and then reshaped with a new face in "The Mind Robber" (1968),

- the Jon Pertwee Doctor encounters the humanoid Solonians who transform into insect-like creatures in "The Mutants" (1972),

- the Tom Baker Doctor meets the Rutans who are able to shape-change at will in "The Horror of Fang Rock" (1977),

- the Colin Baker Doctor's companion Peri grows feathers in "Vengeance on Varos" (1985),

- the Sylvester McCoy Doctor's companion Ace grows cat's eyes in "Survival" (1989),

- and, most dramatically of all, the Peter Davison Doctor finds that the Brigadier has shaved off his famous mustache in "Mawdryn Undead" (1983).

The new series is no less rich in examples, with the David Tennant Doctor meeting shape-changing Krillitane in "School Reunion" (2006), people who have been turned into pig hybrids in "Daleks in Manhattan" (2007), and even a woman who's transformed into a talking paving slab in "Love and Monsters" (2006).

In all of these cases, we're expected to find it intelligible that the person after the transformation is the same person who was there beforehand, despite the change in their bodies. Of course, bodily changes occur in real life too, even if they're not always as dramatic—we grow old, we gain scars or injuries and, like the Brigadier, we sometimes modify our hair. Unless we accept that every time such a change occurs the old body is gone and a new body appears, we're going to have to allow that sameness of body over time doesn't consist in sameness of features over time.

A second problem with insisting that sameness of body over time consists in sameness of features is that more than one body can have the same set of features. Once again, examples of this are found throughout *Doctor Who*. Surprisingly often, people turn out to have doubles; for example, the Hartnell Doctor meets his double, the Abbot of Amboise, in sixteenth-century France in "The Massacre" (1964), the Troughton Doctor meets his double, the twenty-first century world-dictator Salamander in "The Enemy of the World" (1967), the Davison Doctor's companion Nyssa meets her double, Ann Talbot, in 1920s England in "Black Orchid" (1982), and the Colin Baker Doctor just happens to look exactly like the captain of the guard on Gallifrey in "The Invasion of Time" (1978).

As if that weren't trouble enough, people are constantly being impersonated by shape-changing aliens, such as when the Troughton Doctor's companion Polly is impersonated by a Chameleon in "The Faceless Ones" (1967), the Tom Baker Doctor's companion Harry is impersonated by a Zygon in "Terror of the Zygons" (1975), the Davison Doctor is impersonated by Omega in "Arc of Infinity" (1983), and the Tennant Doctor meets a Krillitane who is impersonating the headmaster of an English school in "School Reunion." There's even an entire race of clones in the form of the Sontarans, who definitely don't take themselves to be the same individual: the Sontaran met by Sarah Jane Smith in "The Sontaran Experiment" (1975) states very clearly that he isn't Lynx, whom she met in "The Time Warrior" (1973), but Styre.

In all of these cases—natural doubles and deliberate copies alike—the viewer is easily able to understand that these aren't the same person with the same body, but rather two or more different people, despite the fact that their bodies seem to be physically indistinguishable. Similarly, in real life, we can be confronted with twins or doubles and easily understand that these are two bodies and not one, belonging to two people, not one. So again, it seems that being the same body isn't a matter of having the same form.

Worms in the Space-Time Continuum

Let's take one last stab at finding personal identity through bodily identity. Perhaps we can find sameness of body through tracking continuity of location in time and space. Humans are, after all, four-dimensional worms. No, I don't mean in *Doctor Who*, I mean in real life—hear me out.

Our universe has four dimensions: three spatial dimensions and the dimension of time. We tend to think of our bodies as only being extended in space; they stretch from the tops of our heads to the tips of our feet, from our left side to our right side, and from our back to our front. However, we're also extended in the fourth dimension, time, stretching from the moment we're born (or there-abouts) to the time we die. If you could see the entirety of a human life all at once, what you'd see would be something like a worm in space-time, stretching through every place and every time that the person had occupied during their life.[1]

Given this, it seems tempting to believe that bodily identity over time consists in being part of a single four-dimensional "worm" in four-dimensional space-time. In other words, it's tempting to believe that a body at one time is the same body that existed at an earlier time if both are part of the same continuous object. Applying this to regeneration, we might accept that the body that looked like Christopher Eccleston is the same body as the body that looks like David Tennant because there's spatiotemporal continuity between the two; that is, because the Eccleston body was immediately replaced at exactly the same point in space by the Tennant body. Similarly, we might say that it's spatiotemporal continuity that provides the sameness of the body that looks like a Krillitane and the body that looks like a headmaster in "School Reunion," of the mustached body before the Brigadier has his shave and the mustache-less body after his shave, of your body before and after you cut your finger, and so on.

There's a tidiness to identifying sameness of body with spatiotemporal continuity and sameness of person with sameness of body. However, there're also some big problems with this view. Three in particular might strike those who watch enough (or too much) *Doctor Who*.

- **Firstly, it seems at least conceivable that a person could fail to have any body at all, which would mean that what makes them *them* can't be the spatiotemporal continuity of their body.**

- **Secondly, it seems at least conceivable that a single person might be made up of spatiotemporally discontinuous parts (that means that they might jump about in time and space a bit—who does that remind you of?).**

---

[1] I think that this model of humans in time is forced on us by modern science, particularly Einstein's Special Theory of Relativity. Some philosophers disagree. For a good discussion of the issue, hunt down M.C. Rea, "Four Dimensionalism."

- **Thirdly, it seems at least conceivable that the same body might be inhabited by different people at different times.**

Let's look at each of these problems in turn.

The Problem of People with No Bodies

Problem One for the spatiotemporal-continuity-of-bodies criterion for personal identity is that it seems at least conceivable that a person might exist with no body. In fact, the Doctor runs across people like that all the time.

They may have lost everything below the neck, such as the Master's army of decapitated humans faced by the Tennant Doctor in "Last of the Time Lords" (2007). Alternatively, they may be mere disembodied brains, such as those met by the Hartnell Doctor in "The Keys of Marinus" (1964), or the brain of Morbius, met by the Tom Baker Doctor in, appropriately, "The Brain of Morbius" (1976). Presumably, the Cybermen themselves are essentially human brains in robot shells and, at least during their first appearance with the Hartnell Doctor in "The Tenth Planet" (1966), they see human identity as lasting through a replacement of bodily parts.

It's open to the champion of the spatiotemporal continuity view of identity to insist that spatiotemporal continuity of the brain is what's really important, not the entire body, since it's the brain that actually does the thinking. However, some poor souls in the *Doctor Who* universe don't have any physical form at all. For example, the Refusians met by the Hartnell Doctor in "The Ark" (1966) lost their bodies as a result of an accident, the Great Intelligence met by the Troughton Doctor in "The Abominable Snowmen" (1967) and "The Web of Fear" (1968) likes to live in silver balls but is perfectly capable of floating around bodilessly, the Pertwee Doctor learns that the Time Lord Omega has become nonphysical in "The Three Doctors" (1972), and the Davison Doctor battles the incorporeal snake-spirit "the Mara" in "Kinda" (1982) and "Snakedance" (1983).

Peripheral cases would include creatures with "bodies" made of energy, like the party-crashing Mandragora Helix fought by the Tom Baker Doctor in "The Masque of Mandragora" (1976) and the television-possessing entity known as "The Wire" fought by the Tennant Doctor in "The Idiot's Lantern" (2006).

The Problem of People Who Materialize
Out of Nowhere

A second problem with the spatiotemporal-continuity-of-body view of personal identity is that we can make perfect sense of stories in which people move about in a way that breaks spatiotemporal continuity. In fact, breaking spatiotemporal continuity is what *Doctor Who* is all about. The Doctor can dematerialize in modern London and rematerialize on the planet Skaro in the far future, or Rome in the ancient past, or even in another dimension. If we were to try to plot his spatiotemporal "worm," there'd be a jumble of isolated pieces all over the place without connection to each other. For example, there's going to be a section of "Doctor Worm" that begins suddenly when he lands in Pompeii in 79 A.D. in "The Fires of Pompeii" (2008), without being directly connected to anything that was there in Pompeii before, and ends suddenly when he leaves Pompeii a few days later, without being directly connected to anything that's still in Pompeii afterwards. Whatever it is that makes this disconnected worm section the same person as the disconnected worm section who adventured in 100,000 B.C. in "An Unearthly Child" (1963), it doesn't seem to be spatiotemporal continuity.

TARDIS travel might be thought to be a special case because TARDIS flight seems to take place in its own private timeline, giving the crew time to banter, squabble, and explain the plot. However, there are innumerable other cases in *Doctor Who* in which such travel is instantaneous. In fact, there are examples of this in every era of the television series:

- **the Hartnell Doctor finds a Dalek transmat (teleport) system in "The Dalek Masterplan" (1965),**

- **the Troughton Doctor finds space flight dominated by transmat in "The Seeds of Death" (1969),**

- **the Pertwee Doctor faces blobs who teleport people into the heart of a black hole in "The Three Doctors,"**

- **the Tom Baker Doctor finds an entire planet that teleports around space mining other planets in "The Pirate Planet" (1978),**

- **the Davison Doctor learns that a renegade Time Lord is using a time scoop to abduct people from time and space in "The Five Doctors" (1983),**

- **the Colin Baker Doctor meets a tyrant who eliminates rebels by teleporting them randomly in time and space by throwing them into the timelash in "Timelash" (1985),[2]**

- **the McCoy Doctor gets teleported to another planet by small cats in "Survival,"**

- **the Eccleston Doctor's companion, Rose, gets teleported to the Dalek flagship in "Bad Wolf" (2005),**

- **and the Tennant Doctor gets transported through space and time to the 1960s by the Weeping Angels in "Blink" (2007).**

However outrageous these adventures might be, the stories make sense to us. We understand that the character who steps into a transmat chamber is the same character as the one who instantly steps out of another transmat chamber a million miles away, despite the lack of spatiotemporal continuity. So again, the concept of sameness of person doesn't seem to require spatiotemporal continuity.

The Problem of Possession

A third problem with the spatiotemporal-continuity-of-body account of personal identity is that it seems conceivable that a spatiotemporally continuous body might have different people inhabiting it at different times. In fact, this happens all the time on *Doctor Who*. In such cases, not only do we have personal identity without spatiotemporal continuity of body, we have spatiotemporal continuity of body without personal identity.

Perhaps the most impressive example of this is the Tom Baker Doctor's enemy Eldrad from "The Hand of Fear" (1976), who goes through five bodies in six episodes: first an unseen alien in a spacecraft, then a disembodied hand, then the body of Sarah Jane Smith, then a female body made of rock and finally a male body made of rock. The Master is similarly certain that he can survive a change of bodies and happily steals the body of Nyssa's father in "The Keeper of Traken" (1981). The Davison Doctor's companion Tegan posi-

---

[2] If you're a true *Doctor Who* geek, you have cried "No! Not the timelash!" at this point. If you haven't, do it now. (See also "No! Not the mind probe!")

tively makes a hobby of having her body possessed by alien entities, being possessed by the Mara in "Kinda" and again in "Snakedance." Similarly, in "New Earth" (2006), Cassandra possesses the body of both the Tennant Doctor and his companion Rose. (Since Cassandra is just a human being like the rest of us, this is probably the most amazing event in the history of *Doctor Who*. I can't work out how she did it. I've been trying to possess the neighbors all morning and I'm getting nowhere.)

It's worth stressing again here that the argument isn't that disembodied existence, teleportation, time-travel, possession or any other form of spatiotemporal discontinuity must be possible in real life just because they're possible on *Doctor Who*. Rather, the point is that since stories that feature these things are perfectly understandable as stories, spatiotemporal continuity mustn't be essential to our conception of personal identity. If I tell you that the Doctor found a square circle, or met a married bachelor, or landed on a planet of mammal insects, you'd have no idea what I meant. My statements would make no sense because it's part of the idea of a circle that it isn't square, of a bachelor that he isn't married and of a mammal that it isn't an insect. On the other hand, if I tell you that the Doctor disappeared from London in his TARDIS and reappeared in New York, or that Omega survived without his body, or that Sarah Jane Smith's body was possessed by Eldrad, you understand the story I'm telling perfectly well. This suggests that spatiotemporal continuity isn't part of the concept of personal identity, and so personal identity isn't a matter of spatiotemporal continuity.

Are You Your Memories?

If we don't accept the spatiotemporal continuity model, in what else might we try to find personal identity? One possibility is that we find it in memory. For instance, we might declare that to be *you* is simply a matter of having *your* memories. That'd certainly handle a lot of the problem cases we've looked at above.

The David Tennant Doctor might not look like the original William Hartnell Doctor, but as we saw in "The Fires of Pompeii," he still remembers that, as the Hartnell Doctor, he was responsible for the burning of Rome in "The Romans" (1965). In "The City of Death" (1979), the Tom Baker Doctor who steps out of his TARDIS in Renaissance Italy is spatiotemporally discontinuous with the Doctor who stepped into his TARDIS in modern Paris, but he still remembers boarding in Paris with the intention of traveling back through time. Similarly, the bodiless Omega remembers all too clearly being the bodied Omega who was abandoned by the ungrateful Time Lords, and Eldrad, in all his/her bodies, remembers all too clearly being the Eldrad who was exiled by the ungrateful Kastrians. What's more, the memory criterion seems to be (at least sometimes) endorsed by the Doctor himself. After all, in "The Five Doctors," the Davison Doctor tells his companion Tegan "a man is the sum of his memories you know, a Time Lord even more so," while in "The Planet of the Ood" (2008), the Tennant Doctor tells his companion Donna, "memory and emotions . . . without it, you wouldn't be Donna." Then again, the Doctor told us in "The Dalek Invasion of Earth" (1964) that Earth is the only planet with magnetic poles, so let's not just take his word for anything.

In fact, there are significant problems with the memory account of personal identity too, and the Doctor should know about them because plenty of problem cases pop up in his adventures. Most obviously, sometimes people lose their memory but remain the same person. For example, the Tom Baker Doctor has the memory of his time as president of Gallifrey wiped at the end of "The Invasion of Time" (1978), but remains the same person who was president. Similarly, the Tennant Doctor has the memory of his entire life wiped so that he can pretend to be human in "Human Nature" and "The Family of Blood" (both 2007), but is still the same character.

As if that weren't complication enough, it also seems to be possible to gain someone else's memories without really being them. For example, the Chameleons gain the memories of the Troughton Doctor's companion Polly in "The Faceless Ones," Eldrad gains the memories of the Tom Baker Doctor's companion Sarah Jane Smith in "The Hand of Fear," while the Daleks plunder the memories of the Davison Doctor himself in "Resurrection of the Daleks" (1984). Yet despite this memory stealing, the Chameleons don't become Polly, Eldrad doesn't become Sarah Jane Smith, and the Daleks don't all become the Doctor.

Are You Your Personality?

It might be argued that the memory criterion is right in spirit, but simply doesn't go far enough in demanding mental similarity. In all the examples I've given, the original owner of the memories is very psychologically different from the recipient of the memories, even after the memories are stolen. Polly cared about saving the Earth and being fashionable, while the Chameleons who had her memories cared about conquering the Earth and was unconcerned with fashion. Sarah Jane Smith never had much ambition to wage war across the galaxy, which wasn't true of Eldrad even after s/he took Sarah's memories. Similarly, even when the Daleks had taken the Doctor's memories, they still had very non-Doctorish priorities, preferring the extermination of all other life forms to traveling the universe in a police box.

Would we be more inclined to believe, for instance, that Eldrad had become Sarah Jane Smith if Eldrad now valued everything that Sarah Jane Smith valued and believed everything that Sarah Jane Smith believed? We probably would be more inclined, but at least two problems remain even if we demand very close psychological similarity.

One problem is that it seems possible for two people to have the same psychological characteristics. For example, even if Eldrad were to take on Sarah Jane's entire personality, that wouldn't get rid of the organism that the Doctor has always called "Sarah Jane," the one that isn't blue and glittery and is wearing overalls. Could they both really be Sarah Jane Smith? I don't think so and a hypothetical case might make clear why. What if you knew that you were going to be executed by the Daleks tomorrow, but the Doctor told you, "Don't worry! I happen to know that Eldrad copied your entire personality yesterday, so now Eldrad is you! So even though the Daleks are going to exterminate you tomorrow morning, you'll survive after all, since Eldrad is you and Eldrad will still be alive."

Would you be satisfied by this state of affairs or would you object: "Wait! Eldrad isn't me! I'm me, and when the Daleks exterminate me tomorrow, I won't have survived at all. Eldrad will have lived but I'll be dead!" That's certainly the sort of objection that I'd make, only more pitifully. But if we're right when we make this protestation, then having *our* personality isn't enough for being *us*, and we must keep looking if we want to find the secret of personal identity.

A second problem with the view that personal identity consists in close psychological similarity is that people can change personality dramatically over the course of their lives. Mundane examples might include middle-aged businesspeople who suddenly drop out of the rat-race to find themselves, or wild party animals who turn to religion. Examples from *Doctor Who* would include Mavic Chen

from the Hartnell adventure "The Dalek Masterplan," who decides
to side with the Daleks after a lifetime of serving humanity, or Stein
from the Davison adventure "Resurrection of the Daleks," who
decides to side with humanity after a lifetime of serving the Daleks.

The most dramatic example from the new series would be from
the Tennant adventure "The Last of the Time Lords," in which it is
revealed that after many lifetimes of evil, the Master has just spent
a lifetime of gentle goodness in the persona of Professor Yana, only
to turn once again to a life of evil. Professor Yana is psychologically nothing like the Master fans have grown to know since he first
faced off against the Pertwee Doctor in "Terror of the Autons"
(1971), but the entire story hinges on our understanding that it is
indeed the same character. It looks then, as if personal identity may
not rely on psychological similarity either.

Doctor Who and the Ultimate Answer

Confused yet? We've only scratched the surface of the problem.
You'll easily come up with a huge number of new philosophical
problems regarding personal identity just by watching the Tom
Baker stories "Robot" (1974), "The Ark in Space" (1975), "The
Planet of Evil" (1975), "The Android Invasion" (1975), "The Seeds
of Doom" (1976), "The Face of Evil" (1977), "The Talons of Weng-
Chiang" (1977), "The Invisible Enemy" (1977), "The Leisure Hive"
(1980), "Meglos" (1980) and "Logopolis" (1981), none of which we
got to above. The eras of other Doctors are almost equally fruitful.

So, what's the answer? In what does personal identity consist?
There's no single answer that all philosophers agree on. Some
philosophers support views we discussed earlier, believing that there
are replies to the objections I raised, while other philosophers have
opinions that there just wasn't space to include. I've got my opinion,
of course, but arguing for it here would take us way off topic.

My point here isn't to try to sell you on what I think, but to help
you appreciate the problems so that you can make up your own
mind. And, of course, to make as many *Doctor Who* references as
possible. In that spirit, I bid you to go forth and explore and hunt
for the truth, and who knows, like the Doctor in "The Two
Doctors" (1985), "The Three Doctors," and "The Five Doctors," you
just might find yourself. Or, like the Doctor in "The Happiness
Patrol" (1988), you might find a massive robot made of licorice.
Who can say?

3
Who's Who on Gallifrey

RICHARD HANLEY

Although I grew up mostly in Australia, I grew up mostly British. And if you grew up British in the 1960s, you grew up with *Doctor Who*. Not being into *Doctor Who* would've been like not being into *cricket*! I watched the show religiously, played at being a Dalek under a upside-down laundry basket, got all cranky when they replaced Willliam Hartnell with Patrick Troughton, watched it less religiously for a while, and then resumed my obsession when John Pertwee came along (though he wasn't in color in Australia). Tom Baker was even better (and definitely in color), but then after him . . .

I'm very glad about the recent worldwide resurgence of *Doctor Who*, with Christopher Eccleston, David Tennant, and now Matt Smith. Looking back now, I see that together with *Star Trek* and *Lost in Space*, *Doctor Who* helped kindle my life-long interest in science fiction, and my career in metaphysics. But this chapter isn't about me.

Instead, I will investigate what counts as personal survival for a Time Lord. Breaking down "personal survival" raises two distinct metaphysical issues: first, what a *person* is, and second, what *survival* is.

Let's assume for now that survival is *persistence*, by which I mean the existence of one and the same thing at different times. Personal persistence is the existence of one and the same person at different times. And here on Earth, three basic alternative accounts have been given: body, mind, and soul.

We'll examine these in turn, but first, some preliminaries.

Who's in a Name?

Doctor Who isn't, of course, Doctor Who. ("If he's a time traveler, why didn't they call him Doctor *When?*" my daughter once demanded). Mostly, he's just "the Doctor." But for identity purposes, "the Doctor" is problematic, since it's not a typical proper name. Perhaps it's a proper name; perhaps it's a title, as Harriet Jones suggests to the Tenth Doctor; perhaps it's a definite description. If it's a title, then it needn't even contain a veridical description. "The Greatest Show in the Galaxy" (1988) needn't be the greatest show in the galaxy! If he *is* a doctor, then at least the description fits, but it doesn't fit uniquely, at least in many contexts in which it's used.

Moreover, if "the Doctor" is a veridical title or description, then correctly applying it to successive regenerations may not reflect numerical identity. Just as two distinct persons can be successive Kings ("The King is dead—long live the King!"), two distinct persons might be successive Doctors. That's what Harriet Jones suggests. Also, we shouldn't read too much into the fact that we distinguish the Doctors from each other for certain purposes, for instance by using "the Tenth Doctor." Sometimes we distinguish Smith the man from Smith the boy.

So we can't just read the metaphysics off the name. We need to examine the story.

What's the Story?

Most of us would agree that there's no Doctor, no TARDIS, and no Gallifrey. Yet I've just been writing as if there were, and this isn't some quirk of mine. We all—not just nerdy sci-fi fans—do this kind of thing, and do it a lot.

I'll just assert without argument my view on this: we're all engaged in a kind of pretense, and when we're so engaged, we speak *as if it were the case that the fictional story is a reliable report*. Hence, roughly, what's true in a story is what would've been true had the story been non-fiction.

A consequence is that there're many determinate facts about what's true in a fiction. But interpretation of a fiction is still a very tricky business, bringing in facts about the *background* (in my view, facts about actuality), and requiring what Kendall Walton has called a "good nose."

That's hard enough, but some fictions are serialized, and get curiouser and curiouser. *Doctor Who* can be treated as a whole bunch of smaller fictions, a natural lower limit being an episode. But we commonly regard these episodes as summative to make a larger story, *the* story that's *Doctor Who*. It has multiple authors, has gone into hiatus, then returned, and has looked quite different in different versions. Rather like the Doctor himself!

But not just any *Doctor Who* story counts, and hence we have the notion of *canon*. In canonical serialization there is *symmetry* in dependence between the parts of the story. What's true in later episodes obviously depends upon what's true in earlier ones, but in canonical serialization, what's true in earlier episodes also depends upon what's true in later ones.

So, for instance, when the Tenth Doctor tells Rose about the process of regeneration ("Children in Need Mini Episode," 2005), it's completely appropriate to regard what he says (given that he's to be trusted about it) as applying to all the regenerations of all the Doctors. This is most helpful, because I'll focus especially on the Tenth Doctor.

(I can't resist mentioning here one remarkable thing the Tenth Doctor says to Rose. Upon regeneration, he quickly finds a mole in the middle of his back, between his shoulder blades. In the philosophical literature on truth in fiction, the usual example is a popular serialization, the Sherlock Holmes stories of Sir Arthur Conan Doyle, and one of the noted indeterminacies is that Holmes neither does nor doesn't have a mole in the middle of his back!)

However, when authors produce non-canonical *Doctor Who* stories, what's true in their stories depends upon what's canonical, but what's true in the canon does *not* depend upon what's true in their stories. Call such non-canonical stories the *secondary* literature.

Next, what's true in the canon doesn't at all depend upon what's stated in the *tertiary* literature, by which I mean the wealth of (often very intelligent) commentary on the canon. And here's perhaps the most controversial aspect of my claim: no matter how otherwise "authoritative," the *interpretive* remarks of an author have no special weight. (I don't care what J.K. Rowling says *now*, Dumbledore is not gay unless the way she wrote *the story* made him so!)

However, perhaps authors and other creative entities have some say in *which* stories count as canonical. Steven Moffat, for instance, says in *Doctor Who Magazine* #389, that "Time Crash" (2007) is canonical—does that *make* it so? According to the Whoniverse Wiki, "If a story is officially licensed by the BBC as a *Doctor Who* story, then it counts as canonical."[1] But I doubt that this is sufficient. To be sure, there's *some* notion of canon captured by this, but in my view there's a world of difference between what's officially endorsed and what's part of the canon. The Whoniverse account would allow that if the BBC markets a tea-mug bearing a narrative inscription—a very short *Doctor Who* story—*that* would count as canonical! In any case, in what follows, I'll exclude from the canon novels, webcasts, comic books and the like, BBC-endorsed or not. Spin-offs like *Torchwood* are more plausibly canon, and it'd be harmless to allow them. More importantly, I shall count mini-episodes such as the "Children in Need" special which focuses upon the regeneration from the Ninth to the Tenth Doctor.

Next, a general point about *visual* fictions like *Doctor Who*. In one way they're more determinate than written fictions, since you can *see* what some character or place looks like. But lots of indeterminacy remains, and a new interpretive difficulty is introduced: the visual-media conventions of depiction. One aspect of this phenomenon is that screen time isn't always a good guide to story time. For instance, when the screen fades into black and then into a different, brightly-lit scene—all in a few seconds—we correctly infer that a whole night has passed.

In deciding what's true about regeneration, then, we must be cautious when considering questions such as: *How long did it take?* The tertiary literature on regeneration contains all manner of claims about regeneration based upon a commitment to screen time as guide to story time. I take regeneration time to be largely indeterminate, and so will largely ignore it.

Finally, a somewhat technical complication arises for a small minority of fictions, and *Doctor Who* is in this minority. The idea of "changing the past" that's sometimes employed in *Doctor Who* is a notion I call '*annulling* the past' (as in "The Year that Never Was," 2008); and it's an incoherent one. You can't make it both the case and not the case that a particular event occurred, in exactly the same context or sense. Not even a time machine will allow you to do *that*.

---

[1] <http://tardis.wikia.com/wiki/Doctor_Who_Wiki>.

The complication is that one bit of silliness ought not to infect the whole story. Clearly it's true in the story that the Doctor is from Gallifrey, and not from Earth. But in classical logic, every proposition whatsoever follows from a contradiction. So to keep a sensible story, we either eliminate the contradiction or else do not permit everything to follow from it. I will assume that this can be done, keeping the world of *Doctor Who* safe for our interpretive purposes.

What's in Regeneration?

According to the story, a Time Lord can regenerate twelve times (the Master's shenanigans notwithstanding). Not only is this handy for replacing actors, but it permits relatively tragic storylines in which the Doctor is in a fatal condition, such as in "The End of Time" (2009).

Twelve is an utterly arbitrary limit, and I'd like to see it go permanently by the wayside. (It would be enough to keep the number down that there are significant costs to regeneration in terms of pain, or memory loss, or companion trauma—after all, it's *a bit dodgy.*) Perhaps there's a sneaking suspicion that a regenerated Doctor is, because an imperfect copy, somehow *imperfect*, corrupt, and the next even more so, until not enough of the original remains?

Our judgments about persistence seem to permit a total turnover in bodily composition over time. Our bodies, for instance, are composed now of substantially different cells from, say, ten years ago. Growing up, I often heard it said that we recycle all our body cells in a seven-year period. It seems that isn't true, but nobody would be particularly worried about it, anyway. If science announced tomorrow that we recycled all our cells in a seven-month period, we aren't going to conclude that no body persists longer than seven months.

The interesting question is, why not? The answer is that, for bodily persistence, bodily *continuity* is important. Suppose that we label a certain body B1, and a certain later body B2. If B2 and B1 share any of the same cells, we say that they *overlap*, or are *connected*. Suppose B1 is connected with B2, and B2 is connected with still later B3. It nevertheless is possible that B1 and B3 *aren't* connected.

For instance, in our fantasy of seven-month recycling, suppose B1 and B2 are separated by six months, and B2 and B3 by the same. Though they're not *connected*, B1 and B3 are *continuous*, since there are *overlapping chains of connectedness* between them. (By analogy, think of how to make a hundred-foot rope from much shorter lengths of string. You have to have overlapping strings!)

Indeed, once we grant that continuity is enough, it wouldn't matter if we recycled our cells every seven weeks, or days, or hours, or minutes, or seconds. And given that Time Lord bodies are subject to entropy, too, then presumably we can give the same account of Gallifreyan bodily persistence.

A problem arises, though, when we get to regeneration. According to the Tenth Doctor, "every single cell" was replaced in his regeneration from the Ninth Doctor ("Children in Need Mini Episode").

Again, think of the rope analogy. With no overlap at all between strings, there's a break in continuity, and at best you've two ropes that happen to be laying end-to-end. If there's not a single cell in common between the Ninth and Tenth Doctors, then it seems that bodily continuity is lost in the process.

This strongly suggests that Gallifreyans don't regard bodily continuity as *necessary* for personal persistence. That leaves two basic alternatives: either they rely upon *mental* continuity, or upon something else entirely. But is bodily continuity *sufficient* for bodily persistence? No . . .

What's Continuity Without Persistence?

In "The Christmas Invasion" (2005) the Doctor's right hand is cut off during his duel with the Sycorax leader. Call the pre-duel Doctor D1, the severed hand D2, and the victorious Doctor D3. Surely D1 and D3 are one and the same Doctor; D2 is a just a bit he left behind, much the way we humans leave skin cells and whatnot all over the planet as we live our lives. But D2 *is* bodily continuous with D1, since it's connected with it (it has cells in common with it).

Let's call connectedness between an earlier and later body *strong* if it involves at least fifty percent of the earlier body. And let's call continuity *strong* when it consists of overlapping chains of strong connectedness; otherwise it is *weak*. The example of the Doctor's hand tells us that weak connectedness isn't always enough. Is it ever enough? In "Journey's End" (2008), a whole new body is grown from, among other things, the Doctor's severed hand, and we're repeatedly assured that the regrown Doctor *is* the Doctor.

Can this be right? Suppose it means that one and the same body is in two places at once. That's old hat, in a time travel story. There's at least one way to make simple sense of being in two places at once due to time travel: suppose that a Gallifreyan body is a *space-time worm* extended in time as well as in space. That is, suppose that it has temporal parts in addition to having spatial parts. Then, there's no contradiction in two different temporal parts, if the Doctor is in two places at once, any more than there's a contradiction in his right and left hands being in two different places at once.

But in "Journey's End," it's not time travel but rather *replication* that produces the extra body. And it's doubtful that we can make sense of a *single* space-time worm that's multiply located as a result. All in all, it seems better to say that the regrown Doctor's body isn't one and the same body as the Doctor's.

(By the way, in the same episode, the Doctor calls the Doctor/Donna, "a human being with a Time Lord's brain." I take it this isn't meant literally—Donna seems closer to the mark when she says she has the Doctor's *mind*.)

Where's the Soul?

Given that it's not sameness of body, perhaps there's some of sort of Doctor *essence* that explains his persistence through regeneration. One hint in this direction is the weird appearance of the Watcher when the Fourth Doctor regenerates into the Fifth ("Logopolis," 1981).

Another is in "Human Nature" (2007), when the Doctor uses the Chameleon Arch, which "rewrites my biology—literally changes every single cell in my body. I've set it to *human*." It also gives the Doctor in the person of John Smith *amnesia*, so that he doesn't remember being the Doctor.

It's tempting to think that this is a case where neither body nor mind persists. So, if it's a case of personal persistence nonetheless, something else is implicated—call it the *soul*. Perhaps it's better to call it a *soul pellet*, to distinguish it from a common postulation that the mind and soul are one.

There's a long tradition of belief in soul pellets here on Earth, so maybe there is on Gallifrey, too. Part of the motivation comes from Leibniz's Law, which tells us that if A and B are numerically identical, it can't be true that A has some property that B lacks (or vice versa). It follows that difference in properties entails numerical distinctness. But, think of all the properties you now have that you didn't have when you were five years old. You're bigger, stronger, hairier. You have all sorts of beliefs that you earlier lacked. So you're bodily different, *and* mentally different. So how can it still be *you*?

The temptation is to think that all these changes are associated with some underlying, unchanging thing that is the *real* you: the soul pellet. If the Doctor has—*is*—a soul pellet, then he could persist without continuity of body or mind. He could *be* John Smith, even if John Smith has a distinct body and a distinct mind. The problem is, he could *be* anyone at all, and we wouldn't know it. The only ways we normally have of identifying and re-identifying persons is through bodily and mental evidence. Of course, John Smith *looks* like the Doctor, but as we saw with the regrown Doctor, that's not enough for persistence. Soul pellets, even if they existed, simply wouldn't help.

The case of the Watcher is more difficult. The Watcher *seems* to have a distinct body. In any case, it suffers from the same problem as a soul pellet. If the Doctor *is* the Watcher, and the Watcher can be somewhere else, how do we ever know we have *the Doctor*?

What Do You Have in Mind?

That leaves us one remaining option—personal persistence essentially involves the *mind*, and this is surely what Gallifreyans believe. When Rose demands of the Tenth Doctor that he bring back the real Doctor, he says, "It's still me." "You can't be," Rose replies. "Then how could I remember this: the very first word I ever said to you? Trapped in that cellar, surrounded by shop-window dummies, ooh—such a long time ago? I took your hand, I said one word—just one word. I said, *Run!*"

In "The Christmas Invasion," the Tenth Doctor is challenged by the Prime Minister in almost identical words. The Doctor tells her: "Harriet Jones—we were trapped in Downing Street, and the one thing that scared you wasn't the aliens, it wasn't the war—it was the thought of your mother being on her own."

Both Rose and Harriet Jones take this evidence to override the contrary evidence from his bodily appearance. When the Tenth

Doctor recalls things that only the Doctor would know, they (perhaps too readily—since they have both experienced enough weirdness) accept that he *is* the Doctor.

The view that persistence of persons depends upon memory was proposed in 1690 by John Locke.[2] Locke is generally taken to have proposed that a later person A is identical with an earlier person B if and only if A remembers being B.

Note that we're using *memory* in a restricted way here, assuming that memory is *factive*, meaning you can't remember something that didn't actually happen. (Of course, you can *seem* to remember it.) Locke's memory criterion characterizes personal identity in terms of mental *connectedness,* and his critic Thomas Reid quickly pointed out the problem we noted above for bodily connectedness: it is possible for A to remember being B, and B remember being C, but A not remember being C.[3] This is especially likely in a case of normal forgetting, where an old man might remember being a young man, but not being a young boy.

That would be like the case of bodily disconnection we considered earlier. But in the case of mental connection, a different kind of case is disconcertingly common: amnesia, like that of John Smith. Smith doesn't remember being the earlier Doctor, so by Locke's account he *isn't* the Doctor. But the later Doctor remembers being Smith (he seems to retain memories of who Joan is, who the Family of Blood are, and so on), so he *is* Smith. And the later Doctor remembers being the earlier Doctor, so he *is* the earlier Doctor. That can't be right.

To get around failures of transitivity, *neo*-Lockeans like myself use a criterion of mental *continuity* (once again, overlapping chains of connectedness). Even though there's a sharp break in connectedness between John Smith and the earlier Doctor, *because* the later Doctor remembers being various stages of John Smith and also remembers being various stages of the earlier Doctor, there are, in fact, overlapping chains of connectedness between John Smith and the earlier Doctor. Whew! (So, Joan Redfern is being a bit melodramatic when she says, "John Smith is dead.")

But what about cases where the amnesiac never recovers the crucial lost memories? Suppose John Smith had just gone on being *John Smith?* Here the neo-Lockean has two choices. Either he takes

---

[2] *An Essay Concerning Human Understanding,* Chapter XXVII.

[3] *Essays on the Intellectual and Active Powers of Man,* Volume 1, p. 397.

it on the chin, and just grants that severe amnesia is loss of the original person; or else he allows that there's more to your mental life than remembering who you are, and that other states can support mental connectedness and continuity. John Smith remembers how to speak a natural language, for instance, and he got that from the Doctor.

Who Is Jackson Lake?

In "The Next Doctor" (2008), Jackson Lake thinks he's the Doctor, but we discover that he really isn't. He's experiencing a kind of fugue state, thanks to a personal trauma and a bit of Cyber-technology, the infostamp. In a more ordinary fugue case, the new personality is more or less made up of whole cloth, presumably out of the brain's ability to confabulate to protect us. That'd be more like the case of John Smith. (Though fugue patients often can't remember the fugue, once they recover their old selves, and we might have to resort to other states to claim persistence through it.)

But Lake takes on an existing persona, and, more disturbingly for the neo-Lockean account, one that seems related in the right way to the original Doctor.

Let me explain. Suppose that the Doctor encounters a crazy, obsessed fan. This fan believes with all his heart and soul that *he* is the Doctor. (The Fifth Doctor thinks he has encountered just such a fan in "Time Crash"!) But the fan has limited access to the Doctor's actual adventures, and so "remembers" mostly made-up nonsense. Of course, the fan is *not* the Doctor, not even qualifying for mental continuity with him.

However, in Lake's case, the infostamp gives him "everything you could want to know about the Doctor." Intuitively, Jackson Lake isn't the Doctor, but why not? Doesn't he have what it takes, in terms of mental continuity? To find the answer, we have to consider another weird sort of transformation that turns up in *Doctor Who*.

What's in Teleportation?

The tertiary literature on *Doctor Who* tells us that teleportation is a form of "instantaneous matter transport," or some such. Rubbish. That'd be the dumbest technology anyone ever invented, for two reasons. First, it'd never make sense for short-range transport, since it'd be incredibly expensive in terms of the energy costs of converting matter into energy and back again. The speed advantage just wouldn't be worth it.

And it wouldn't make sense for long-range transport, because there's a much better alternative: just send the information, and use recruited matter at the other end to build a replica. Much cheaper!

The idea of teleportation—which I shall from now on understand as information-only transmission—gives most people the heebie jeebies. It seems to them too much like death, especially when I explain that if you're worried about there being two of you, don't—we're going to painlessly kill the original.

But this is one of those times when ordinary intuition is in conflict with itself. Consider a case Locke described in 1690. He imagined a scenario familiar to us from umpteen Hollywood movies: a Prince finds himself somehow in the body of a cobbler. Of course, everyone else at first thinks that the person in front of them is the cobbler, but it's really the Prince.

Body-swap movies play this out well. Inevitably, close friends become convinced that the "cobbler" really is the Prince, and so do we, the audience! We readily grant that the Prince goes where his mind goes. If we were to seek out the Prince's body and find he thinks he's the cobbler, this would just confirm our suspicions. But it isn't necessary. Suppose that conspirators have snuck in and killed the Prince during the night. Now he won't be able to swap bodies back again, but on the other hand, he survived what would otherwise have ended him!

Did you notice that the scenario I've just described is structurally identical to teleportation? So if you can survive it, you can survive teleportation. Make up your mind.

Who's Your Closest Continuer?

Suppose we teleport you, by scanning you and then sending the information. But we don't kill you *here*, and the replica is produced *there*. What gives? The clear ordinary intuition is that the one *here* is you, and the one *there* isn't. I think this is true.

This would be like seeking out the Prince's body, and discovering that *he* also thought he was the Prince, knew everything the Prince would know, and so on. We would conclude that he's right, and the cobbler-body person is wrong. So even if Jackson Lake is mentally continuous with some version of the Doctor, he isn't the Doctor.

I think the way to understand this is through what Robert Nozick calls the *closest continuer schema* for identity.[4] Really, it'd be more accurate to call it the closest *close-enough* continuer schema, but that's a mouthful. If I'm right (and I always am), then for Jackson Lake to be close enough, he has to mentally continuous with the Doctor, and there's a case for saying he is. But unless he's the *closest* such continuer, bad luck—and there's a Doctor who's closer. (I'm not sure who it is, since I'm not sure of the complete temporal sequence—a chronic problem with time travelers.)

Now we can make sense of "Journey's End." Neither the regrown Doctor nor the Doctor/Donna is *the Doctor*. Each seems mentally continuous with him, though goodness knows how—unless a Time Lord's consciousness is had by his right hand, reminiscent of Locke noting that if consciousness was contained in the "little finger," then you would go where your little finger goes. (In "The End of Time," the Master regenerates from a ring and a biometric imprint, and somehow this supports mental continuity!) Mental continuity isn't enough, though, and there's a closer candidate around—the one and the only, the Doctor.

What's Persistence Without Identity?

So far, so good. But it may leave you feeling that personal identity isn't what it used to be. After all, *if* Jackson Lake had had enough mental continuity with the Doctor, and had been the closest continuer, then he *would* have been the Doctor!

This makes personal identity rather like the story identity we considered earlier. It seems not a very deep fact about the world, and heavily dependent upon our interests. I think this is true.

The philosopher Derek Parfit has gone so far as to say that persistence isn't really what matters in personal survival.[5] Suppose you undergo *fission* teleportation: we scan you, and we kill you. But two signals are sent, and two replicas produced. Each of the replicas *would have been you* if not for the other, but *it is not you* because of the other.

So you don't persist through such a process. How bad is that? Surely, Parfit argues, it isn't as bad as ordinary death—rather, it's about as good as ordinary survival. So what you really should want

---

[4] *Philosophical Explanations.*
[5] Derek Parfit, *Reasons and Persons*, pp. 199–201.

in personal survival is not persistence, but that someone exists in the future who is mentally continuous with you.

There're ways to preserve the role of persistence in personal survival. David Lewis holds the view mentioned earlier that persons are space-time worms, individuated by mental continuity.[6] In the fission case above, there was no single you prior to the fission. What we called "you" was in fact two overlapping persons sharing a person stage, much the way that two distinct highways might share a stretch of road surface.

But what happens in "Journey's End," according to Lewis's view? That depends. He might regard "the Doctor" as undergoing triple fission, so there really was no single Doctor in the first place. Or he might employ some version of the closest continuer schema, to preserve the ordinary intuition that neither the regrown Doctor, nor the Doctor/Donna, really is *the Doctor.*

---

[6] "Survival and Identity."

4

Is the Doctor Still the Doctor—Am I Still Me?

DAVID KYLE JOHNSON

K'ANPO RINPOCHE: The Doctor is alive.

SARAH JANE: No, you're wrong. He's dead.

K'ANPO RINPOCHE: All the cells of his body have been devastated . . . but you forget he is a Time Lord. . . . His cells will regenerate. He will become a new man.

BRIGADIER: Literally?

K'ANPO RINPOCHE: Of course, he will look quite different . . . and it will shake up the brain cells a little. You may find his behavior somewhat . . . erratic. . . .

SARAH JANE: Look, Brigadier, look. I think it's starting.

BRIGADIER: Well, here we go again.

—"Planet of the Spiders," 1974

According to K'anpo Rinpoche, each time the Doctor regenerates his cells are replaced and his brain structure is rearranged. Consequently, each Doctor has been quite unique. The First was a crotchety old man—a white-haired grandfather giving those young whipper-snappers "what for." By contrast, the Tenth was an exuberant young man—a great-haired lover, brash and impetuous. In between, he's been a clown (Sixth), a pleasant uncle (Third), a cricket player (Fifth), a scatterbrained jelly-baby-offering comedian (Fourth), and Moe from the Three Stooges (Second).

But does regeneration make the Doctor, literally, a different person? K'anpo Rinpoche suggests the difference is merely metaphorical. He'll behave and look different, sure, but he won't be literally a different person—like twins are literally different persons. The Doctor still is the Doctor, regeneration after regeneration. If we saw the First and Tenth Doctor together, however, there'd be nothing to make us think they are, literally, the same person. They're more different than they're the same—more different than you and the person across the room. You and he or she aren't the same person, right? So how could each regeneration of the Doctor be, literally, the same person?

Who Cares?

So you're my replacements? A dandy and a clown?

— The FIRST DOCTOR, to the Second and Third ("The Three Doctors," 1972)

What we're asking is how the "replacements" could all be one in the same person. Non-*Who* fans might wonder, "Who cares?" But think about yourself at age ten. You acted differently, had a different worldview, a different personality, and different beliefs. As you learned, your brain structure was rearranged. In fact, gradually, your body completely replaced all of its cells using material and energy you ingested.[1] Just like the Doctor, *you regenerate*; and "you at ten" is less like "you now" than that person across the room. How could *you at ten* and *you now* possibly be the same person?

So our question about the Doctor's identity is very relevant. By answering it, we can answer an important question about ourselves: How is it that we retain our identity over time?

I'm a Soul Man

THIRD DOCTOR: Jo, it's all quite simple. I am he, and he is me.

JO GRANT: And we are all together, coo coo cachou?

SECOND DOCTOR: What?

JO GRANT: It's a song by The Beatles.

---

[1] How long does this take? Such things are hard to pin down. Different types of cells replace themselves at different rates, and brain cells are not replaced—once gone, they're gone—but are maintained. All in all, however, over time, your body fully discards and replaces all of the material that makes it up.

Second Doctor: Really? How does it go?

—("The Three Doctors")

A common answer is that *me at ten* and *me now* are the same person because we have the same soul. So perhaps what makes the Third and the Second Doctor the same person is their having *the same soul*. If persons (and Time Lords) are "ensouled" beings, this answer is fair enough. And the assumption that we have souls is widespread indeed. Yet, it's hardly ever questioned and not many can even articulate what a "soul" is supposed to be. If we don't even know what souls are, how do we know that persons have them?

The "soul"—as first defended by Plato (429–347 B.C.E.) and later defended by Descartes (1596–1650)—is the immaterial part of you.[2] It's not comprised of atoms and has no spatial location, but it's "where" decisions are made, self-control is exercised, emotions and sensations are felt, "where" memories are stored and recalled, reasoning occurs, your personality is housed and religious experience is generated. It can interact with the body, causing it to move; when your soul decides to raise your arm, your arm will rise. But it's not dependent upon your body for existence, so when you die, it "floats away." This was the conception accepted for thousands of years, and some version of this is what people who believe in a soul accept today.

But the problem with using "souls" to account for personal identity is that the concept of *soul* has been totally debunked. One might say it started when a rail road spike shot through Phineas Gage's head. A chunk of his forebrain was rendered inactive (pulverized), and Phineas was changed from "a purposeful, industrious worker into a drunken drifter," unable to control himself or make decisions. "Ladies were advised not to stay in his presence" and he would devise plans which were "no sooner arranged than they [were] abandoned."[3] "Wait a minute," people said. "If the soul—this separate from the body non-material thing—is where decisions and self-control happen and personality is housed, how could damage to Phineas's brain, a physical thing, affect them?" The answer: It couldn't. Those things must be housed in the brain—the part that Phineas lost—not the soul.

---

[2] See Plato, *Phaedo* and René Descartes, *Meditations on First Philosophy* .
[3] Rita Carter, *Mapping the Mind*, pp. 25–26.

That was just the start. Wilder Penfield found where our sensations of touch are housed, along with where some memories are stored. (Stimulating different parts of the brain directly can bring about a touch sensation on your hand or a distant childhood memory). Centers for emotion have been found, as well as for reasoning and intelligence. There's even a part of the brain responsible for religious experience. People who have seizures in that area "enjoy" a life of repeated "religious experiences" and deep "significance." You can even bring about such experiences by stimulating that part of the brain with magnets.[4] For every "thing" that we thought went on in the soul—which would be a separate-from-the-body, immaterial thing—we've found that it actually goes on in the brain—a completely-tied-to-the-body, material thing. As Tom Wolfe put it, "Sorry, But Your Soul Just Died."[5] And since it's dead, it will not suffice for an answer to our question.

Remember the Good Ole Days?

FIFTH DOCTOR: I've never met anyone else who could fly the TARDIS like that.

TENTH DOCTOR: Sorry mate, you still haven't.

FIFTH DOCTOR: You didn't have time to work all that out. Even I couldn't do it.

TENTH DOCTOR: I didn't work it out. I didn't have to.

FIFTH DOCTOR: You remembered.

TENTH DOCTOR: Because you will remember.

FIFTH DOCTOR: You remembered being me, watching you, doing that. You only knew what to do because I saw you do it.

TENTH DOCTOR: Wibbly Wobbly . . .

BOTH: . . . Timey Wimey!

—TENTH and FIFTH Doctor ("Time Crash," 2007)

One big difference between you and the person across the room is that you don't share any memories or mental states. But you do, at

---

[4] See V.S. Ramachandran, *Phantoms in the Brain*, Chapter 9.

[5] This is the title of Wolfe's article as it appears in *Forbes ASAP* (December 2nd, 1996).

least vaguely, with your ten year old self. The philosopher John Locke (1632–1704) therefore suggested that memory access is what accounts for personal identity over time. According to Locke, the reason the Tenth and the Fifth Doctor are the same person is because the Tenth Doctor remembers being the Fifth.

Although the memory link is good reason *to conclude* they're the same person, there are a few problems with saying that is what *makes them* the same person. One such problem was observed by Thomas Reid (1710–1796). Recall transitivity from math. If A=B and B=C then A=C. Likewise, if a first person is identical to a second and a third, then the second and third must be identical as well. But on Locke's criterion it doesn't always work that way.

Recall Donna Noble, who had the memory of her adventures with the Doctor wiped in "Journey's End" (2008) because she became the half human–half Time Lord "DoctorDonna." By Locke's criteria, Pre-Doctor Donna is identical to DoctorDonna because DoctorDonna remembers her life before the Doctor. And Post-Doctor Donna is also identical to Pre-Doctor Donna, for the same reason. So far, so good. According to transitivity, DoctorDonna must be identical to Post-Doctor Donna as well. And that makes sense; even though she acts differently, we don't think Post-Doctor Donna is, literally, a different person. But since Post-Doctor Donna doesn't remember being DoctorDonna, Locke would have to say that they are, literally, different individuals. So Locke's theory gets it wrong.

Paul Grice (1913-1988) modified Locke's theory to try to solve similar problems, and we can modify his to solve the "Donna Identity Problem."[6] Contrary to fact, let's say the Eleventh Doctor can't remember being the First—it was just too long ago. Grice would say that this doesn't keep the Eleventh and the First Doctor from being the same person. The Eleventh can remember being the Tenth, the Tenth the Ninth, and so on, all the way back to the Second remembering the First. There's a "chain of memory" running back that connects the Eleventh and the First Doctor. Grice would suggest that personal identity can run backwards along that chain and thus the Eleventh and First Doctor are identical, even if the Eleventh Doctor doesn't remember the First.

Let us suppose that personal identity can run backwards *and forwards* along a memory chain. If so, the "Donna Identity

---

[6] "Personal Identity," in *Personal Identity*.

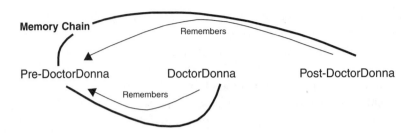

Problem" is solved. Since Post-Doctor Donna remembers Pre-Doctor Donna, and DoctorDonna remembers Pre-Doctor Donna as well, there's a as memory chain that connects Post-Doctor Donna to DoctorDonna.

So, on our modified Grician theory, Post-Doctor Donna and DoctorDonna would be identical.

Yay for us, right? The identity question is answered, right? . . . Not quite.

What about total amnesia? After a severe injury, you might awake unable to remember a single day of your life. If you never regained your memory, the memory chain would be completely broken and on our new criterion that would mean you'd be, literally, a different person. But would you?

To test your intuition on that, consider the following thought experiment inspired by Bernard Williams (1929–2003).[7] In the "Human Nature"/"The Family of Blood" two-parter from 2007, the Doctor traps his memories inside the Chameleon Arch (a.k.a. his pocket watch) and "becomes" John Smith to hide from the Family of Blood. Assuming John Smith's fictional stories about the Doctor don't count as real memories, are John Smith and the Doctor, literally, different persons? Martha Jones, and the others in the show (including John Smith) certainly speak as though they are. But suppose the Doctor knew John Smith was going to be tortured by the Family of Blood. Would the Doctor say, "I'm not worried. I won't even feel anything. John Smith won't be me." Probably not. Even if he thinks regaining his memories would erase John Smith's, he'd probably still dread the upcoming pain because he believes, despite the memory loss, that he will feel it.

I know I would! So unless your intuition is vastly different than mine, memory simply isn't going to be useful in a criterion for

---

[7] "The Self and the Future."

personal identity over time. But if that won't work, and the concept of "a soul" has been debunked, where else can we go?

The Causal Nexus

SUSAN: Is he really . . .

FIRST DOCTOR: Me? Yes. I'm afraid so. Regeneration?

FIFTH DOCTOR: Fourth.

FIRST DOCTOR: Goodness, me, so there are five of me now!

—("The Five Doctors," 1983)

Even the First Doctor admits he's literally identical to his regenerations. Memory can't explain it, but there's something else that connects his regenerations that could explain it: a causal chain. For any given moment in time, the condition of one's body at that moment is mainly brought about, causally, by the condition of one's body at the previous moment. This is especially true of one's brain, where how it's wired and firing one moment causally determines how it's wired and firing the next. Since regeneration is a causal process, regeneration would not break that chain. So maybe it's the fact that the Doctor's regenerations are all linked together with a causal chain that accounts for his personal identity over time.

Derek Parfit suggests this can account for *your* personal identity over time as well. But if this criterion is right, it should give us intuitive answers regarding personal identity, even in weird sci-fi circumstances. Recall "Journey's End" when the Doctor channels his regenerative energy into his severed hand, and it grows into the New Doctor. This entire "meta-crisis" process is a causal one—both the Doctor and Donna explain it—and so by Parfit's criterion, the New Doctor and the Tenth Doctor are, literally, the same person. But are they?

The episode's writer, Russell T Davies, is a bit ambiguous on this point. At Bad Wolf Bay, when Rose denies that they're identical, the Tenth Doctor suggests they are merely similar, saying "He needs you; that's very me." But later, when Rose insists that "the Doctor is still you," the Tenth Doctor replies, "And I'm him." Their divergent answers to Rose's later question about their final words seem to indicate that he was only being metaphorical—but it doesn't matter. They can't be, literally, the same person. Literal identity must pick out one and only one thing; otherwise, we'd land ourselves in contradictions—like we would if we suggested that the Tenth Doctor and the New Doctor are identical. The New Doctor isn't a regeneration of the Tenth Doctor, so he's not "later" in the Doctor's time stream. So what one does, the other never does. But the Doctor can't both be romantically involved with Rose and never have been; he can't both regenerate into the bow-tie-wearing, Amy-Pond-adventuring, Eleventh Doctor and also live out the rest of his life in "Pete's world" with Rose, no bow-ties, and never regenerating.

To defend Parfit's criterion one might suggest that, to preserve identity, an event must have the right kind of causation but the meta-crisis doesn't have it. But why not? And what counts as the right kind of causation? Would tele-transporters—like the T-Mat in "Seeds of Death" (1969) or the transporters in "The Sontaran Stratagem" (2008)—preserve the right causal connection? If they don't, "transporters" are really suicide machines—they kill you and create a replica at your destination. If they do, it's possible to create more than one of you—this happened constantly on *Star Trek*—but again paradoxes ensue. It seems that causation isn't going to supply us with the answer we need, either.

The Whole Show

Have you ever thought what it's like, to be wanderers in the fourth dimension?

—First Doctor ("An Unearthly Child," 1963)

Maybe the answer eludes us because we've been asking the wrong question. Consider this:

• *Doctor Who*, as a TV show, was a black and white kids' show in the early 1960s—with horrendous special effects. In the late 1960s, it was a bit of a monster/detective show and the Doctor often wore costumes to fool his enemies. The early 1970s brought color and a James Bond feel—what with the *Who Mobile* (Betsy), the flying cars, and a regular "arch villain" (the Master). Tom Baker gave us a little more action/adventure and a season-long story arc (regarding The Key to Time). It was even a little scary at times, before it was "camped up" in the late 1970s. The 1980s was more hard core sci-fi and during one of the Colin Baker years, it was more like "Judge Judy" than anything else. It finished the decade as a show mainly dedicated to its hardcore fans, but when it was reincarnated in 2005, it was mainstream and even had respectable special effects.[8] Yes, they all have the same name, "*Doctor Who*," but how could they all be *the same show*—specifically, how could the new and the old shows be the same show?

But when we think about this question, we realize it's kind of silly. What do we mean by, "be the same show?" Are we asking about particular episodes—like "An Unearthly Child" (1963) and "The Big Bang" (2010)? If so, what are we asking about them? Whether they're the same episode? Clearly they're not. In order for the question to make sense, we must be asking whether they're episodes of *the same show*. Thus "show" refers to a collection, a "set" of episodes that airs over a period of time. Asking "is it still the same show" queries whether the current episodes should be placed in the same set to which the old episodes belong.

I think they should. The classic shows (from "An Unearthly Child" to "Survival," 1989) all belong in the same set because there's a causal chain that runs through them. Despite the hiatus, that causal connection remained unbroken when the show was revived in 2005. The changes were no more drastic than those that happened from season to season, on occasion, in the old days. There was even a 1990s movie to fill the gap. To boot, the new episodes are inspired by the old episodes, reference them, and are based on the same concepts: the Doctor, the TARDIS, Daleks, Cybermen, Sontarans, and sexy companions—some of whom have even returned from the classic shows, like Sarah Jane.

Regardless of whether I'm right, the point is that we started with a bad question. Shows aren't things that happen at particular times; they're collections of things (episodes) that happen at particular times. Asking, "are the new and old shows the same show?" doesn't appreciate this fact. We should be asking whether their episodes can rightfully be placed in the same set.

Perhaps the same is true of persons. Perhaps persons don't exist at particular moments, but instead are collections of things that exist at particular moments. If so, "Are the First and Tenth Doctor the same person?" is a misguided question. We should be asking

---

[8] For more on why the series followed this path, see James Chapman, *Inside the TARDIS: The Worlds of Doctor Who*.

whether they're members of the set of objects that is *the Doctor*. What would make them members of the same set? Probably the same thing that made their episodes, episodes of the same show— a causal connection and common elements. Since these are present, it seems that they are the same person; that is, they are members of the set of objects that is the Doctor.

So the Doctor isn't something that can exist at a particular place at a particular time; he's not a three-dimensional object. Instead, he's a four-dimensional object—a collection of three dimensional objects—stretched across time and space, held together by causal connections and common elements. The First, Second, Third, Fourth, Fifth, Sixth, Seventh, Eighth, Ninth, Tenth, and Eleventh Doctors are not "the same person," but parts of the same person. Together, they make up the Doctor.

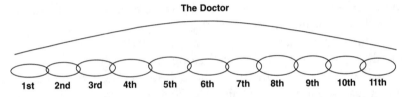

We might say that the Doctor is a four-dimensional "time worm."[9]

Once again, for this theory to work, it's going to have to remain intuitive, even in light of weird sci-fi examples. Consider again "Journey's End," where the New Doctor splits off from the original. The split still creates two persons, but the way we describe them will make much more sense now. They'll both share many parts— in fact, they'll have all the same parts up to the split. But since they diverge after that, they're two different collections of objects and thus two different people—two different time worms.

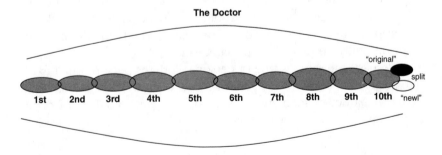

---

[9] This theory is inspired by David Lewis, "Survival and Identity."

Since black and white make gray, you can see how the two Doctors share many parts but aren't the same set of objects. Rose seems unsatisfied because she ends up with the New Doctor who she believes isn't the man she originally met. But the New Doctor is a set of objects, the members of which include the "episodes" of the Doctor with which she had her original adventures. So she really has nothing to complain about.

If persons don't exist as three-dimensional objects, but are four-dimensional time worms, then our original question ("What makes *you at ten* and *you now* the same person?") was ill-formed. You don't exist like you think you do; neither *you now* nor *you at ten* are a person. You're merely parts—time slices or "episodes"—of a person: a four-dimensional object that stretches from your birth to your death. Like the Doctor, we're all wanderers in the fourth dimension.

I Think, Therefore I Exist . . . I Think

Go on, scan me. . . . I don't exist. Therefore, you can't kill me. . . . Brilliant!

—TENTH DOCTOR ("Voyage of the Damned," 2007)

But we've been making one major assumption: that persons exist. Objections to the "four-dimentional time worm" theory, however, seem to entail that persons don't exist at all. I know it sounds strange, but hear me out.

Think about *Doctor Who* as a show again. Do *Torchwood* and *The Sarah Jane Adventures* belong to that same entity? They're related to the original, but are they related in the right way? And what about the *K9 and Company* Christmas special (1981)? What about "Curse of the Fatal Death" (1999)—that parody for the comic relief telethon where the Doctor starts off as Mr. Bean and regenerates five times in less than twenty minutes, once as Hugh Grant? What about *Abducted by the Daleks*, the "Straight-to-DVD spin-off film, in which four women . . . are captured by Daleks, groped by their plungers and forced to engage in soft porn shenanigans."[10] What does it take for a spin-off to be a part of the original show?

---

[10] Chris Howarth and Steve Lyons, *Doctor Who: The Completely Unofficial Encyclopedia*, p. 11.

When you study this kind of stuff, you come to realize that the answers simply depend upon convention. Question: You have a small pile of sand, and you add one grain of sand at a time. At what point does the pile become a heap? Answer: there is no answer. It just depends how the situation is described—where the line is drawn. And there's no right or wrong place to draw the line. *Heaps* aren't discrete entities that "emerge" when you have the right amount of sand. "Heap" is just a word we use to describe collections of sand.

What makes a collection of episodes "a show"? Answer: there is no answer. It depends on how the collection is described, and there's no right way to describe it. On one description, *Torchwood* episodes are a part of *Doctor Who*; on another, they only belong to a separate entity called *The Torchwood series*. And neither description is right because "shows" don't exist as discrete entities.

What if a person-time-worm had a "spin-off"—a causally related but independent break from the original line? Given recent developments in cloning technology, such questions may not be far off. We could go round and round on this issue—but ultimately it'd seem to come down to a matter of description. So when is a collection of objects—of three-dimensional biological time slices—a person? Answer: There is no answer. It just depends on how the collection is described and there's no right or wrong way to describe it. There's a collection of atoms—a "body"—sitting here reading this book; that much is true. But the idea that the body reading this book is somehow tied to an independently existing discrete entity called "a person" is wrong. There're only different, and equally valid, descriptions.

If so, our original question was completely off the mark. But we've already discovered that souls don't exist, and that persons can't exist at specific moments in time. Is the idea you don't exist at all any more radical? Honestly, it probably is. But that doesn't mean it's not true. If you don't exist, things are much simpler. Both the Doctor's and our regenerations raise far fewer questions. However, if this leaves "you" with an unsettled feeling, "I" understand. It might be one of those ideas that, even if we're convinced by the arguments, we'll never be able to accept it. Then again, maybe once "you" get used to the idea, "you" will like it—just like every new regeneration of the Doctor.

Okay. I just reversed the polarity of the neutron flow . . . so you can stop reading now.

EPISODE 2

Wibbly-Wobbly, Timey-Wimey . . . Stuff

The Science, Logic, and Other Really Cool Stuff of Doctor Who

5

Timey-Wimey Stuff

PETER WORLEY

People don't understand time—it's not what you think it is. It's complicated—very complicated. People assume that time is a strict progression from cause to effect, but actually—from a non-linear, non-subjective viewpoint—it's more like a big ball of wibbly-wobbly, timey-wimey . . . stuff.

—TENTH DOCTOR ("Blink")

This is how the Doctor *begins* to explain the nature of time to Sally Sparrow in the exquisite story "Blink" (first broadcast in 2007), and Sally says to herself in response to the TV-screen Doctor, "Started well, that sentence." "It got away from me, yeah," replies the Doctor coincidentally.

In this chapter, I'm going to try to finish the Doctor's sentence that started so well.

Vitruvian Man in the City of Death

Is time travel possible? We could try to answer this question empirically or logically. An *empirical* fact is one that is open to scientific investigation. So if we ask whether time travel is possible and we try to answer it empirically then we'd need to ask whether the technology has allowed for it up to now or would allow for it in the future. In other words, *will technology one day allow for a TARDIS to be built?*

A *logical* fact, by contrast, is one that we know to be true or false without the need for scientific investigation. So, even if technology allowed us to build a TARDIS, *would it actually be possible for a TARDIS to work?*

Imagine that you're hanging around the Doctor in Paris during the story "City of Death" (1979) and you manage to stow away in the TARDIS when he travels back in time. You step outside into a room, littered with Renaissance paraphernalia. You notice that among all the unfinished notes strewn about the place is a painting of a very familiar face, only it's different than how you're used to seeing it: you're looking at an unfinished *Mona Lisa,* and you realize, with a wave of excitement, that you're in the house of Leonardo Da Vinci. As you listen to the sound of footsteps coming towards you, you're relieved to have worked so hard at your *Old Italian (Florentine dialect)* exam at school. As Leonardo enters the room you find you don't need it as he says, "Who are you and what are you doing in my house?" in perfect English but with a bad Italian accent (it's *Doctor Who* after all).

You get into a conversation with the Maestro and you notice, spread out on the table, his design for one of his famous flying machines. You know that flight hasn't been mastered at this time but you also know that in the future the Wright brothers will achieve it in 1903 and it'll be commonplace by 2010.

When you ask the Maestro if flight is possible he answers, "Of course . . ." and goes on to list all the reasons he has for thinking that flight can be achieved, mechanically, by humans. (You resist telling him that one of his flying machines, the hang-glider, will in fact work even though you know he'll never get to see it for himself. The dramatic irony is moving and you feel something of the responsibility of a Time Lord).

But when you ask him if one day someone will be able to make a 'round-square', he looks bemused and says, "That could never happen—it's a *contraddizione logica.* The very definition of a *square* is such that it couldn't contain *roundness*—if it did, it wouldn't be a square. And the very definition of *roundness* is such that it can't contain straight sides and right angles—if it did, it wouldn't be round. This will never be true no matter how far in the future you find yourself."

"What about your *Vitruvian Man,* where you brilliantly use the figure of a man to describe a square *and* a circle. Isn't that a round-square?" You object tentatively, pleased with your reference, hoping that, at this point, he's completed the *Vitruvian Man.* "That's a square *within* a circle." He corrects, clearly knowing what you're talking about, to your relief. "My *Vitruvian Man* contains three concepts: the concept of a *square,* a *circle,* and the concept of *within.*

The single concept of a round-square is simply impossible. Now leave me alone, I'm working!" He says, picking up his paintbrush. Then he looks at you with interested eyes and says, "Ah, but you have a very mysterious smile." You run away quickly. (Leonardo's *Vitruvian Man* was completed in 1487; his plans for the flying machine in 1488 and his *Mona Lisa* (La Gioconda) in 1503–1506. Have another look at the famous painting—do you recognize the smile?)

So now we know the difference between empirical and logical possibility. If something is logically impossible it's called—as Leonardo said—a *logical contradiction*. Another example of a logical contradiction would be: 2 + 2 = 5. And yet another example, so many people believe, is time travel.

Time Loops and Paradoxes

Time travel does seem to lead to logical contradictions. In the story "The Invisible Enemy" (1977) Leela is immune to the virus that threatens everybody else in the story. She contributes her anti-bodies, which in turn save the human race. However, it's from a later stage in the human race's development that she inherits her immunity (the story is happening in her past). So, Leela is both the *cause* and the *effect* of the antibodies: she wouldn't be there if it weren't for the anti-bodies, but at the same time, the anti-bodies wouldn't be there (at the time of her conception) if it weren't for her.

It's a paradoxical loop where the anti-bodies don't seem to have come from anywhere and this is impossible according to our understanding of causation. There's a similar idea in an Anthony Burgess story, *The Muse*, in which a character travels back in time and furnishes Shakespeare with all his plays so that Shakespeare simply copies them out. This would mean that nobody actually *created* Shakespeare's plays. "Blink" is another example of this in *Doctor Who*.

Think about it: *who wrote his lines on the DVD Easter egg?* The Doctor simply reads them from the document he's been given by Sally Sparrow, and they're only on the document because Larry Nightingale copied them from the DVD. Again, nobody actually created them.

One of the basic laws of logic is the *law of non-contradiction*. It states that something can't both be true and false at the same time. In the story "The Edge of Destruction" (1964), the Doctor and his companions find themselves at the very beginnings of the universe itself, so it's safe to say that all the non-Gallifreyan characters, Barbara and Ian, are at a point in time before they were born and it would therefore both be true that *they had been born* and that *they had not been born* and this does seem to contravene the *law of non-contradiction*. Philosophers would say: *it cannot be the case that it's true that both 'p and not p'*.

The Doctor (who obviously knows that time travel *is* possible because he's spent his entire life time-traveling and that would make it contradictory for him to say that it isn't possible) might point out here that the above example is just a *contradiction of statements*. So, you may be contradicting yourself to *say* these two things but that doesn't mean they can't be true. There's a famous example that bares this out.

The ancient Greek philosopher Zeno of Elea (490 B.C.E.) concocted what the Oxford philosopher Gilbert Ryle has claimed is the quintessential philosophical problem. And what makes it interesting to us is that it's a logical problem that leads to a contradiction that seems to entail that something couldn't be true that our experience tells us must be. The problem is called *Achilles and the Tortoise*. Achilles, the great Greek sprinter, is to race a tortoise. Knowing that the tortoise will be much slower, he gives the tortoise a head start. Now according to mathematics, whatever distance has been covered by Achilles as he races to catch up with the tortoise, there's a corresponding smaller distance covered by the tortoise. The problem is that the tortoise *always* moves *away* by *some* degree from Achilles however much closer he is to the tortoise. So it seems that logic tells us that Achilles can never overtake the tortoise, but we all know that reality tells us he can.

Just in case you are asking yourself, *how does logic tell us that? It's not clear to me.* Then let me try to explain in other words. If you have two objects at some distance apart and then you try to move them closer, geometry tells us that the distance between them can always be halved *ad infinitum*. But this means that the two objects could never actually reach each other, though quite clearly they can. Is there any way around these contradictions?

The Paradox Machine

The Master, in "The Sound of Drums" (2007) introduces a plot that is potentially paradoxical: the *Toclafane*—the future descendants of human beings—are brought back in time to destroy their human ancestors, without whom they couldn't exist. Aware that this is paradoxical, the Master converts the TARDIS into a *paradox machine* and its purpose is to resolve any paradoxical problems and thereby allow events to occur that would otherwise be cancelled out by a paradox. So, in our attempt to circumvent the paradoxes of time travel, we're invoking our own paradox machine.

An Australian philosopher, David Lewis (1941–2001), tackled these problems in his article "The Paradoxes of Time Travel." He believed that there are ways in which time travel stories can be seen as consistent, avoiding paradoxes. Lewis's implication is that time travel is, at least, logically coherent—that is to say 'possible'.

The TARDIS Inside and Out

David Lewis suggests that we can overcome the paradox mentioned earlier, with reference to the story "The Edge of Destruction," where it's both true and false that Barbara and Ian have been born, by thinking of time in two senses: *external* and *personal* time.

External time is the time line that the time traveler is traveling *through* either backwards or forwards through time, and personal time is the time line of the time traveler themselves that must always be moving forward. So, the Universe's history (outside the TARDIS) is the *external time* through which the Doctor moves around, the direction of which is at his discretion, but *inside* the TARDIS is his *personal time* that's always moving forward.

We've drawn a *distinction* between two kinds of time: *external* time and *personal* time. Returning to Barbara and Ian's case in the "Edge of Destruction," it's *true in her personal time* that she has been born and it's *false in external time* that she has been born. By drawing a distinction, we've avoided contravening the law of non-contradiction.

In "Silence in the Library" (2008) the Doctor meets a character, Professor River Song, who claims to have met his future self. This is quite a momentous event in the Doctor *Who* series as there are only rare references to his personal time line and almost none to his future incarnations. Another of these rare examples is "Battlefield" (1989) where the seventh incarnation of the Doctor is left a note from a future incarnation in the world of King Arthur where the inhabitants know him as 'Merlin'.

Does Lewis's idea make sense? The first question we might ask is: Can we split time into two simply by thinking about it? David Lewis may be guilty of what philosophers call an *ad hoc* move (literally: for this purpose). This is where you introduce notions simply to get out of a sticky situation or to support something you "like the idea of," rather than because you think it's true. One may object to Lewis's idea by saying that *time* is a single concept and that logic wouldn't allow for it to be split into two arbitrarily (if it can be split into two, then why not into three or four?). And we may ask the further question: exactly what reasons does Lewis give for upholding two kinds of time, other than to make sense of time travel for science-fiction geeks like me?

The Paradox of the Time Meddler

In the First Doctor's serial "The Aztecs" (1964), he repeats the refrain, "But you can't re-write history! Not one line!" David Lewis would agree and suggests that a consistent time-travel story must have one extra feature as well as this one in order to avoid paradoxes, and that is: *the events the time traveler brings about must themselves be the very events that made history as we know it*. An example of this in *Doctor Who* occurs in the story "The Visitation" (1982) in which the events of the story—which includes an alien plot in London of 1666—bring about the Great Fire of London (this fact being disclosed at the story's end where the camera pans to the street name where the fire has started: 'Pudding Lane'). This isn't to be thought of in a *fatalistic* sense (that the Great Fire of London *must happen anyway* and *whatever* events occur will inevitably lead to the realizing of this event), but in the sense that the events of the story are the events that did *in fact* bring about history as we know it, and always have been. This avoids the problem of having to introduce strange and inexplicable forces that *nurture* the events as we know them because they simply *are* the events that made history. Another example like this is in "The Chase" (1965) in which it's revealed that the Daleks are responsible for the disappearance of the crew on board the ship that turns out to be the *Mary Celeste*.

Accepting Lewis's idea, there follows a problem for the stories in that it excludes those where it's explicit that causal events are different from history but that the consequent events of history still occur. And it might seem that any interference from a time traveler is likely to cause things to be different in the future if we consider the complexity of causal circumstances. A *Whoian* example of this kind of problematic story is "The Time Meddler" (1965), which has a mischievous Time Lord character who tries to influence the Battle of Hastings in 1066, unsuccessfully. The crucial point here is that a person deliberately interferes with the facts of history as we know them, but the correct events still occur though the causal chain has been altered.

There's a very interesting exchange between the Doctor and his companions in "The Reign of Terror" (1964) that considers some of these problems though they all seem to be equally in the dark about it. "Events will happen, just as they are written," declares the Doctor in his peremptory way that is characteristic of the First Doctor incarnation. "Supposing we'd written Napoleon a letter telling him, you know, some of the things that were going to happen to him," muses Ian. "It wouldn't have made any difference, Ian," replies Susan. "He'd have forgotten it, or lost it, or thought it was written by a maniac." Barbara then adds: "I suppose if we'd tried to kill him with a gun the bullet would have missed him?" To which the Doctor says, rather vaguely, "Well, it's hardly fair to speculate, is it?"

The problem of changing history is also hinted at in "The Shakespeare Code" (2007) where Martha is concerned that their being in the past could have devastating consequences, as she notices, "It's like in the films. You step on a butterfly; you change the future of the human race." The Doctor simply replies, "Tell you what, then: don't step on any butterflies. What have butterflies ever done to you?" This being a reference to a Ray Bradbury short story, *A Sound of Thunder,* in which a character steps on a butterfly in the prehistoric past only to find that this has caused the world in his present to be altered unrecognizably. And this in turn is a reference to *chaos theory,* which is famous for the idea that a butterfly flapping its wings on one side of the world causes a storm on the other, highlighting the incredible complexity of causal chains.

Another classic paradox of time travel—that Lewis talks about—is also briefly mentioned in "The Shakespeare Code." Continuing the previous conversation Martha says, "What if . . . I don't know . . . what if I kill my Grandfather?" "Are you planning to?" quips the Doctor facetiously. Martha says, "No," and the Doctor replies, "Well then," conveniently avoiding exploring some of the less palatable consequences of time travel. But Martha has hit upon an important problem with time travel: if you kill your own grandfather then you've eliminated an essential cause of your own existence. The paradox should be clear.

It would seem to be an unfortunate consequence of time travel stories that allow for even the smallest interference of historic events that they'd inevitably bring about significant changes to future history. But once the time travel story is conceived as the very events that brought about history *as we know it* then we seem to be left with none of these sorts of problems: history isn't changed by the meddling time traveler, merely instantiated.

Turn Left

We shall take a left turn here because some people attempt to avoid this problem of the subtleties of time meddling by appealing to the notion of *possible worlds* and *parallel universes*.

In philosophy two very commonly used notions are that of *contingency* and *necessity* and they're used in relation to *truth*. A contingent truth is one that *could have been otherwise*, and a necessary truth is one that *could not have been otherwise*. And in order to flesh this out, philosophers talk about *possible worlds*.

Possible worlds were introduced to philosophy by the German Enlightenment philosopher Gottfried Leibniz (1646–1716). He asserted that ours is "the best of all possible worlds." This idea was entertainingly ridiculed by Voltaire (1694–1778) in his satirical story *Candide*. In the story "Turn Left" (2008), we have a good example of a possible world: one in which Donna didn't meet the Doctor and as a result, a whole bunch of other things happen to her. The events that occur in the possible world of "Turn Left" are contingent: that is to say they're events that we have no problem conceiving as being able to happen but are events that didn't happen in the 'real world'. It's perfectly conceivable that Donna turns right at the junction instead of left. Whenever you do something where it's conceivable that you could have done otherwise, philosophers say that *there is a possible world in which you did turn right instead of left*.

Philosophers aren't suggesting that these possible worlds are actual and exist somewhere in a parallel universe but that they're *conceivable*. Philosophers would express this by saying that possible worlds are a *logical construction* and not actual. . . . All philosophers, that is, except the Doctor and David Lewis.

Actual Actualists

The Doctor and David Lewis are what are known as *actualists* about possible worlds: they believe that possible worlds actually exist, and one way of conceiving of this—certainly for the purposes of exploring the possibility of time travel—is that every time a contingent event occurs, such as making a decision to turn right instead of left, possible worlds are created where the contingent events that you didn't instantiate are instantiated. It's as if time-streams split to realize all the different contingencies that are possible. This is dealt with in the series when explaining how the different incarnations of the Doctor meet in the multiple-Doctor stories such as "The Three Doctors" (1973).

Strictly speaking, there is an important distinction between possible worlds and parallel universes as possible worlds are logical and parallel universes are actual. This distinction is blurred, however, when we introduce *possible world-actualists*, such as Lewis.

Alternative Time

There's a fascinating discussion between the Doctor and Sarah in "Pyramids of Mars" (1975) where they're discussing whether or not they need to stop the evil Sutekh from his attempt to destroy the world in 1911. Aware that she's from 1980 Sarah says, "But he [Sutekh] didn't, did he? I mean we know the world didn't end in 1911." Using the TARDIS, the Doctor shows her the future as it would be if they don't stop him and it's like the distant future visited by the time traveler in H.G. Wells's *The Time Machine*: "A desolate planet circling a dead sun," as the Doctor says. He then makes an explicit reference to alternative futures that seems to imply the existence of parallel universes in the *Doctor Who* universe: "Every point in time has its alternative, Sarah. You've looked into *alternative time*."

The Doctor is an *actualist* because he has traveled into possible worlds and therefore has personal experience of their existence, notably in "Inferno" (1970), "Rise of the Cybermen" (2006), and, of course, "Turn Left." This is therefore more of a scientific hypothesis than a philosophical one, and this brings me to the scientific entity of *parallel universes,* which have been hypothesized because of some unusual behavior in sub-atomic particles that can apparently only be explained by the existence of parallel universes. (It's important to understand that this isn't *proof* of parallel universes but is only a hypothesis). David Lewis is an *actualist* for purely philosophical reasons that I shall not go into. Suffice it to say that he's unique among philosophers for holding this view. And the Doctor loves a maverick. As *Doctor Who* fans, we're also *actualists* about possible worlds for no other reason than it's fun and it allows many of the Doctor *Who* stories to make sense. But what has it got to do with our paradox machine?

Well, if there are parallel universes then this may get us out of the problem of time loops and the problems of time meddling, because if changes to the events of history inevitably create changes to our present then the changed events and the unchanged could conceivably co-exist, albeit in parallel universes. So, whenever a time traveler goes back in time and turns right instead of left, the subsequent chain of events spin off into an alternative parallel universe and thereby avoid paradoxes (and allow for the possibility of more spin-off series—because there aren't enough already).

We Wouldn't Be Here Without Time Travel

According to the story "City of Death" (1979), not only is time travel *possible* for human beings (and not just Time Lords and Ladies), but it turns out that time travel is *essential* for the existence of the human race. It's an explosion caused by the villain of the story, Scaroth (the last of the Jagaroth), that contributes the essential radiation that brings about life in our solar system, and although a possible paradox looms in the story—with Scaroth encouraging and using human-made time travel to try to avert the explosion which would thereby eliminate the causal factor that enables him to do this—it's avoided by the thwarting of Scaroth's plans by Duggan punching him (a disconcertingly prosaic explanation for life on Earth) and so is a consistent time travel story according to Lewis's conditions.

Now that we've shown time travel to be, at the very least, philosophically possible we've cleared the way for the building of a real time machine. So, put down the book, get out some blue planks of wood and a flashing light, and get to work. Just keep an eye out for Scaroth—you can't miss him, his face looks like a bowl of green spaghetti with an eye in the middle (which brings me to the question: *How was he able to see out of his human disguise with two eye-holes?*[1] Mmm . . . now there's a philosophical question).[2]

---

[1] I would like to thank seven-year-old Isaac Williams for this critical observation.

[2] I would also like to offer a huge thanks to Mark Trotman and Aled Williams for their help making sure the *Doctor Who* references were accurate. Any errors will be mine and not theirs.

6
Could the Daleks Stop the Pyramids Being Built?

PHILIP GOFF

The Daleks decide to time travel to the past in order to conquer Ancient Egypt, and in the process of doing so they exterminate every single Egyptian slave builder and stop the pyramids from being created. As the result of their evil destruction a new history without pyramids begins to unfold. Our only hope is that the Doctor can go back and foil the Daleks' evil plan. But will he succeed?

Such a story seems, on the face of it, paradoxical. On the one hand we want to say that the Daleks have made it the case that *there were no pyramids* in ancient Egypt: they've stopped them from being built at all. But on the other hand we want to say that *there were Pyramids* in ancient Egypt: they existed before the Daleks went back to the time before the pyramids and stopped them from being built. We seem to face a contradiction: it both was and wasn't the case that there were pyramids in ancient Egypt.

Whether or not we can avoid this paradox depends on our theory of time. Neither of the two most popular philosophical theories of time, *presentism* and *eternalism*, are able to make sense of changing the past. However, there is a middle way between these two views, *the growing block theory*, which allows us to make sense of this possibility of time travelers altering history.

There's No Time Like the Present

Presentism is the theory of time closest to common sense. According to presentism only events in the present moment exist: only the event of your reading these words, and everything simultaneous with it, are part of reality. Events in the future, such as your finishing this chapter or the setting up of human colonies on Mars, don't exist (although they perhaps *will* exist). Events in the past, such as your reading of the first line of this chapter or the Battle of Hastings in 1066, don't exist (although they *did* exist). For the presentist, there's an absolute fact about what time is 'now': quite simply 'now' is the only time that exists.

If presentism is the correct view of time, then time travel isn't possible at all. If the past and future don't exist, then we can't travel to them (you can't go to a land that doesn't exist). If the Doctor lives in a presentist world, then stepping into the TARDIS and setting the co-ordinates for ancient Egypt would be tantamount to committing suicide; he'd be traveling straight into non-existence.

What's So Special about Now?

Eternalists believe that all events in time exist equally. The Battle of Hastings in 1066, the setting up of human colonies on Mars, and your reading of this chapter, are all equally real. For the presentist 'now' is *absolute*, but for the eternalist 'now' is *relative*. For William the Conqueror, the eleventh century is 'now'. For the people setting up the first human colonies on Mars, the fifty-first century is 'now'. For you reading this chapter (unless my reputation survives my death by a bit) the twenty-first century is 'now'.

For the eternalist, 'now' functions a bit like 'here'. For me as I write this chapter, London is 'here'. Perhaps you're reading this in New York, in which case New York is 'here' for you (and 'there' for me). For the people in Timbuktu, Timbuktu is 'here'. There's no absolute fact about where 'here' is. God couldn't look down on space from Heaven, and say, "Ah, there's where 'here' is," pointing to some specific place slightly left of the Milky Way. Similarly, according to the eternalist, when God looks down on the whole of time, he doesn't look at the twenty-first century (or any other time) and say, "Oh yes, that's when 'now' is."

Presentism seems closer to our common-sense picture of time, but eternalism is arguably closer to our science. If there's an absolute present, as the presentist supposes, then it consists of a large number of events—my writing this chapter in London, Emma in New York getting on a bus, Yujin in Japan eating breakfast—which all happen *at the same time*. But according to Einstein's special theory of relativity, for any two events, say my writing this chapter in London and Yujin's eating breakfast in Japan, there's no absolute fact of the matter as to whether those two events happened at the same time or at different times. If there's no absolute fact of the matter as to whether two events happen 'at the same time', then there can be no absolute fact of the matter over which events are happening 'at the present time'. It looks as if Einstein's theory rules out there being an absolute present, and so is inconsistent with presentism.

In an eternalist world, all times exist and so time travel is possible. All that needs to happen for an eternalist world to contain time travel into the past is that causation sometimes work 'backwards': some of the causal processes in that world begin at a later time and end an earlier time). If the Doctor's operating the TARDIS controls in the twenty-first century causes the TARDIS to appear in the eleventh century, then we can truly say that the world contains time travel into the past.

While eternalism allows for *travel* into the past, it doesn't allow for time travelers to *change* the past. This is because eternalism is a *static* picture of time, which is to say the facts about time as a whole don't change. The facts about time as a whole are eternally laid out before God, as it were. If God looks to ancient Egypt, he either does or doesn't see the pyramids. It can't be the case that 'earlier' God sees the pyramids in ancient Egypt, and 'later' God sees no pyramids in ancient Egypt because they've been destroyed by the Daleks. There is no 'earlier' and 'later' in this context, after all God is looking down on the whole of time! The story of the Daleks changing the past by preventing the pyramids from being built is incoherent on the eternalist view of time.

This doesn't mean that time travelers can't *affect* the past, according to the eternalist picture of things. It might be among the eternal facts of time that the Doctor began his life in the far future and then went back in time and helped build the pyramids. We can make coherent sense of this so long as it doesn't involve a change in the eternal facts of time. Either it's among the facts of time that the Doctor helped build the pyramids or it isn't. It can't 'earlier' be the case that the Doctor didn't help build the pyramids, and 'later' the case that the Doctor did help build the pyramids; 'earlier' and 'later' make no sense when we're talking about the whole of time. In an eternalist world, time travellers like the Doctor and the Daleks can *affect* the past, but can't *change* the past.

The Growing Block Theory—A Middle Way

The presentist picture doesn't allow us to go to the past at all, because the past doesn't exist. The eternalist picture doesn't allow us to change the past, because the facts of time are unchangeably fixed. What we need is a theory of time in which the past exists, and so is there for us to pop over to, but in which time isn't static and unchangeable. This is exactly what we get from the growing block view of time, which is a kind of middle way between presentism and eternalism. The basic idea is that events in the past and present exist, but events in the future don't. The Battle of Hastings and your reading this chapter are part of reality, but the setting up of human colonies on Mars isn't. The flow of time is a continuous process of new events coming into being and remaining in existence.

The growing block view of time gives us everything we need to make sense of genuinely changing the past. The past exists, so we can get into a TARDIS and go back and visit it. But the events of time aren't static and unchanging, but flowing and dynamic. When God looks down at the world he witnesses the growing course of history, as more and more events come into existence. Just as in the presentist conception of things, in the growing block world there's an absolute fact about when 'now' is, but for a slightly different reason. For the presentist, 'now' is the only time that exists. For the growing block theorist, 'now' is not the only time that exists (the past exists too), but 'now' is the most recent time to have come into existence. Each "now" is the latest addition to reality.

What happens when the Daleks travel back into the past and exterminate the builders of the pyramids? If causation in the past works as it does in the present, the Daleks' intervention will create a new causal history without pyramids. Assuming that change happens at exactly the same rate in the past as it does in the present, this new history will replace the old history at exactly the same rate as the absolute present advances. If the absolute present is in the twenty-first century A.D. when the Daleks intervene in history in the twenty-first century B.C., then, by the time the absolute present reaches thirty-first century A.D. (one thousand years later), the new history (the one lacking pyramids) will have advanced to the eleventh century B.C. (one thousand years later, remember B.C. years count backwards!). By the time the absolute present reaches the forty-first century A.D. (another thousand years later), the new history will have advanced to the first century A.D. (another thousand years later). It's only when the absolute present reaches the sixty-first century A.D. that the new history will reach the twenty-first century A.D.

Crucially, because they advance at exactly the same rate, the new history will never catch up to the absolute present, and so will never completely 'write over' the old history. When the 'new history' (the one lacking pyramids) is up to the first century A.D., the second century A.D. onwards will still contain the 'old history' (the one where people have historical records of there being pyramids). If there're no time travelers, the flow of time will be just the flow of new events coming into existence in the present. But if there are time travelers journeying to the past and intervening in the course of history, then the flow of time will also be the flow of new histories slowly replacing old ones (at exactly the same rate as new events come into existence in the present). And so, even if the Doctor is unable to foil the Daleks and stop them preventing the pyramids from being built, it'll always be possible for him to get back into the TARDIS, return to the absolute present, and find himself in a world which is causally continuous with the old history, containing memories and historical documents which make reference to pyramids.

Of course, this is not how *Doctor Who* script writers generally present things. Generally, in time travel stories the old history is completely eliminated by intervention in history—in the first *Back to the Future* film Marty McFly slowly starts to fade as the history containing him is wiped from existence. But this is just because script writers are not thinking carefully enough about the metaphysics of time. If *Doctor Who* script writers adopted the growing block view of time as I have described it, then they could write time travel stories free from concern about the potential paradoxes of time travel (they wouldn't, for example, have to resort to avoiding paradox by introducing flying monsters to sterilize wounds in time, as we find in the "Father's Day" story from 2005).

To Be in the Past or Not to Be in the Past— What Is the Question?

Suppose the Daleks destroy the pyramids, so that they no longer exist in the past. The new history with no pyramids slowly begins to replace the old history with pyramids. But in the absolute present, because the people are causally continuous with the old history (remember, the ever advancing present will always contain people causally continuous with the old history because the new history will never be able to catch up with it), they'll have historical documents referring to the pyramids. Are those historical documents now incorrect, given that the pyramids are no longer contained in the past? Surely there's still a sense in which those documents are correct because, although there *are* no pyramids in the past, *there used to be pyramids in the past.*

To make sense of the growing block view of time we need to distinguish two senses in which an event can be said to 'be in the past'. First, an event might 'be in the past', in the sense that it occurred in the concretely existing past. In this sense, the pyramids, once the Daleks have destroyed them, cease to 'be in the past'. Call this sense of being in the past, 'concrete past existence'. Second, an event might 'be in the past' in the sense that it used to exist in the concretely existing past. Even when the Daleks destroy the pyramids, it still remains true that, first time round (as it were), the pyramids were part of the concrete past. Call this sense of being in the past 'abstract past existence'. Even after the Daleks have destroyed the pyramids, we can say that the historical records of pyramids in the absolute present are correct, because the pyramids still have abstract past existence (even though they lack concrete past existence).

Hold on: Didn't the Doctor and Rose travel to the year five billion to witness the end of the Earth? ("End of the World," 2005). It may seem as if the growing block view of time is limited because it can't allow travel to the future. This is of course true in a sense: we can't travel to the future of the absolute present, because the future of the absolute present doesn't exist. However, we need not suppose that *our* present (2010) is the absolute present. Perhaps the Time Lords of Gallifrey exist (or rather existed before they were annihilated from all of space and time in the Time War) in the absolute present a billion years ahead of our present. In this way we can make sense of the Doctor's adventures in our future as well as our past.

The Daleks Can Stop the Pyramids from Being Built!

If only the present moment exists, then the Daleks couldn't travel to the past and stop the pyramids being built, because the past no longer exists. If the past, present, and future all exist equally, then it could be among the eternal facts of time that the Daleks traveled to ancient Egypt, but they couldn't stop the pyramids being built (given that they were built), because the facts of time as a whole are eternal and unchanging. If the past and the present exist, but the future doesn't, then the Daleks can travel to ancient Egypt (because it's there to travel to), and they can also change it (because time in such a world is dynamic and flowing rather than static and unchanging). The growing block theory of time allows us to make sense of the Daleks stopping the pyramids from being built. But don't panic; even if the growing block theory is true, I'm sure the Doctor won't let them get away with it!

7

The Doctor on Reversed Causation and Closed Causal Chains

WILLIAM EATON

The Doctor is usually too occupied with practical concerns to participate in any serious metaphysics, and justifiably so. But in "Blink" (2007), the practical concerns themselves require the Doctor to present some of his views on the nature of time, time travel, and causation. The Doctor is trapped, without his TARDIS, in 1969, and the TARDIS itself is in danger of being destroyed, taking the Earth's solar system along with it. The Doctor's only chance to retrieve the TARDIS and prevent the calamity is to convince a woman in 2007 named Sally Sparrow to send it back to him. In the course of doing this he explains the nature of time. The explanation is brief and, due to his pressing predicament, left unjustified. All we get concerning the Doctor's philosophy of time are the following fragmentary claims:

> People don't understand time. It's not what you think it is. [It's] complicated, very complicated. People assume that time is a straight progression of cause to effect. But from a non-linear, non-subjective viewpoint, it's more like a big ball of wibbly-wobbly, timey-wimey stuff. ("Blink," 2007)

This is all we get, the Doctor doesn't have time to elaborate—and as we'll see, there's a sense in which it isn't possible for him to elaborate. The statement is so brief one might hesitate to describe it as a coherent philosophy of time at all. But I think the Doctor says just enough to make describing his philosophy of time possible. His statements are open to a number of interpretations, but David Lewis provides a model by which we can develop the statements into an insightful theory of time, which many philosophers today might agree with.

Let's start by considering Lewis's philosophy of time. According to Lewis, the universe is a four-dimensional manifold of events. There're the normal three spatial dimensions of height, width, and depth, and there's also one temporal dimension. This view is sometimes called *four-dimensionalism*. It's actually very similar to the original model H.G. Wells himself describes in *The Time Machine*. People usually move in one direction in time, but it's at least possible to move in both.

In his article, "The Paradoxes of Time Travel," Lewis's goal is to show that time travel is logically possible, which means the apparent paradoxes raised by time travel can be solved. According to Lewis's view there's only one temporal dimension that, like the spatial dimensions, is more or less fixed. This can be contrasted with other views of time travel, less plausible in my opinion, in which events, such as decisions or actions, can branch or split, creating multiple temporal dimensions.

Anatomy of a Time Traveler

To explain the possibility of time travel, Lewis introduces the important distinction between *external time* and *personal time*. By external time Lewis means the complete, objective temporal dimension comprising the entire history of the universe. Personal time shouldn't be seen as a separate temporal dimension existing outside of external time. It's composed, rather, of the events that comprise the personal history of the time traveler. It might be helpful to think of personal time as the time measured by the traveler's watch. For example, imagine a time traveler, perhaps Martha Jones, who lives normally for twenty-seven years and time travels for the first time in 2007, after she turns twenty-eight. If she travels back in time to 1969 then parts of the twenty-eighth year of her life actually occur before she was born. As Lewis puts it:

> A time traveler, like anyone else, is a streak through the manifold of space-time, a whole composed of stages located at various times and places. But he is not a streak like other streaks. If he travels toward the past he is a zig-zag streak, doubling back on himself. If he travels toward the future, he is a stretched-out streak. And if he travels either way simultaneously, so that there are no intermediate stages between the stage he departs and the stage he arrives and his journey has zero

duration, then he is a broken streak. ("The Paradoxes of Time Travel," p. 69)

Thus a time traveler's personal time can bend back on itself in such a way that two different stages of personal time can even occupy the same point in external time. To see how this is possible, Lewis compares it to a train track that curves around, eventually intersecting itself. The point that is five miles down the line might be at the same location as the point ten miles down the line. But this intersection of points does not require positing an additional spatial dimension. Likewise, a stage of a time traveler's personal time can intersect with an earlier or later stage without requiring us to posit an additional time dimension. This occasionally happens to the Doctor when he meets other regenerations of himself. Lewis's distinction between personal and external time allows us to see how this is possible.

Another important consequence of four-dimensional time travel is the possibility of reversed causation. According to Lewis, travel into the past necessarily involves instances in which effects precede their causes. Normally, causes precede their effects—so much so that some philosophers claim that this is part of the very meaning of word *cause*, and reversed causation can be ruled out because of the meanings of words. But if time travel is possible there can be instances in which the effect actually precedes the cause. And this is very important for understanding the Doctor's philosophy of time. Lewis asks us to imagine a time traveler who gets punched in the eye just before traveling into the past. The effect of a black eye might happen years or even eons before he was punched. Notice that the distinction between personal time and external time explains this unusual phenomenon. In terms of personal time the black eye occurred after the punch, just as it usually would. But from an external, objective point of view, that is, viewing all of space-time as a whole, the black eye exists before the punch.

Consider another example, a thirsty time traveler about to travel into the past. As the time machine is activated, he drinks an *Old Speckled Hen*. From the standpoint of personal time nothing unusual has occurred. The traveler was thirsty and then satisfied his thirst by drinking an excellent English ale. But the standpoint of external time yields a bizarre and borderline paradoxical result. The traveler's thirst becomes satisfied before, possibly eons before, he ever became thirsty.

I think that reversed causation is precisely what the Doctor has in mind when he explains that time isn't what people normally think it is. Non-time-travelers assume time is a straight progression from cause to effect because they don't need to distinguish between personal and external time. From the subjective and linear point of view of personal time, their assumption is essentially correct. There *is* a straightforward progression from cause to effect. But from the non-linear and non-subjective point of view of external time, strange phenomena such as reversed causation, are entirely possible. In other words, the Doctor's big ball of wibbly-wobbly, timey-wimey stuff is Lewis's four dimensional manifold of events.

Let's Do the Time Warp Again!

An important consequence of reversed causation is that if it's possible, then completely closed causal chains also become possible. A closed causal chain is sequence of causes and effects in which the normal chain of events loops back on itself in such a way that the chain, as a whole, is the cause of itself. Imagine meeting a future version of yourself, whose TARDIS suddenly materializes in your room. After telling you how much fun time travel is, the traveler gives you instructions on how to build or grow your own TARDIS. You follow the instructions and then, after years of work, travel back in time to deliver them to yourself. Where does the information contained in the instructions originally come from? According to Lewis there's simply no answer. The apparent uncaused, spontaneous existence of the information is very strange, but it's logically possible, and showing this, after all, is Lewis's only goal. Lewis thinks we shouldn't be surprised that a world in which time travel occurs is very strange.

Sure enough, "Blink," and by extension the Doctor's explanation of time, hinges on a closed causal chain. The Doctor is sent back in time without his time machine, a time traveler's worst nightmare. The only way for him to retrieve the TARDIS is to communicate with a woman named Sally Sparrow in 2007 and persuade her to send it back to him. What makes this communication possible is a closed causal chain.[1]

---

[1] There are at least three examples of abnormal temporal communication in "Blink": 1. The Doctor's message to Sally written on the wall; 2. Kathy Nightingale's letter to Sally; and 3. The Doctor's DVD *Easter egg*. For simplicity I'm just looking at the Easter egg here.

Though trapped in 1969, the Doctor communicates with Sally by sending her a DVD *Easter egg*. As Sally watches the video, the Doctor is able to communicate with her because he already has a complete transcript of the conversation, which he reads from an autocue (teleprompter). During the conversation Larry Nightingale adds what Sally says to his transcript of the Easter egg. Then, in the future, Sally herself gives the Doctor the now completed transcript before he becomes trapped in the past, enabling him to undertake the creation of the Easter egg, starting the chain *again*. The normal chain of causes and effects here loops back on itself forming a closed system, and the Doctor cleverly exploits this feature of space-time to communicate with Sally Sparrow. Once again, Lewis's four-dimensionalism provides a model by which we can clearly see how this is possible.

However, the theory of four-dimensional time travel does have significant philosophical problems, the most famous of which is the dreaded *Grandfather Paradox*. Sometimes called the *Bilking Argument*, the paradox goes like this: if a closed causal chain was possible, then it should also be possible to interrupt such a chain of events, thereby disrupting or bilking the loop. The classic example involves a foolish time traveler who travels into the past and kills his own grandfather before his grandfather can procreate. If he can kill his grandfather, and it certainly seems possible for one person to kill another, then his grandfather would never procreate and as a result he would never exist to travel back in time and kill his grandfather in the first place. It seems that the time traveler both can and can't kill his grandfather. Traditionally, philosophers have thought that such a contradiction shows that time travel is impossible.

In case you're bothered about issues such as autonomy, agency, and intentionality, other versions of the paradox have been developed that don't involve abnormal temporal suicide. Some examples take human intentionality out altogether by focusing instead on inanimate objects such as rockets or even time-traveling positrons. But for our purposes let's just imagine a world in which the Doctor refuses to accept the transcript from Sally Sparrow. If this happened it would bilk the chain, the Doctor wouldn't be able to make the video, Larry wouldn't be able to complete the transcript and Sally would then have no transcript to deliver.

This is more than merely an obstacle standing in the way of the Doctor's plans of escaping 1969. The mere possibility of bilking a closed causal chain threatens to generate a logical contradiction that would make time travel impossible. Lewis attempts to solve the problem by claiming that the paradox rests on an equivocation of the word *can* and thus leads to no real contradiction. He explains the equivocation using a linguistic analogy:

> An ape can't speak a human language—say, Finnish—but I can. Facts about the anatomy and operation of the ape's larynx and nervous system are not compossible [able to exist or happen together] with his speaking Finnish. The corresponding facts about my larynx and nervous system are compossible with my speaking Finnish. But don't take me along to Helsinki as your interpreter: I can't speak Finnish. (p. 77)

Lewis both can and can't speak Finnish, yet there's no paradox or contradiction involved because the word *can* is being used in two different ways. Likewise, a time-traveler both can and can't murder his grandfather, and the Doctor both can and can't refuse to accept the transcript, yet there is no contradiction and the paradox is solved.

But this also reveals a kind of fatalism that four-dimensional time travel seems to entail. Strictly speaking, from the point of view of external time, it's not possible for a time traveler to travel to the past and murder his grandfather. Likewise, it's not possible for the Doctor to refuse to take the transcript. The fact is, at least on Lewis's view, that the Doctor received the transcript and that's that. No amount of time traveling can ever change it. The sense in which he can refuse to accept the transcript is analogous to the sense in which Lewis can speak Finnish. So, if Lewis is correct then closed causal chains do not entail logical contradictions and time travel is logically possible. But mere logical possibility is cold comfort for someone wanting to explain that closed causal chains aren't just possible but actually exist. And it's particularly nippy when you're explaining this to someone stranded in a 1969 shop job. Here the similarity between the views of the Doctor and Lewis start to break down. According to Lewis:

> The paradoxes of time travel are oddities, not impossibilities. They prove only this much, which few would have doubted: that a possible world where time travel took place would be a most strange world, different in fundamental ways from the world we think is ours. (p. 67)

Lewis doesn't believe that time travel occurs in the actual world, but the Doctor certainly does. The views of the Doctor and Lewis aren't identical, but they're very similar. And this similarity allows us to use Lewis's four-dimensionalism as a model to elaborate and elucidate the Doctor's view. But we shouldn't expect a perfect fit between them.

Another difference between the views of Lewis and the Doctor may be the possibility of additional temporal dimensions. As I have shown, Lewis's view doesn't include multiple temporal dimensions or the threat of their creation. But these both seem to be possibilities for the Doctor. When "Blink" is seen in context with other adventures such as "Father's Day" (2005) and "The City of Death" (1979), the fabric of space-time seems more fragile, and the threat of bilking seems to be a real and dangerous possibility. But the Doctor is still basically a four-dimensionalist, and at least under normal circumstances multiple temporal dimensions don't exist. No bilking occurs in "Blink," and the closed causal chain involved is completely unbroken and consistent within a single temporal dimension.

Diagnosis

By briefly considering the views of two additional philosophers we can see precisely where the Doctor's philosophy of time fits into the contemporary scholarship. Paul Horwich has completed a careful investigation of multiple examples of closed causal chains and defends them against several objections. In his article "Closed Causal Chains," Horwich agrees with Lewis that such causal chains can't be ruled out. He sums up his view in the following way:

> Theories that countenance what are naturally termed 'closed causal chains' cannot be dismissed on *a priori* [based on reason alone] grounds, and cannot invariably be ruled out by the *a posteriori* [based on experience] bilking argument. The latter argument shows that closed causal chains imply uncaused correlations. But the import of this result is not uniform. In some cases the proper conclusion is that such a phenomenon is incompatible with what we know. In others we may infer that closed causal chains do not and will not occur—but we cannot conclude that a spacetime structure permitting them is not actual. And in a third class of cases the bilking argument has minimal force; for the uncaused correlations to which it draws our attention are not improbable. The overall moral is that the bilking argument, even in its strongest form, should not be regarded as a *general* argument against backward causation and closed causal chains. Its significance

can be assessed only with respect to specific hypotheses. ("Closed Causal Chains," p. 267)

Horwich agrees with Lewis that closed causal chains are logically possible. Also, like Lewis, he thinks the existence of closed causal chains might entail strange coincidences and uncaused correlations. For example, each and every time the time traveler tries to murder his grandfather something always goes wrong. This happens no matter how many times he tries. Such coincidences are very strange but aren't impossible. They are, however, highly improbable. Horwich and Lewis agree that while reversed causation and closed causal chains are possible, they don't occur in the actual world.

Perhaps the view that best resembles the Doctor's in the contemporary scholarship is that of Jenann Ismael. Ismael has completed the most detailed analysis of closed causal chains to date, a feat with which the Doctor himself would be impressed. Not only does she agree that the bilking argument doesn't create a contradiction and closed causal chains are possible, she also thinks that the existence of time travel, including reversed causation and closed causal chains, is probable. She doesn't even think, as Lewis and Horwich do, that closed causal chains create problematic coincidences. Ismael would be the least surprised of the three, were she to communicate with the Doctor using a causal chain similar to Sally Sparrow's.

Ismael claims that while it's true, for example, that something would always prevent the would-be parricidal assassin from succeeding no matter how many times he tried, it involves no strange coincidences, anomalies, or mysterious forces. Such multiple failures only appear strange because we're focusing on a class of events that already rules success out. Consider, for example, a class consisting of the number of days that I failed to finish grading the midterm exams of my *Metaphysics* course last semester. When we look at any member of this class there's always some cause that prevents me from grading the exams on that particular day, but there's no mysterious force or strange coincidence involved. Each failure to finish grading is produced by perfectly ordinary causal laws. I just focused on a class in which grading the exams was ruled out from the start. Likewise, according to Ismael, failure to kill the grandfather is built into the description of the cases Lewis and Horwich are considering, so no actual anomalies or strange coincidences occur. Thus, closed causal chains aren't only logically possible but also, given some interpretations of general relativity, physically probable (Ismael, pp. 306–08). The Doctor, of course, would be sympathetic with these claims. The biggest difference between the views of Ismael and the Doctor is that, according to the Doctor, closed causal loops aren't just probable, they actually exist.

Prognosis

David Lewis provides a four-dimensional model which can be used to expound the Doctor's brief statements concerning the nature of time. According to the Doctor, the universe is a big four-dimensional ball of wibbly-wobbly space-time. People assume that time is a linear progression of causes and effects because they're looking at the world only from the point of view of their own personal time. But from the non-linear point of view of external time strange things, such as reversed causation and closed causal chains, can and do occur. These strange features of the universe allow the Doctor to know surprising things, such as what Sally Sparrow will say, long before the event occurs.

The Doctor's view fits nicely alongside other contemporary views of time travel. This is significant because it means that if the Doctor's philosophy of time is correct then several contemporary philosophers are on the right track and we now live in the exciting period of history in which the nature of time, at long last, begins to be understood. Like the Doctor, Lewis and Horwich think reversed causation and closed causal chains are possible. Like the Doctor, Ismael thinks that reversed causation and closed causal chains aren't only possible but also probable. The Doctor takes the next step and proposes that they aren't only probable but also actual. If the Doctor's philosophy of time is correct then we live in a very strange world. But as *Doctor Who* fans, we shouldn't be surprised.

8
Logically, What Would a Cyberman Do?

GREG LITTMANN

I'm a logician by trade, and if there's one thing *Doctor Who* fans know about logicians, it's that we're allied with the Cybermen. It is, after all, the Brotherhood of Logicians, presumably our future professional association, who try to take over the Earth by bringing the Cybermen back to life in "The Tomb of the Cybermen" (1967).

As of 2010, none of the professional organizations I belong to are hatching any plots—at least, none that I'm aware of. Yet at some time in the future, according to "Tomb," it'll be the logicians who betray the Earth. Why are we doing it? Our leader and top agent, Eric Kleig, explains to Patrick Troughton's Doctor: "Logic, my dear professor. Logic and power. On Earth, the Brotherhood of Logicians is the greatest mass-intelligence ever assembled. But that's not enough by itself. We need power—power to put our ability into action." Are Kleig and the Brotherhood of Logicians really being logical? The Cyberman Controller thinks so and approves our proposal, telling Kleig, "You are a logician. Our race is also logical. You will be the leader of the new race."

Logic leads to worse things than that in *Doctor Who*. The Cybermen are said to be logical creatures—and look how *they* behave. They've become a race of emotionless soldiers devoted to conquering the universe, destroying other species or forcing them to become Cybermen too. Their schemes involving Earth alone include draining Earth of all power in "The Tenth Planet" (1966), sabotaging Earth's weather in "The Moonbase" (1967), annihilating Earth's population with a bomb in "Earthshock" (1982), crashing Halley's comet into us in "Attack of the Cybermen" (1985) and, of course, simply invading to turn us all into Cybermen in "The

Invasion" (1968), "Silver Nemesis" (1988), "Rise of the Cybermen" (2006), "The Age of Steel" (2006), "Army of Ghosts" (2006), and "Doomsday" (2006).

If this is being logical, then being logical doesn't sound very appealing. But would a logical creature really behave like the Cybermen do? If not, how would a logical creature behave? Or, to put it another way, what's the "logical" way to live? That's the question I'll be examining here by contrasting the views of philosophers Thomas Hobbes, John Stuart Mill, and David Hume, asking what they'd think of Cyberman "logic" and how Cybermen might've looked if they'd been designed according to the principles espoused by these philosophers; how *they* might have designed the Cybermen differently, given a chance.[1] While my examples come from *Doctor Who*, the issue of living logically has real-world importance. After all, we all have to decide if we care about living logically or not, and if we do want to live logically, we'd better know what "living logically" requires of us.

Before proceeding, we'd better decide what's meant by being "logical." I take it that when the Cybermen use the term "logical," they're using it in its most ordinary sense, whereby "logic" is synonymous with "reason," and to be logical is to make judgments that are reasonable. I'd better mention that philosophers use the term "logical" in several more technical senses, but I don't believe that the writers of *Doctor Who* have generally been aware of these more technical senses, nor does their dialogue regarding logic make sense if the word is understood in a more technical way.

In "Doomsday" (2006), when the Cybermen and Daleks meet for the first time and the Daleks refuse to identify themselves, a Cyberman complains, "That is illogical. You will modify." I take it that the Cyberman means something like, "Come on dude, be reasonable. Tell me your name." If the Cyberman instead means something like, "I want you to derive your conclusions in accordance with the rules for any artificial, formal language," I no longer understand the scene, both because there's no reason for the Cyberman to want that, and because there's no way in which he could know if the Dalek had done it or not. Therefore, I'll be using

---

[1] It is irrelevant why these famous philosophers have been given the chance to redesign the Cybermen. If it bothers you, assume the High Council of Gallifrey is somehow behind it. Or, if it floats your boat, the Meddling Monk, Omega, the White Guardian, a glowing yellow Rose, or a floating Tennant Doctor.

the terms "logical" and "reasonable" (and "logic" and "reason") interchangeably. This is important because the philosophers we'll be looking at spoke of acting in accordance with "reason" rather than in accordance with "logic," as the Cybermen do, and I'm treating that as merely a terminological difference.

We Will Survive

If this is indeed what the Cybermen mean by "logic," then the Cybermen believe that life should be lived in accordance with reason. Thomas Hobbes (1588 to 1679)[2] believed that life should be lived in accordance with reason too. Reason, thought Hobbes, tells us to do whatever is in our own personal best interests. Our most fundamental best interest is to survive, so the most fundamental command of reason is that we ensure our own survival.

This need to survive gives rise to what Hobbes called the "Laws of Nature." He wrote "A Law of Nature is a general rule, found out by reason, by which a man is forbidden to do that which is destructive of his life or takes away the means of preserving it or to omit that by which it may be best preserved." Hobbes listed nineteen Laws of Nature that he'd discovered through reason, but the first three are particularly basic to his plan for a reasonable society.

The first Law of Nature is that one must always seek peace and defend oneself against danger. Although Hobbes thought it was reasonable to seek peace, that doesn't mean he thought humans are peaceful by nature. Rather, he thought that without strong government to keep order, humans naturally live in a state of violent anarchy, a "war of every man against every man." In fact, Hobbes thought that harming others to help yourself is the reasonable thing to do if you can get away with it. Without police to stop you, why not steal? If your neighbor looks like a threat, why not kill him first?

---

[2] Thomas Hobbes, a professional tutor, lived from 1588 to 1679. This means that as an eleven-year-old in 1599, he might have attended one of Shakepeare's plays with David Tennant's Doctor and Martha, only to be terrorized by the invasion of the Carrionites during the events of "The Shakespeare Code" (2007). It's also possible that he later played cards with William Hartnell's Doctor, Ben, and Polly in a Cornish pub during "The Smugglers" (1966). It's even possible that in 1666, at age seventy-eight, he joined the angry mob chasing Peter Davison's Doctor, Tegan, Nyssa, and Adric through the woods in "The Visitation" (1982).

The reasonable person in such a society would be a dangerous, untrustworthy opportunist like the grim mercenary Commander Lytton from "Resurrection of the Daleks" (1984) and "Attack of the Cybermen," the treasure-seeking thug Sabalom Glitz from "The Mysterious Planet" (1986) and "Dragonfire" (1987), or the Dalek-collecting tycoon Henry van Statten from "Dalek" (2005). Understandably, Hobbes saw life in such a society as "solitary, poor, nasty, brutish, and short." However, he also thought that reason offered us a way out of this hellish chaos, through a social contract.

Hobbes's second Law of Nature is that we should be willing to make social contracts with other people, giving up liberties equally in the interest of the common good. So, for example, we might all agree to surrender our freedom to kill one another, to drive on whichever side of the road we like, and to touch others if we've been infected by a Crinoid, like Mr. Keeler in "The Seeds of Doom" (1976). Reason tells us to make such deals even though we'll lose some freedom by doing so, because living in a society that follows rules like these is in our own best interest. After all, none of us wants to be murdered, run down, or transformed into a giant predatory bush (no you don't—think it through). Hobbes's third Law of Nature is that we must keep these contracts we've made. He thought that the only way to ensure the contracts are kept is for society to appoint a dictator with absolute power. This is, of course, just the sort of dictator that Eric Kleig thought "logic" demanded for Earth.

We are Human-Point-2. Every Citizen will Receive a Free Upgrade.

So how do the Cybermen match up to Hobbes's conception of a life lived in accordance with reason? In other words, just how logical would Hobbes think the Cybermen really are? They do better at some times than others. When we first see them facing off against William Hartnell's Doctor in "The Tenth Planet," they look like perfect Hobbesian heroes. Though they're attacking Earth, they do it only to preserve their own lives. Cyberman Krang explains: "This close proximity of our two planets means that one has to be eliminated for the safety of the other. The one to be destroyed will be Earth. We cannot allow Mondas to burn up." When the Doctor's companion Polly pleads with the Cybermen not to let millions of humans die, one Cyberman replies, "We are only interested in survival. Anything else is of no importance. Your deaths will not affect us."

Furthermore, these Cybermen seem to show a fine understanding of Hobbesian social contracts. What the Cybermen (or their Mondasian ancestors) appear to have promised one another is to mutually give up many liberties for the sake of order and survival. The Cybermen co-operate closely and follow rules to the letter, submitting to complete regimentation and offering absolute obedience to authority. Appropriately enough from Hobbes's viewpoint, Cyberman promises are only considered binding within the social contract of Cyberman society—"Promises to aliens have no validity," one Cyberman reminds another as they prepare to betray the Master in "The Five Doctors" (1983). In the new series, John Lumic, once converted, is clearly the Hobbesian dictator of Cyberman society, holding absolute authority over them and receiving absolute obedience. "I will bring peace to the world. Everlasting peace and unity and uniformity" he decrees from his enormous throne of pipes in "Doomsday."

Feelings? I Do Not Understand that Word

What would Hobbes say about the Cybermen's most distinctive modification, the removal of all emotion? A somewhat Hobbesian justification is offered by the Cybermen themselves. "Our brains are just like yours, except certain weaknesses have been removed," one explains to Polly in "The Tenth Planet." Nevertheless, Hobbes would be horrified by what they've become.

When Hobbes considered what's valuable in life, he wrote that good is whatever people desire and evil whatever they hate: "whatsoever is the object of any man's appetite or desire, that is it which he for his part calls good: and the object of his hate and aversion, evil."[3] If Cybermen lack emotions, then presumably they can't desire anything. Since it's desire alone that makes things valuable in Hobbes's view, a life without desire would be a life without value.

Locate and Destroy All Animal Organisms!

Hobbes would approve of the Cybermen less and less as their history progresses. Arguably, the Cybermen are still just trying to sur-

---

[3] A view also held by Sutekh the Destroyer in "Pyramids of Mars" (1975).

vive in the three Cyberman stories after "The Tenth Planet": "The Moonbase," "Tomb of the Cybermen," and "The Wheel in Space" (up against Troughton's Doctor). However, by the time they invade Earth in Troughton's "The Invasion," they've already established themselves and are now set on conquering everything they can get their silver hands on. By Tom Baker's "Revenge of the Cybermen" (1975), they make clear that their ambition includes conquering the entire cosmos. They still see themselves as creatures of logic, but now, logic tells them not just to survive but to make war on everyone else. Hobbes would be horrified. The business of the Cyberman state is now effectively eternal warfare and eternal warfare is eternal threat to your personal survival. The Cybermen may have made mutual sacrifices for the common good, but they made the wrong sacrifices, and Hobbes wouldn't call them reasonable. To be fair, it's the plan of Cyberman creator John Lumic in "The Age of Steel" to "bring peace to the world. Everlasting peace . . ." through Cyberman conquest. However, if you're reading this book, you already know where Lumic's plans really led.

If Thomas Hobbes Had Designed the Cybermen

If Hobbes had been allowed to redesign the Cybermen to be genuinely logical, their history would be different. They might still have attacked humanity in "The Tenth Planet," "The Moonbase," "Tomb of the Cybermen," and "The Wheel in Space," if that seemed to offer them the best chance for survival. However, as soon as they'd established themselves away from their doomed home planet, they'd have avoided warfare where practical, seeking peace and security instead.

In the new series, the Cybermen we've been watching didn't arise on Mondas but on a parallel Earth. If these Cybermen were reasonable, in Hobbes's terms, they'd see no logic in trying to convert other humans. After all, for Hobbes, reason tells us to seek our own good. The new Cybermen should be able to see that they'd be better off keeping the gift of conversion to themselves. Of course, this would require disobedience to their ruler, John Lumic, and Hobbes didn't generally believe in disobedience to authority, but he also stated, "The obligation of subjects to the sovereign is understood to last as long as, and no longer, than the power lasteth by which he is able to protect them." Since the Cybermen no longer need Lumic's protection, they've no further reason to respect his authority.[4] So, rather than killing the president of Great Britain when they crash Jackie Tyler's birthday party, it seems more likely that the Cybermen would've entered into immediate negotiations, demanding billions of pounds in return for letting British scientists study them.

Have You No Emotions, Sir?

John Stuart Mill (1806–1873)[5] came to a very different conclusion about the sort of life that reason recommends. On his view, reason recommends spreading happiness. The only proof that something's worth having, according to Mill, is that people want it. What people value, he thought, is happiness, and concluded that pleasure is the only good and suffering the only evil. This might make Mill sound like a selfish hedonist, but in fact, he thought it unreasonable to treat other people's happiness as any less important than your own. Since only happiness has value, it doesn't matter whose happiness it is. Far from advocating selfishness, he advocated universal concern for others and campaigned for political change to improve the wellbeing of the poorest and most disadvantaged members of society. The most reasonable sort of life, according to this view, is a life devoted to doing good in the world, like hippy scientist Cliff Jones from "The Green Death" (1973), the chairbound Keeper of Traken from "The Keeper of Traken" (1981), or the Doctor himself.

Mill believed that people should enjoy themselves as well as help others. Even while enjoying oneself, though, Mill's life of reason is no wild party. While he thought that all pleasures are good,

---

[4] For a different interpretation, see Chapter 18 in this volume.

[5] John Stuart Mill lived from 1806 to 1873. If he'd been traveling in the north of England as a young man, he might have stepped on a mine in the forest and been turned into a tree during "The Mark of the Rani" (1985). In 1866, at the age of sixty, he might have dropped by to see Professor Maxtible socially, and so bumped into Patrick Troughton's Doctor, Jamie, and Victoria during "The Evil of the Daleks" (1967). If he'd gone to visit Cardiff in 1869 at age sixty-three, he might have run screaming out of a theater, pursued by ghosts, Christopher Eccleston's Doctor, and Rose during "The Unquiet Dead" (2005). If Mill had boarded the *Mary Celeste* in 1872 at the age of sixty-seven, he would have seen William Hartnell's Doctor, Ian, Barbara, and Vicki run by in "The Chase" (1965), just before the ship is overrun by Daleks with the loss of all life still onboard. Lucky for him he didn't get on.

he thought that some pleasures are better than others. In particular, he thought that "higher pleasures," pleasures that exercise the intellect, like studying philosophy or reading poetry, are more valuable than "lower pleasures," pleasures that don't exercise the intellect, like gambling or drinking or watching Adric explode again.

There Are Some Corners of the Universe which Have Bred the Most Terrible Things

So what would Mill think of the Cybermen? Like Hobbes, he'd be appalled at what they've become and would see nothing logical about their actions. He'd look at the endless warfare Cybermen wage and would be repelled—Cybermen are agents of misery. This is ironic given that the elimination of suffering is presented as one justification for conversion from human to Cyberman. "Why no emotions?" Rose asks David Tennant's Doctor in "Rise of the Cybermen." "Because it hurts," he replies. A Cyberman explains: "We think of the humans. We think of their difference and their pain. They suffer in the skin. They must be upgraded."

It's possible that Mill might approve of surgical alterations that prevent negative emotions. After all, Mill thought that unhappiness is the only thing that's intrinsically bad and that it's only reasonable to reduce unhappiness if we can. However, Mill wouldn't find it reasonable for the Cybermen to have removed their positive emotions as well. In removing their ability to feel happiness, they've abandoned the very thing it would have been reasonable to pursue. "When did you last have the pleasure of smelling a flower, watching a sunset, eating a well-prepared meal?" demands Peter Davison's Doctor of Cybermen in "Earthshock," making a similar point.

If John Stuart Mill Had Designed the Cybermen

Mill would've thought it reasonable to design the Cybermen to be happy. Since Mill thought that "higher pleasures"—intellectual and cultural pleasures—are more important than "lower pleasures" that don't challenge the mind, he might also find it reasonable to sacrifice some lower pleasure if it was likely to bring about more higher pleasure.

Mill might think that extending life by replacing organic parts with cybernetic ones would be worthwhile even if it required the loss of certain bodily pleasures, such as those of smell, taste and touch. If so, Mill's Cybermen might not look very different from the Cybermen we're used to seeing. However, instead of devoting their extended lifespans and high intelligence to developing schemes for conquest, Mill's Cybermen might compose exquisite poetry, debate philosophy, or study science just for the joy of it (as opposed to studying science to design viruses, head-mounted firearms, and killer robot silverfish). Their society wouldn't resemble a fascist state, but the sort of peaceful, intellectual civilizations we've seen on Traken in "The Keeper of Traken," on Logopolis in "Logopolis" (1981) or even (sometimes) on Gallifrey itself.

The thing that Mill would consider most important to give the Cybermen is the one thing they're most famous for lacking: a concern for the suffering of others. Mill's Cybermen would've listened when Polly begged them in "The Tenth Planet" to think of the millions of human lives their plan would destroy. They'd then calculate whether it would bring about more unhappiness to destroy Earth or Mondas and would sacrifice whichever of those planets that would cause the least suffering. Admittedly, they'd probably decide to destroy Earth, predicting that their own world would have a happier future.

Even if Mill's Cybermen would've tried to wipe us out in "The Tenth Planet," they'd have gotten on with us much better in subsequent adventures where their survival wasn't at stake. Rather than trying to enslave or destroy humanity, Cybermen who are reasonable by Mill's standard would want to help us so as to raise the level of happiness in the universe, starting by sharing their miraculous medical technology. They might be strange neighbors, but they'd be kind ones. Of course, kindness can be misguided and so we might still fear that the Cybermen would "help" us by force in accordance with their idea of what we should be.

You Will Become Like Us

Such mandatory "help" is common in Cyberman stories, such as when Eric Kleig, in "The Tomb of the Cybermen," is judged by the Cyberman Controller to be good Cyberman material, whether Kleig wants to become a Cyberman or not. The theme of involuntary "help" is even more prominent in the new series, in which Cybermen speak of "upgrading" humans into Cyberman form in order to reduce the subject's suffering.

John Lumic, inventor of the Cybermen, is himself converted without consent in "The Age of Steel," his protests dismissed by his creations with the words: "This man worked with Cybus Industries to create our species. He will be rewarded by force." Similarly, Kleig, who presents himself as humanity's benefactor, thinks that logic tells him to be "master of the world" so that he can enact his plans. He's so eager to enforce his way of thinking that he wants a world in which, as the Doctor describes it to him, "no country, no person would dare to have a single thought that was not your own. Eric Kleig's own conception of the . . . of the way of life!" Would Mill agree that reason instructs us to be so coercive towards other people?

He wouldn't. Mill thought that reason tells us to do just the opposite. He thought that human beings are the best judges of what will make them happy; taking away people's freedom and making decisions on their behalf for their own good tends to make them miserable instead. Like Eric Kleig, Mill sought political position to bring about his plans for changing society—he became a member of the UK parliament. However, far from agreeing with Kleig that reason demands a totalitarian state, Mill campaigned for a freer society, advocating such things as voting rights for women and the abolition of the slave trade. He wrote, "The only part of the conduct of anyone for which he is amenable to society is that which concerns others. . . . Over himself . . . the individual is sovereign."

In particular, Mill thought it vital for people to have the right to express their opinions whether the authorities agree with it or not, since it's by the free exchange of ideas that truths can most easily be distinguished from falsehoods. He wrote: "If any opinion be compelled to silence, that opinion may, for aught we can certainly know, be true." Cyberman society, and thus "logical" society, is sometimes shown to be closed to new ideas and so immune to change. "The Cybermen won't advance. You'll just stop. You'll stay like this forever," cries David Tennant's Doctor in "The Age of Steel." Mill's Cybermen, on the other hand, would prize new ideas and would constantly seek to change and improve their own society.

Some "logical" races in *Doctor Who* aren't even *able* to form their own opinions, just because they're too alike. "We think the same. We are uniform," explains a Cyberman in "The Age of Steel." In "Destiny of the Daleks" (1979), Tom Baker's Doctor finds that two Movellan robots can't even play rock-paper-scissors, since logic leads them to always make the same choice. The Cybermen see it as only logical to wipe out *our* individuality too through a process of conversion. Since "The Tenth Planet," they've been promising "you will become like us." Mill, however, believed that reason requires us to foster individuality, on the grounds that it's the most effective way of allowing people to reach their potential. Far from wanting uniformity, he criticized China for having too much of it, complaining that "its progress has become stationary by making its people all alike, all governing their thoughts and conduct by the same maxims and rules." Mill's Cybermen wouldn't suppress individuality; they'd revel in it. Far from insisting that we be like them, they'd be delighted by our strangeness and eager to share ideas and viewpoints with us.

The Cybermen Won't Advance. You'll Just Stop.

David Hume (1711–1776)[6] had yet another take on the life of reason. Hume believed that reason doesn't tell us to do anything at all. Reason may tell us how the world is, but only the emotions can suggest action. Upon observing a murder site, we might be able to use our faculty of reason to explain how and why a murder was committed, but no amount of reasoning based on the observed evidence can demonstrate that it'd be better to catch the murderer than encourage them to kill. Such judgments depend on having an emotional preference for one state of affairs over another—in this case, a preference for people not being murdered.

If David Hume Had Designed the Cybermen

If David Hume had designed the Cybermen to be perfectly reasonable but emotionless, they'd do nothing at all. They'd have no impetus, since they'd care about nothing. Mondas would simply drift past the Earth in "The Tenth Planet." Human scientists would

---

[6] David Hume, a best-selling historian in his day, lived from 1711 to 1776. He was Scottish, and in 1746, at the age of thirty-five, might have helped Patrick Troughton's Doctor, Ben, Polly, and Jamie to escape from the Redcoats in "The Highlanders" (1966), except that Hume always kept far away from battles. Hume lived in France from 1734 to 1737 and may have vied for the affections of Madame de Pompadour, losing out to David Tennant's Doctor, who kept appearing in her fireplace in "The Girl in the Fireplace" (2006). If Hume had burst in on them unexpectedly in a fit of jealousy, he and the Doctor could have had a fist fight.

no doubt eagerly attempt to contact this newly discovered form of alien life, but the Cybermen wouldn't even wave back at our telescopes. When the new Cybermen are brought to John Lumic, he'd bark orders at them only to be ignored by creatures who, lacking emotions, care no more about what he wants than about whether they live or die. Cybermen built to be reasonable but lacking emotion would be a race indistinguishable from statues, fit only to serve as shop mannequins.

Of course, it'd be open to Hume, like Hobbes and Mill, to build his Cybermen as entirely reasonable but also to give them emotions. There's nothing unreasonable about doing so according to Hume's model, since reason alone doesn't tell us not to do anything—at most it helps us to work out *how* we can do whatever it is we want to do. These Cybermen would desire whatever they'd been programmed to desire and no desire they pursued would be unreasonable. Conquering the universe, spreading happiness and prosperity to all, or holding endless dress-like-the-Doctor contests with other Cybermen, they could follow any goals at all without ever being illogical.

Knowing Hume, he probably would've made them desire to be a race of historians, scouring the past to learn what makes a society function best, changing their ways accordingly (see Hume's *The History of England*). He would've given them a desire to combat superstition and religion by providing reasoned arguments for members of other species (see Hume's *The Natural History of Religion* and *Dialogues Concerning Natural Religion*). He would've also given them a love of art and a keen interest in artistic criticism (see Hume's *Of the Standard of Taste*). None of these goals would be reasonable or unreasonable, logical or illogical by Hume's standard. They're simply goals for which Hume had an emotional liking—a liking he would pass on to his Cybermen.

This Is the Age of Steel

So where does that leave us? How would a logical, reasonable species act? In other words, what would a Cyberman do if Cybermen were really as logical as they claim? Would the logical society of the Cybermen be an orderly dictatorship, caring nothing for the well-being of outsiders but avoiding warfare except when survival is at stake? Or would it be a benevolent society of individualistic scholars who seek only to enjoy intellectual pleasures and to spread happiness throughout the universe? Or would they be a race of creatures who never act, who float by on their doomed planet without the slightest interest in the Earth or in their own survival? Or would their society have a different form altogether?

If you work it out for sure, place your answer in a time capsule and leave it in trust for the Brotherhood of Logicians. In a few hundred years we're going to break into the Tomb of the Cybermen on Telos and we need to know what to expect when we do.

9

Ain't We All the Same? Underneath, Ain't We All Kin?

BONNIE GREEN and CHRIS WILLMOTT

What are species and how do we identify them? These may seem simple questions given that we distinguish between species of plants and animals every day. Dogs (*Canis familiaris*), for example, seem as distinct from horses (*Equus caballus*) as broccoli, a cultivar of the species *Brassica oleracea*, is from carrots (*Daucus carota*). The identification of individual organisms as members of these species also seems quite straightforward. It'd be hard to mistake a dog for a horse, much less a horse for a carrot!

The differences between species are all the more striking when dogs, horses, carrots and broccoli are contrasted with *Homo sapiens*, our own species. When making distinctions between organisms that are human and those that aren't, we do so intuitively and instinctively and without needing to think about the criteria we use to make those distinctions. However, in the philosophy of biology, these criteria are up for grabs. Philosophers continue to debate three issues which make up the 'species problem':

1. **What are species?**

2. **How can members of a species be reliably identified?**

3. **Do species really exist in nature, or are they merely imposed on nature by our own sytem of classification?**

In spite of their differences dogs, horses, carrots, broccoli, and humans all share a common origin on the planet Earth. In this way, they're all unlike the extraterrestrial species found in *Doctor Who*, particularly Daleks; the 'salt-shaker' beings that have terrorized the

Doctor (and the audience) since their first appearance on UK television in 1963.

As mutated organisms living in polycarbide travel machines, Daleks seem to be the antithesis of everything human. Ruthless, logical, and emotionless the Daleks are driven by a single goal: the extermination of inferior species and total domination of the Universe at any cost. They look and behave very differently to humans, have a different history and origin, and appear biologically incompatible with *Homo sapiens* in almost every way. However, in their quest to become the dominant species, the Daleks have made several attempts to integrate the best of other species, including humans, into their own. These experiments produced hybrid organisms, notably human-Daleks and Dalek-humans in "The Evil of the Daleks" (1967) and "Daleks in Manhattan" (2007), and drew attention to the three aspects of the species problem noted above.

What Are Species?

Taking the liberty of assuming that you, the reader, are a member of the species *Homo sapiens*, what is it that makes you human? Do you possess some intrinsic quality that's both universal among humans and unique to our species? Or, is it your place in a line of human ancestors, which goes back through your parents, grandparents, and beyond, and forms a part of a diverse population of *Homo sapiens*? Or, is it because you share both physical and developmental similarities and an evolutionary heritage with the other humans around you?

Each of these approaches provides a different account of what makes a species a species. These questions capture three prominent views of species within the philosophy of biology: seeing them as *natural kinds, individuals,* or as *sets.* The popularity of each of these positions has waxed and waned over time, often as the biological sciences have changed and developed. Lately, it's the view of species as natural kinds that has become the most difficult to maintain. However, as we shall see, in *Doctor Who* this view has yet to become extinct, and has indeed been recently resurrected in a new, modern form.

But first, what does it mean to say that species are 'natural kinds'? In philosophy we distinguish between *particulars* and *kinds*, where kinds are groups of particulars that share some set of intrinsic properties that make them what they are. In the philosophy of biology, the particulars are usually biological organisms, and the kinds are often taken to be species. A common way of thinking about species is as *natural kinds*, where 'natural' tells us that a kind corresponds to a real grouping that is independent of human classification.

An example of a natural kind is 'mountains'. There are numerous particular mountains (both on Earth and on other planets throughout the solar system) that are assumed to be intrinsically similar in some—perhaps—unobservable way, and to exist independently of human beings. Following John Locke in *An Essay Concerning Human Understanding*, natural kinds can be contrasted with so called *nominal kinds*. Nominal kinds are conventional: they are categories picked out by human concepts, whose particulars share no intrinsic, underlying similarity. Human artifacts, like tools or machines, are examples of nominal kinds.

So, are species natural kinds? Common sense suggests that they are (this is also the traditional answer within the philosophy of biology). That humans and *Doctor Who*'s Daleks form distinct and identifiable groups irrespective of our knowledge of them seems obvious. But, does each group share some intrinsic property? And, if they do, what is this quality that makes these apparently distinct species different from one another, and in such a way that the distinction is preserved over time and space? One answer appeals to the *essence* of species. That is to say that each species has an intrinsic 'nature' possessed by each and every member, and only them, which is unchanging regardless of where the species or its particulars are found geographically and historically. Historically this type of *kind essentialism*—which, in this context, is called 'species essentialism'—has been extremely pervasive within both philosophy and biology. It's derived from an Aristotelian view of natural kinds, in which the nature of a species was God-given and immutable, and responsible for all the traits that a species displays. This essentialist view of species is very often our intuitive understanding, particularly when it comes to our own 'human nature'. Thus, it isn't surprising to find it in *Doctor Who* as well.

Finding the Human Factor

In the seven-part story "The Evil of the Daleks," first broadcast in the UK in 1967, the Daleks entertained us with precisely this essentialist position on species. In this episode the Daleks believed so strongly in the reality and importance of human nature as an essence, that they designed an experiment to identify all the components of the 'human factor'. An admirable goal perhaps, but—unlike the many philosophers and biologists who've tried to clarify the basis of our common essence—the Daleks don't do this for the good of mankind. As always, the Daleks are looking out for themselves and, when he's first coerced into helping them with their experiments, the Doctor assumes that they wish to isolate, extract and add the human factor to their own Dalek nature. This would allow them to absorb all the qualities that make humans able to triumph over the Daleks, the 'superior beings'. Unfortunately he's wrong, and the Daleks real plan is far more sinister. Their intention is to use the isolated human factor to identify the essence of their own species—the 'Dalek factor'. This they plan to spread throughout humanity, turning all humans into Dalek-humans who'll obey their every command.

The Daleks could've chosen any human being for their experiment, however they select Jamie, the Doctor's slightly gullible Scottish companion. Unwittingly, Jamie is put through a behavioral test: a trial which involves rescuing the daughter of a Victorian scientist, whose house the Daleks have adopted as their base and laboratory. As the episode opens we learn that the beautiful young Victoria has been captured by the Daleks. She's being held by them, though apparently unharmed. Jamie, who along with the Doctor has been transported back in time to the Daleks' stronghold, is mesmerized by a resemblance of Victoria and so is easily tricked into becoming her savior. Unbeknownst to Jamie, the Doctor and the Daleks are monitoring and recording every thought and feeling that he experiences as he faces the obstacles placed between him and Victoria. In this story it's these thoughts and feelings that form the human factor—the essence of humanity. This essence is depicted as a combination of qualitative behavioral, emotional and moral characteristics. These include "courage, pity, chivalry, friendship," and "compassion," alongside an instinct for self-preservation. Together they're presented as both, intrinsic to, and unique and universal within, the human species.

With the help of the Doctor, the Daleks succeed in encapsulating the human factor into small postitronic devices that they implant into three of their own species. These three Daleks—which the Doctor names Alpha, Beta, and Omega—are instantly transformed. They develop human characteristics as a result of taking on the essence of our species. However, the Daleks get a good deal more than they bargained for, as Alpha, Beta, and Omega begin to display another human trait—one that's typical of the "young children" that the Doctor claims they are.

The humanized Daleks begin to ask 'Why?' Like many human parents, the other Daleks are—at first—simply irritated by the constant questioning. However, the consequences quickly get far more serious, and this questioning becomes the basis for the Daleks' downfall. The human-Daleks rebel against the dalek-Daleks and a civil war destroys them all. Hoist by their own petard, the Daleks discover that being human is far from simple.

The Death of Essentialism . . . and Its Resurrection

Just as the Daleks were thought to have been wiped out in the Time War (a fact revealed in 2005 by the Ninth Doctor, played by Christopher Eccleston), many philosophers of biology thought that essentialist views of species had also been consigned to the dustbin of history. In 1859 Charles Darwin published his theory of evolution in the seminal work *On the Origin of Species by Means of Natural Selection*. These ideas undermined the belief that species were defined by fixed properties or essences that didn't, and couldn't, change over time. By the 1930s, evolutionary theory dominated biology. It emphasized both diversity and adaptation as the source of species differentiation and survival, as well as a common origin for all species.

Since then some philosophers have come to view species as individuals or sets rather than as essences, because of the lack of biological evidence for any necessary and sufficient species properties. However, in the final decades of the twentieth century, a new type of essentialism appeared. Enter 'genetic essentialism', which—on the back of developments in molecular biology and genetics—told us that "DNA defines who we are" and positioned the human genome as "the ultimate explanation of human being."[1]

Sadly neither DNA nor the genome could ultimately live up to its billing as the essence of species. Today both philosophers and

---

[1] Both quotes from Ted Peters, *Playing God? Genetic Determinism and Human Freedom*, p. 8.

biologists accept that there's vastly more variation between and within species, more gene flow, and more genetic mutation and recombination, than was originally thought possible. Fortunately for both the creators and fans of *Doctor Who*, however, the series deals in fiction rather than scientific fact. The new series of *Doctor Who*, which began in 2005, resurrected both the Daleks and their experiments with the human factor, though this time located the essence of the human species in our genes.

That the Daleks are master genetic engineers is something of a cliché in the world of *Doctor Who* . . . well, since the 1980s at least. The Daleks' advanced skills in this area were dramatically displayed in the episode "Resurrection of the Daleks" (1984) when they cloned humans and altered them to become Dalek agents. Genetic essentialism—the view of species essence as located in the genes—first appeared in "Dalek" (2005), the sixth episode of the new series. In this adventure the "last" Dalek in the Universe absorbs Rose Tyler's DNA in order to reactivate itself and escape from the confines of Henry van Statten's alien museum. As Rose's human DNA starts to take hold in the Dalek it begins to feel and act very strangely. The Dalek exclaims, "You have given me life. What else have you given me? I am contaminated!"

The Doctor tells the Dalek that it's becoming somewhat human as a result of taking in the genetic material. It reacts violently, and replies, "I shall not be like you. Order my destruction." Reluctantly the Doctor and Rose comply. Inexperienced as she was at the time, Rose is distressed by the death of the creature. Just as in the "Evil of the Daleks," this Dalek had also bitten off more than it could chew when it absorbed the essence of humanity.

In the double episode "Daleks in Manhattan" (2007) and "Evolution of the Daleks" (2007), the audience is treated to a more literal replaying of events from the "Evil of the Daleks." On this occasion the time-traveling Daleks establish their laboratory in 1930s New York rather than Victorian England, and use DNA rather than encapsulated thoughts and feelings to transfer human and Dalek factors between species. Much of the action centers on Dalek Sec—a member of the Dalek Emperor's inner circle, the Cult of Skaro. This elite band of Daleks has been specially designed to imagine new ways for the Daleks to become the dominant species in the Universe, though here they reinvent the idea of triumphing over humanity by introducing the Dalek factor to our species. The climax of the first episode is Dalek Sec's transformation from pure-Dalek to a hybrid human-Dalek form. Sec accomplishes this in spectacular style by absorbing a human being whole. This apparently includes all of the unfortunate man's DNA, as well as his bipedal form and quintessentially human sense of style. The hybrid Sec emerges from his travel machine wearing a snappy pinstripe suit and two-tone Spectator shoes, and declares, "I am a human-Dalek."

From a scientific point of view, the possibility that human traits and characteristics might emerge automatically in a transgenic organism like Dalek Sec—a being whose genome incorporates DNA and genes of both human and non-human origin—is laughable. But, although most scientists (and philosophers) love a good joke, *Doctor Who*'s use of our DNA as intrinsically human and humanizing shows just how pervasive this genetic take on species essentialism can be. In the second of the two episodes, "Evolution of the Daleks," the process is reversed and the genetic essence of the Dalek species is also revealed. "Empty human shells" are filled with Dalek DNA, via an infusion of "chromatin solution." This process transforms them into 'Dalek-humans' who (in contrast to the human-in-Dalek-form that Sec becomes) are apparently the essence of the Daleks in bodies that belong to the human species.

Although this is far from the end of the story for either the hybrids in "Daleks in Manhattan" and "Evolution of the Daleks," or alternatives to essentialism in the philosophy of biology (through the views of species as individuals or sets), we shall leave this first aspect of the species problem here. Suffice it to say that the question of what species really are remains contentious in philosophy. Particularly since essentialism appears to retain its popular currency, not least in the Daleks' ongoing quest for the human factor in *Doctor Who*.

Species Concepts and the Reality of Species

Another debate revolves around the criteria used to identify members of different species. Here philosophers are more concerned with particulars than kinds, and specifically the features and characteristics that can be used to correctly (or at least reliably and consistently) place those particulars within species groups. John Dupré describes this aspect of the species problem as "more straightforwardly biological."[2] Most philosophers—taking their

---

[2] John A. Dupré, "Species: Theoretical Contexts," p. 312.

lead from colleagues in the life sciences—accept that a variety of different concepts and criteria concerning similarity and difference (both within and between species groups) may be applicable in species membership and identification. Choosing between them is another contentious issue.

There are a number of different facets to this part of the species problem.

Firstly, what are the 'species concepts' that underlie different sets of membership criteria?

Secondly, is one concept and set of criteria more correct than the others?

And thirdly, if we allow many different species concepts and sets of identification criteria to coexist, does this undermine the reality of species as a natural category?

In terms of the Daleks in *Doctor Who*, one way to explore these questions is through the relationship between Daleks and members of another species that lives on Skaro: the Thals.

The British TV audience's first visit to Skaro was in 1963, during the seven episodes in the series "The Daleks." There they met both the Daleks and the Thals; two intelligent populations engaged in a nuclear war that had lasted for five hundred years. Although the Daleks and the Thals describe themselves as different 'races'—a term we usually use to discriminate between different sub-populations within the species *Homo sapiens*—they're probably better thought of as distinct, though related, species.

That Daleks and Thals are radically different on at least the first two criteria is obvious in "Genesis of the Daleks" (1975), and also the other episodes in which the Daleks and Thals appear together. Where the Daleks are cold and emotionless, and thrive on extermination and domination; the Thals are warm and empathetic, peace-loving and diplomatic. Thals are also graceful and beautiful, while the Daleks are squishy, octopus-like, blobs of organic matter that require special 'travel machines' just to get around.

As well as being morphologically and behaviorally distinct, evidence that the Doctor uncovers in "The Daleks," suggests that Daleks and Thals may have originated from different ancestors. While rooting around in the Thals' historical records, the Doctor discovers two images: one is of the "original Thal male," the other the forbear of the Daleks. So, Daleks and Thals do seem to be distinct species.

What about *biological* species concepts? Are Daleks and Thals separate species according to the reproductive criteria used here? As expressed by its creator, Ernest Mayr, in *Systematics and the Origin of Species*, the biological species concept centers on the "reproductive isolation" of species groups. At the risk of passing judgment on the sexual preferences of the Daleks and Thals, it doesn't seem likely that these species would either choose to, or be capable of, interbreeding (and even if they were, it's doubtful that the details would be suitable for family viewing). It also appears that these two groups have been geographically cut off from each other for many years—another feature that suggests they're reproductively isolated. The Daleks and Thals preserve this situation by building their own city-habitats. They rarely leave their own cities, and the two encampments are separated by a vast and dangerous wasteland. Here again, we might conclude that Daleks and Thals are separate species according to popular biological species concepts.

There are many different ways of distinguishing between species. Richard Mayden lists twenty-two different species concepts in current use.[3] How, then, are we to choose between them? Particularly when—as in the case of the Daleks and Thals—different species concepts highlight the differences between species in different ways? Is there one correct way of identifying the members of a species—a position called *species monism*? Or, should we take a *species pluralist* stance and accept that the many different concepts can be complementary, with different concepts being used for different purposes? Though philosophy doesn't offer definitive answers to these questions, they can be seen as some of the most important aspects of the species problem, in that they affect how we think about the reality of species. If we accept pluralism, and embrace many different ways of placing particulars into species groups, this might seem to undermine the reality of species. If an organism can fit into many different groups depending on the criteria used, is the species category really all that significant?

---

[3] "A Hierarchy of Species Concepts."

They May Not Be Human, but Could Daleks Be People Too?

In the quote that we've used as a title for this chapter, a human in "Evolution of the Daleks," sums up the significance of the species problem. It's much more than just a theoretical issue debated by philosophers. The positions we take on both, the ontological nature of species, and the concepts and categories that are tenable and relevant, impact upon our views on the reality of species. And, since the reality or unreality of this category has implications for the security of any metaphysical boundary we place between species, this affects how particulars in the real world—as well as the fictional one created in *Doctor Who*—get classified and consequently treated. The importance of these issues is clearest in relation to the boundary we place between humans and non-humans. That is, those organisms we classify as *Homo sapiens* and those that we don't.

The boundary between humans and non-humans is both descriptive and normative. It describes when and where humans and non-humans differ, though it also has consequences for how we *should* live our lives. To illustrate this, philosophers often refer to our relationship with one of our closest living 'sister' species, the common chimpanzee *Pan troglodytes*. But we'll take the human-Dalek Sec as our example. So far we've only looked at Sec's status descriptively, but consider this from a normative point of view: what would be the consequences for Sec of being designated human or non-human within our society? In the first case—if he were accepted into the species *Homo sapiens*—would he be entitled to the same education, healthcare, and voting rights as the rest of us enjoy? Conversely, if he were excluded from our human club, would he risk becoming a laboratory animal or a creature in a zoo?

These questions aren't traditionally associated with the species problem in the philosophy of biology, though they're close to the hearts of many moral philosophers and animal ethicists, including Peter Singer. These philosophers recognize that those of us in the club *Homo sapiens* enjoy many rights that are withheld from other organisms. And, although those organisms are free from the corresponding duties, they lack the protection from exploitation that the status 'human' is supposed to confer. These philosophers ask us to consider whether this disparity is fair, given that it depends solely on species membership. Going back to carrots, broccoli, horses, and dogs, it's a little ridiculous to grant them voting rights, but in the case of Dalek Sec things aren't so clear cut. If he were to be accepted into our society, could we justify withholding rights from him simply because he wasn't a member of the species *Homo sapiens?* Singer and others use the term 'speciesism' for the view—which they reject—that mere membership of the species *Homo sapiens* alone provides sufficient grounds for our privileged status in the natural world.

Many animal ethicists now suggest that *personhood* might be the most 'humane' species concept available today. Personhood acknowledges the normativity of the species category, and instead suggests that rights and duties should be allocated to persons rather than species. The criteria for membership in the category persons could include intellectual and linguistic abilities, as well as the capacity for pain and suffering. According to this, some organisms that don't belong to the species *Homo sapiens* would be 'elevated' into our club. These might include dolphins and chimpanzees—animals whose intellectual abilities are thought to be at least as advanced as those of human children, and whose capacity for pain is widely acknowledged.[4]

However, there's a more controversial flip side to the allocation of rights to persons rather than species. While the inclusion of higher animals might be celebrated, the exclusion of some humans—including patients in persistent vegetative states and those with advanced dementia or very severe learning difficulties—is likely to be rejected as entirely unacceptable. Thankfully there are no serious plans to rearrange society along these lines. But, accepting personhood's inclusive aspects for a moment, Daleks (if they existed) would seem to be ideal candidates for membership. "Extermination" aside, let's face it, they are intelligent, goal-oriented, and very determined—all characteristics we prize highly in our children and ourselves. Who knows, perhaps in the world of *Doctor Who*, a future American President might be a Dalek . . .[5]

---

[4] Peter Singer, *Practical Ethics*, pp. 114–19.

[5] With thanks to the GENIE CETL at the University of Leicester, for their support of the BioethicsBytes project of which this work forms a part.

10

To Be Is *Not* to Be Perceived?

PAULA SMITHKA

Almost every species in the universe has an irrational fear of the dark. They're wrong, 'cause it's not irrational. It's Vashta Nerada.

—THE DOCTOR to Donna ("Silence in the Library," 2008)

Fear of the unknown has plagued humanity since we showed up on the scene of this play of existence. If there are things unknown, then for the most part, they go unperceived. Metaphysics, the nature of reality, and epistemology, what we know about reality, are intricately bound together in human experience and Time-Lord and aliens' experience in the Whoniverse. Why postulate the existence of something which we can't perceive? Wouldn't that be an irrational thing to do?

After all, as the good bishop, George Berkeley (1685–1753) has taught us, "to be is to be perceived." Objects must be perceived by minds in order to make the ontological claim that they exist. So, to claim objects exist with no perceptual evidence would be an irrational move to make; well, at least for an empiricist. Rationalists, who contend that reason is one's best and most reliable source for knowledge, might deduce the existence of some empirically transcendent thing, like a noumenal realm, as Immanuel Kant did. However, we'll mostly leave Kant out of this discussion. If there's no perceptual evidence, then to posit the existence of something would be irrational—why would one think something exists if there's not a shred of perceptual evidence? As a matter of fact, one wouldn't. If you tell your friends that "leprechauns exist," they'll tell you you're crazy, precisely because there's no evidence to support your claim. Now, if you're coming up with a story about some new fictional creature, then your friends understand you've restricted your domain of discourse to the realm of fiction, and so existence claims are restricted to existence-as-fiction claims.

The Vashta Nerada ("Silence in the Library," 2008) can't be perceived, but the Doctor claims that fear of the dark isn't irrational. "It's what's in the dark; it's what's always in the dark . . ." The difference is we have *indirect* perceptual evidence for their existence. The distinction between *direct* and *indirect* perceptual evidence in science and philosophy of science is an important one. Though the Doctor, Donna, Professor River Song and her team can't see the Vashta Nerada directly, in the same way they can perceive one another in the library, they see the *effects* of the Vashta Nerada—the ghosting skeletal remains of Miss Evangelista and later, Dave, the consumed chicken leg, and the number of shadows. "Count the shadows," the Doctor warns. They're "Piranhas of the air—Vashta Nerada—shadows that melt the flesh."

The Weeping Angels, ("Blink," 2008), however, play havoc with the notion of indirect perceptual evidence, undermining, perhaps even falsifying, Berkeley's claim that "to be is to be perceived." The Weeping Angels exist and function precisely when they are *not* perceived.

One's approach to the ontological status of unobservables, a.k.a. theoretical entities, determines whether one is a realist or antirealist. Does science provide true theories about the world? If so, then the postulated unobservables probably exist and one is a scientific realist. Or, are theories merely effective pragmatic tools for enhancing our understanding? If so, then theories needn't be true to be useful and posited unobservables needn't be thought of as existing. Both the Vashta Nerada and the Weeping Angels are unobservables; can we know they exist?

It's What's in the Dark

What's in the dark is beyond our customary senses; so, the question is: must we remain in perceptual darkness? The answer depends upon your philosopher of choice. John Locke (1632–1704) reasoned that the various properties of objects perceived by us, like color, taste, and sound, are really in the perceiver. They're functions of the primary qualities which are actually in objects, like extension (taking up space), texture, solidity, etc. Locke was a fan of Robert Boyle's (1627–1691) *corpuscular* theory. Small particles (corpuscles) given off by objects would light on our sense organs, like our eyes, and cause us to perceive color; so, color is in us, the perceiver, and not "objectively" in the object. What's in the dark, so to speak, is 'substance'. 'Substance', Locke claims, is an "underlying I know not what," reasoning that properties must be properties of *something*. Notice I said 'reasoning'. Locke makes the *inference* that properties have to be in something that's "more basic"; we don't, and can't, perceive that "underlying substance." So, why bother to postulate the existence of something for which there's no perceptual evidence? This is precisely Berkeley's point—don't bother. "To be is to be perceived."

In his *Three Dialogues Between Hylas and Philonous*, Berkeley very cleverly undermines the materialist claim that there's mind-independent matter. The character, Hylas (meaning 'matter' in Greek), defends the view that objects exist independently of their perceivers. Philonous (meaning 'love of mind') manages to get Hylas to concede that all properties, including the primary ones that Locke discusses, like extension, motion, solidity, etc., too, are a "matter of mind," for example:

PHILONOUS: Since therefore it is impossible even for the mind to disunite the ideas of extension and motion from all other sensible qualities, does it not follow that where the one exist there necessarily the other exist likewise?

HYLAS: It should seem so.

PHILONOUS: Consequently, the very same arguments which you admitted as conclusive against the secondary qualities are, without any further application of force, against the primary, too. Besides, if you will trust your senses, is it not plain all sensible qualities coexist, or to them appear as being in the same place? Do they ever represent a motion or figure as being divested of all other visible and tangible qualities?

HYLAS: You need say no more on this head. I am free to own, if there be no secret error or oversight in our proceedings hitherto, that all sensible qualities are alike to be denied existence without the mind.

Berkeley sums it up quite nicely in *The Principles*:

> . . . it will be objected that from the foregoing principles it follows things are every moment annihilated and created anew. The objects of sense exist only when they are perceived; the trees, therefore, are in the garden, or the chairs in the parlor, no longer than while there is somebody by to perceive them. Upon shutting my eyes all the furniture in the room is reduced to nothing, and barely upon opening them it is again created.

"Don't blink," as the Doctor warns Sally Sparrow about the Weeping Angels ("Blink"). "Don't even blink." The Doctor's warning takes on a new meaning when applied to Berkeley's philosophy. Blink, and the whole world would disappear—all of the objects and our perceptual knowledge of them, gone! Despite our blinking, some objects seem to persist whether we observe them or not, like the stars, planets, and the natural world in which we live. These are ideas in God's mind, according to Berkeley. While *we* can't be sure of what isn't perceived, because it really *is* all a matter of mind, we can be confident that those more "permanent-seeming objects" are maintained by the omniperceiver, God. Of course, we can't *perceive* God, but we've a *notion* of Him, or so Berkeley claims. Even though "to be is to be perceived," we seem to remain in the empirical "dark" about God; there seems to be little or no perceptual evidence for the existence of God, and, at best, it'd be indirect; rather like the indirect, perceptual evidence for the Weeping Angels.

Stay in the Light

David Hume (1711–1776) thinks that Berkeley is correct about rejecting a Lockean idea of physical substance, as an "underlying I know not what." However, for the same perceptual reasons, Hume remains skeptical, he *must* remain skeptical, about the existence of a Berkeley-conceived God who sustains the perceptible world. For, if God exists, He must be a "matter of fact" and so, we should have perceptual evidence for His existence.

William Paley's (1743–1805) endeavor to provide such, albeit indirect, empirical evidence for the existence of God in his famous "Argument from Design," also known as the "Watchmaker Argument," from his *Natural Theology* (1802), claimed that the complexity and regularity of the universe can best be accounted for by an intelligent designer, just as a watch, with all of its parts and intricacies, must have a watchmaker. David Hume lived too early to read Paley, but he answered some of Paley's arguments in advance, criticizing them in his *Dialogues Concerning Natural Religion* (1776). For Hume, if claims about what exists can't be traced back to the evidence of our senses, we must be skeptical about those claims—like the claim that God exists. Hume famously states:

> When we run over libraries, persuaded of these principles, what havoc must we make? If we take in our hand any volume of divinity or school metaphysics, for instance, let us ask, *Does it contain any abstract reasoning concerning quantity or number?* No. *Does it contain any experimental reasoning concerning matter of fact and existence?* No. Commit it then to the flames, for it can contain nothing but sophistry and illusion.

So, we can consider Hume to be asking us to "Stay in the light," with respect to what we take to be justified beliefs, just as the Doctor warns Donna, Professor River Song, and her team members, to stay in the light in order to avoid being consumed (literally!) by the Vashta Nerada. But surely, there are unobservable things for which we have reasonable indirect perceptual evidence!

Count the Shadows

Science regularly postulates the existence of empirical unobservables. The key is the degree of the "shadowy" nature of the indirect empirical evidence one presents in support of the hypothesis. The more shadows, the less probable the hypothesis; fewer shadows means the hypothesis is more plausible. Consider some "garden-variety unobservables" we now take for granted but historically may have been more problematic: wind—we can't directly *see* it, but we can feel it, and we're able to see its effects; gravity—it keeps us and the things around us in place and it takes a great deal of force and acceleration to break its grip when we attempt to leave the Earth; microbes—Louis Pasteur (1822–1895) had considerable difficulty convincing people of their existence, particularly that the Anthrax bacillus was responsible for killing farmers' sheep. Advances in technology make these once unobservable entities observable.

More recently postulated theoretical entities or unobservables include quarks and strings in theoretical physics, as well as black holes. We can't perceive them, so why say they exist? Because their suggested existence is consistent with what physicists have observed, and the existence of these entities help us to explain anomalies in what has been observed. The discovery of Neptune was largely due to anomalies observed in the orbital patterns of Uranus, which was taken to be the most distant planet. The hypothesis was that if there was another planet beyond Uranus, its gravitational force acting on Uranus would explain the observations. Mathematical calculations by Urbain Le Verrier (Paris) led to Johann Galle's observation of Neptune in 1946 from the Berlin Observatory. Did we *know* there was another planet before Galle observed it? No—that's Berkeley's point. But the best explanation to account for the observational data—orbital anomalies of Uranus—was the existence of another planet. The probability of the correctness of the hypothesis that there was another planet was high, based on the perceptual evidence and the mathematical calculations based on that data. There weren't too many *shadows* on that hypothesis.

Starting from observations, quarks and black holes are more of a stretch than Neptune, however. Strings are even worse than quarks and black holes. A goal of science is to explain phenomena in nature. As long as a hypothesis is consistent with perceptual evidence, has explanatory power, is testable by different scientists, doesn't lead to contradictions, and is fruitful, that is, leads to further inquiry, the hypothesis is likely to be accepted for the time being. There may be other competing hypotheses as well. In this case, which hypothesis does the best job? Empirical science doesn't deal in many certainties (unlike mathematics), so it's all about probability; the hypothesis with fewest *shadows* is the best one.

Is There Truth in the Shadows?

Are quarks, strings, and black holes real? What about the Vashta Nerada? These are questions about what really exists. There's also the question: how do we know they exist, if they do? It depends on whether you're a scientific realist or antirealist about the entities postulated in the theories. A goal of science is to explain phenomena in nature, but isn't it also to provide us with true theories about the world? We want to know what causes anomalies in our experience of the world; the Doctor, Donna, and the team members of Professor River Song's group want to know what's causing the unusual deaths of their comrades.

Scientific realism accepts that scientific theories are true or approximately true; they provide us with a literally true, or approximately true, picture of the world. Wilfrid Sellars said: "To have good reason to accept a theory is to have good reason to believe that the entities it postulates are real." Paul Churchland argues that the continued success of a theory is due to its being probably true and the likely existence of the theoretical entities postulated. Bas van Fraassen is an antirealist. Theories needn't be true to be useful; neither do we need to have the attitude that we *believe* them to be true. All theories need to be is "empirically adequate," van Fraassen contends. In other words, as long as they explain the phenomena, that is, "do their jobs," they're adequate. The epistemic attitude we have toward them is *acceptance* of their "empirical adequacy"; we don't need to *believe* them to be true.[1] I think the Doctor, unlike van Fraassen, is a scientific realist.

Don't Blink

The Weeping Angels are the monkey wrench in Berkeley's claim, "to be is to be perceived," and, in a way, for rational scientific inquiry. For them, to be is *not* to be perceived! *Molto bene*, writer Steven Moffat! When they're perceived by an observer, any creature, they cease to function *as* Weeping Angels; "they literally turn to stone," the Doctor says on the DVD Easter Egg. He describes them as "lonely assassins" and "creatures of the abstract," "as old as the universe." They prey upon the really existent potential life energies that humans (and presumably other creatures) would've used to finish their days along their projected normal life trajectory. The Weeping Angels disrupt that normal life trajectory, hijacking the victim's potential life energy to fuel their own existence. How the Weeping Angels live on really existent *potential* energy is an interesting philosophical topic in itself. You and I require *actual* energy to live and grow! And, the TARDIS is full of that potential energy, which is why the Weeping Angels want it and why the Doctor needs Sally Sparrow in 2007 to send the TARDIS back to him in 1969 where he and Martha are stuck—having been sent there "by the touch of an angel," just as Billy Shipton was, who then helps the Doctor by creating the DVD Easter Eggs as a message to Sally.

---

[1] Churchland, "The Ontological Staus of Observables"; van Fraassen, "To Save the Phenomena" and "Arguments Concerning Scientific Realism."

Sally sets out to photograph an old house, because she likes old things. While there, she finds a message on the wall warning the reader to beware the Weeping Angel and to duck; "really, duck." The message is for her. "Duck, now!" She does, avoiding a rock allegedly thrown by the Weeping Angel, located outside the window. But, as soon as she looks, the Weeping Angel has turned to stone and appears to be a mere statue. In the Easter Egg, the Doctor explains: "They are quantum locked . . . their greatest asset is their greatest curse"—they go unperceived and are swift assassins, but perceived, even by each other, they literally turn to stone. And, "you can't kill a stone," he says.

Returning to the house the next day with Kathy Nightingale, friend and co-"girl-detective," Sally seeks more empirical evidence regarding the strange message and the events of the night before. "Why come here?" Kathy asks. "I like old things. They make me sad," Sally says. "So, what's good about sad?" asks Kathy. Sally responds, "Sad is happy for deep people." Then the door bell rings. Sally goes to answer the door; Kathy remains behind, only to have her potential energies stolen by the Weeping Angels—her life trajectory was hijacked. They send her to the past; from 2007 London to 1920 Hull. The person at the door is Kathy's own grandson who promised his grandmother to deliver a letter to Sally Sparrow at precisely that date and time at that house. Yes, this is a closed causal chain.[2] Imagine receiving a letter detailing your friend's life, marriage, and her children when she was just with you a moment ago! You'd think it a (sick) practical joke; Sally does, as any rational person would.

The Weeping Angels seem to exist in Kant's noumenal realm—beyond anyone's perceptual experience. Why would we bother to postulate something which by definition is beyond perceptual experience? No good empiricist would, as we've seen with Berkeley and Hume. Yet, there are anomalies in Sally Sparrow's world that suggest something isn't quite "normal" and requires an explanation. Like the anomalies in Uranus's orbit, Sally has the letter from Kathy, the message on the wall, the Easter Egg messages placed in DVD's where she and the Doctor seem to be dialoguing in real time, but aren't, and the statues which *seem* to change locations—the angel statue has moved, she tells Kathy when they're at the house, "It's moved since yesterday; it's got closer to the house,

---

[2] See Chapters 5 and 7 in this volume.

I'm sure of it." Then she notices angel statues on a church across the street from the police station, and in a blink, they're no longer there. "Okay, cracking up now," Sally says to herself. Then there's the phone call from Billy Shipton, the detective she met while at the police station trying to report Kathy's disappearance, using the very strange letter from Kathy as evidence. He's in the hospital, old and dying. She met him only that day—in her time. He brings a message from the Doctor, to "look at the list"; the list is of seventeen DVDs, all of which she owns and all have the Doctor's Easter Egg on them. Larry Nightingale, Kathy's brother, is the one who discovered the Easter Egg and gave her the list of the DVDs. The indirect perceptual evidence begins to accumulate supporting the hypothesis that the Weeping Angels, though unobservable entities, actually might exist and don't merely "save the phenomena," as van Fraassen would have put it.

Doomed to Be Perceived

Detective Billy Shipton showed Sally the garage with vehicles which, over the years, had been abandoned by people who visited the old house. Along with the cars is the blue Police box. Billy can't open the box because he doesn't have the key. Sally doesn't realize it at first, but she has the TARDIS key, which she took from one of the statues at the old house.

Via Easter Egg, the Doctor directs Sally and Larry to the TARDIS. With key in hand and a disk found by Larry, Larry plugs in the "security program" as the Weeping Angels close in and encircle the TARDIS. The "security program" says that it's good for one ride in the TARDIS (a lie, by the way). Instead, the TARDIS begins to disappear. "He's leaving us behind!" Sally exclaims. "Doctor, no!" The TARDIS has vanished, and Kathy and Larry are on the ground, surrounded by Weeping Angels. "Quick, look at them!" Sally screams. "I don't think we have to," Larry responds. The Weeping Angels, now in a circle, perceived each other when the TARDIS disappeared. They've turned to stone with their stone eyes wide open, locked in constant perception of one another. Larry says, "the Doctor tricked them; they're never gonna move again."

To be is to be perceived, Berkeley says; but *not* if you're a Weeping Angel. To be perceived is your doom. To be is *not* to be perceived.

11

Could There Be Carrionites?

SIMON HEWITT

Does the time the Doctor bumped into Shakespeare help us to understand the philosophy of mathematics? Numbers keep cropping up for the Doctor. His lucky number, we learned in "The Creature from the Pit" (1979), is 74,384,338. Admittedly this represents something of a change from seven, which was revealed as his lucky number in "The Power of Kroll" (1978).

At other times numbers have mattered for the Doctor for rather less superstitious reasons. Think back to "The Doctor's Daughter" (2008). Here the Doctor, Donna, and Jenny are confronted with a puzzling sequence of numerals on the walls of the underground tunnels of Mezzaline: 60120717, 60120716, 60120714, 60120713, 60120724. These turn out to be dates, showing that the war between the humans and the Hath has been going on for a grand total of seven days. And there are numerous other examples of numerical encounters in the TARDIS's log book. Among the most interesting is the one when the Doctor meets the Carrionites.

Enter the Carrionites

It's actually a little bit cheeky describing the Carrionite encounter as numerical. This is because the reason that the Carrionites are philosophically interesting is that they *don't use* numbers. Humans, as the Doctor explains to Martha, use numbers to understand the universe and to get power over it. (If you're not prepared to believe the Doctor on this one, flick through any science textbook and notice how often mathematics is used.) Carrionites, on the other hand, use words for the same purpose. Words are very powerful for the Carrionites, which is why they want to get their hands on William Shakespeare, a master of words. Thankfully, the Doctor has other ideas. Now, what fascinates me about the Carrionites is that they seem highly relevant to one of the most important questions in the *philosophy of mathematics* (or *maths*, as we say in Britain![1]): is it possible to give a completely adequate scientific account of the universe—like the Skasis Paradigm from "School Reunion" (2006)—without mentioning numbers? Obviously, it'd be very difficult for us to do this. We humans seem naturally to use numbers to do science. Numbers make things easier. Nobody denies that. But (some philosophers would say) perhaps that's just because of the way we are, because of the way we evolved with tiny little brains that are difficult to get around in. The real question is this: is it possible, in theory, to do science without numbers? Perhaps you'd have to have a brain like Morbius and live as long as the Face of Boe to actually do it. But is it possible?

In 1980 the philosopher Hartry Field published a book called *Science Without Numbers*. As the title suggests, Field argues that it's possible to do science without doing mathematics at the same time. Ever since then, there's been a lot of debate about whether Field was right. This debate has often been highly complex and technical, involving detailed discussion of cutting-edge science and mathematics. But basically the question boils down to this: could there be Carrionites? Could there be creatures which understand the universe and have power over it (possibly in a slightly less exciting way than the Carrionites in "The Shakespeare Code," 2007) without having to use mathematics in the process? The reason that philosophers worry about this is that many of them think that if we absolutely need to mention numbers when we explain the universe in an attractive way, we ought to believe that numbers exist.

The position that numbers exist is often known as *Platonism*, after Plato (around 428–348 B.C.E.), who held a version of this view. Generally, when people talk about numbers 'existing' they don't mean that numbers exist in space and time (like police boxes,

---

[1] The British may have a quaint form of English, but we have compensated for this by providing the universe with several individuals who have saved it—on one occasion using nothing more than a yellow truck.

paving slabs, and Madame de Pompadour). Instead, they mean that numbers exist outside of space and time. This might sound like a rather odd thing to think, and it's the oddness of this form of Platonism which causes many philosophers (like Field) to try to show that we don't need to believe in it. On the other hand, odd things sometimes are true, as anyone who has traveled with the Doctor knows.

Interesting Isn't It? Allons-y, Alonso . . .[2]

If we couldn't give a complete account of the universe without mentioning Cybermen, then we ought to believe that Cybermen exist. In exactly the same way, if we can't give a complete account of the universe without mentioning numbers, then we ought to believe that numbers exist.

Arguments of the sort just presented are known as *indispensability arguments* for platonism and are differentiated from classic Platonism with a lowercase 'p'. Indispensability arguments are associated in particular with Willard Quine (1908–2000). In *Science Without Numbers*, Field attacks indispensability arguments as ferociously as a red-eyed Ood faced with its slave-master.

Think of an indispensability argument as consisting of three numbered stages:

1. **We ought to believe that everything necessarily mentioned, when giving our best scientific account of the universe, exists.**

2. **It is necessary to mention numbers when giving our best scientific account of the universe.**

3. **Numbers exist.**

If stages #1 and #2 are true, it follows that #3 is true, more surely than trouble follows the Master. So if somebody wants to believe that numbers don't exist they have to at least deny that either #1 or #2 is true, or they *can* deny that *both* are true. Field lays in to #2. He does this by providing an example of how (he thinks) physics can be done without using mathematics. In other words, he does a bit of Carrionite physics.

---

[2] I've always wanted to write that.

Time and Space, but No Relative Dimensions

As his example, Field takes what's called the *Newtonian theory of gravity*, and argues that you don't need to use mathematics to state the theory. If more proof than the existence of cakes with ball-bearings on top were needed that human beings are ingenious creatures, then Field's argument would be a good thing to put forward. It's deeply complex and not for the faint-hearted, but it shows how somebody might go about doing science without doing mathematics. Philosophers think that what Field has done is significant, not just because it allows Krillitane head-teachers the glimmer of hope that they might be able one day to understand everything without force-feeding children oil to make them good at mathematics, but also because it's a blueprint for how to attack step #2 of the indispensability argument mentioned above.

But it's only a blueprint. It's no more the real thing than Charlotte Abigail Lux lives in a real house. The reason for this is that the Newtonian theory isn't true. Anyone who told you otherwise—as most science teachers do at most schools—lied. Moral: don't believe everything you hear. (Especially not from that Mr. Saxon!) While it's approximately true—you won't go far wrong using it to help you understand average-sized objects which aren't moving very quickly, things like robot dogs and Daleks—it's been replaced in modern physics by Einstein's famous General Theory of Relativity. The General Theory of Relativity is the best theory of gravity we have; it's also a theory anyone who wants to comprehend the Doctor should appreciate.

In his book *The Science of Doctor Who*, science writer Paul Parsons very helpfully explains that the General Theory of Relativity has the potential to explain how the TARDIS could be bigger on the inside than the outside and how travelers (like the Doctor) could carve non-standard paths through space and time (which, in the General Theory of Relativity, are not actually two things but one multi-dimensional thing—'spacetime'). On a more mundane level, the General Theory of Relativity can explain some astronomical observations a lot more straightforwardly than the Newtonian theory of gravity. It's almost certain that the General Theory of Relativity isn't the last word on gravity. At the moment, physicists are trying to construct a theory of gravity which sits comfortably alongside certain other bits of physics; so-called 'quantum gravity'. However, it's clear that the Newtonian theory is a thing of the past, so Field hasn't succeeded in translating a current scientific theory into mathematics-free language.

This doesn't mean that Field hasn't achieved anything. He definitely *has* given us some idea of the kind of thing somebody might do to a scientific theory in order to get rid of the mathematics in it. It's just that he hasn't done it with a *current* scientific theory. He hasn't done any real Carrionite physics, so we're a long way away from showing that stage #2 of the indispensability argument for platonism is false.

Not So Much Timey-Wimey, as Teeny-Weeny Stuff

What's that I hear you asking? Has anyone discussed whether we could do away with mathematics in real, up-to-date, physical theories? *Molto Bene!* That's exactly the right question to ask. Because unless we have a good reason to believe that #2—the claim that we can't do science without numbers—isn't true, the possibility of Carrionite physics looks to be on shaky ground. It gets worse for the Carrionites: philosophers have argued that #2 seems pretty solid, because one of our most fundamental physical theories, Quantum Mechanics, is as full of mathematics as the Abzorbaloff is full of people.

Quantum Mechanics, in rough terms, is a part of physics which helps us understand the behavior of very small things. It could well be a lot more than that: some physicists, and some philosophers who are interested in physics, think that it applies to ordinary everyday objects as well. For all we know, Quantum Mechanics might explain how some of the weirder things which have happened to the Doctor are possible. But at the very least, it predicts how things like photons, electrons and quarks behave. And Quantum Mechanics is full to the brim with mathematics: full to the brim, that is, with incredibly complicated mathematics. The prospects of doing away with this mathematics, while keeping a physical theory that's powerful enough to explain and predict the things which Quantum Mechanics does, strikes a lot of people as not very good; maybe even impossible.

But some people, following the Doctor's lead, like impossible. Mark Balaguer claims to have done for a very important bit of mathematics in Quantum Mechanics what Field did for the mathematics in the General Theory of Relativity. In his book *Platonism and Anti-Platonism in Mathematics*, he turns on the use of things called 'Hilbert Spaces', which I won't attempt to explain, but which are a development of the idea of vectors, which may be familiar from school. Like a Dalek blasting away at the amassed ranks of Cybermen, Balaguer eliminates this mathematics from scientific theory. Now *that's* a bit of Carrionite physics to be proud of. The only problem is that some people don't think Balaguer has done what he claims.

There are two basic worries about Balaguer's work which cast doubt on whether his attempt at Carrionite physics is everything it claims to be. The first is that it rules out some *interpretations* of Quantum Mechanics. In one sense, Quantum Mechanics is nothing more than a formal theory which tells us how certain things behave. Now, if the Doctor has taught us anything it's that things sometimes behave very strangely, and Quantum Mechanics is with him on this. In order to explain how the world can be such that things behave as Quantum Mechanics describes, people have suggested a variety of interpretations of Quantum Mechanics. On one interpretation, there are things out there ('hidden variables') which explain the oddity. On another interpretation, parallel worlds do the job. And there are other interpretations, most of them equally weird and wonderful.

The odd thing about Balaguer's mathematics-free version of Quantum Mechanics is that it rules out some of these interpretations. Not only does this mean that Balaguer's new Quantum Mechanics is unlikely to appeal to people who support one of these interpretations, it means that Balaguer's Quantum Mechanics is significantly different from normal Quantum Mechanics. We think that the TARDIS is good at translating because it lets people hear in one language what is said in another. There's no loss of meaning. It should be a bit like that with 'translating' a scientific theory into a mathematics-free version. Obviously the mathematics-free version won't 'mean' exactly the same thing as the standard version, because it'll avoid making reference to numbers. But we'd expect the mathematics-free theory to say the same kind of thing about the physical universe, to have similar advantages and have a comparable openness to interpretation. But it appears that this isn't true of Balaguer's Quantum Mechanics.

The second worry is that Balaguer's new Quantum Mechanics might not be what it says it is. It's always worth checking whether something is what it claims to be: that looks like Santa walking down the street playing a trombone, but . . . Remember that

Balaguer claims to have done away with mathematics in his theory, and so to have made progress towards attacking stage #2 of the indispensability argument. There's doubt about whether he's really done this. It all gets horribly complicated at this point, but in essence it seems as though Balaguer hasn't got rid of the mathematics to everyone's satisfaction.

But even if Balaguer has carried off doing a bit of Quantum Mechanics without doing mathematics, the foes of the indispensability argument still have a long way to go. Balaguer focuses on one part of Quantum Mechanics, not even the whole of Quantum Mechanics, let alone the whole of physics. The person who wants to defeat stage #2 of the indispensability argument has a tough job. And it could be a lot tougher than some people realize. A lot of people—not just philosophers—assume that all of science boils down to physics. We might study things like biology, polymer chemistry, or advanced sonic technology, but the things we study when we study these subjects are the way they are because of the kind of thing studied by physics. Donna behaves as she does solely because of what lots of little particles in her body are doing. Krelatine oil has the properties it does, similarly, because of stuff going on at the sub-atomic level.

The view that everything in science is physics is sometimes called *microphysicalism*. This is a popular position, but that doesn't make it true. It's a popular position that car SatNavs are harmless. If microphysicalism is false, people who want to attack the indispensability argument have an even tougher time of it. Not only do they have to get rid of the mention of mathematics from physics, they have to do it with the other sciences as well. But biology and chemistry contain lots of mathematics. As for the social sciences— can you really imagine economics without mathematics? It'd be easier to imagine a celibate Captain Jack.

Aww, . . . Poor Monster. Should We Feel Sorry for the Carrionites?

So far we've looked at stage #2 of the indispensability argument, and quite right too, because it's stage #2 that—in effect—claims there couldn't be Carrionites. Even so, somebody could attack stage #1 of the argument, which says we ought to believe that everything necessarily mentioned, when giving our best scientific account of the universe, exists. Actually, philosophers normally put things a bit more precisely than this; they say that we should believe in things we need to mention in a particular way (called 'quantifying over') in a formal logical language. A few people have actually gone about attacking stage #1 as well. With reckless abandon, however, I'm going to ignore them. If you're interested, you can read about this—as well as much more that I've skimmed over here—in Mark Colyvann's book The *Indispensability of Mathematics.*

The reason that I'm skimming over attacks on stage #1 of the indispensability argument is that there's a far more interesting question to ask about the argument. Suppose that the argument doesn't work. Suppose that it really is possible to do science without using mathematics. There really could be Carrionites. The interesting question is this: so what? Even if there were Carrionites, even if we no longer need numbers to do science than modern Daleks need a stair-lift to climb stairs, does that mean that numbers don't exist? Why should it?

Here's an argument that numbers would exist *even if* we didn't need them to do mathematics. If there were Carrionites, they'd be missing out on something. Question: what? Answer: mathematics. Even if the Carrionites could understand the entire physical universe, and exercise control over it without using numbers, they'd be deprived of a type of knowledge which humans (and Time Lords) have; knowledge of mathematics. We don't just know things like: 'At standard pressure, water boils at 100°C' and 'A healthy human heart contains two ventricles and two atria' (notice, by the way, that numbers naturally creep into even the most simple scientific statements). We also know things like '2 + 2 = 4' and 'there's no largest prime number'. When we know things like this, aren't we knowing *about* numbers in the same way as chemists know *about* water, biologists know *about* hearts and experts in Earthonomics know about Earth (or ought to)? But, if this is right, don't there have to be numbers for us to know *about?*

There might be a lot wrong with this sort of argument, and many philosophers have claimed that there is. But isn't it worth asking: don't we think that mathematicians discover true things, that they really know things? Working mathematician Marcus du Sautoy says this about mathematics, "These truths are simply waiting to be unearthed, and no amount of creative thinking will undermine their existence." Earlier in the same book he also said:

Some philosophers might take issue with such a Platonist view of the world—this belief in an absolute and eternal reality beyond human existence—but to my mind that is what makes them philosophers and not mathematicians. (*The Music of the Primes*, p. 7)

Harsh words! And, in fairness to the anti-Platonists, there are in fact mathematicians who don't agree with platonism. But du Sautoy's words are food for thought.

Let's give almost the last word to Elton Pope:

When you're a kid, they tell you it's all grow up, get a job, get married, get a house, have a kid, and that's it. No, the truth is the world is so much stranger than that, so much darker, and so much madder. And so much better! ("Love and Monsters," 2006)

That's the thing about the Doctor, he opens doors to a whole new universe. He shows people that there's just so much out there, waiting to be discovered. The Doctor helps people discover things about themselves, but he also helps them discover things about other stuff. Rose learns about Daleks, for example.

There's a lot of stuff to be discovered. Perhaps some of this stuff is mathematical. Perhaps there are numbers. And if there are—whether or not we need them to do science, whether or not Field and Balaguer are correct—then the Carrionites are missing out. Poor things! Although, perhaps it serves them right for doing horrible things to the Doctor, Martha, Shakespeare, and other innocent humans.

Either way, there're no easy answers. One of the gripping things about philosophy of mathematics is that, just when you think you've got somewhere, there's a problem with your view. There's a problem with every view everyone's ever come up with. So don't worry if you haven't found any of the positions I've written about very convincing. Another thing the Doctor does is force people to think for themselves. And that's what you're going to have to do on the question of whether numbers exist. But as you think, it's worth being aware that even the Carrionites fell back on numbers in the end. They needed to use Shakespeare because of his command over language, because it was words (and not numbers), which would gain them power over the portal. Yet, in spite of this, the last words of "Love's Labours Won" were these:

The light of Shadmock's hollow moon doth shine on to a point in space betwixt Dravidian Shores and Linear 5930167.02, and strikes the fulsome grove of Rexel 4; co-radiating crystal activate!

Numbers, it seems, just won't go away. Not even for Carrionites.[3]

---

[3] Thanks to Ian Potter for pointing out that even the Carrionites couldn't do without numbers, and to Matt Kimpton for the discussion of the Doctor and numbers in general.

It's a Different Morality. Get Used to It, or Go Home!

The Ethics of Doctor Who

12

The Ethics of the Last of the Time Lords

KEVIN S. DECKER

A frail old man lost in time and space. . . . He seems not to remember where he has come from; he is suspicious and capable of sudden malignancy. . . . He remains a mystery. From time to time the other three [time travelers] discover things about him, which turn out to be false or inconclusive. . . . They think he may be a criminal fleeing from his own time.

—C.E. WEBBER, notes on creating *Doctor Who*[1]

The man who abhors violence, never carrying a gun. . . . You take ordinary people and fashion them into weapons. Behold your children of time, transformed into murderers. . . .

—DAVROS ("Journey's End," 2008)

When the whole universe is at stake, how does the Doctor make moral decisions about who's saved and who must sacrifice? Do his anti-authoritarianism and constant wandering express a sustainable notion of what a flourishing life could be? Is he a hero or a genocidal murderer (or both)?

From its very beginnings in a fog-shrouded junkyard in Totters' Lane, the Doctor's adventures have flouted television conventions: historical serial or fantastic futurism? Fantasy, drama, or horror? Given this ambiguous heritage, it's perhaps appropriate that the ethical messages the Doctor sends are equally nebulous. Like the police box shell of the TARDIS, the alien morality that the Doctor

---

[1] Quoted in Gary Gillatt, *Doctor Who from A to Z*, p. 11.

represents has unseen dimensions that no one would suspect lay behind his unassuming façade.

As a Time Lord, the Doctor's role as the ultimate outsider complicates the situation: Gary Gillatt, a cultural historian of *Doctor Who* notes, "In many ways, the Doctor is defined by our distance from him . . . we are rarely given access to his thought-processes or motivations, which in turn only adds to the character's enigmatic appeal." Complex motivations make it difficult to apply traditional ethical theories to judge the Doctor's conduct. Not only are the Doctor's intentions both complex and usually private, but also they often relate to unique situations in which conventional rules don't seem to apply. The Doctor clearly seems to reject the idea that there's any clear formula for making the right decision every time and expresses this in many ways: in "Warrior's Gate" (1981) he quips, "One good solid hope is worth a cart-load of certainties."

The Doctor's unique relationship to *time* also presents obstacles to using ethical theories that emphasize the importance of consequences to whether an action is right or wrong. Assessing our decisions or administering praise and blame in terms of consequences assumes a linear, cause-and-effect notion of how the universe works. But *Doctor Who* often demonstrates linear cause-and-effect as a convenient fiction—for example, in the cases of the TARDIS jumping a time dimension in "The Space Museum" (1965), or the insight into our timeline provided by alternate universes of "Inferno" (1970), "Rise of the Cybermen" (2006), and the Master's Paradox Machine in "The Sound of Drums" (2007). The Fourth Doctor expresses the now-classic formulation of this problem in "Genesis of the Daleks" (1975):

> Listen, if somebody who knew the future pointed out a child to you and told you that the child would grow up totally evil . . . to be a ruthless dictator who would destroy millions of lives. Could you then kill that child?

Given his propensity for talking about the integrity of the "web of time" ("Attack of the Cybermen," 1985) as "wibbly-wobbly, timey-wimey stuff" ("Blink," 2007), the Doctor's perception of time must give him insight into the relationship between intention and consequence that we don't share.

Perhaps there's another approach that better captures the *ethos* (of the same Greek root as *ethical*) of *Doctor Who* as a whole.

Maybe the Doctor's ethics can be found between the poles of the Romantic's ideal of embracing self-realization and the beauty of uniqueness and the existentialist's cosmic *angst*—focused on the deep aching realization of both our finitude and our freedom. In this respect, the Doctor's morality, as I see it, is an "ethics of ambiguity."

Just This Once! Everybody Lives!

Those eager to associate *Doctor Who* with the values of written science fiction in the mid-twentieth century might be tempted to take the Third Doctor's impressive line, "I am every kind of scientist!" as definitive of the show's ethos. *Positivism* was the name given by Auguste Comte (1798–1857) to the theory that any claim, to be meaningful, must be able to be verified by logical proof or scientific testing. Although the Doctor clearly prizes good reasoning and gets through many scrapes through technological McGuffins (like sonic screwdrivers and reversing the polarity of the neutron flow), it seems clear he's not a positivist. From the First Doctor's stirring assertion, "I don't believe that man was made to be controlled by machines" ("The Keys of Marinus," 1964) it makes more sense to infer that it's the Doctor who has mastered scientific theory and technology, and not vice-versa. Inasmuch as a non-human can be a humanist, the Doctor is, and not a positivist.

Beyond this, bold decisions were made in re-imagining *Doctor Who* both in 1996 ("Doctor Who: The TV Movie") and in the new series begun in 2005 in order to give the Doctor a more emotional side and to explicitly stress the emotions and the relationship dynamics between characters, especially between the Doctor and companions.

Sci-fi author Kim Newman sees a major shift starting with the character of the Eighth Doctor, who's "impulsive, open (if the heart is the center of feeling, this would explain why McGann has emotion enough for two), eager to share knowledge even if he knows he should keep it to himself. . . ."[2] In the new television series, Christopher Eccleston and David Tennant have also consistently injected more pathos into the role.

These humanistic and passionate elements of *Doctor Who* converge in the ideals of Romanticism, an intellectual movement span-

---

[2] Kim Newman, *Doctor Who*, p. 112.

ning a few decades before and after the turn of the nineteenth century. The Romantic temperament was born in Britain and Germany out of the collapse of the Enlightenment's adulation of *reason*. This occurred in the wake of the French Revolution, especially the irrationality and excess of its Reign of Terror (which, as we know, the First Doctor was helpless to prevent). *Doctor Who's* parallel construction, I would argue, has the Doctor's Romantic character evolve from his initial alienation from Gallifreyan society. In post-2005 *Doctor Who*, blatantly Romanticist themes emerge from the utter destruction of that same society. So, for example, the very first time we see the Doctor openly weep is in "The End of the World" (2005) when Jabe confronts him about the destruction of the Time Lords.

If a single ideal can represent Romanticist ethics, it must be an ideal that has indefinite potential for richness and depth. This ideal is found in the quest for what it means to become more fully human. In face of the collapse of the ideal of society organized by principles of reason, historian of ethics Warren Ashby tells us:

> there arose the ideal and reality of the individual in his or her uniqueness, with potential and realized richness and depth. . . . Each of these individuals broke previous rational limits and discovered new ways of feeling and thinking. In each there emerged new perceptions of what life essentially was and might be. (*A Comprehensive History of Western Ethics*, p. 441)

The Romantics share with later existentialists the idea that human nature isn't a given, but that its shaping is essentially in the hands of each free, expressive person. So begins a fascination with the *quality* of experience as well as with the social conditions that made this quality better or worse.

They weren't merely affirming the cliché, "Do what you love." Indeed, the characteristic "longing" of the Romantic wasn't for any *particular* experience, but for the "infinite" itself, "a feeling and a yearning that had to be realized through finite, small things" (p. 444). In his connection with vast and alien cosmic forces, the Doctor often pronounces how different he is from his (mostly) human companions: "I'm a Time Lord. . . . I walk in eternity" ("Pyramids of Mars," 1975); "The ground beneath our feet is spinning at a thousand miles an hour, and the entire planet is hurtling around the Sun at sixty-seven thousand miles an hour, and *I can feel it*" ("Rose," 2005). In the face of this, it's remarkable how often the Doctor immerses himself in "finite small things," like a cup of tea, flowers, home cooking ("Battlefield," 1989) and of course, little shops. "For some people, small, beautiful events are what life is all about!" the Fifth Doctor reminds us in "Earthshock" (1982).

It's by exploring our feelings about the experience in question, as well as focusing on the indefinite and ambiguous qualities of the experience that we begin to catch a fleeting glimpse of the infinite. Romantics like poet Percy Bysshe Shelley would disagree with the positivists and traditional moral philosophers who think that our reason and sense experience are enough to tell us how to live a flourishing life. Instead, as Shelley declares in his poem "The Sensitive Plant":

> For love, and beauty, and delight,
> There is no death or change: their might
> Exceeds our organs, which endure
> No light, being themselves obscure.

The human faculty of *imagination* is underappreciated, Shelley thinks. "Reason is the enumeration of quantities already known," he writes, while "imagination is the perception of the value of those qualities. . . . Reason is to Imagination as the instrument to the agent, as the body to the spirit, as the shadow to the substance." It's clear that this ideal is operative in *Doctor Who*'s more subtle characterizations: it's more work for the audience of *Doctor Who* to have to look carefully at a character or a race, to be willing to revise our judgments about them ("Captain Jack is bisexual—am I okay with that? He *is* very witty and clever . . ."). The attitude common to both existentialism and Romanticism—in the face of the limitations of our all-too-human perspective—is a stance of *openness to surprise* in face of the unique experiences of others. The Doctor, as Romantic, exemplifies this attitude perfectly, and it's when he wears it on his sleeve that he provides the most galvanizing moral example for the rest of us.

Yet sometimes even the Doctor's behavior surprises us. Happily, the literature of the "Romantic Gothic" in which *Doctor Who* is steeped helps explain this as well: the Gothic motif is often focused on the notion of the "divided consciousness." Heroes and villains in this world are often portrayed as mirror images of each other, with only shades of gray separating them. "Because the dividing line between heroic revolt and manic villainy could never be demarcated," John Tulloch and Manuel Alvarado write, the "Romantic Gothic generated a degree of angst, guilt and alienation around its central narrative oppositions which attached doubted to its heroic performance and emotional sympathy to its villainous ones." [3]

The mystery of the show's central character thrives on this kind of uncertainty, from the First Doctor's flirtation with the cold-blooded murder of a caveman ("An Unearthly Child," 1963) to the Third Doctor's close identification with Omega, the lost Gallifreyan solar engineer; from the scheming artfulness of the Seventh Doctor to the Tenth Doctor's inability to know when to stop kicking a dead Racnoss ("The Runaway Bride," 2006). Allies and enemies in the Doctor's universe are equally ambiguous—races such as the Monoids, Sensorites, and Silurians and even the Daleks have members both benevolent and malicious.

Have You Ever Thought What It's Like . . . to Be Exiles?

Novelist James Baldwin wrote that "nothing is more unbearable, once one has it, than freedom." To grasp the other side of the Doctor's adventures in time and space, we should focus on the notion of *freedom*, an emphasis common to both Romanticism and existentialism. The TARDIS is emblematic of this freedom: from the very first episodes, we see that the Doctor's time and space machine gives him limitless opportunities to travel everywhere and everywhen—a freedom most of us would love to possess. [4] This is freedom in the sense of absence of limitations (that is, the opposite of *coercion*), of not being tied down to a specific place or time but having the liberty to wander and explore. But existentialists like Jean-Paul Sartre (1905–1980) have pointed out that freedom also refers to a *positive ability* to act on my choices and—even more importantly—to have a range of options for act-

---

[3] John Tulloch and Manuel Alvarado, *Doctor Who: The Unfolding Text*, p. 137.

[4] The significant obstacle to this freedom for the Doctor in his first three incarnations is, of course, his spotty knowledge of how to work the Ship (the knowledge is actively repressed by the Time Lords during his exile on Earth). In "An Unearthly Child," the Doctor explains to Barbara and Ian why he can't use the TARDIS to take them back to their own time: "You see, this isn't working properly. Or rather the code is still a secret."

ing that is not arbitrarily limited by forces outside our control. This is what the essayist and lecturer Ralph Waldo Emerson meant when he proclaimed that we must be free ". . . even to the *definition of freedom*."

Sartre's and Emerson's redescriptions of freedom call attention to the ways in which traditional moral theories can restrict our notion of what "ethics" is all about: are we simply to *avoid* forbidden actions, as rule systems such as the Ten Commandments require? But then, what should we *do*? The content of a meaningful life isn't something that we gain from sets of rules. Must we focus on doing our absolute duties, as Immanuel Kant recommends? This ignores the possibility that we might have insoluble *conflicts* of duties, but also fails to deal with the possibility that within Kant's own ethical system, we might be simultaneously commanded to both do and refrain from doing an action—surely a deep problem! Are we simply to act for the greatest happiness, as John Stuart Mill would have it? This exposes us to the possibility that the happiness of the many may consistently depend upon the oppression of the few, a situation that the Doctor encounters far too often as evidenced by "The Mutants" (1972), "The Sunmakers" (1977), "The Happiness Patrol" (1988), and many other episodes. Rejecting the very idea that moral theory might be helpful in grappling with our own "dreadful freedom," Sartre instead offers a compelling story of a young, French student who came to him for advice during World War II:

> The boy was faced with the choice of leaving for England and joining the Free French Forces—that is, leaving his mother behind—or remaining with his mother and helping her to carry on. He was fully aware that the woman lived only for him and that his going-off—and perhaps his death—would plunge her into despair. He was also aware that every act that he did for his mother's sake was a sure thing, in the sense that it was helping her to carry on, whereas every effort he made toward going off and fighting was an uncertain move which might run aground and prove completely useless. (*Existentialism Is a Humanism*, pp. 29–30)

What choice did Sartre advise his troubled student to make? The answer may be surprising; to understand it, we must make a short hop in the TARDIS to the existentialist's views on *choice* and *value* before returning. I want to explain these views by first looking at answers to the question, "Why did the Doctor leave Gallifrey?"

In fact, more than forty years after the show's premiere, we still know little about the Doctor's reasons for his primarily lifestyle choice of "wandering through space and time in a rackety old TARDIS" ("The Five Doctors," 1983). At first, both the Doctor and his grand-daughter Susan speak longingly of one day returning to their unnamed home world, from which they have been exiled. The Doctor's confessed inability to control the TARDIS suggests that he left home in less than ideal circumstances, and is a stark contrast with his aspersions to a higher science (such as when he says to Ian in the original pilot episode, "I tell you, before your ancestors had turned the first wheel, the people of my world had reduced movement through the farthest reaches of space to a game for children."). In "The Two Doctors" (1985), he identifies himself as a "pariah"—suggesting a deep cultural or philosophical divide between himself and his people. Here, the Doctor clearly represents a forlorn individual like Sartre's student: both must face up to both the opportunities and the dreadful responsibilities of being free.

But things aren't so clear! In "The War Games" (1969), the Second Doctor is seized by the Time Lords and put on trial for interference in the course of established history. He claims to his companions that he left Gallifrey *voluntarily*—because he was bored! Adding to the retcon-fusion is that in the aforementioned "Two Doctors," the Doctor claims not only to be a pariah but also to be *on a mission for the Time Lords*! Further, often radical developments for the Doctor's relationship with his own people are implied by *Doctor Who: The TV Movie* (1996) and "Rose" (2005). What are we to make of the inconsistency of the Doctor's motives and indeed, his entire history?

Again, we could loosely paraphrase Emerson: "A foolish consistency is the Peking homunculus of little minds."[5] Existentialists agree with Emerson and the Doctor that inconsistency and ambiguity is to be treasured because it's a close reminder of our own freedom to revise our identity and our future. And as James Chapman writes in his cultural history of the show, "The cultural politics and narrative ideologies of *Doctor Who* . . . serve to encourage difference and non-conformity. This is evident . . . in

---

[5] Okay, the actual quote invokes a "hobgoblin of little minds," but what's a chapter on *Doctor Who* without a mention of Mr. Sin, the crazed, pig-brained dwarf from "The Talons of Weng-Chiang" (1977)?

the characterization of the Doctor himself as an eccentric and a social outsider."[6]

Because existentialists put a premium on the unique character of subjective, concrete experience as well as on passion, they see that it's *our choices themselves* that confer value on a situation. The opposite perspective, embraced by most traditional ethical theories, is that value is a pre-existing good that we reach for when we act correctly. What could be wrong with this common-sense approach? Against it, Sartre tells his student to avoid relying on religious doctrines or philosophical theories for advice: not only do they lead us to different outcomes based on arbitrary presuppositions, but they're a way of transferring the ultimate responsibility for value and choice onto something *other than us*. To use them to avoid making a choice, or to avoid the full responsibility for that choice, is to engage in what Sartre calls "bad faith," the act of denying the aching truth of our freedom. Sartre's advice is simple but troubling: make *some* choice and *assume responsibility* for the choice. Hiding behind pretended absolutes or allowing others to make the decision for us is equally inauthentic—again, bad faith!

In discussing how different kinds of people react to the fact of ultimate responsibility, existentialist Simone de Beauvoir (1908–1986) characterizes "the adventurer," who gleefully "casts himself into the world." She couldn't have described the Doctor more precisely. He's contrasted with what she calls the "subman," an apathetic person who "manifests a fundamental fear in the face of existence, in the face of the risks and tensions which it implies." The Doctor is also contrasted with what Beauvoir calls a man of "petit bourgeois seriousness," who "gets rid of his freedom by claiming to subordinate it to values which would be unconditioned"; in other words, he doesn't live by the book.[7] No, the "adventurer" faces his fears and throws away the TARDIS manual:

> Hoping for no justification, he will nevertheless take delight in living. He will not turn aside from things which he does not believe in. He will seek a pretext in them for a gratuitous display of activity. . . . He finds joy in spreading through the world a freedom which remains indifferent to its content. (*The Ethics of Ambiguity*, p. 58)

---

[6] James Chapman, *Inside the TARDIS: The Worlds of Doctor Who*, p. 7.

[7] Simone de Beauvoir, *The Ethics of Ambiguity*, pp. 42, 46.

Unlike Beauvoir's definition of the adventurer, the Doctor really does care (usually!) about the consequences of his choices upon other people. This is the difference that he makes in an "indifferent" universe, in which "planets come and go. Stars perish. Matter disperses, coalesces, forms into other patterns, other worlds. Nothing can be eternal" ("The Trial of a Time Lord," 1986).

"Howzat!" Prometheus Is a Fast Bowler

One conclusion we should draw from all this is that the Doctor's morality can't be reduced to a formula or a theory. In his existentialist leanings, the Doctor acknowledges both his ultimate freedom *and* responsibility for his choices by rejecting Time Lord values and defining himself through his relationships and his wandering. As a Romantic, the Doctor seeks the infinite in small events—whether in the joy of running through corridors or in the tragic loss of "Love's Labour's Found"—and recognizes that, since his own path to self-actualization must be idiosyncratic, everyone else's must be as well. But in what sense does this lead us to an ethics that we can learn from?

Well, the figure in Greek mythology that the Doctor resembles most, in his existentialist and Romantic trappings, is *Prometheus*.[8] A Titan, Prometheus challenged the all-powerful, all-knowing Zeus, stealing fire from Olympus to give to humans to use as they pleased. In eternal punishment, Zeus chained Prometheus to a rock, where his liver was eaten by an eagle, a painful process carried out daily as Prometheus, immortal, regenerated after each attack. The punishment wasn't quite "eternal," since Hercules killed the eagle and freed Prometheus from his chains. The Prometheus myth is most resonant with us today as a humanistic reversal of the Biblical myth of the Fall: the theft of enlightenment, whether Zeus's fire or the fruit of the tree of knowledge, may be seen as a crime by some, but in its consequences, it *liberates* humans, giving us a degree of control over our identities that is both delightful and dreadful. The gift of fire from a Gallifreyan Prometheus—in the Doctor's words, "a whole galaxy to explore, millions of planets, eons of time, countless civilizations to meet!" ("The War Games,"

---

[8] This Greek name has two derivations, both of which are fascinating in comparison to *Doctor Who*: in its more linguistically certain one, it means "to steal." But another relates it to the Greek word for "foresight."

1969)—is an existentialist allegory for escaping from the imposed mediocrity of much of our mass culture. It's also a Romantic's metaphor for cultivating our imagination and creating provocations against biased and prejudiced imagination, whether our own or that of others.

The virtue of discussing popular culture in philosophical contexts is that it provides an accessible way for anyone to challenge dominant paradigms of thinking. The Doctor's proclivity for seeing his companions and adventures through the lenses of Romanticism and existentialism is itself a challenge to the dominant ways of talking about ethics in schools, universities, and the professions because all too often, morality is treated as something distinct from the social, biological, and cultural conditions from which it emerges.

When we talk about what's valuable, the difference between good versus evil, or what a flourishing life would look like, we're aided by alliances not only with popular culture, but also other, non-philosophical disciplines like anthropology and cognitive science. These bodies of knowledge help put flesh on the all-too-thin bones of ethical rules and standards—they make our exploration of morality *concrete*. And because *Doctor Who*'s unique narrative twist is the juxtaposition of the familiar and the otherworldly (Jon Pertwee was quoted as saying that Daleks aren't scary, but finding a Yeti on your loo in Tooting Beck *would* be), we shouldn't overlook the likelihood that such juxtapositions may be hidden in the most unassuming of guises. As the show's first story editor David Whitaker tells us, "Everyone expects . . . to see large, gleaming spaceships orbiting planets. But what if the spaceships were here already, disguised as ordinary artifacts? And what if their occupants were already walking among us, keeping cautiously in the background to avoid notice and suspicion?"[9] The Doctor's ethics are inspiring to us primarily because he often treats us better than we deserve, realizing, as we must force ourselves to realize, that humans are bigger on the inside than on the outside.[10]

---

[9] Jeremy Bentham, *Doctor Who: The Early Years*, p. 61.

[10] I want to thank Kennedy Stomps for the original idea for this chapter; I appreciate comments and suggestions on earlier drafts from Ethan Decker and the editors and their refereees.

13
Empathy, Ethics, and Wonder

LAURA GEUY AKERS

I know what it's like—everything you're feeling right now. The fear, the joy, the wonder—I get that!

—TENTH DOCTOR ("Planet of the Ood," 2008)

It was a better life. And I—I don't mean all the travelling and . . . seeing aliens and spaceships and things—that don't matter. The Doctor showed me a better way of living your life.

—ROSE TYLER ("The Parting of the Ways," 2005)

For those who are, in effect, immortal, questions of ends and means must be especially acute. When you've already seen "all that is . . . all that was . . . all that ever could be" ("The Parting of the Ways," 2005), how can you keep your life fresh and meaningful? And how should you interact with those whose lives are almost as ephemeral to you as mayflies are to ordinary humans?

Philosophers have long considered the question of how to make one's life fulfilling. In his *Nicomachean Ethics*, Aristotle taught that the good life is one of engagement in activities that accord with virtue, and others have emphasized the pursuit of justice, honor, and other ideal ends. Psychologists like Edward Deci and Richard Ryan propose three basic human needs: competence in one's actions, relatedness (connections with others), and autonomy (feeling we're acting without pressure from others).[1] An extensive body of cross-cultural research confirms that meeting these three needs is important to individuals' well-being.

---

[1] Deci and Ryan, "The 'What' and 'Why' of Goal Pursuits," pp. 227–268.

Earlier in his long life, the Doctor hardly seemed to face this issue. Bored with his home planet and something of a rebel among the Time Lords, the Doctor always seemed content with himself. Since the final Time War, however, which destroyed Gallifrey and (almost) all of the other Time Lords, these existential issues have become especially pressing. The Doctor is now fully self-directed and painfully alone. How then should he live his life?

Paths Not Taken

The Doctor strongly rejects the worldviews of his opponents. He condemns the Daleks for their genocidal belief that "Human beings are different, and anything different is wrong" ("Dalek," 2005). He's likewise appalled by the Cybermen, who believe that "upgrading" from humanity must involve removing all emotion and differences, in the interest of "Everlasting peace—and unity—and uniformity" ("Age of Steel," 2006). The Doctor cherishes creativity, even eccentricity, and abhors blind conformity and schemes that treat living beings as means toward others' ends.

In "School Reunion" (2006), the Doctor encounters the Krillitanes, who are using British schoolchildren to help them solve the Skasis Paradigm so that they can "shape the universe and improve it." The Doctor understands the temptation but refuses to help them. He doesn't believe it's appropriate to act on such a scale, to engineer solutions and impose them on others.

Even more germane to the question of Time-Lord ethics is the Master, a rival Time Lord whose way of life is diametrically opposed to the Doctor's. As his name implies, the Master seeks to conquer and dominate, while the Doctor, like a good physician, responds to needs, works to restore situations to a state of well-being, and then moves on.

This isn't to say that the Doctor has been entirely consistent in his approach to life. In his First incarnation, he was "rude, angry, dangerous, and malevolent," and in his Second, "puckish, quixotic" and "slyly self-deprecating."[2] The Third was gentlemanly, and the Fourth, downright cavalier. Even in his Tenth incarnation, he can still succumb to the temptation to make godlike judgments, as when he condemned The Family of Blood to eternal imprisonment

---

[2] Kim Newman, *Doctor Who*, pp. 3, 40.

("The Family of Blood," 2007) As Donna Noble said when he destroyed the Racnoss in "The Runaway Bride" (2006), "Sometimes, I think you need someone to stop you." Overall, however, he seems much more cautious than in his earlier days. Perhaps he's more realistic about his wisdom, or perhaps the Great Time War has caused him to fear his own power.

Our Doctor and Ethics

One key to understanding the Doctor's personality is his ethical stance. The Doctor's sense of right and wrong shapes how he spends his time, how he treats his companions, and how he uses and limits his use of his vast powers.

One of the most prominent approaches to ethics today is rule deontology. This approach says that people can know what's right by reference to principles: universally valid rules to ensure that everyone acts fairly and impartially, regardless of feelings or special circumstances. The Doctor seems to live by some rules, such as not carrying a weapon, but he doesn't require others to follow the same rules, and his interpretation of those rules depends on context (for instance, he uses a satsuma tangerine to cause an enemy to fall to its death in "The Christmas Invasion," 2005).

Another approach to ethics focuses on consequences, where actions aren't inherently right or wrong; only their results determine whether they're good or bad. In this utilitarian perspective, the aim is to maximize that which is "good," whether this is pleasure, well-being, or some other valued end. The Doctor, however, doesn't seem comfortable with this sort of moral calculation, and a person with his privileged perspective might find both good and bad consequences from any action. As the Fourth Doctor says, after declining to destroy the Daleks at their moment of creation, "I know also, that out of their evil, must come something good" ("Genesis of the Daleks," 1975).

A third approach, virtue ethics, focuses on each person's moral character. In this view, a well-lived life involves developing one's virtues to the utmost. The Doctor, however, lives his life at such a pace that introspective reflection isn't practical. He also doesn't seem interested in contemplating the coherence of his long-term identity, preferring to live in the moment. Early in their acquaintance, in "The End of the World" (2005), Rose Tyler asks the Doctor who he is, and the question makes him angry. He responds, "This is who I am, right here, right now, all right? All that counts is here and now, and this is me!" Clearly, each moral decision the Doctor makes must feel right at the moment he makes it, because he doesn't seem to concern himself with improving his character.

Rather than a rule-based ethic of abstract principles, a calculated cost-benefit approach, or a virtue ethics of concern for optimizing his personal integrity, the Doctor's ethics are focused on particular others; that is, on being responsive to the needs of others in whatever situation he finds himself. He responds to individuals, not abstractions, and for the Doctor, emotion is the very key to appropriate moral response.

The Doctor's ethical stance can be characterized as relational ethics, an ethics of care. As originally developed by Nel Noddings and other feminist scholars, care ethics finds its roots not in impartial and abstract principles but in how we are moved to act by our feelings in real-world situations. Noddings explains:

> Many persons who live moral lives do not approach moral problems formally. Women, in particular, seem to approach moral problems by placing themselves as nearly as possible in concrete situations and assuming personal responsibility for the choices to be made. They define themselves in terms of *caring* and work their way through moral problems from the position of [one who cares].[3]

Care ethicists assert that it's both natural and reasonable to show a greater sensitivity to the relationships in which one is embedded. As Michael Slote[4] explains, it's our empathic response to the needs we see in those near to us that leads us to prioritize them over those we merely hear about, although empathic concern may be expanded to provide a foundation even for policies of social justice. The Doctor shows us that an ethics of care can apply to any relationship, however brief, in which one makes a personal connection.

In other words, an ethics of care is an approach that involves meeting others in what Martin Buber calls an "I-Thou" stance, a mode of direct, intersubjective encounter. As Buber describes it:

---

[3] Nel Noddings, *Caring*, p. 8.
[4] *The Ethics of Care and Empathy.*

If I face a human being as my *Thou* . . . he is not a thing among things, and does not consist of things. Thus human being is not a *He* or *She*, bounded from every other *He* or *She*, a specific point in space and time within the net of the world; nor is he a nature able to be experienced and described, a loose bundle of named qualities. But with no neighbor, and whole in himself, he is *Thou* and fills the heavens. This does not mean that nothing exists except himself. But all else lives in *his* light.[5]

In contrast, there's also the "I-It" stance, the mode in which we can think *about* people and things. We can experience them, describe them, consider their qualities. Without the I-It perspective, we can't survive in the world, but this stance also underlies instrumental thinking, the perspective from which we manipulate, manage, and use. When we're in I-It mode, we have no openness to the reality of others' subjective worlds; the world is a world of things.

The Doctor rejects instrumentalism; people are not "things" to him. When he and Donna find an enslaved Ood half-dead in a snowbank, he makes sure she understands the Ood is "a 'he,' not an 'it'" ("Planet of the Ood"). He always tries to be attentive to the feelings and uniqueness of others. Even in a moment of considerable stress, about to surrender to Daleks waiting outside the TARDIS (in "Journey's End," 2008), he treats those with him as individuals, not a group, addressing each in turn with his full attention. He speaks first to Donna: "You were brilliant." He then turns to Jack Harkness: "And you were brilliant." Last, he speaks to Rose: "And you were brilliant." This mindful awareness of each person, each relationship, is the essence of the Doctor's ethical self-expression.

Some of the Doctor's most painful dilemmas have also arisen from his ethical stance. These issues illustrate some of the concerns that philosophers have raised about an ethics of care. Sarah Lucia Hoagland notes that when the intimate is not expected to care for the carer in return, the relationship can be oppressive.[6] Although the Doctor treats his companions as Thou, he maintains a distance and doesn't encourage them to reciprocate, and there's always an imbalance of power between them. In an ultimate

---

[5] *I and Thou*, p. 8.
[6] "Some Concerns About Nel Noddings' *Caring*," pp. 109–114.

exercise of power over another, he erases Donna's memory of their adventures, just as earlier Time Lords did with the companions of the Second Doctor, Jamie McCrimmon and Zoe Heriot ("The War Games," 1969). He does this for Donna's own good, but would she agree?

Many critics have felt, too, that practicing care ethics can leave people vulnerable to abusive relationships, or as Barbara Houston puts it, "we feel responsible for the moral goodness of those who abuse us, exploit us, harm us."[7] In "Last of the Time Lords" (2007), the Doctor chooses not to kill the Master, his long-time nemesis, who has just kept him imprisoned for more than a year. Rather, he tells him, "Now I'll have someone to care for." Only the action of Lucy Saxon, the Master's human wife, spares the Doctor from a commitment to keep the Master permanently within the TARDIS, to forever safeguard the rest of creation.

Ethics and Wonder

The Doctor's I-Thou stance toward his companions is closely related to his stance toward the universe in general, a non-instrumental approach to life and beauty that can be best characterized as a highly developed sense of wonder. As defined by the *Oxford English Dictionary*, wonder is "the emotion excited by the perception of something novel and unexpected, or inexplicable; astonishment mingled with perplexity or bewildered curiosity."

Moral philosopher Martha Nussbaum believes that experiencing wonder helps us expand our scope of ethical concern. Wonder, as she puts it, "helps move distant objects within the circle of a person's scheme of ends."[8] If something engages us with wonder, we open ourselves to experiencing that phenomenon in all its immediacy, and we approve. Just as an I-Thou sensibility reflects an openness to particular humans in all their depth and individuality, an openness to wonder implies an openness to—and appreciation of—phenomena as they fully are, whether a rainbow, a snowflake, or the grandeur of the Sapphire Waterfall, which the Doctor tries to visit on "Midnight" (2008).

In general, we experience wonder when our expectations are violated in a positive and aesthetically compelling way. We might

---

[7] "Caring and Exploitation," p. 116.
[8] *Upheavals of Thought*, p. 55.

feel wonder when we see something that doesn't fit into known categories, like a new form of art or a hitherto unimagined creature, or when an experience is better than one could possibly expect. Very often, too, wonder happens when we come across things that don't fit our usual sense of scale, when we step out of our ordinary perspective to encounter the reality of the vast or the infinitesimal, the eternal or the ephemeral.

Another source of wonderment is the appreciation of complexity. As the Scottish philosopher Ronald Hepburn notes, "The wonder aroused by the discerning of intelligible patterns in nature has . . . been one main motivation in scientific inquiry."[9] Wonder can be compatible with science, if by science we mean the activity connected with curiosity and a desire to understand, rather than a drive to reduce everything to propositions and equations, to render the universe predictable and tamed. Science doesn't necessarily sustain wonder: Categorization, manipulation, and a striving for objectivity often mean treating phenomena as things, not individuals. For the Doctor, however, science involves curiosity, caring, and respect for the phenomena he discovers. He's an ethical scientist, a scientist who prioritizes the unpredictable vitality of wonder over the firm possession of dry knowledge.

Wonder is not the only emotion associated with encountering the unexpected. A creature that doesn't fit within our taxonomy might be judged to be monstrous, and the idea of an entire ecosystem living in a drop of water might fill us with dread or horror. Our cultural and personal predispositions may lead us not into wonder but anxiety. The anthropologist Mary Douglas noted that cultures often condemn "any object or idea likely to confuse or contradict cherished classifications,"[10] treating them as anathema, even dangerous, and needing to be restrained and purified. Immanuel Kant had such a bias. He felt that although we may feel respect for the very large, we also feel "a kind of contempt" for "the level of the infinitely little."[11] Seeing wonder instead of the monstrous, frightening, or degraded requires the right attitude, an enthusiasm and openness that the Doctor has and shares with others.

---

[9] *'Wonder' and Other Essays*, p. 141.

[10] *Purity and Danger* p. 36.

[11] *Critique of Judgment*, pp. 80–81.

In his *Critique of Judgment* and earlier writings, Kant concerned himself not with wonder itself but with a closely related concept especially relevant to the Doctor, the sublime. This compelling emotional state, very much like awe, can arise in two kinds of situations: when we encounter the raw force of nature while knowing ourselves to be safe and secure (the "dynamic sublime"), and when we realize that our imagination is insufficient to take in the scope of something that our intuition perceives as a whole (the "mathematical sublime"). As Kant put it, "where the size of a natural object is such that the imagination spends its whole faculty of comprehension upon it in vain, it must carry our concept of nature to a supersensible substrate (underlying both nature and our faculty of thought) which is great beyond every standard of the senses." In other words, the phenomenon is too great for us to understand. All we can do is stop in amazement and realize that this is the case.

The Doctor, however, is a Time Lord. He's lived for many human lifetimes, and his brain contains a far greater capacity for understanding than any human could endure (as Donna discovers to her despair in "Journey's End"). Many phenomena that would leave humans bewildered are comprehensible to him. To the extent that he can, in fact, grasp things that for us would "strain the imagination to the utmost," the experience of the sublime would elude the Doctor. To him, much of the universe could simply be ordinary.

The Doctor's ability to resist this outlook reveals one of the most important benefits he gains from human companionship. His mortal friends aren't just a buffer against loneliness—they are, as he would say, "so much more," giving him access to the human scale as a reference point. By seeing the fabulous beings and places of the cosmos through human eyes, he can renew his own sense of wonder, his fascination and engagement with the infinite possibilities of existence in the universe as he encounters it. The Doctor's companions, in a very important sense, give his life meaning.

Wonder and the Doctor's Companions

In the wake of the events that led to the destruction of his home planet, the Doctor comes to Earth and meets Rose Tyler. He's recently experienced a considerable trauma, and it's taking him some time to reestablish his ethical bearings. On their first adventure in time, he decides to impress her by taking her to the Earth's last moments, essentially a tourist event, wonder as a commodity. This isn't a thoughtful choice, as Rose finds the idea quite upsetting. Perhaps the Doctor is on some level seeking empathy for the loss of his own home, and out of sympathy for his loss she agrees to continue travelling with him. She finds herself fascinated—not only can the Doctor visit other times, but he has an entirely different perspective on time. As she remarks on their next adventure, "Think about it, though. Christmas. 1860. Happens once. Just once, and it's gone. It's finished. It'll never happen again. Except for you. You can go back and see days that are dead and gone and a hundred thousand sunsets ago . . . no wonder you never stay still" ("The Unquiet Dead," 2005). For Rose, the ability to re-experience time is a source of wonder, and this wonder infuses her relationship with the Doctor.

Later in the same adventure, Rose realizes that the Doctor's ethical sense has gone askew. He wants to let the Gelth inhabit a few of the bodies of Cardiff's dead, and to use a young woman, Gwyneth, as their portal. Rose protests, and he responds, "It's a different morality. Get used to it." Of course, he does come to realize that Gwyneth isn't a thing to be used, especially when she heroically sacrifices herself to save the Earth from the Gelth invasion. Finally, by "Dalek," Rose succeeds in recalibrating (healing?) the Doctor's ethical sensibilities, insisting he show mercy to the last of the Daleks, to treat it as an individual. He resumes his characteristic sensitivity to relationships and circumstances, sparing the life of the Slitheen posing as Margaret Blaine (in "Boom Town," 2005) and intending to spare the Sycorax leader ("The Christmas Invasion") until the latter double-crosses him.

At the time of their meeting, Rose had not yet begun to act in the interests of people beyond her immediate circle. In a broader moral sense, it was as if her life had not yet begun. The Doctor serves as a catalyst for the development of Rose's imperative to act, but more importantly, he's also its foremost focus. True to her I-Thou orientation, when he regenerates she can recognize and accept him for who he is, not being distracted by the superficials of his appearance (though she does appreciate them).

Martha Jones, by contrast, is a medical student when she first meets the Doctor. Her motivation for action in the wider world is established, and she's already committed to a universally oriented ethics of service. Martha appreciates beauty and novelty, and her eager suggestion that they visit the Doctor's home world

("Gridlock," 2007) hints at her capacity for wonder, but she doesn't need wonder to inspire her to act. The Doctor values Martha's enthusiasm, skills, and dedication, but he can't make the empathetic connection with her that he had with Rose, probably in part because Martha doesn't find wonder energizing in the way that Rose did.

The Doctor's relationship with Donna Noble is, yet again, different. Donna sees herself as a very ordinary person, an office temp from Chiswick, a view reinforced by her calculating mother, Sylvia. Donna's grandfather, Wilfred Mott, has a much different influence on Donna, spending each night gazing at the skies through his telescope, speculating hopefully about the existence of aliens.

Donna is initially eager to join the Doctor and see the glories of time and space, but their early travels disappoint her. First she's disheartened by the tragedy of Pompeii, and then she's so distressed by the plight of the Ood that she begs to go home until she finds that it's actually possible to help them. Donna, however, has a virtue that Rose and Martha lacked. Her ethics focus on the particular, as do the Doctor's and Rose's, but Donna can respond to the needs she encounters without the inspiration of wonder and beauty, even (as we saw so poignantly in "Turn Left," 2008) when the person asking is a stranger and the path is frightening, even when responding means that she must die. Donna is, indeed, noble. It's not that she's selfless: It's vitally important to her to be special. Donna's deepest motivation is to be able to believe that others might feel wonder in their encounters with *her*.

The value the Doctor finds in his relationships with ordinary humans becomes all the more apparent when contrasted with how he interacts with the Time Lord Romana, a companion of his Fourth incarnation, as well as with Captain Jack Harkness, an experienced human time traveler. When the Doctor first met Romana, they bickered and attempted to assert dominance over each other, until she diagnosed their problem as "a negative empathy" ("The Ribos Operation," 1978). Jack, of course, he mistrusted. The Doctor couldn't respect a self-described con man ("The Empty Child," 2005), especially one so interested in flirting with Rose. In "Utopia" (2007), Jack complained, "You abandoned me," the Doctor replied indifferently, "Did I? Busy life. Move on." Not until "Journey's End" does the Doctor treat Jack as a trusted friend.

The centrality of wonder in the *Doctor Who* ethos is further shown in the relationship of Sarah Jane Smith and Maria Jackson, in *The Sarah Jane Adventures*. Sarah Jane kept her neighbors at a distance, until Maria saw her with an alien one night in the garden. Both were entranced by the beauty of the star poet from Arcateen V, and their shared wonder at the fairy-like alien made them kindred spirits.

The importance of wonder is also illustrated by what the loss of the Doctor does to each of the companions. Sarah Jane had a difficult adjustment at first, as she tells him when they meet again ("School Reunion"): "You took me to the furthest reaches of the galaxy, you showed me supernovas, intergalactic battles and then you just dropped me back on Earth. How could anything compare to that?" Once she reconciles herself to life without the Doctor, however, she creates her own career that balances sustaining her sense of wonder with a commitment to investigation and action, emulating the Doctor in her Earth-based life. Martha misses the Doctor as a person and regrets the relationship she wishes they could've had, but her life resumes right where she left off. She completes her medical training and becomes a doctor herself. As for Donna, although Wilfred laments that she's lost "all those wonderful things she did" ("Journey's End"), the Doctor knows she'll be fine—she never needed him, or wonder, but only to value herself.

Rose, on the other hand, is completely lost without the wonder. Her world goes grey; she can no longer connect to it. For her, life on Earth would now be "Get up—catch the bus—go to work—come back home—eat chips and go to bed" ("The Parting of the Ways"). She'd never learned to focus on the big picture, to find meaning in an abstract commitment to service as Martha did. Although in the ethos of the series, the personal is always sufficient grounds for motivation, in Rose's case the personal imperative was fused with the identity of the person who awakened her to its call, and without him, life lost its meaning.

After the conclusion of "Journey's End," Rose has regained her Doctor but lost her access to the grandeur of the cosmos. Rose and the "human Doctor" will have to learn together how to find a sustaining sense of wonder in the human scale and in the intimacy of their I-Thou relationships. This will itself be something new and strange for him—never before has the Doctor opened himself up to being someone else's Thou. Now they'll have time to explore a genuine mutuality and the possibilities of love.

A Better Way of Living Your Life

As possessors of vast knowledge and considerable power, Time Lords might do whatever they please, pursuing grand schemes and ruling over lesser mortals to gain their own selfish ends. Our Doctor chooses a different path. He serves as a fine example for how to make the most of our more modest existences. Through an empathetic sensitivity to particulars and individuals, by being responsive to the needs of persons, not abstractions, each of us can have a life that's meaningful.

If we're open to wonder, we can each be, as the Doctor would say, "brilliant."[12]

---

[12] I would like to thank two websites for providing access to transcripts of *Doctor Who* episodes: *Doctor Who (2005+) Transcripts* at <http://who-transcripts .atspace.com>, and *the Doctor Who Transcripts Project* at <http://dwtpscripts .tripod.com>. I also appreciate feedback from Jonathan Woodward on an early draft of this chapter.

14
Doctor, Who Cares?

J.J. SYLVIA

> **DOCTOR:** I have one thing to say to you. . . . You know what it is.
>
> **MASTER:** (*hurriedly*) Oh, no you don't!
>
> —("Last of the Time Lords," 2007)

The Doctor is unique among Time Lords because he involves himself in the affairs of the universe despite this being prohibited by Time Lord policy. It's precisely this involvement that's so important about him. Although his personality can differ somewhat from one incarnation to another, the Doctor is essentially a compassionate and caring being—he cares for the particular individuals he meets as well as the universe as a whole. It's precisely this penchant for caring which leads the Doctor to involving himself in the universe— and undoubtedly he makes the universe a better place for it.

The ethics of caring, a relatively new philosophic development, is a system expressed by feminists who believe that traditional ethical systems are male-biased and don't account for the way women experience the world. Of course, most who support a feminist ethics don't believe the differences this system reflect can be split right down the gender line—it's simply an easy generalization to make. The Doctor, then, is all the more interesting because he, as a man, represents an ideal example of the ethics of caring.

The Sanctimonious Doctor

MASTER: Doctor.

DOCTOR: Master.

MASTER: I like it when you use my name.

DOCTOR: You chose it. Psychiatrists' field day.

MASTER: As you chose yours. The man who makes people better. How sanctimonious is that?

—("The Sound of Drums," 2007)

Both men were able to choose their own names and as the Doctor points out, there's clearly some significance to these choices. A master rules over people while a doctor typically cares for people—and we see this in the Doctor—he struggles and works to make people better time and again. Rita Manning, in *Speaking from the Heart*, explains that caring involves: "acting in some appropriate way to respond to the needs of persons and animals, but can also be extended to responding to the needs of communities, values, or objects" (p. 62). A concrete example of this action is found in parenting. Parents must consistently respond to the needs of their children in order to help them grow and later, hopefully, flourish. Although it's possible for a doctor not to care at all about his patients—one just has to think of Dr. Gregory House—this is another relationship that can typically be understood as one exemplary of caring.

But what exactly does an *ethics* of caring entail? Carol Gilligan pioneered the movement in her book *In a Different Voice*. Prior moral theories have reflected what Gilligan calls theories of justice, which generate strict systems or rules which can be used impartially to direct a person to the right action. In analyzing the responses of people to moral scenarios with which they were presented, Gilligan began to notice a divide between the responses of men and women. Psychologist Lawrence Kohlberg ranked different levels of moral development, and this divide tended to put most women in a category of lower moral development than most men.

Gilligan asserts that the problem lies not with women, but with the classification system used by Kohlberg. Kohlberg's system relies entirely on what Gilligan deems an ethics of justice. This ethics of justice has some merit, but it's incomplete without also including an ethics of care. In essence, she believes any complete moral theory will include both an ethics of justice and care.

Just as parents need children in order to actually be considered to be parents, a doctor needs patients to be a doctor. A relationship between the care-giver and the cared for develops, and it's this relationship that's of utmost importance for an ethic of care. Consider the following example: the Doctor is forced to decide between saving one of his companions or a random stranger he's never met. Obviously he'd try to save both if at all possible, but imagine that simply were not possible. Who ought he to save in that situation? A traditional system of justice, such as utilitarianism, would have a difficult time giving advice as to which he would be obligated to save. Utilitarianism, developed by Jeremy Bentham and elaborated by John Stuart Mill, suggests that the correct action is the one which promotes the greatest good for the greatest number of people. Every person, including oneself, carries the same amount of ethical weight in this system. Because utilitarianism is impartial, the Doctor couldn't use its system of rules to distinguish between his companion and the stranger. On the other hand, an ethics of care would acknowledge that the most prominent moral feature of this scenario is the relationship between the Doctor and his companion. His most important obligation is specifically to care for *his* companion, and thus the decision of which to save is by no means arbitrary. In that situation an ethics of care would suggest that he save his companion.

On the Necessity of Companions

Of course, this all poses somewhat of a problem for a lone traveler—a being mostly unnoticed by the majority of the population of earth. How can the Doctor consistently manage to care for so many people with whom he has no relationship at all? We all know that one of the most interesting things about the Doctor is that he has companions on his travels. Producer Russell T Davies notes in an interview, "What's the point of seeing the whole of the cosmos and all of history if there's no one to share it with, no one to join in with the wonder and awe, no one's hand to hold when it gets terrifying? Underneath all the Doctor's wit and vigor, I think there's quite a lonely man, the last of his kind, wandering inside the only TARDIS in existence. He needs companionship."[1]

The Doctor has a tendency to develop these "companionships" where the role of care-giver and cared for frequently flips back and forth. We don't have to understand the Doctor as simply a care-

---

[1] <www.radiotimes.com/content/show-features/doctor-who/russell-t-davies-on-companions>.

giver to fit him within the framework of an ethics of care. We're all sometimes care-givers and sometimes cared for, possibly even simultaneously on different levels of interaction. Sometimes the Doctor saves the companions, but sometimes they save him, and certainly he seems to learn from them. Billie Piper, the actress who plays Rose, comments, "Rose and the Doctor teach each other. She's quite closed off from the world, but she could, potentially, be someone brilliant. He shows her how to do that. And equally, she shows him how to be sympathetic, how to have morals and show and express his emotions."[2] The real question is how the Doctor can care for so many people—the whole human race and more—without a relationship to each of those he cares for.

Perhaps because the Doctor is able to develop these relationships with his companions in a one-on-one basis, he can apply that ethics of care, that understanding of the relationship, to the larger population and others in need. As Manning puts it, "although we do not know the sufferer, we can assume that the sufferer shares essential characteristics with someone who is close to us" (p. 68). Perhaps it's through his companions that the Doctor learns to care for the world at large. Manning argues that we have a prima facie obligation to help a creature in need that can't help itself. The Doctor certainly seems to be meeting this obligation—just how many times has he saved our world?

Manning's explanation seems to match up to the way we normally experience things. We experience the problems of those who are close to us, and through those relations we feel sympathy for others who are in plight whether we've met them or know anything about them. Although there may be more reasoning involved in the overall analysis, this might also explain why we feel more upset by harm done to animals like dogs or cats than, say, lobsters. We care for dogs and cats as our pets and develop a relationship there. We'd likely cringe at dropping a dog into a pot of boiling water, but doing the same with a lobster might only cause us to salivate in anticipation of a meal. Perhaps part of the explanation for those divergent reactions is that we have a care relationship with one but not the other. Seen through this lens, the Doctor's

---

[2] <www.radiotimes.com/content/show-features/doctor-who/companion-rose-tyler>.

relationships with his companions would be a vital element in his caring for humanity on a larger scale.

Sad Is Happy for Deep People

> I absorbed all the energy of the Time Vortex, and no one's meant to do that! Every cell in my body's dying.
>
> —NINTH DOCTOR ("The Parting of the Ways," 2005)

Is sacrifice required in order to care for others? Is the process of caring itself a sacrifice? Certainly the Doctor is no stranger to the notion of sacrifice. In "The Parting of the Ways," he takes the energy of the Time Vortex from Rose, which kills him and causes him to regenerate. He's made similar gestures in the past as well. In "The Caves of Androzani" (1984) there's only enough spectrox toxæmia antidote to save one person, so the Doctor gives it to his companion Peri, causing himself to die and regenerate. Of course, this may be easier for the Doctor to do than most others, because he knows he will be able to regenerate. Yet, in "Mawdryn Undead" (1983), the Doctor is willing to give up his very regeneration energy in order to save companions Tegan and Nyssa. Does an ethics of care require sacrifice this great?

There can be no straightforward rule to answer this question, because it'll depend in large part upon the relationships involved in the particular situation. Manning argues that "where the need is great and the ability to meet it sufficient, we are required to sacrifice" (p. 73), but she doesn't think this must be a form of life. We could continually donate money to needy children in Africa until we were as poor as they, and this would seem to meet Manning's requirements. However, in continually donating all the money we make, we'd be taking on this sacrifice as a way of life, which isn't what would be intended. In fact, this could cause "caring burnout" which would deter or even prevent us from being able to care in the future. We must make our own decision about sacrifice in the moment, taking into full considerations the relationships this sacrifice will affect.

The Doctor seems almost immune to such a burnout, but there's evidence it possibly exists somewhere inside of him. In one episode, we see the Ninth Doctor get both scared and angry, and he tries to exterminate what he believes to be the last Dalek:

I've got to do this, I've got to end it. The Daleks destroyed my home,
my people. I've got nothing left. ("Dalek," 2005)

The Doctor is upset because his home, his people, those to whom
he was most connected, are gone, and for him it's a moment of
weakness in which he wants simple revenge rather than to care
about his enemy, as he has in other circumstances. In this case it's
his companion Rose who stands in the way and tries to prevent
him from exterminating the Dalek, while quite possibly at the same
time becoming even more like the Dalek. Certainly we could see
this as an example of caring burnout. The Doctor has cared so
much for so many people, but it takes extraordinary circumstances—the extermination of all of his people—to even see a
chink in his armor.

A further suggestion is that if this sacrifice occurs in a recipro-
cal relationship, it can actually make us stronger. Of course, we can
easily see this happening on the show. The Doctor will care for one
of his companions, but at some point they'll have to care for him
as well. Through this relationship, a trust or bond builds and
they're able to face bigger and badder villains knowing they'll be
there to care for one another if needed. Although we don't all face
down monstrous enemies across time on a day-to-day basis, we
can relate to a similar sort of caring for bond that seems to develop
between people.

The Fury of the Time Lord

BAINES: He never raised his voice. That was the worst thing. The fury
of the Time Lord. And then we discovered why. Why this Doctor,
who had fought with gods and demons, why he'd run away from
us and hidden—he was being kind.

—("The Family of Blood," 2007)

Although the Doctor can certainly bring forth his fury in battle, he
always tempers this fury with compassion. The Family of Blood
learned that the Doctor ran from them not out of fear, but out of
kindness. He was going to let them die off and attempted to hide
in human form so they couldn't track him down in their last days.
Unfortunately they found him anyway, and in his fury he did punish them, but he did so by imprisoning them in chains, an event
horizon, mirrors, and a scarecrow.

We repeatedly witness the Doctor trying to help his most bitter enemies:

> Dalek Caan. Your entire species has been wiped out. And now the Cult of Skaro has been eradicated. Leaving only you. Right now you're facing the only man in the universe who might show you some compassion. 'Cause I've just seen one genocide. I won't cause another. Caan, . . . let me help you. What do you say? (The Tenth Doctor in "Evolution of the Daleks," 2007)

The Doctor offers compassion to the last of the species with which the Time Lords were at war. He responds in a similar way to the Master, who has just spent a year using the Toclafanes to destroy Earth:

DOCTOR: And you know what happens now.

MASTER: No! No! (*grovels*) No! No!

DOCTOR: You wouldn't listen.

MASTER: No!

DOCTOR: Because you know what I'm going to say.

MASTER: No! (*curls into fetal position. The Doctor lands, walks over to the whimpering Master and wraps his arms about him.*)

DOCTOR: I forgive you. ("Last of the Time Lords," 2007)

The show had been building up to this one thing the Doctor had to say, and it really seemed as if we were about to witness the ultimate demonstration of the fury of the Time Lord, but instead, the Doctor is compassionate and empathetic! No one else agrees; they all want to execute the Master so that he can never do something like this again. In the end, the Master's human wife, Lucy, does shoot him before anyone can stop her.

To try to understand what the Doctor's motivation may be, we can draw upon a distinction between natural caring and ethical caring made by Nel Noddings in *Caring*. Natural caring is something we can all understand—it's when we can easily care for another. Our relationships with others *cause* us to care for them. It's not all that difficult to care about our child or spouse; in fact, it may be hard *not* to care about those to whom we are close. This is natural caring. We can understand why the Doctor goes out of his way to save Rose or Martha, but it's much more difficult for us to understand his forgiving the Master or reaching out to Dalek Caan. In doing this, the Doctor is exhibiting an ethical caring. Ethical caring occurs in the absence of natural caring. One has to think back to a time when they were able to be an ideal care-giver and try to apply that same standard in the new situation. Even if the Doctor doesn't naturally care for Dalek Caan, he can sympathize with him and attempt to understand what he's been through and how he's gotten to this particular point in life. It's this sympathy which helps bring out the ability for ethical caring.

Toward Caring

DOCTOR: You're my responsibility from now on. The only Time Lord left in existence.

JACK: Yeah, but you can't trust him.

DOCTOR: No. The only safe place for him is the TARDIS.

MASTER: You mean you're just gonna . . . keep me?

DOCTOR: Hmm. If that's what I have to do. (*Looks to Jack*) It's time to change. Maybe I've been wandering for too long. Now I'll have someone to care for.

—("Last of the Time Lords," 2007)

Although the Doctor himself may not think of his own actions that way, he's actually caring for all of humanity—among other species—in his time travels. Yet, the fact that he's willing to care for the Master, even after the Master has destroyed most of the Earth and used a sonic screwdriver to make the Doctor very old, is quite telling. The others, from Lucy to Jack to Martha Jones and her family, all seem to believe that the Master needs to be killed because he can't be trusted. The Doctor alone is able to view this situation from a different perspective. Perhaps he's benefiting from the synergy of two meshing methods of ethics, or perhaps he's simply displaying a blatant example of the ethics of care. It can't be as simple as the Doctor's being opposed to killing an evil creature, as we've seen him do just that time and time again. A great deal of concern for the Doctor lies in the fact that the Master is the only other living Time Lord. This *relationship* between the Doctor and the

Master defines the way the Doctor sees the appropriate moral reaction. Quite possibly if the relationship were different, the Doctor's reaction and punishment would be different—which is entirely characteristic of an ethics of care rather than an ethics of justice.

Yet, I felt a strong sense of relief when Lucy finally shot the Master. If he were alive, I was imagining it'd only be a matter of time until he was able to cook up another scheme or escape from the Doctor despite the Doctor's best efforts. In that sense, I feel as if a strong counter argument could be made that killing the Master really was the best course of action. Of course, since the Master is also a Time Lord and can regenerate, this likely isn't the last of him.

This system of an ethics of care is fairly new in the philosophic world, but the explanatory power it offers is quite telling. As one can tell by looking at it through the lens of a moral exemplar such as the Doctor, it offers an explanation for why we both act and believe we should act in certain ways which traditional ethics of justice would have difficulty explaining. Very often the Doctor might not take the course of action that offers the greatest good for the greatest number, but an ethics of care can explain to us how we can still hold up these actions as morally praiseworthy from a different perspective. What's really interesting about an ethics of care is that it gives us a chance to reflect on a different way of thinking about moral issues. At the very least, it helps explain a certain intuitive notion that would explain why we think the Doctor should save a companion instead of a complete stranger. The Doctor's adventures through time and space give us examples of how these ethics might be applied in a wide variety of zany circumstances!

15

Why the Doctor and Rose Tyler Kant Be Together

DONNA MARIE SMITH

Time travel. Wondrous worlds. Menacing monsters. Amazing adventures. For over four decades *Doctor Who* has captured the imaginations of viewers of all ages. This unique television show introduced us to fantastical technology like the TARDIS and the sonic screwdriver, dangerous enemies like the Daleks and the Cybermen, endearing companions like Sarah Jane Smith and Rose Tyler, and, of course, the mysterious Time Lord from the planet Gallifrey known as the Doctor.

Yet, *Doctor Who* also offers insights into how we—the Doctor's beloved humans—can learn to lead ethical lives. Throughout the new episodes of *Doctor Who*, as produced by Russell T Davies, Julie Gardner, and Phil Collinson, we find out how the concepts of love, individual sacrifice, and the social good play a role in helping the Doctor and his companions to be good people.

As the last of the Time Lords, the Doctor feels it's his duty to protect innocent beings from the Evil present in the universe. He believes that the welfare of society, both human and alien, transcends any personal attachments and desires. Time and again, the Doctor faces dangerous situations, many of which involve the invasion or destruction of the Earth by nefarious aliens like the Slitheen or the Sontaran. Yet, most of his adventures are straightforward thwart-the-bad-guys scenarios. On occasion, though, the Doctor has to make difficult personal sacrifices when trying to resolve these grave conflicts. In "Doomsday" (2006), he faces a most heartbreaking moral dilemma when he must choose between being with his beloved companion Rose Tyler and his moral duty to save the people of Earth from being "exterminated" by the Daleks and "deleted" by the Cybermen.

Groundwork of a Time Lord's Morals

To understand from a philosophical viewpoint why the Doctor and Rose ultimately can't be together, let's take a more in-depth look at the Doctor's worldview and moral character. As fans of the show, we know that he's a Time Lord, one of the "ancient and powerful race of beings from the planet Gallifrey who tended to observe events in the universe rather than become involved, teaching in their Academy the importance of calm detachment."[1] Of course, this was before they became embroiled in the Last Great Time War with the Daleks. Since our Doctor participated in that war, his view of the world was shaped not only by the ancient teachings of the Time Lords but also by the epic conflict with the Dalek race. No longer could he and the other Time Lords practice "calm detachment," a virtue held by Buddhist practitioners here on Earth. In fact, the Doctor was at the forefront of the final battle that led to the destruction of both his and the Dalek races. Lifelong participation in war and a narrowly focused objective—to defeat the enemy—most likely skewed the moral philosophy of the Time Lords. Anger, grief, remorse, and hatred veiled their ancient societal values.

Perhaps having spent many years observing human nature and sharing human companionship, the Doctor's worldview may have been tempered by the general good nature of the people of Earth. Being an extremely intelligent and curious person, the Doctor might even have sought out the counsel of Earth's great thinkers, such as the ancient Greek philosophers Socrates, Plato, and Aristotle.[2] These esteemed philosophers formed the foundation of Western philosophy, teaching and writing about the values and actions that make a person good. Certain virtues, they believed, are characteristics of a good person, or in other words, a person with a good will. Plato (429–347 B.C.E.) developed and wrote about the ideas of his mentor, Socrates (469–399 B.C.E.). In his influential work *The Republic*, he discussed the four virtues one should strive

---

[1] Gary Russell, *Doctor Who: The Encyclopedia*, p. 172.

[2] The Fourth Doctor encountered Socrates in the Gareth Roberts short story, "The Brain of Socrates" in *Short Trips: The Muses*.

to attain, namely, wisdom, courage, temperance, and justice. Aristotle also wrote about ethical philosophy, highlighting the significance of a virtuous life as a means of attaining happiness. In *Nicomachean Ethics*, Aristotle explained that "virtuous acts require conscious choice and moral purpose or motivation, and that man has personal moral responsibility for his actions."[3]

David Tennant's Doctor possesses exceptional wisdom and a strong sense of justice. Time and again, he displays courage when faced with moral or physical conflicts, like when he saved Madame de Pompadour from the Clockwork Robots in "The Girl in the Fireplace" (2006), or when he confronted the ancient demon in "The Satan Pit" (2006). Yet, the Doctor still acts unrestrained at times. He's had to learn how to control his rage at the loss of his home world, for example, and not to get mired down in self-pity in the face of unbearable loneliness. The time spent with his companion, Rose, helped him to develop a more compassionate—and temperate—moral center. "You made me better," he explains to Rose in "Journey's End" (2008).

A Rose by Any Other Name Would Still Be Virtuous

The Doctor has had many companions during his years of wandering the universe, but he has a particular affection for the inhabitants of Earth. He has fond memories of his human companions, but the blonde shop girl he meets in early twenty-first century London—Rose Tyler—is arguably someone whom he deeply loved. Because of the moral dilemma between his duty to save the world and his desire to be with Rose, his choice to leave her leads to unfathomable heartbreak—even more so because he has two hearts!

Rose, too, faces the choice between saving humanity and being with the man she loves. When the spirited and carefree Londoner first encounters the Time Lord, she believed, like any other young human, that she has all the time in the world. She would travel through space and time, experiencing grand adventures, seeing marvelous sights, and braving grave dangers. She'd be with the man she loved. She'd be with the Doctor forever. Or so she thought.

---

[3] 1998 edition, p. 12.

After her first year of traveling with the Doctor, Rose has matured into an adult. She learns from being with him how to be a virtuous and responsible person, particularly when faced with hard decisions. In "Parting of the Ways" (2005), Rose tells her mom Jackie Tyler and her friend Mickey Smith that, even though the Doctor sent her back home to protect her from the Daleks, she must return to the future to try to help him. Rose explains why she made this choice:

> The Doctor showed me a better way of living your life. You don't just give up. You don't just let things happen. You make a stand. You say no. You have the guts to do what's right when everyone runs away.

In deciding to help the Ninth Doctor save the humanity of the future, she chooses duty over personal safety. When she absorbs the Time Vortex and ultimately destroys the Daleks and their Emperor, she sacrifices her life to save the Doctor and humankind. Fortunately, the Doctor saves her by kissing her and ingesting the Time Vortex into himself, thereby forfeiting his own life for Rose and the good of human society. With this episode, we see a fore-shadowing of the courageous young woman who chooses the self-less, moral path when, during her adventures with the Tenth Doctor, the Daleks once again threaten to eradicate humanity during the Battle of Canary Wharf in the haunting two-part episode "Army of Ghosts" and "Doomsday" (2006).

By the time we meet up with Rose and the Doctor on present-day Earth, Rose has learned a great deal about what it means to be a good person. Her travels through time and space have given her the opportunity to encounter new people and ideas. She's also worked through ethical problems and moral dilemmas during her adventurous experiences with the Time Lord. When the Daleks and the Cybermen invade Earth "via the Void"—the nothingness between time and space dimensions—Rose bravely stands up to these deadly foes. She's savvy and courageous when confronting the Daleks who want to exterminate humanity and keep the Earth for themselves. Her relationship with the Doctor is what helps her to achieve this moral strength.

Love in the Time of Daleks

A deeper look into the Doctor and Rose's relationship and their love for one another will reveal why they can't ultimately be together and have a fairy-tale ending for their story. Throughout his long life, the Doctor grappled with the idea of loving a human companion, knowing that a human has a much, much shorter lifespan. In "School Reunion" (2006), the Doctor explains to Rose why he couldn't stay with his former companion Sarah Jane Smith, as well as why it was now difficult for him to love Rose. "You can spend the rest of your life with me," he tells her, "but I can't spend the rest of mine with you. I have to live on. Alone. That's the curse of the Time Lords." Despite this, the Doctor wants Rose to stay with him, and they continue their journey together.

The Doctor learned from his travels throughout the universe that love comes in many forms. The ancient Greeks divided love into three different forms: *eros* (romantic love), *philia* (friendship), and *agape* (love of beauty or of God). Unlike his relationships with former and future companions like Sarah Jane Smith, Martha Jones, and Donna Noble which can be classified as *philia,* the Doctor forges both a special fondness, or *philia,* with Rose and a deep romantic attachment to and desire for her, what the Greeks would describe as *eros.*

Yet, before the Doctor realizes how much Rose means to him, he falls in love (experiences *eros*) with another human female, as we see in the Hugo Award-winning episode "The Girl in the Fireplace." During a trip to the fifty-first century, the Doctor, Rose, and Mickey encounter a time window on a space ship. This window leads to eighteenth-century France and to a captivating woman named Reinette, or as history knows her, Madame de Pompadour. The Doctor has to protect Reinette from the Clockwork Robots—the ship's repair androids—and in doing so, becomes enamored of her. In the course of trying to save her and the people of the court of Versailles, the Doctor breaks through another time window on the space ship, even though he knows that he'll no longer have a way back to the ship. He's therefore stranded in Reinette's time. His love for Reinette and his subsequent actions are what medieval philosophers would call chivalrous love (or *agape,* love of beauty and purity). Like a knight saving a damsel in distress, the Doctor chooses to save his lady by charging on a white horse through the one remaining time window. Thus, the Doctor acts out of duty despite closing off the only way back to his time period.

Before the Doctor can come to terms with this seemingly rash decision to save Reinette, she surprises him with a way back to the future. Having preserved the original time window, that is, her childhood fireplace and mantle clock, she offers the Doctor a way back to Rose and the TARDIS. She sacrifices her desire to be with her "lonely angel" because she knows it's the noble and right course to take. From her actions, the Doctor learns about love and personal sacrifice. Madame de Pompadour teaches him how to love selflessly and to be a better person because of this love.

Critique of Gallifreyan Reason

German philosopher Immanuel Kant (1724–1804), who was one of the most pre-eminent philosophers to discuss morality and ethics in a detailed, scientific way, believed that people develop moral judgment in two ways: they learn how to be good from experience (what he calls "empirical philosophy"), and they know how to be good through *a priori* knowledge, that is, deductive logic or reason (what he calls "pure philosophy").[4] Kant further explained that "worth of character is shown only when someone does good, not from inclination, but from duty." He distinguished between what he called a "hypothetical imperative," or wanting to act in a certain way to achieve a moral end, and a "categorical imperative," or acting in a certain way to attain the greater good because you "ought to regardless of the consequences."[5] Duty to others, to society often comes in conflict with personal desires, and the Doctor and Rose's love for one another is no exception. In terms of Kant's ethics, "love and similar attitudes such as friendship are in tension with morality. Love seems to impel one to be partial: to give greater weight to the interests of one's beloved."[6]

Throughout her two Earth years of travel, Rose falls in love with this amazing man who takes her on great adventures and shows her a better way to live her life. She feels a deep attachment to him, more so than with any of her human boyfriends, like Adam Mitchell or even Mickey Smith. The Doctor means everything in the world to her. Gradually, their love binds them together, not only in their travels throughout the universe, but on the moral path. In turn, the path of goodness and duty to their fellow beings enriches their love for one another.

---

[4] *Groundwork of the Metaphysics of Morals*, pp. 55–56.

[5] Mel Thompson, *Teach Yourself Ethics*, pp. 80–84.

[6] George Boas, "Love."

As we see in each subsequent adventure, both the Doctor and Rose not only act out of duty as a result of their experiences together but because, as rational beings, each has an innate sense of right and wrong. Even though their many adventures have transformed their love into a shared goal of making the world a better place, it does so at a cost. Since their love for one another deepens over time, and since they're bound together in that love, this attachment becomes a potential barrier to making the right choice when faced with a moral decision. The more the Doctor and Rose love each other, the greater the risk of experiencing personal loss if their love, according to Kant, comes into conflict with their moral duty. Kant's moral theory, what in philosophical terms is called "deontology," is based on the idea that we have the freedom, or "autonomy," to choose between what we "ought" to do (what is "right" action) or what we "ought not" to do (what is "wrong" action), regardless of our personal desires or "inclinations." Therefore, while their love helps to inform the Doctor's and Rose's individual sense of moral responsibility, it's their love that ironically causes their eventual separation. The Doctor and Rose ultimately act out of their own sense of justice and not specifically out of their feelings for each other.

Journal of Impossible Things

The Doctor and Rose decide to face the ultimate moral choice when they take a stand against the Cybermen and the Daleks during the Battle of Canary Wharf, as poignantly depicted in "The Army of Ghosts" and "Doomsday." When they learn that the Daleks have broken through a Rift in the space-time continuum—and the Cybermen from a parallel Earth happen to tag along—they choose to try to find a way to save both their world and the parallel world from these lethal foes and from the harmful effects of the Rift. In the chilling two-part episode "The Rise of the Cybermen" and "The Age of Steel" (2006), the Doctor, Rose, and Mickey first encounter these Cybermen when the TARDIS crashes on a world in a parallel universe. "Travel between parallel worlds is impossible," the Doctor explains, "because the worlds were sealed off from each other when the Time Lords died." This impossible happenstance leads to the eventual impossibility of their romantic relationship. They simply can't be together because they each choose to risk their special bond with each other for the sake of the greater good, namely, to save humanity. This grave choice becomes their "categorical imperative." They sacrifice their personal desires because this is what they "ought" to do; this is the right path for them to take.

As the story of "Doomsday" reaches its heart-wrenching climax, Rose decides to help the Doctor destroy the Daleks and the Cybermen despite great personal risk. The Doctor tries to send Rose along with her mother and Mickey to the safety of "Pete's World"—the parallel world on the other side of the Rift where Rose had previously met her alternate "father." The Doctor wanted her and the others who were affected by "Void Stuff," or the "background radiation" that a time traveler absorbs, to have a chance at life on the parallel Earth, even though it meant being separated from his beloved, as well as having to confront his own inner void of loneliness. Yet, Rose refuses to leave him to complete the dangerous task by himself; therefore, she uses one of the transmat devices to traverse the Void and to pop back into her world to help him. The Doctor must seal the Rift between the two worlds after sending the Daleks and Cybermen, who were also affected by the "Void Stuff," back into "Hell." He does so by using the Void Machine to open the breach in space-time. The machine, located in the Torchwood Tower, in the Canary Wharf section of London, has two levers that the Doctor and Rose must set in order to open the Rift. They each have to hold on to a special magnetic device attached to the wall of the Lever Room in order to not get sucked in to the "dead space" along with the deadly invaders.

Unfortunately, the lever of the Void Machine nearest to Rose goes off-line, and she has to get it working or the Doctor's plan will fail. She tenuously grasps the lever of the machine. If she doesn't re-activate the machine, both worlds will be destroyed, one by the Daleks and the Cybermen and one by the harmful effects of "Void Stuff." Despite this brave effort, her fingers slip free of the lever. Rose glances one last time at the Doctor, knowing that her life is over. In her eyes, though, the Doctor sees that what really frightens Rose isn't dying but being separated from him. Suddenly, violently, the Void tears her away from the lever, from the Doctor, from her world. Only at the last possible second is she rescued by Pete Tyler, her "father" from the parallel Earth. Rose was spared from death but is severed from the love of her life. While it's the Rift between parallel worlds that physically separates the Doctor and Rose, the philosophical rift between love and morality is what causes them to "be sealed off forever" from each other.

Parting of the Ways

Because of their sense of duty and their voluntary willingness to act for the sake of the greater good, the Doctor and Rose experience an unfathomable personal loss. As Kant sums up, they "perform the action [saving humanity], irrespective of all objects of the faculty of desire [their love for one another], and it is their sense of duty [their will to do good to keep their family, friends and the other people of the Earth safe that their] wills stand, so to speak, at a *parting of the ways* . . . where every material principle [their personal desires] is taken away from [them]."[7] Even when Rose finds a way to return to her home universe to help the Doctor save not only her Earth but all of reality from being exterminated by the Daleks in "The Stolen Earth" (2008) and "Journey's End," she and the Doctor can't be together. The Doctor sends her and his half-human, half-Time Lord hybrid back to "Pete's World," because the New Doctor, who was "born in battle" and filled with anger and vengeance, mercilessly destroyed the entire Dalek race during the battle to save humanity from these ruthless killers. The Doctor "told Rose that she was the only one who could make the New Doctor a better man, as she had before done with him,"[8] when she convinced him not to kill the Dalek prisoner in the episode "Dalek" (2005). Thus, the lovely Rose and her New Doctor get to live out their lives together. Unlike the Doctor who can live for hundreds of years, and who ages at a completely different rate than that of humans, the hybrid Doctor has a human life span, has only one heart, and can't regenerate. This New Doctor can also tell Rose what the other Doctor couldn't: that he loves her. As actor David Tennant explains, the Doctor "sacrifices his relationship with Rose for the greater good. He ends up with nothing. . . . Again."[9]

Our Doctor, then, is left on his own by the conclusion of the story. Not only does he have to leave his current companion, Donna Noble, back on Earth but also once again loses Rose, the love of his life. Despite the impossible loneliness and loss he'll have to once again endure, the Doctor lets Rose go in order for her to be safe and because it was the right thing to do. Consequently, the Doctor "feels the pain only someone with a morally good heart can feel very

---

[7] Kant, *Groundwork*, p. 68.

[8] Doctor Who Wiki, "Rose Tyler" <http://tardis.wikia.com/wiki/Rose_Tyler>.

[9] "End of an Era" (BBC Wales, July 5th, 2008).

deeply."[10] Because he loves her, the Doctor knows that the personal sacrifice he suffered in order to save her and the people of Earth pales in comparison to his duty to the greater good, to the restoration of order in the universe. He made these difficult decisions regarding his companions "without wavering or even doubting" (p. 129) because, to do otherwise, he would fail to do his duty.

Allons-y into the Starry Heavens

A famous quote by Immanuel Kant eloquently epitomizes the Doctor's ethical philosophy and guiding principles:

> Two things have filled my mind with ever new and increasing admiration and reverence: the starry havens above me and the moral law within me." (*Critique of Practical Reason*, p. 133)

The Doctor, despite sacrificing his great love and personal happiness, knows that he must strive to overcome the bitterness and despair that would bring down a lesser man. For he must continue to do what he as a Time Lord must do: travel through space and time, exploring the fantastic and brilliant universe and experiencing wondrous adventures in his TARDIS.

---

[10] *Critique of Practical Reason*, p. 128.

16

Should the Daleks Be Exterminated?

ED WEBB and MARK WARDECKER

The Daleks have been with the Doctor since the beginning. It was in *Doctor Who*'s very infancy, its second serial, that the First Doctor, William Hartnell, and his companions first encountered these aliens, so mutated that they must live within saltshaker-shaped metal carapaces for mobility and defense, on their war-torn and devastated home world of Skaro.

These creatures, who quickly became the Doctor's most popular nemesis, were at this time bent upon world domination by genocidally destroying their wartime enemies, the Thals. Since then, the Doctor has encountered the Daleks numerous times, while the Daleks have set their sights on dominating much more than just the planet Skaro. These confrontations include at least two occasions on which he must resolve the question of whether a genocidal species itself deserves to be wiped out. He reaches two different conclusions. The difference between the two highlights the warning the Daleks present to us.

In the Doctor's dilemma we find out more about humanity, and our own great potential for evil, than about either Time Lords or Daleks. The Daleks show us what we're capable of becoming, when technology and social engineering aren't tempered with humility and compassion—to urge the destruction of the Daleks is to say that we might deserve the same fate.

The Dilemma

In "Genesis of the Daleks" (1975), arguably one of the bleakest stories in Tom Baker's tenure as the Fourth Doctor, the Daleks' creator, Terry Nation, decided to re-write the story of their origin, presenting the Doctor with an acute dilemma. He's commissioned by the Time Lords to go back to the moment of the Daleks' origin and destroy them at birth. In Part 6 of the story, he's in a position to destroy the hatchery in which Daleks are being grown. He pauses, before setting off the explosion, to explore with his human companion, Sarah Jane, the dilemma he faces.

DOCTOR: Have I that right?

SARAH JANE: To destroy the Daleks? You can't doubt it.

DOCTOR: But I do. You see, some things could be better with the Daleks. Many future worlds will become allies just because of their fear of the Daleks.

The Doctor presents a classic conundrum of time-travel science fiction: if someone tells you that a baby will be a future dictator, causing mass misery, can you kill it? Sarah Jane's answer is that this is no baby, these are the Daleks, "the most evil creatures ever invented. You must destroy them. You must complete your mission for the Time Lords." The Doctor is unconvinced: "Do I have the right? . . ." Sarah Jane argues: "If it were a disease or some sort of bacteria you were destroying you wouldn't hesitate." The Doctor is not swayed: "But if I kill, wipe out an intelligent life form, then I become like them. I'd be no better than the Daleks."

At this moment of truth, the Doctor is relieved of the decision by a dissident scientist who arrives with the news that the Daleks' creator, Davros, has agreed to talks about ending the program. The Doctor is grateful, "more grateful than I can tell you," to be relieved of his burden of decision (although it turns out to be a temporary reprieve). We shouldn't let ourselves off this hook. Would we commit genocide to prevent future horrors, including future genocides?

Only One Race Can Survive

For the Daleks, this isn't a dilemma at all. In "The Daleks" (1963), the wasted, fall-out irradiated surface of Skaro and the mutation of the Dals into the Daleks suggest a Cold War theme similar to that which dominated American science-fiction films of the 1950s and 1960s. But as Kim Newman points out, "a nation that had suffered the Blitz and the direct threat of Nazi invasion still harked back to World War II for its nightmares."[1]

Like the Nazis, the Daleks are bent on wiping out another people, the Thals. It was the warrior Thals that the philosopher Dals fought in the devastating "Neutronic War." Following the war's neutronic holocaust, the Thals evolved into a humanoid species of peaceful farmers, while the Dals retreated into their city and mutated into the Daleks. To survive, the technologically and scientifically superior Daleks built tank-like carapaces for themselves and lived off supplies hoarded within the city. It's in these food stores that the Thals, facing limited supplies of arable land, are interested, while the Daleks are interested in procuring the anti-radiation drug that allows the Thals to live in the open.

The Doctor's granddaughter, Susan, is used as a dupe to retrieve the drug and lure the Thals to a summit with the Daleks. The Thals enter the city in order to bargain for provisions, and their leader, Temmosus, learns too late that there's no negotiating with or appeasing the Daleks. It's up to the Doctor's companion, Ian, to convince the surviving Thals of the danger they face and that they must abandon their pacifism and fight.

After testing the Thals' anti-radiation drug on themselves with disastrous results, the Daleks realize they've mutated to the point where they can't survive without high levels of background radiation and decide to detonate another, massive neutron bomb: "We do not have to adapt to the environment. We will change the environment to suit us." When the Doctor is captured and learns of this plan, he rebukes the Daleks with "That's sheer murder." To which a Dalek replies, "No. Extermination." For the Daleks, eliminating what they perceive as an inferior species isn't "murder," but a much less personal, more industrialized "extermination" of a pest. They're motivated both by hatred of the other and by a will to survive that demands the removal of any potential threat.

In the climactic battle the Daleks are all killed when their power supply is damaged. When one of the Daleks pleads with the Doctor to save them he replies, "Even if I wanted to, I don't know how," and in a pattern that will be repeated several times in such serials as "The Dalek Masterplan" (1965) and "Evil of the Daleks" (1967),

---

[1] Kim Newman, *Doctor Who*, pp. 31–32.

the Daleks fall victim to their own scheme, while the Doctor need do no more than passively watch things unfold.

In their second appearance, "The Dalek Invasion of Earth" (1964), the comparison between the Daleks and the Nazis is much more explicit. In this serial the Daleks are occupying the Earth of 2164. Human beings have been enslaved and forced to labor in a mine which comprises the whole of Bedfordshire. Signs of occupation are everywhere. Daleks stridently proclaim again and again that "Resistance is useless" and that they "are masters of Earth." They attempt to firebomb London, recalling the Blitz and the fire bombings of Axis cities such as Dresden and Tokyo. There's an active Resistance, who attempt to sabotage the Dalek spaceship, and collaborators. Many humans have been turned into "Robomen" by the Daleks. But even some who haven't been assimilated in this way collaborate with the occupiers, such as two women who turn over the Doctor's companion, Barbara, and another Resistance member to the Daleks in return for food. The Daleks enslave and humiliate all of humanity for the Earth's natural resources, planning to outfit the hollowed-out planet with an engine and use it as transportation. Afterwards, they intend to implement their final solution—the extermination of all humans. In the end, the Doctor prematurely triggers the explosive device the Daleks were going to use to hollow the Earth's core and engineers a revolt of the Robomen, defeating the invaders and destroying their ship. The story presents few moral ambiguities—a classic tale of occupation and resistance.

A New Beginning

Telling a more complex story than the two serials described above, "Genesis of the Daleks," a re-imagining of the Daleks' origin, unambiguously portrays the Kaleds (the Dals of the earlier serial) as Nazis. In this serial, the "thousand year" war is still in progress and has reached a state of attrition that makes Skaro's battlefields look more reminiscent of World War I than those of World War II. High-technology coexists with relatively primitive weaponry as two exhausted peoples each pursue survival through the eradication of the other. Humanoid (pre-mutated) Kaleds are dressed in black uniforms and jackboots, carry Lugers as a sidearm, and greet each other with fascist salutes. There's even clearer evidence of hatred of the other, as Kaleds irradiated during the long war with the

Thals, or "Mutos," have been banished to "keep the Kaled race pure." Their hatred of the Thals is no more subtle, with an officer boasting that the Kaleds will "wipe the Thals from the face of Skaro" and "Our battle cry will be 'total extermination of the Thals!'"

But "Genesis" allows for greater complexity by making the Thals almost as despicable, genocidal, and totalitarian as the Kaleds. For instance, the Thals use the Mutos and Sarah Jane in forced labor in a lethally irradiated missile silo, building their own devastating "distronic" weapon to wipe out their foes "in seconds."

The story also introduces a crucial figure, the horribly disfigured Kaled super-scientist, Davros, who'll create the Daleks. This is an essential point of difference between the two origin stories. Scientists will be the ones to bring about the ultimate destruction, the ultimate evil, and *deliberately* so. Davros's team has projected the effects of the ravaged environment onto their species' future and discovered the mutated "final form"—a small, feeble, and hideous being. Davros has invented the metal armor that'll give the mutated Kaleds a means of motion and self-defense—the Mark III Travel Machine. But his ambitions are larger, and darker. He's manipulated the genes of the mutated Kaleds to make them pitiless and amoral. His totalizing vision has a remorseless logic. Davros is creating a "Master Race" that will "survive only by becoming the dominant species. When all other life forms are suppressed, and the Daleks are the supreme rulers of the universe, then we will have peace. War will end."

Exterminate! Exterminate! Exterminate!

What "Genesis" makes clear in rewriting the Daleks' origin myth is that they're evil *by design*. Davros has engineered all traces of conscience out of their genotype, leaving only creatures intent on domination of the universe, primarily by exterminating all life forms in their path. Why would he do that, particularly when it's easily predictable that, in the tradition of Faust and Frankenstein, it must end badly for him, exterminated as an imperfect life form by his own creation, his crippled hand stilled before it can connect with the wonderfully kitschy "Total Destruct" button as he realizes, too late, his fatal error?

Remember that, in "The Daleks," the serial that introduced the creatures to a nation cowering behind their couches in a Britain still rebuilding from World War II and terrorized by the ever-present threat of nuclear annihilation, we saw two peoples locked in an eternal, fatal struggle for domination. The motivation for the Daleks' genocidal plan, to wipe out what little life remains on the ravaged planet through a massive neutronic explosion, is their need to survive. Permanently irradiating the planet will make it more hospitable to them (and only them). This is the pessimistic view of the "state of nature" as described by the political philosopher Thomas Hobbes in *Leviathan* (1651), his response to the destruction and chaos of the English Civil War.

In a world of limited resources—in other words, any world imaginable outside the most utopian of fantasies—one doesn't have to posit any innate evil in human nature (no Original Sin, for example) to predict conflict. The survival imperative is enough to induce competition over resources, enough to produce violence and mutual destruction. For Hobbes, the answer was a strong state—a ruler to use force and fear to keep people in line. In a situation of civil war, or of the strategically balanced and mutually-destructive war between Thals and Daleks, there's no such outside power to bring order out of chaos. So for Hobbesian political Realists such as the Daleks, survival remains dependent on the destruction of the other. Hence their plan to irradiate the planet, wiping out their rivals in a final solution.

But the Daleks, despite their signature cry of "Exterminate!" aren't all about destruction. They're also about order—"perfect little Hitlers" as Kim Newman puts it—"Though they seem to be individuals, they act as one" (p. 32). They'll be supreme, because no other species can match their power or their ruthless pursuit of their goal. And while their vicious efficiency will make them hated and feared throughout the universe, the second origin story offers a warning for humans that goes beyond evil intent. For they represent not only the obvious parallel—Nazis, or other genocidal totalitarian regimes of twentieth-century earth. More broadly, for Terry Nation, they "represent government, officialdom, that unhearing, unthinking, blanked-out face of authority that will destroy you because it *wants* to destroy you."[2] This isn't the passionate drive to destroy of the Berserker or the fanatic, but the bureaucratic imperative to make things tidy, orderly, complete.

---

[2] Peter Haining, *Doctor Who: The Key to Time—A Year-by-Year Record*, p. 21.

Daleks are creatures of unquestioning dedication to rules and order. In the name of procedure or orders or regulations or efficiency, the greatest horrors can be perpetrated, and very effectively so. The chilling real-world parallels include the functionaries who operate death camps, torture chambers, show trials, and the other machinery of modern authoritarian states. But they might also represent other inhabitants of what the sociologist, Max Weber, famously referred to as the "Iron Cage" of modernity—all those involved in modern bureaucracy, and more broadly in the instrumental rationality (ends justifying means) that drives so much of modern life. In this, the Daleks aren't exciting monsters at all—they're bureaucratic drones. Their "evil" is in their single-minded pursuit of the logical solution to their problems of survival and order. Mostly they're following a facile plan to reach their collective goal; mostly just carrying out orders. This is the terrifying truth to which political philosopher Hannah Arendt wished to draw our attention in her famous observation on the trial of Adolf Eichmann for his part in the Holocaust: "It was as though in those last minutes he was summing up the lesson that this long course in human wickedness had taught us—the lesson of the fearsome, word-and-thought-defying *banality of evil*."[3]

Scarred Relics of Ourselves

The warning of the Daleks isn't about the dangers of genetic engineering. Hitler didn't genetically engineer concentration camp guards to be without compassion. There are more subtle technologies at work in the construction of the banal, bureaucratic human monsters whose echo we recognize in the Daleks. The Daleks are so terrifying in part because they're at once alien and all-too-recognizable. They are our terrors of what humans can become, if combined irresponsibly with runaway technology and with schemes to "perfect" the species through transformation of the self. The Daleks combine the destructive power of technology in their armor-plated travel machines and death rays, with the physically weak, emotionally stunted, and amoral mutant inside—a projection of what can happen to the human soul in certain environments, in certain possible futures or, indeed, pasts.

---

[3] "Eichmann in Jerusalem," p. 365.

Many of the most insightful analysts of the technologies and environments that mutate the human soul in these ways were, like Hannah Arendt, refugees from the cataclysm that overtook Europe in the Twentieth Century—in particular Max Horkheimer and Theodor Adorno, leading lights of the "Frankfurt School" of political sociology, and co-authors of *Dialectic of Enlightenment.* For it was the European birthplace of the Enlightenment, of modern ideas of freedom, tolerance, and human rights, that also spawned totalitarianism and the peculiarly effective techniques of high-tech, modern mass murder. The two halves of this pair were there at the start: the French Revolution brought both the *Declaration of the Rights of Man and the Citizen* and the industrialization of death in the form of the guillotine (this symbol of efficient state murder is the ancestor of the gas chamber, of the gulag, of napalm). It isn't that science and technology and reason are in themselves evil. Far from it. As Jacob Bronowski argued toward the end of his landmark television series, *The Ascent of Man* (1973) reflecting on an ash pit at Auschwitz, it isn't knowledge, but the aspiration to total knowledge, "the knowledge of gods," that ends in the gas chambers. The great evils of the age of totalitarianism came when humans disregarded Cromwell's plea: "Think it possible you may be mistaken." Bronowski urges us to cure ourselves of the "itch for absolute knowledge and power."

Horkheimer and Adorno warned of the dangers of what they termed the "culture industry," the industrialization of cultural production, the irresistible pressure toward conformity in modern societies. Even apparently benign systems that afford choice, individuality, and self-expression can have the perverse effect of enforcing or incentivizing conformity, through market or other social mechanisms. Consider the operation of fashion to limit self-expression, the boundary-setting power of literary, artistic, or academic canons, or the creative deadening induced by inflexible regimes of intellectual property rights. Our social environment imposes certain choices on us: are not the avatars or uniforms or images we "choose" to project in social spaces, online and off, equivalent to Dalek carapaces, protective, allowing travel, concealing any ugliness and weakness within? If we couple their insights with those of Michel Foucault, in *Discipline and Punish* and elsewhere, showing how modern institutions like the school, the prison, and the clinic work to transform the inner as well as outer life of citizens, we can begin to see how the disciplinary technologies of the modern state and other powerful institutions (such as corporations) can be equivalent to Davros's genetic manipulations in excising the individual conscience, or at least suppressing it, of eliciting the drive to conform, the obedience that'll ultimately commit murder for the state, even mass murder, if so ordered. Just like the Daleks, humans can be *made* monstrous.

Which of You Will Do It?

Humans can be monstrous enough to commit genocide. What of gods? It's not difficult to perceive the practically immortal, time- and space-traveling Doctor as god-like. His superior vantage point and detachment allow him to make horrible calculations, sometimes sacrificing individuals for the greater good. He sees space-time in a way that's beyond human comprehension, understanding the sweep of history as from the point of view of a being that's outside both space and time, and yet who can intervene in and manipulate them. For all his genuine attachment to his various human (mortal) companions, he's ultimately a lonely being, a perpetual traveler, an observer to whom individual human and similar beings, with their limited life spans and understandings, must seem puny and ant-like. In "Genesis," the history-changing, god-like figure comes clearly into focus when he's tasked by the Time Lords with interfering with the Daleks' evolution, because they "foresee a time when they will have destroyed all other life forms and become the dominant creatures in the universe." And yet he questions that right of intervention. He must weigh costs and benefits as we must, but on the unimaginably vast scale of the whole history of the universe.

Next to this terrifyingly powerful, but charmingly irreverent and benign figure, Davros's aspirations to the status of god seem both tragicomic and desperately frightening. The Doctor feels the weight of his power upon him. Davros aspires to ultimate power without responsibility. Consider the following exchange between Davros and the Doctor, when the latter has been captured and Davros has discovered that he could learn secrets of the Daleks' future from his time-traveling visitor. Davros tortures the Doctor's human companions to force him to disclose these secrets, seeing his compassion for them as a weakness, and one that mustn't be allowed to plague his Dalek creations: "You are afflicted with a conscience."

The Doctor appeals to Davros to change his plans for the Daleks: "Why not make them a force for good throughout the universe?" "I could do it," admits Davros. Why, then, make them evil? Davros explains: "Evil? No. No, I will not accept that. They are conditioned simply to survive. They can survive only by becoming the dominant species. When all other life forms are suppressed, and the Daleks are the supreme rulers of the universe, then we will have peace. War will end." This fits the Hobbesian view—destruction as a means of survival in a competitive and lawless universe. But it doesn't end there. The Doctor, speaking to Davros as a fellow scientist, appeals to his reason by presenting an analogy. What if you could create a virus so deadly that it would destroy all other life? Davros answers in a speech that rises to a hysterical peak:

> Yes. Yes. To hold in my hand a capsule that contained such power. To know that life and death on such a scale was my choice. To know that the tiny pressure of my thumb, enough to break the glass, would end everything. Yes, I would do it. That power would set me up above the gods. And through the Daleks I shall have that power.

Here's a moment when the difference between malign and benign reason is thrown into sharp relief. The Doctor, a more knowledgeable and powerful scientist (or god) would never create the doomsday virus, much less exploit it for absolute power. His cocky irreverence covers a deep reverence for life in all its crazy variety, and a passionate affection for silly, flawed, dangerous humans. But if the Doctor were himself more human, would he be as monstrous as Davros?

The Genocidal Doctor

In "Journey's End" (2008), in a plot that recalls "The Dalek Invasion of Earth," Davros has been rescued and revived by Daleks who have also perfected time travel, making them an even deadlier enemy who has wiped out the Doctor's own people in the Time Wars. Davros and a rebuilt Dalek army have again determined to move the Earth (along with twenty-six other planets) in order to use it as a weapon of vast power. After plunging the TARDIS and the Doctor's latest human companion, Donna, into the molten core of "The Crucible," a sort of Dalek mother ship, Davros reveals his plan to align the planets he's hijacked to use as a transmitter for his "reality bomb" that's capable of dissolving "every form of matter" within every single dimension, leaving nothing behind but The

Crucible and its horde of Daleks. Here's what may have been truly at stake during the Time Wars: "This is my ultimate victory: the destruction of reality, itself!"

Before the device has fully charged, the TARDIS rematerializes to reveal both Donna and a *second* Doctor. As the TARDIS was on the point of breaking up in the fiery heart of The Crucible, the Doctor's hand, severed during his previous regeneration and stowed onboard, suffused Donna in residual regenerative energy, generating a duplicate, half-human Doctor and making Donna part-Time Lord, with a knowledge rivaling the Doctor's own.

The part-human Time Lord and part-Time-Lord human now save reality. Donna commandeers a Dalek control panel, powers down the reality bomb, returns every planet but Earth to its proper co-ordinates, incapacitates the Daleks, and once more places the Doctor in the position of deciding whether the Daleks shall live or die. Only this time, it's the half-human Doctor. He barely even hesitates. Considering the massed Dalek army to be too great a threat, he flips a switch blowing every one of them to bits. The true Doctor is horrified by this genocidal act and rushes from the TARDIS into the flaming debris of the disintegrating Crucible to rescue Davros, who dies screaming, "I name you forever: You are the destroyer of worlds!"

The Doctor exiles his half-human self to a parallel universe. The Time Lord–human hybrid is a being too terrible, too dangerous to be permitted to exist in this universe.

The Ninth Doctor was born out of the Time Wars that have seen his people and (so far as he knows) the Daleks wipe each other out. This was the angriest Doctor yet, often on the edge of violence. The Tenth Doctor is more like the affable Fourth Doctor who faced the decision in "Genesis." His part-human counterpart that emerges from the crucible, though, is also born in war, also infused with a vengeful spirit. Far more crucially, though, he's infused with humanity. Just as Sarah Jane urged the Doctor to abort the Daleks at the dawn of their existence, not seeing past their evil deeds to the larger picture that troubled the Doctor, so now it's the human within that enables the Doctor to commit genocide.

The Dalek Within

We should not . . . no, *cannot* exterminate the Daleks. We *are* the Daleks, at least potentially. What we can and must do is guard against the Dalek tendency within. That means guarding against the harnessing of the survival imperative, and the fears it fuels, to the dangerous politics of xenophobia and illusions of our own perfectibility. It means accepting and protecting difference, not pursuing uniformity. It means also recognizing and avoiding the dehumanizing effects of the application of cold reason alone to human problems, effects magnified by the modern technologies of bureaucracy, mass education, and mass communication.

As the anthropologist James C. Scott warned us in *Seeing Like a State*, even the most well-intentioned projects of human progress can have horrific effects when married to the power of the modern state and applied on a mass scale as if all citizens were homogeneous and perfectible. Given the temptations of hubris and untamed reason and given our susceptibility to social engineering, our humanity contains within it the potential to make us all Daleks. But our humanity also contains the potential to fight the Daleks wherever we encounter them, through compassion, curiosity, and creativity. The latter qualities may be one reason why the Doctor is so fond of our puny species. The former are why he should be wary of us. After all, it was only with a dose of humanity that the Doctor of "Journey's End" was able to bring himself to do what the Doctor of "Genesis" was unable to do—to exterminate the Daleks.

17

Why the Daleks Will *Never* Beat Us

SARAH HONEYCHURCH and NIALL BARR

> We're talking about Daleks. The most evil creatures ever invented.
>
> —SARAH JANE ("Genesis of the Daleks," 1975)

What's wrong with the Daleks? Why do they trundle around the universe shouting "EX-TER-MIN-ATE" whenever they bump into things that don't live in metal boxes and look like them? The problem is, Daleks will never learn—they're just not capable of understanding why the Doctor gets on so well with other species.

The Doctor *loves* humans, but Daleks haven't got a clue what love is or why it matters. Poor things—Davros made them to win a war, and fighting is all they can do. When he made them, he left out a whole load of important stuff that humans have. Okay, so humans aren't perfect—we fight from time to time, but at least some of the time we're capable of getting on with other people and animals.

In "The Mutants" (1972) we're told that the Daleks were philosophers. Well, if they were, they can't have been very good ones, or they'd have come up with a better catch phrase. It's not worth bothering to tell the Daleks what's wrong with their thinking—they wouldn't listen because they're too busy shouting—but we'll tell you.

So what's the important stuff missing from Daleks? Why do they think that they're so superior to other species? It's because of their belief that superiority is based solely on logical ability and similarity of appearance—and that these are the only two things that are worthy of consideration. According to the Daleks, anybody who doesn't look or think like them is necessarily inferior and therefore, should be exterminated. They don't understand that other species might be subjects worthy of moral consideration, too.

The Doctor understands both Dalek-mentality and human-mentality, and this is why he succeeds where Daleks fail—he appreciates those human traits that Daleks overlook. Humans realize that love and compassion are an important part of our lives, and that these play a part in our everyday lives when we're working out how we should act. And, unlike Daleks, humans and the Doctor have the capacity to realize that other species might also count. The problem with the Daleks is that they are speciesist—and that's a really, really bad thing to be.

What on Earth Is Speciesism?

Not all 'isms' are bad, but some are. Sexism is bad, racism is bad, and Nazism is really, really bad. Terry Nation said that he modelled the Daleks on the Nazis, and you can definitely see the resemblance.[1] Furthermore, the uniforms that the Kaleds wear in "Genesis of the Daleks" (1975) are evocative of those worn by the Nazis, and this is no coincidence.

Nation spent his childhood in Wales during World War II, and was deeply affected by this experience. He felt the Britain of his youth was an isolated island threatened by a single-minded, unfeeling enemy that threatened to destroy or subjugate everything that didn't fit with its idea of what was right. So, it's not surprising that when he creates the ultimate enemy of the Doctor, he models it on the Nazis. And, in so doing, he creates an enemy which suffers from a defect in reasoning.

Daleks would hate to be told, by mere humans, that we consider ourselves culturally and morally superior to Daleks, but we do think this. The role emotions play in moral reasoning makes us superior to the Daleks. Our capacity for emotions is why we think humans and the Doctor, together, continue to beat those pesky tin machines.

'Speciesism' is a word that was first coined by Richard Ryder in the context of the philosophy of animal rights.[2] Peter Singer, a prolific writer on the subject of animal liberation, also uses the concept of speciesism to argue that we humans aren't the only species in

---

[1] Howe, Stammers, and Walker, *Doctor Who: The Sixties*, p. 31.

[2] <www.richardryder.co.uk/speciesism.html>.

the world which has interests that matter. In our modern age, he says, we recognize that racism and sexism aren't acceptable moral attitudes. The next step, Singer writes, is to extend to other species—to non-human animals—the same equality of consideration that we should show to our fellow humans. The relevant moral principle, according to Singer, isn't whether other animals are intelligent, or rational, as some philosophers have thought, but whether they have the ability to feel pain. Human infants, after all, don't have the capacity for reason, but we don't, on these grounds, think that it's morally acceptable to harm them. On the contrary—we believe that although they can't think or speak for themselves, we still have a duty to care for them—to ensure that, to the best of our ability, they are nurtured.[3]

Singer calls humans 'speciesist' if they don't think that the interests of animals should be considered when we act. If humans are speciesist, then the Daleks are super-speciesist. Daleks consider themselves to be at the top of the logical and intellectual heap, and humans, as well as other species, are simply inferior. We just think there's more to life than Dalek-logic. Our cat's not very good at logic, but we don't (often) feel like exterminating her—she can feel pain so we shouldn't starve her or pull her tail; instead, we should feed her and stroke her; we're responsible for her well-being. If animals can feel pain and we know this, then that means that we might have a moral responsibility towards them. This allows us to start thinking about ethics in the right way.

Now, of course, we're not saying that cats are exactly like humans and should have exactly the same rights; just that, when we're thinking about how to treat them, we should realize that they also have interests that matter. Surely survival and avoiding pain would count as interests that animals have. Though we might conclude in some situations, that our human interests outweigh the interests of the animals in question, we ought not to simply write them off as mere objects having no interests of their own. Humans are the beings with moral agency; and as moral agents, we should recognize that this means that we shouldn't intentionally harm beings that feel pain, if we can avoid doing so. Thus, we have a moral duty to care for them, or at least an obligation not to interfere with them if they pose no threat to us as individuals or as a species.

---

[3] Singer, *Practical Ethics*.

Why the Daleks Are Speciesist

Daleks don't get this bit. They think it's fine to bully us, scare us, and kill us. Being bullied, scared, and killed, hurts us, and that's bad—morally bad. Of course, it's really not their fault—they were created by Davros specifically to be killing machines.

Davros thought that Skaro was the only planet in the universe that contained sentient life. So he never anticipated the problems Daleks would cause once they started to travel throughout space and time ("Genesis of the Daleks," 1975)—becoming the ultimate enemy. But we should reflect upon Davros's design flaw in creating the Daleks with such limited moral reasoning, so that we don't make similar mistakes. What Singer suggests, and what the Daleks exemplify, is that an ethics based merely on similarity of body, similarity of beliefs, or level of intelligence isn't suitable for the world in which we live. In today's world, with the level of information we have, and the amount of interaction with other cultures and species, we should take care that we don't assume that we necessarily know best. Just because we may disagree with other cultures, species, or non-human aliens, it doesn't warrant or justify imposing our own personal human standards on everybody else. But that's what Daleks and Cybermen do.

Cybermen don't always exterminate other species, but what they do to humans is just as bad. In assimilating humans, they kill everything about them that makes them human—they turn them into machines with no identifying features. Both the Cybermen and the Daleks were originally created for similar reasons. Just as Davros saw the Daleks as the ultimate evolution of the Kaleds, John Lumic created the Cybermen as the next level of humankind—as Human-Point-2.

As explained in the episode "The Age of Steel" (2006), John Lumic selected those character traits that he believed would allow the Cybermen to best survive, and used an emotional inhibitor, fitted into their chest units, to suppress their ability to feel emotions. John Lumic did this because of the painfulness of the conversion process and the likelihood that a human would become insane upon awakening in a metal body. However, the result is the same as the Daleks. John Lumic envisioned his Cybermen as the ultimate upgrade that would allow humanity to achieve its full potential. But without emotions the Cybermen, like the Daleks, are unable to *share* the universe with other intelligent beings.

Without the capacity to feel pain and pleasure and without the capacity to empathize with, or feel compassion for, other species, Daleks and Cybermen can only see other species as threats to exterminate or inferiors to assimilate. And because of this inability, neither Daleks nor Cybermen are able to envisage sharing a world with species that are unlike themselves. Both species assume that the human ability to feel emotions is a character flaw, but it's not. It's the capacity to feel, coupled with the ability to think logically, that enables at least some humans, often with the help of the Doctor, to understand that the universe is big enough to share, despite differences and conflicts.

Emotions Matter

So how is the capacity to feel emotions relevant to moral reasoning? Okay, you might say, "having emotions such as love and compassion make us nicer people, but surely emotions are just irrational impulses that should be disregarded when we're working out our moral theory." Many philosophers have thought so. However, both ancient and contemporary philosophers have plausibly argued that the emotions can, and should, play a role when we're thinking about how to treat other people. One such philosopher is Martha Nussbaum. She argues that the emotions aren't just unthinking impulses, but that they also include an element of belief and interpretation—they're a type of judgment.[4]

An emotion such as fear, for example, isn't just a mindless response to the environment; it involves a belief that something scary looms, and that action should be taken to remove oneself from danger. This doesn't mean that we should always trust our emotions—they can be wrong, just as other types of belief can be. But it does allow for the possibility of training our emotions to become appropriate responses to the world around us. As Aristotle wrote, the enlightened person is one who'll respond in the appropriate manner to each situation.[5] This is what's missing from Daleks and Cybermen—the ability to adapt their behavior according to the situations in which they find themselves.

---

[4] Nussbaum, *Upheavals of Thought*.
[5] *Nicomachean Ethics*, Book 2, Chapter 2, line 1104a.

Is There Any Hope for the Daleks?

In fact, there're some examples of Daleks learning from humans. In "Dalek" (2005) the Doctor is horrified to find that one of the artifacts in van Statten's museum is a Dalek. Van Statten acquired the Dalek at an auction and had been trying, unsuccessfully, to make it talk. It's only when the Dalek sees the Doctor and recognizes the enemy of the Daleks that it begins to talk. Although the Doctor urges van Statten to destroy the Dalek, van Statten refuses to do so and captures the Doctor instead. The Dalek then tricks Rose Tyler into touching it, and by so doing, is able to use her DNA to regenerate and escape from its cage. Immediately, it proceeds with typical Dalek behavior, exterminating all of the humans it encounters. However, the Dalek then begins to change as a result of having absorbed Rose's human DNA. For the first time it experiences emotions—pain, loneliness, and, most importantly, empathy with Rose. No longer is it a pure Dalek ready to follow the Dalek master plan; now that the Dalek can feel emotions, it longs only for its own destruction—it can no longer cope with being part of the Dalek order.

And likewise in "Daleks in Manhattan" (2007), we encounter a Dalek who can feel. In this story, the Daleks in the Cult of Skaro find themselves stranded in 1930s New York, on the apparent brink of extinction, with only four Daleks left. Their leader, Dalek Sec, forms a plan by which to make the Daleks supreme again. They construct a huge genetics laboratory and attempt to breed new Dalek mutants.

When this project fails, they contact a human called Diagoras and recruit him to find human specimens for their final experiment. They separate these captives into two groups according to their level of intelligence. They experiment with those of lower intellectual ability by fusing their DNA with pig DNA, creating Pig Slaves that can walk on two legs but have limited powers of speech. The humans of higher intellect are held in suspended animation, awaiting the Final Experiment—infusion with Dalek DNA, in order to create a new race: a Dalek-human army that'll be faithful to the Dalek project of total domination. Before harnessing the power necessary to implement this plan, Dalek Sec absorbs Diagoras and forms a Dalek-human hybrid.

However, in absorbing human DNA, Dalek Sec gets far more than he anticipated. Now, the Dalek can feel emotions—including compassion. As with the Dalek touched by Rose, Dalek Sec changes his beliefs once he's able to feel emotions. He now realizes that the original Dalek plan was flawed, and that Daleks can actually learn from human emotions. He therefore works with the Doctor on a plan to revise the Final Experiment, in order that a new race of thinking, feeling Daleks can be created. However, the rest of the Cult of Skaro reject Dalek Sec's plan and decide, in typical Dalek fashion, that such a race will be inferior to pure Daleks. They therefore intervene in order to thwart this plan, and the events which follow end with the death of Dalek Sec and two other Cult members, Jast and Thang. Yet again, the failure of the Daleks to recognize the importance of empathy leads to their downfall.

Why the Doctor Is So Special

So, why's the Doctor so different from Daleks and Cybermen? Is it because he's a Time Lord, and Time Lords recognize the importance of the emotions and of not being speciesist? It seems not. The other Time Lords that we meet seem quite different from the Doctor, often seeming to have more in common with Davros or the Cybermen. Why should this be?

Other Time Lords who've left their home planet are far from admirable people. One of the first ones that we meet is the War Master from "The War Games" (1969), and he has ambitions to build a human army by selecting the best soldiers from across human history and using that army to conquer the Galaxy. Next, the Master, who we meet many times and who, like the Doctor, survived the Time War, also has ambitions to be a ruler. So, too, does the Rani. All of these Time Lords, like Daleks and Cybermen, fail to recognize the importance of other species, treating them only as play things for their own amusement. However, these Time Lords, like the Doctor, are rebels operating outside the laws of their people, and so shouldn't be taken as typical.

The remainder of the Time Lords seem to be highly insular people, who take little interest in the universe outside Gallifrey, and oppose the Doctor's tendency to become involved. We learn in "The War Games" (1969) that the Time Lords have a strict law of non-interference in the affairs of other species, and it's for breaking this law that the Doctor gets exiled to earth. However, in "The Five Doctors" (1983) we're also given hints of a dark past, when the Time Lords saw themselves as being superior to other races, and operated war games of their own, kidnapping other beings from across space and time to fight for the Time Lords' entertainment inside the Death Zone on Gallifrey. These games were ended by Rassilon, the first Lord President of the Time Lords, who also developed the technology used for time travel. As the "players" in the games were collected using a device called the "Time Scoop," which was able to collect beings from other times, we must assume that Rassilon's technology was also required to start them. It may be that it's the guilt they feel about such past crimes of their race that make the Time Lords so reluctant to become involved with the rest of the universe.

Time Lords, other than the Doctor, seem to fall into one of two extremes: either cutting themselves off from the universe beyond Gallifrey, or rebelling against that life and trying to become an absolute ruler, invariably arguing that under their ultimate dictatorship the universe would be a peaceful and happy place. The Doctor is more involved, he's seen and lived with other races and observes the impact of these events on the individual people as well as on whole planets and races. He has an empathy that the other Time Lords have never permitted themselves to develop, and so, is able to resist most temptations from either extremes. "The Waters of Mars" (2009) is a good example of one occasion when he couldn't resist.

We never understand fully why the Doctor is different than the other Time Lords, but perhaps it's because when he left the Time Lords, his interests were that of a scientist or a philosopher, whose ultimate goal was to learn and understand the worlds around him—rather than that of a person hungry for success in the form of wealth or power. Whatever it was that initially made him different, we think that it's his continued involvement with humans—in particular with his companions in the TARDIS—that enables him to emotionally develop as he does. As time goes on, he develops into an individual with a totally different point of view from the rest of his race. Once he realizes the importance of the emotions, he becomes the champion of the underdog, and on many occasions, a savior of the human race. And, unlike other Time Lords, the Doctor doesn't see helping other species as mere meddling, for sometimes it's morally required.

At the end of "The War Games," the Doctor is forced to allow himself to be caught by the Time Lords, as only they can restore the thousands of soldiers to their correct times on Earth. The

Doctor is formally charged with interfering in the affairs of other planets, which is a violation of Gallifrey's most important law of non-interference. He defends himself by arguing that there's sometimes a real need to interfere, to fight evil and prevent races such as the Daleks and Cybermen from succeeding. The Time Lords ultimately accept this argument, and subsequently use the Doctor as their tool to interfere when they see that intervention is called for.

Because the Doctor has respect for other species, he's not speciesist in Singer's sense of the word: he recognizes that other species, although they may be intellectually inferior to Time Lords, still have interests that matter. Just as we humans should care about how we treat animals, whatever their intellectual ability, so the Doctor takes seriously his ability to help others. And because the Doctor has a developed sense of empathy, which other Time Lords, and most Daleks and Cybermen lack, he's able to respond appropriately and work with other species, rather than patronize them or use them as mere pawns in a game. The moral is that logical ability isn't the be all and end all. Our human capacity for emotions, empathy, and compassion should also be valued.

18
Cybermen Evil? I Don't Think So!

COURTLAND LEWIS

The Doctor's argument that Cybermen are evil fails to take into account the motives behind why Cybermen act the way they do. Despite Cybermen being portrayed as emotionless, conquering, killing machines, a careful examination of Cyber-nature shows that we humans share many more important beliefs and motivations with the Cybermen, than what we may've thought. Though we find some of the Cybermen's actions morally wrong, they shouldn't be judged solely on a few bad characteristics; we should also consider what good qualities they may have. To be responsible in our critique of Cyber-culture we must attempt to understand Cyber-nature.

The Ethics of Cybermen

It's true that Cybermen do a lot of really bad things, like persistently "upgrading" humans and killing anything and everything else that doesn't serve their interests. However, just because they perform bad actions doesn't necessarily mean that they're evil.

Utilitarianism is an ethical theory that maintains an action is morally right if it maximizes good consequences (namely, happiness or pleasure) for the most people, while minimizing bad consequences (pain). The agent needs to consider all relevant outcomes of an action and the interests of those who will be affected by the action. Each person's interests are weighted equally; no one person's interests are intrinsically more valuable than any other's. Thus, the action that produces the greatest amount of good (happiness or pleasure) for the most people must be chosen. An example of utilitarian reasoning is seen when the Doctor ponders whether he should destroy the Dalek race in "Genesis of the Daleks" (1975). In this episode, the Doctor and Sarah Jane have an intriguing discussion to determine the fate of the Daleks. The Doctor realizes that by exterminating the Daleks "hundreds of millions of people, thousands of generations can live without fear, in peace, and never even know the word 'Dalek'," yet, he also realizes that not exterminating the Daleks produces its own set of equally good consequences: ". . . some things could be better with the Daleks. Many future worlds will become allies just because of their fear of the Daleks." The Doctor ponders: if I destroy the Daleks, am I maximizing the good while at the same time minimizing the bad? Sarah Jane tries to help the Doctor resolve his conundrum by offering reasons why destroying the Daleks maximizes the good, saying, "Think of all the suffering there'll be if you don't . . . [kill the Daleks]." The Doctor, however, rejects this type of consequentialist utilitarian reasoning and opts for a different ethical standard, based on duties.

Whereas utilitarianism maintains that morally *right* action always equals *good* action, duty-based ethical theories maintain that performing the right action for the right reasons, namely out of a sense of moral obligation, is primary, and the consideration of consequences should be ignored. Duties can be formulated in various ways, but according to Immanuel Kant (1724–1804), in *Groundwork of the Metaphysics of Morals*, they have three features: they're objective, universal, and respect the autonomy and rights of others. In the ethical conundrum above the Doctor considers more than consequences. He replies to Sarah Jane, "Have I that right? . . . Do I have the right? . . . If someone who knew the future, pointed out a child to you and told you that that child would grow up totally evil, to be a ruthless dictator who would destroy millions of lives, could you, then, kill that child?"

The Doctor's dilemma is that, even though he knows what the Daleks will do if they're allowed to exist, he's not sure that he has the *right* to destroy a creature (a proto-Dalek) that has yet done no wrong. The Doctor asks Sarah Jane, and indirectly the viewer: if given the chance to go back in time to Adolf Hitler's birth, is it morally acceptable to kill a person who hasn't yet committed any crimes, though will do so? He can think of many good consequences for killing and for not killing the Daleks, but he doesn't feel he has the moral right to kill them, especially since they're (so far) innocent of any wrongdoing. The Doctor believes he has a duty to protect innocent lives, even if they're the lives of creatures that will become Daleks. This decision is one a duty-based ethicist would make.

Just as we saw with utilitarianism, the relationship between the right and the good is important. In the case of duty-based ethics, the *right* action doesn't equal the *good* action. One can do what's right and still suffer or cause others to suffer. Allowing the proto-Daleks to live continues the existence of the Daleks, who later cause a lot of pain and suffering for others, which is bad, but, for the Doctor, it would be morally wrong to exterminate a species that has done no harm. In duty-based ethics, 'right' can be separated from 'good', and 'wrong' from 'bad', and as a result, we must rethink our understanding of the rightness and wrongness of Cybermen's actions.

From a duty-ethics perspective, it should now be clear that even though the Cybermen perform many bad actions, which cause harmful consequences, it doesn't mean they're necessarily morally wrong, even though the writers of *Doctor Who* want viewers to think this way. They portray Cybermen as selfish, oppressive "psychological egoists" (acting only in their own self-interests), bent on destroying humans. They attack Earth, forcibly "upgrade" humans to Cybermen, and kill the ones that can't be upgraded. This stereotype is misguided.

A more in-depth examination suggests Cybermen act on a different moral principle: altruism. Altruism is opposed to egoism in the sense that altruists act in the interests of others. Altruists consider the desires and needs of others and act in such a way to make sure these needs and desires are met; indeed, sometimes at the expense of their own desires and needs. Now I expect most readers to have their jaws fully dropped, mouths agape: "What?!" I admit that my claim is, well, shocking—perhaps like walking into the TARDIS for the first time. But once we understand the Cybermen better, we'll see that their actions—at least the ones directed towards humans—really are consistent with altruism.

The Geneses of the Cybermen

The examination of Cyber-nature must begin with the origins of the Cybermen, and there are three explanations offered from the classic, new, and comic book series of *Doctor Who*, respectively. In the classic series, Cybermen are humans who lived on Earth's twin planet Mondas. After the planet drifted away from Earth's orbit, the population of Mondas began replacing their "weak" human parts (such as arms, legs, and heart) with superior cybernetic parts, and constructed a means to suppress human emotions—a rather nasty human psychological weakness. Eventually, the citizens of Mondas transformed themselves fully into Cybermen. Not only do Cybermen believe their cybernetic parts are superior to human-parts, but their transformation gives them the ability to live a life guided by pure logic, free from pain, fear, and for the most part, death ("The Tenth Planet," 1966). The effect of these changes cre-ates the incorrigible belief in the Cybermen themselves that they're the most superior beings in the universe, which for some Cyber-enthusiasts isn't that far-fetched.

The new series offers a different genesis of the Cybermen. Instead of arising on a parallel planet, the Cybermen arise in a par-allel universe. In this parallel universe, John Lumic, a technological wizard and creator of many cybernetic and synthetic inventions, creates the Cybermen out of his desire to avoid the pain associated with aging and death. Lumic is confined to a wheelchair and kept alive by a variety of devices, and because of the "weakness" of his body, he devises a cybernetic device that stores his brain and saves him from pain and death. According to Lumic, the brain is the locus of humanity, and if it can be preserved, then humans can be trans-formed into superior Cybermen ("The Rise of the Cybermen" and "Age of Steel," 2006). What's more, during the preservation of the brains of each human, Lumic "upgrades" them by implanting an emotional inhibitor to keep the now *new* Cybermen from feeling any emotional pain, and he replaces their human body with a cybernetic one. Hence, Cybermen feel neither physical nor emo-tional pain, and they live indefinitely. So again, we see that Cybermen view themselves as superior beings because they lack emotions and so have overcome the weaknesses of human frailty, pain, and suffering.

Grant Morrison's comic book series offers a radical explanation of the genesis of Cyberman that suggests they're the result of the evolutionary process, and are destined to one day be the greatest agents of peace to ever exist! Morrison bases this evolutionary tale on the Doctor's encounters with the Voords in "The Keys of Marinus" (1964) and the Cybermen in "The Invasion" (1968). According to Morrison, Cybermen evolved from the Voord (a race of amphibious assassins) as a result of the use of a "world-shaper machine" that accelerates time and causes rapid environmental changes.[1] Between the Doctor's first visit to Marinus (in "The Keys of Marinus") and his last visit in Morrison's comic book, the Voord have evolved into the early developmental stages of Cybermen, and Marinus has evolved into the planet that'll become known as Mondas. When the Doctor realizes what's happening, he tries to stop the continued evolution of the Voord/Cybermen, but the Time Lords keep him from doing so. Angry that he's not allowed to stop the development of the Cybermen, the Doctor quickly leaves before finding out that the Cybermen will some day become creatures of pure thought, and the most advanced peace-loving race in the universe.

Barring any new revelations about the nature of Cybermen, there are three related beliefs of Cyber-nature. First, Cybermen believe that pain (both physical and emotional) should be eradicated. Second, they believe all things capable of pain are weak and must be upgraded so that they'll no longer be susceptible to pain. Third, they believe emotions must be inhibited, for they too are a weakness. Cybermen believe that they're a superior race, and that their way of life is superior to that of humans because they've achieved what all humans strive for: a life free from pain and death. This overarching belief dictates how Cybermen treat humans, and why they believe it's acceptable to treat humans as lesser beings.

More importantly, as the comic-book series shows, these beliefs don't necessarily entail that the Cybermen are evil. It's these beliefs that form the basis of Cyber-nature, which will form the foundation for the Cybermen's future: supreme agents of peace. Therefore, we shouldn't be too surprised to find morally good characteristics within the Cybermen's belief system.

It's probably difficult for most readers to accept the tale that Cybermen evolve into highly advanced beings of pure thought, who are devoted to peace because of how Cybermen are commonly presented. However, if we can mentally suspend what we've been taught about the Cybermen for almost fifty years, and look at them in a new light—as eradicators of pain and suffering—and not merely as Cyber-bullies, then it's possible to see Cybermen in a more altruistic way, as agents dedicated to helping those who are "suffering."

---

[1] Grant Morrison, *Doctor Who*, Issue 2 (IDW, 2008).

Humans seek relief of physical pain by going to physicians or dentists and emotional pain by going to psychotherapists or priests. Cybermen, on the other hand, offer their own unique cure to both physical and emotional pain; one that's much more effective than human cures—in the sense that one doesn't have to worry about such pains ever again. By looking at Cybermen in this way, their actions shift from being about human destruction to being about helping humans achieve what we all strive for—a life free from suffering, pain, and death. They're quite efficient at their job because they're not hindered by emotional considerations of what's lost when one achieves the total freedom of pain that one strives for. From their point of view, then, they're quasi-saviors to the human race.

Their conquests, then, should *not* be viewed as mere killing sprees, but as altruistic campaigns to grant weaker beings what they've long wished for—a pain-free, immortal existence. An example of this can be seen in "Age of Steel." Cyber-creator Lumic begs with the Cybermen *not* to upgrade him, but it's obvious that he's in pain and about to die. So, in order to help cure him, they upgrade him. Now, we humans might not like the methods the Cybermen use, but it must be remembered that Cybermen consider themselves to be superior to the weak humans who suffer and die. They're acting in our own best interests and so see themselves as "humanitarians," or rather, "Cybertarians." If we were Cybermen, we'd agree.

One final note, Cybermen shouldn't be confused with human attempts to advance the human species along one particular conception of humanity: most notably, the Nazi movement. The Nazis promoted an agenda that focused on improving *German* society by eradicating undesirable aspects of it and promoting particular Nazi "virtues." Cybermen, on the other hand, don't discriminate between races, genders, or ethnicity—they're an equal opportunity "upgrader," just like the Borg in *Star Trek*. The Cyberman, unlike the Nazis, understand the human desire to avoid physical and emotional pain, and are able to give humans what they so desperately desire. So, Cybermen strive to improve, not destroy, the lives of *all* humans, not to build up or destroy specific national or ethnic groups.

Is There a Doctor in the House Who Can Help?

The Doctor's clearest argument against the existence of Cybermen appears in the episode "Age of Steel." The Doctor never talks of good and bad, or right and wrong, but his argument goes something like this:

1. **It's good for living creatures to strive for a life free from sickness and death.**

2. **It's bad for living creatures to not strive for this.**

3. **Cybermen lack this striving aspect.**

4. **Therefore, Cybermen are bad.**

It's quite easy to get caught up in the show and to take this argument to be a good argument, especially when David Tennant is the one presenting it! However, once one takes a closer look, it becomes obvious that the Doctor is making a radical claim that there's such a thing that's *good* to *strive for* but *bad* to *achieve*. It's clearly true that there are things that are bad to strive for that are also bad to achieve. For instance, I often find myself striving for fried fish sandwiches but acquiring too many of them is bad for my health. So, if something's bad for my health, then my striving for it seems bad too, assuming I want good health. In this case, I'm striving for something *bad*, and it's *bad* to achieve. The Doctor, on the other hand, suggests that the striving for something good, like health, is good, but the actual achieving of health is bad, which sounds strange indeed!

Careful reflection on the Doctor's claim offers little help. If it's good to strive for something, then it must also be good to achieve it. The only plausible counterexample is that knowledge might be something that's good to strive for, yet bad to achieve. Take for instance the episode "The Five Doctors" (1983), where multiple regenerations of the Doctor come together to gain knowledge of immortality, which the Time Lord, Rassilon, keeps hidden in his castle. Of course, the Doctors are being manipulated to gain this knowledge by someone evil, which turns out to be Lord President Borusa, and it's Borusa who's really seeking out Rassilon's knowledge of immortality. In the end, Borusa gets the knowledge of immortality and the immortality he desires, but he ultimately regrets getting it, for it means he will live for an eternity as a stone figure on Rassilon's tomb.

This *appears* to be a clear example of the seeking of some knowledge that's good, but at the same time is bad to achieve, but it's not. The knowledge is good because it's the same thing that the Doctor claims all humans strive for (a life free from pain and death), and it's bad because to achieve it, one must continue one's existence as a stone figure. However, the achievement of the knowledge isn't what's bad: the Doctors, their companions, and the viewers now have knowledge of Rassilon's immortality, and none of them are worse off for having such knowledge. The only ones who are harmed in the entire episode are a lot of poor Cybermen who are slaughtered by the Raston Warrior Robot in the process of Borusa achieving his knowledge, a few Daleks, and Borusa himself. However, Borusa is the only one that's directly harmed by Rassilon's method of achieving immortality. But it's not the knowledge that's bad; it's the immortality as an immobile stone for all eternity that's bad. Hence, seeking knowledge fails to offer an adequate counterexample.

There's nothing bad about not having pain and not dying: I count it a good day when I avoid both! The problem with the Doctor's argument is with his claim that not having the striving aspect to avoid these is bad (premise 2). If the Doctor is correct that it's good to strive for a life free from pain and death, then it *must* also be the case that it's good to actually achieve a life free from pain and death. It appears that the only way to make the Cybermen's achievement morally wrong is to say that it's morally wrong to strive for a life free from pain and death; but then premise 1 of the Doctor's argument is false. The result of this change means that any human who goes to a physician, takes medicine, or avoids pain and death, is in some way immoral! To avoid this unsettling conclusion, we must reject the Doctor's second premise, and accept that if it's good to strive for something, then it's good to achieve it. Hence, the Doctor's argument against the Cybermen fails.

Coupled with the altruistic characteristics of Cyber-nature illustrated above, the Doctor's argument against the Cybermen is itself in major need of an "upgrade." Cybermen merely achieve what most humans strive for, and they can't be faulted for that. However, Cybermen can be faulted for the manner in which they act after having achieved a life free from pain and suffering, and since these actions are the cause of their status as "evil," we must next take a look at them.

Two New Cyber-Approaches: Enlightenment and a Good Ad-Campaign

I realize my claim that Cybermen act in an altruistic fashion is controversial, and if Cybermen indiscriminately killed humans merely because they considered them an inferior species, then there'd be no room to mount any sort of defense: they'd simply be genocidal maniacs. However, our examination of their motives and actions shows they're not. In fact, indiscriminately killing humans would be illogical for them: they'd be endangering the future of their own species by destroying prime Cyber-stock. It'd be like adult humans killing teenagers because they're irrational—we'd simply be destroying ourselves as a race. The *Doctor Who* episodes that feature the Cybermen illustrate that they are primarily interested in upgrading humans and increasing their Cyber-population, not merely killing them, even though they're more than willing to kill humans if they get in the way (as in "Revenge of the Cybermen," 1975). I suggest that the Cybermen need a new approach to promoting the benefits of upgrading, and this approach requires a new level of philosophical Cyber-enlightenment.

In the field of medical ethics, autonomy—the freedom and responsibility of individuals to govern themselves—is a central characteristic of the patient-doctor relationship.[2] When a patient has to undergo some sort of medical procedure, doctors are required to fully inform patients about their medical condition, treatment options, and possible negative consequences of the medical procedure. The thought behind this is: if patients are fully informed, they'll be capable of making well-thought out decisions about what medical procedures should or shouldn't be performed. In this way, the patient's autonomy is enhanced, and a patient willingly agrees to undergo the prescribed medical procedure.

What the Cybermen need to do is adopt a similar approach. Cybermen want to perform an invasive medical procedure that has the benefits of prolonged life without pain and suffering, with the side-effects being the pain associated with the procedure and the complete loss of emotions. Cybermen, then, should be thought of as doctors of a sort, who are capable of performing a procedure that promises to "cure" many human ailments. As with

---

[2] Beauchamp and Childress, *Principles of Biomedical Ethics.*

many medical procedures, upgrading is painful, but if patients know the risks involved in the procedure, yet desire the final result, and if they're fully informed about the procedure, they can responsibly choose to be upgraded. If the Cybermen allowed humans to choose whether or not they were upgraded, as humans do when deciding whether or not to undergo a medical procedure, then upgrading might be morally acceptable.

Like doctors, Cybermen are altruistic in the sense that they really believe they're helping an inferior species gain a better life by removing the pain and death that the human species itself strives to be rid of. Cybermen, however, unwittingly violate the rights that their converts believe they have, because they rarely, if ever, get the informed consent of converts. Instead, they parentalistically force the conversion process onto others. In other words, Cybermen think they know what's best for humans, and for the good of humans they force them to become Cybermen. This parentalism is not bad in-itself, but there's a more morally acceptable way for the Cybermen to act.

One thing Cybermen could do to combat this "bad press" is to respect the perceived rights of humans to choose *not* to upgrade. By starting an advertisement campaign aimed at informing the public about the "benefits" of being a Cyberman, and then, offering upgrades to only those willing to undergo the procedure, the Cybermen would avoid violating the autonomy of humans, and therefore, the right to bodily integrity that humans believe they have. This approach would also maximize the good for both Cybermen and humans: Cybermen would've helped humans achieve their goals, and upgraded humans will have been willing participants in the procedure. Hence, the upgrades cease to violate the moral principles they used to violate.

Cybermen have never tried this, but that's probably because it'd sound pretty far-fetched to them. The simple fact is Cybermen see humans as a weak and inferior species, and until humans mature enough as rational creatures to be capable of reasonably considering the benefits of becoming a Cyberman, then it will be difficult for Cybermen to move beyond their parentalism. Such an advertising campaign, though, will help in the maturation process, and might make for an intriguing *Doctor Who* episode!

Finally, much of the Cybermen's unwillingness to change their worldview is a result of their dedication to logic as the pinnacle of wisdom, which could be remedied by becoming more enlightened about their own existence and what a dedication to logic implies for Cyber-nature. Logic aids in the pursuit of the meaning of life, it doesn't provide the meaning of life.[3] Cybermen, mistakenly, think a strict adherence to logic, and nothing else, is the meaning of life, and they don't seem willing to consider the possibility that logic is merely the tool in which higher-beings arrive at different explanations of the good life. For them, the meaning of life is to be free from pain and death, and because of this belief, they're driven to convert and relieve humans of such things. What the Cybermen need is some Cyber-philosophers or Cyber-psychologists, or maybe Spock, to help them evolve into the enlightened peace-loving beings that the Time Lords claim they'll become.

With the nature, beliefs, and motivations of the Cybermen understood, we must engage ourselves with Cybermen in a new way. Instead of fighting them with our fists, guns, and sonic screwdrivers, we need to figure out a way of communicating to them the principle of respect for the autonomy of beings that are, let's face it, potential Cyber-people. For whatever reason, humans deserve the right to choose life as a Cyberman, free from pain and death, or continued life as a human, with all of our "weaknesses." This engagement with the Cybermen might force us to change how we treat other (inferior?) species too, which implies that, by carefully understanding Cybermen, not only have we come to understand them better, but we've also come to understand ourselves a little better too.[4]

---

[3] Walter Robinson, "Death and Rebirth of a Vulcan Mind."

[4] I offer many thanks to Paula and Jenny for their help in "upgrading" this chapter.

Human Beings, You're Amazing. Apart from That, You're Completely Mad

What the Doctor Teaches Us about Existence

19

Regeneration and Resurrection

MICHAEL HAND

There are certain losses in childhood that stay with you not only because of their aching sadness, but because, even in the throes of despair, you realize they have changed you, become part of you, in a mysterious way enriched and enlarged you. They stay with you because, as well as being the end of something wonderful, they are the beginning of something new and unknown and exhilarating, something whose fascination lies precisely in its contrast with what has gone before. Such is the end of your first romance, the day your family moves from the house you were born in, and the moment it dawns on you that there are problems in life your Mum and Dad can't help you with. And such is the episode of *Doctor Who* in which *your* Doctor regenerates.

Everyone (by which I mean everyone with access to BBC television and a modicum of taste) has a Doctor they think of as theirs. *Your* Doctor is the one you hold to be the truest embodiment of the Doctor's essence and, normally, the one who accompanied you through your formative years. As we learn in the mini-episode "Time Crash" (2007), even the Doctor himself, in one of his later incarnations, thinks of an earlier incarnation as *his* Doctor. The Tenth Doctor looks back on the Fifth as the point at which he stopped trying to be "old and grumpy and important" and acquired the traits he now thinks of as most centrally his own.

My Doctor is the Fourth, the Doctor of jelly babies and yoyos and impossibly long scarves. All the Doctor's incarnations have possessed an incorruptible decency and respect for the value of life (notwithstanding momentary aberrations on the parts of the First and Sixth), but in the Fourth Doctor, as portrayed by the magnificent Tom Baker, these qualities are allied with a charm, confidence, and mischievousness unmatched by his predecessors or successors. (the Doctor's multiple incarnations, of course, overlap roughly but not exactly with portrayals of the character by different actors: not exactly because the First Doctor has been portrayed by at least two actors, and three if you count Peter Cushing in *Dr. Who and the Daleks* (1965) and *Daleks—Invasion Earth 2150AD* (1966), which you shouldn't for several reasons, chief among which is his utterance of the abomination: "Hello, I'm Dr. Who.") The Fourth Doctor saw me through the tricky transitional years from toddler to preteen and represented to me everything in life that seemed worth emulating and aspiring to.

So when, in the final scene of the final episode of "Logopolis" (1981), the Fourth Doctor plunges from the scaffold of the Pharos Project satellite dish, merges with the Watcher and regenerates into the Fifth, my sense of loss was palpable and overwhelming. I suffered, I think, an embryonic form of bereavement. But there was, too, an undeniable thrill of anticipation, an awareness that a new age was dawning and an openness to the possibility that it might be just as extraordinary, in its own way, as the one on which the sun was setting. The face of the Fifth Doctor gradually becomes visible, a smile spreads across his lips, and he props himself up on his elbows to see what's going on; and the world changes forever.

Regeneration, then, is an immensely powerful dramatic device. It is key to the enduring appeal of *Doctor Who*, and to its vice-like grip on the imaginations of those who love it. And regeneration is also an idea of significant *philosophical* interest. Specifically, it's an idea that can help us with the question of the logical possibility of life after death.

Not Impossible . . . Just a Bit Unlikely

Belief in some form of life after death is very common in the religions of the world, and for good reason. Suppose it's true that there is a god (or a pantheon of gods), intimately concerned for the welfare of human beings and possessed of mighty supernatural powers. Such a god couldn't fail to be moved by the appalling and pointless suffering, unjustly distributed goods, unpunished cruelties and unrewarded kindnesses characteristic of life as we know it. So it's fair to expect that he will, at some point, intervene in human affairs to right wrongs, remedy ills, and reward virtue. He can't do this merely by transforming the conditions of life on earth for some future generation, or even for the present one, because this would leave out of account the agonies and injustices suffered by previous generations. What's needed is the establishment of a heavenly realm in which the dead are given new life, human nature is perfected, and health, happiness and justice are enjoyed by all. Life after death is therefore strongly implied by the existence of a benevolent deity.

Since almost everyone who believes in an afterlife also believes in a god of some sort, the fact that coming back from the dead contravenes the laws of nature isn't especially troubling. Gods, after all, are in the business of working miracles; that they aren't bound by the laws of nature is just what's meant by saying that their powers are supernatural. What is, or should be, troubling to believers in an afterlife is the suggestion that their belief may contravene the laws of logic, that life after death may be logically as well as scientifically impossible.

The problem, in a nutshell, is whether it makes sense to suppose that the Joe Bloggs who will live eternally in heaven could really be the same person as the Joe Bloggs who currently lives next door to me. There are at least two reasons for thinking he couldn't. First, one of the things we know about the afterlife (in the form suggested by belief in a god) is that human nature will be perfected: those who populate it won't harm one another, won't pursue their interests at one another's expense and won't suffer injustices at one another's hands. At present, however, my neighbor Joe is some way off perfection. Although a jovial fellow, he's hard-living and hedonistic, gives little thought to the consequences of his actions and is largely insensitive to the feelings of others. His life is geared to pleasures of the flesh, dominated by basic instincts and unreflective desires, and he frequently, albeit inadvertently, upsets, fails and disappoints the people who care about him. He is, in short, the sort of person one hopes not to be approached by for a character reference. No doubt an all-powerful god could change Joe from the person he is now into a person fit for heaven: but this, one is tempted to say, would be to turn him into someone else. A Joe purged of his flaws, it seems, would no longer be Joe.

Second, when Joe dies, the atoms of which he's now composed will be dispersed through the biosphere, perhaps by burial and decomposition, perhaps by cremation and the scattering of ashes. In itself, the dispersal of atoms may not be an insurmountable problem: we can readily imagine a god gathering up Joe's parts and putting him together again. The real difficulty is that many of Joe's atoms are likely, in due course, to find their way into the bodies of other people. Hamlet famously and gruesomely describes one of the myriad ways in which organic matter passes from one person to the next:

> **HAMLET:** A man may fish with the worm that hath eat of a king, and eat of the fish that hath fed of that worm.
>
> **KING:** What dost thou mean by this?
>
> **HAMLET:** Nothing but to show you how a king may go a progress through the guts of a beggar.[1]

The stuff of which we're made is the stuff of which others have been made before us and still others will be made after us. This means that, when the time comes for Joe's parts to be reassembled in heaven, a good number of them will already be spoken for. This doesn't rule out the possibility of a god creating a *replica* of Joe, using different, unspoken-for matter, but a newly-created replica of Joe, however exact, isn't easily thought of as the same person as the Joe who died. The problem of the unavailability of Joe's atoms is, again, logical rather than practical: it just doesn't make sense to say that a god might simultaneously reassemble several decomposed human beings who were successively made of the very same stuff.

This is the philosophical problem. How might the idea of regeneration, as encountered in *Doctor Who*, help us with it?

I Was Dead Too Long This Time

Perhaps the first question that comes to mind is: Does regeneration involve death? Do the successive incarnations of the Doctor represent actual cases of life after death, or just analogues of it?

This is a vexed question in *Doctor Who* lore. Most of the Doctor's regenerations to date give little support to the suggestion that the process involves death. In the regeneration scene closest to my heart, the Fourth Doctor declares "It's the end": but this could as easily refer to the end of a chapter in the Doctor's life as to the

---

[1] *Hamlet*, Act IV, Scene III.

end of life itself. In "Planet of the Spiders" (1974), the Third Doctor gives every appearance of having died, but K'anpo assures Sarah that "He is not dead." And the Second Doctor, in "The Power of the Daleks" (1966), compares his regeneration from the First to the metamorphosis of caterpillars into butterflies, implying an unbroken continuation of life. But there's one regeneration that gives powerful support to the death hypothesis: that of the Seventh Doctor into the Eighth in "Doctor Who: The TV Movie" (1996).

Following an emergency landing in San Francisco in December 1999, the Seventh Doctor steps out of the TARDIS into the midst of a gun battle and is immediately shot in the chest. Badly wounded, he's rushed to hospital and into the operating theater. The cardiologist who operates on him, Dr. Grace Holloway, is understandably unfamiliar with Time Lord physiology, and the procedure doesn't go according to plan. The Doctor goes into seizure, flatlines, and is pronounced dead at 10:03 P.M. His body is taken down to the morgue and stored in the refrigerator. Sometime after 1:00 A.M., his corpse is reanimated and he regenerates.

A little later, the Eighth Doctor offers Grace the following explanation for his befuddled state of mind: "I was dead too long this time. The anaesthetic almost destroyed the regenerative process." This explanation not only confirms that the Doctor was indeed dead for the three plus hours prior to his regeneration, but also clearly implies that regeneration *always* involves death, albeit usually for a shorter period of time.

It may be, then, that regeneration is a literal form of resurrection: the Doctor comes back from the dead each time he regenerates. But the relevance of regeneration to our philosophical problem doesn't depend on acceptance of this view. What's important about regeneration, for our present purposes, is what it tells us about how much change a person can undergo while still remaining the same person. Whether the radical transformation of the regenerative process involves an actual dying and rising, or just something analogous to one, is by the by.

A Dandy and a Clown

Consider now the first of our logical worries about the preservation of identity between this life and next. The worry, you'll recall, was that Joe, a man of many flaws, must be made flawless as a condition of his entry to heaven, and that this seems to require his becoming a different person. The idea of regeneration helps us to see that this worry is unfounded.

The Doctor's incarnations are very different from one another. They differ in height, weight, age and appearance; and, crucially, they differ in personality. The First Doctor is irascible and cantankerous, yet at the same time benevolent and avuncular; the Second is playful and puckish, mercurial and cunning; the Third is commanding and aristocratic, a daredevil and a dandy; and so on. Yet despite the wide variation in the Doctor's personalities, we have no difficulty in accepting that they belong to successive incarnations of the same person. The Doctor's identity, the thing that all his incarnations have in common and by virtue of which they qualify as incarnations *of the Doctor*, can't reside in his personality, for his personality has changed dramatically on ten occasions. Identity must therefore be logically distinct from personality.

It isn't only the idea of regeneration that shows up this distinction. We're led to the same conclusion if we reflect on character transformations brought about by religious conversion, on the symptoms of multiple personality disorder, or on personality changes resulting from brain injury, pharmaceutical intervention, or courses of psychotherapy. In these cases, as in the case of regeneration, significant discontinuities of personality do nothing to undermine continuity of identity. We don't doubt that the virtuous, god-fearing convert of today is still the same person as the vicious, godforsaken unbeliever of yesterday.

Regeneration, then, is just one of several illustrations of the difference between identity and personality, but one that's particularly vivid and compelling. If the Doctor can go from formidable, charismatic and decisive to vulnerable, sensitive and uncertain in one tumble from a satellite dish scaffold, there's no reason why Joe can't go from sinner to saint in one act of an almighty god.

It Will Shake Up the Brain Cells a Little

If identity doesn't consist in personality, what does it consist in? What *is* the thing that all the Doctor's incarnations have in common and by virtue of which they qualify as incarnations of the same person? One plausible answer to this question, and an answer supported by the idea of regeneration, is the body. What makes someone the same person as she was a year ago, even if her personality has changed out of all recognition in that time, is the fact that she still has the same body.

My claim that the idea of regeneration supports this answer may seem odd. The Doctor's body, after all, undergoes some very significant changes when he regenerates. The physical differences between successive incarnations are striking, sometimes striking enough to be used to comic effect, as in the encounters between the Second and Third Doctors in "The Three Doctors" (1973) and "The Five Doctors" (1983). Does this count against the suggestion that identity consists in sameness of body?

No. Regeneration involves bodily changes but not a change of body. The Doctor's body is reconfigured in the process of genetic reshuffling, but it isn't replaced. The atoms of which the Doctor is composed immediately before regeneration are the very atoms of which he's composed immediately after it. It's precisely this bodily continuity that accounts for our readiness to see the ten Doctors to date as successive incarnations of the same person.

This is bad news with regard to our second logical worry about life after death, that for most of us resurrection will be prohibited by the unavailability of the stuff of which we're made. Insofar as regeneration supports the view that identity consists in bodily continuity, it offers no way around this problem. If Joe's atoms are unavailable for reassembly because they're needed to reassemble people who lived long before him, it's difficult to see how Joe could possibly be resurrected from the dead.

But perhaps we've been too hasty here. The Doctor's body isn't the only thing he retains through regeneration and therefore not the only possible locus of his identity. He also retains his memories. Each incarnation remembers the actions and experiences of his predecessors, and remembers them as *his* actions and experiences. He remembers their knowledge and beliefs, their skills and competences, their attachments and loyalties. Could his identity consist, then, in continuity of memory? This possibility holds out the prospect of a solution to the problem of the unavailability of bodies for resurrection, a solution I shall call the 'replica theory of life after death'.

But He's Not You

The replica theory assumes that the basis of identity is continuity of memory. What makes Joe Joe isn't his personality or his body, but his memories. A god seeking to resurrect Joe is therefore obliged neither to leave Joe's personality intact nor to reassemble the parts of his decomposed body. He can create a brand new version of Joe, a replica, composed of different matter and free of all character defects, and simply program the replica with Joe's memories. Since continuity of memory is sufficient for identity, the heavenly replica counts as the same person as the earthly original, and Joe has been successfully resurrected. This account of life after death certainly avoids the unavailability-of-bodies problem. But will it do? Is continuity of memory really sufficient for identity? A recent episode of *Doctor Who* sheds some light on the matter.

In "Journey's End" (2008), an instantaneous biological metacrisis results in the generation of a replica Doctor. The replica grows from the original Doctor's severed hand, into which a quantity of unused regeneration energy has earlier been channelled. He has the same appearance as the Doctor, the same memories, knowledge and attachments, and almost the same character (but not quite: he, unlike the Doctor, is prepared to commit genocide against the Daleks). He differs from the Doctor in being part human and having only one heart.

If the replica theory were sound, we should now be in the odd situation of having to say that the Doctor and the replica are the same person; or at the very least that they're two individuals with equally strong claims on the Doctor's identity, equally entitled to whatever the Doctor is due and equally liable for whatever he owes. But we, or at least most of us, have a powerful intuition that it would be wrong to say this. We're inclined to think of the replica as a new and different person, possessing the Doctor's memories but not thereby identical with the Doctor.

Compare this intuition with the one we have about John Smith in the episode "Human Nature" (2007). Pursued across the universe by a deadly foe, the Doctor attempts to evade capture by transforming himself into the human being John Smith, a schoolteacher in early twentieth-century England with a fictional personal history and no recollection (except in his dreams) of his life as the Doctor. Martha is charged with guarding the fob watch in which his Time Lord configuration is stored and ensuring that he transforms back into the Doctor when it's safe to do so. Despite the fact that he has none of the Doctor's memories, I think our intuition is to say that John Smith *is* the Doctor. He and the Doctor are the same person because they have the same body. Our different common-sense judgments about John Smith and the replica suggest that, in practice at least, we favor bodily continuity over continuity of memory as the basis of identity.

Our unease about regarding the replica as the Doctor is shared and articulated by Rose in "Journey's End." The Daleks defeated and the stolen earth returned to its solar system, the Doctor takes Rose back to the parallel universe that has become her home and entrusts the replica to her care. His intention, apparently, is that the unconsummated and largely unspoken love affair between Rose and him should now be fully realized between Rose and the replica. As it dawns on Rose what the Doctor has in mind, she puts up some resistance:

> **DOCTOR:** (*to replica*) You were born in battle, full of blood and anger and revenge. (*to Rose*) Remind you of someone? That's me, when we first met. And you made me better. Now you can do the same for him.
>
> **ROSE:** But he's not you.
>
> **DOCTOR:** He needs you. That's very me . . .
>
> **ROSE:** But, it's still not right, because the Doctor is still you.

Rose feels that the replica isn't the man she fell in love with. He may share the Doctor's appearance, personality, and memories, and he may love her as deeply and sincerely as the Doctor loves her, but he is nevertheless a different person. The man she loves is the person about to leave in the TARDIS with Donna. Although Rose is eventually persuaded (perhaps a little too easily) to accept the replica as a substitute for the Doctor, with the bonus that, being part human, he'll grow old and die with her, it's still with profound sadness that she gazes at the dematerializing TARDIS and bids the Doctor a silent farewell.

Can we rationally defend the view that the replica isn't the Doctor? Intuition is all well and good, but perhaps it's mere prejudice that disinclines us to accept the identity of replicas with the originals whose memories they share (a kind of replicaphobia, if you will). Why shouldn't we be willing to say that replicas *are* the people they replicate? One reason is that many of the memories of replicas are, in an important sense, *false* memories. It's tempting to say that they're false because they're the memories of other people, but this won't quite do because it begs the question: the replica theory denies precisely that those replicated are 'other people'. But we can make a similar point without begging the question. All of our actions and experiences involve our bodies in some way, and to remember them as our actions and experiences is to remember them as involving our bodies. But if we're replicas, our bodies were *not* involved in the actions and experiences we remember as involving them; and to that extent the memories are false.

This element of falsity in the memories of replicas gives some rational support to the intuition that replicas and originals aren't the same people. But it doesn't quite clinch the case. Determined defenders of the replica theory can bite the bullet here: they can accept that the personal memories of replicas are false but insist that this is irrelevant to the question of identity. What makes replicas and originals the same people is the fact that their memories are *subjectively* identical. The difference only appears when one considers the memories objectively, when one asks how truly they represent the remembered events. And this, replica theorists can assert, has no bearing on the matter.

The replica theory therefore offers one route, though not a very promising one, by which believers in life after death can escape the unavailability-of-bodies problem. But it's not the only route open to them. One contemporary philosopher, Peter van Inwagen, has suggested a different way out of the problem, and one that's compatible with the view that identity consists in bodily continuity.

Here They Are . . . Ready to Outsit Eternity

The unavailability-of-bodies problem looks insurmountable if we assume that the god intending to resurrect the dead only arrives on the scene at the end of the world, by which time the same atoms have been components of many human bodies. But what if, rather than waiting in the wings until the final act, this god has been busy throughout the course of human history, harvesting and storing bodies in readiness for resurrection at the appointed time?

This is the possibility van Inwagen invites us to consider.[2] Perhaps what happens is that, at the moment of death, our bodies are removed from the biosphere and immediately replaced with different ones. Or perhaps it's not our whole bodies that are

---

[2] Peter van Inwagen, "The Possibility of Resurrection."

removed and replaced, but just our brains and central nervous systems, or whatever organs are necessary for our still being ourselves in the next life. The bodies that are dispersed through the biosphere, by burial and decomposition or cremation and the scattering of ashes, are not *our* bodies, but mere simulacra. Our bodies are safe in the care of a god who will miraculously preserve them until the day of resurrection.

Van Inwagen's theory has come in for a bit of flak. His critics have remarked disparagingly on the way it casts the resurrecting god in the role of cosmic cryonicist, deep freezing corpses until he's ready to defrost and revive them. The suggestion is that the practice of cryonics is somehow disreputable, primitive or unethical, so it would be beneath an all-powerful god to resort to quasi-cryonic methods. But little is offered to substantiate this suggestion. What precisely is objectionable about the idea of a god guaranteeing the availability of our bodies for resurrection by removing and preserving them? The Doctor, at least, sees cryonics in a rather more positive light. When, in "The Ark in Space" (1975), he finds the last survivors of the human race cryonically frozen aboard the space station Nerva, it prompts him to offer one of his most moving tributes to humanity:

> Homo sapiens. What an inventive, invincible species. It's only a few million years since they crawled up out of the mud and learned to walk. Puny, defenceless bipeds. They've survived flood, famine and plague. They've survived cosmic wars and holocausts. Now, here they are, out among the stars, waiting to begin a new life, ready to outsit eternity. They're indomitable. Indomitable.

The divine cryonicist theory, then, offers a solution to the unavailability-of-bodies problem that doesn't require abandonment of the bodily continuity view of identity, thus putting to rest the second and more difficult of our logical worries about life after death.

To show that something is logically possible isn't, of course, to show that it's true, or is likely to be true, or can reasonably be thought to be true. The hypothesis of an afterlife-promising god can't be dismissed on the grounds that the afterlife promised is logically impossible; but there may be other good reasons to dismiss it, or no good reason for advancing it in the first place. On the question of the existence of a god, the Doctor has scrupulously refrained from passing judgment for almost half a century; in this, as in so much else, I shall follow his example.

20
And, Before I Go . . .

PAUL DAWSON

When the Doctor regenerates, does he die? If not, what survives the process?

Regeneration is unsettling for *Doctor Who* fans. I cried when the Third Doctor regenerated ("Planet of the Spiders," 1974), and was moved again, over thirty years later, as the Ninth Doctor give way to the Tenth ("The Parting of the Ways," 2005), and the Tenth to the Eleventh ("The End of Time," 2010). Maybe ten-year-old me just didn't understand what was happening; but why should the adult me be saddened by the regenerations of 2005 and 2010? The Ninth Doctor described regeneration as a "sort of way of cheating death," so why worry?

You're My Replacements

One common view is that regeneration instantaneously changes the Doctor's appearance and, to a lesser extent, personality. This assumes that one subject, the Doctor, persists through such changes—that the Doctor is *the same individual* on both sides of the regeneration. But this is questionable. The newly regenerated Second Doctor refers to his predecessor in the third person, while the departing Ninth Doctor tells Rose that he won't see her again, and speaks of himself in the past tense, seeming far from sure that whatever emerges on the other side of the process will be *him*. And the Doctor's own uncertainty is even clearer when, so to speak, "one Doctor" encounters "other Doctors." The First Doctor refers to the Second and Third Doctors as his *replacements*, for example ("The Three Doctors," 1973).

Is it possible, then, that the different Doctors are not the same individual at all? Perhaps the "old Doctor" *does* die, before the "new Doctor" takes his place.

Let's analyze this possibility using two philosophical notions. First, a *designator* is any word or phrase used to pick out something. "Davros" is a designator, as is "the creator of the Daleks." The difference between them is that the first is a *proper name*, and the second is a *definite description*. Second, a *possible world* is any complete state of affairs that's logically possible—any way that it's logically possible for the world to be. The actual world, given its actuality, is of course logically possible, but some philosophers think there's an infinity of other possible worlds. For example, since it's logically possible that Britain has a President rather than a Prime Minister ("The Age of Steel," 2006), there's a possible world in which Britain has a President.

According to philosopher Saul Kripke, *proper names* pick out the same individual in all possible worlds containing that individual, while definite descriptions pick out different individuals in different possible worlds. Proper names are therefore *rigid designators*, while definite descriptions are *non-rigid designators*. Thus the proper name "William Shakespeare" picks out William Shakespeare in all possible worlds which include that individual (including worlds in which that individual isn't named "William Shakespeare"), whereas the definite description "The author of *Love's Labour's Lost*," while it picks out Shakespeare in the *actual* world, picks out Christopher Marlowe in some other possible world.

So, a rigid designator, such as proper name, seeks out *the same individual* in all possible worlds, whereas a non-rigid designator, such as a definite description, takes *a given role* to all possible worlds, and discovers whoever or whatever occupies that role in each of them. In the actual world the definite description "the Prime Minister of the UK in 2010" finds David Cameron, but in another possible world, it finds Gordon Brown, because he might have won the 2010 General Election. In yet another possible world, this description designates Harriet Jones, MP for Flydale North. (Yes, we know who she is.) And in some possible worlds, nothing fits this role. In Pete Tyler's World—the parallel world which

---

[1] Saul Kripke, *Naming and Necessity*.

becomes home to Rose and Jackie Tyler—the UK has a President rather than a Prime Minister.

Is "the Doctor" rigid or non-rigid? Does it pick out *the same individual* wherever that individual is to be found, or designate *a role or a job* that different individuals might occupy at different times and in different places? As I said, at times even the Doctor seems unsure of the answer. Focusing on the dialogue quoted above, it's plausible to interpret the Ninth Doctor as worrying about just who's going to replace him—to *inherit his job*. Later, the Tenth Doctor tells Wilf that after regeneration "some new man goes sauntering away" ("The End of Time").

Regarding "the Doctor" as non-rigid also explains our curious practice of talking in terms of the First Doctor, the Second Doctor, and so on. This sounds like "the First President of the United States," "the Second President of the United States"—that is, like talking about different occupants of the same role. And if we ask how the First Doctor has one heart ("The Edge of Destruction," 1964), while the others have two, how the Seventh Doctor is more than a Time Lord ("Remembrance of the Daleks," 1988), while the Eighth Doctor is half-human (the TV Movie), and so on, a "non-rigid designator theorist" might answer that the First Doctor is human, and all subsequent occupants of the role designated by the definite description "the Doctor" are regular Time Lords, apart from the Seventh and the Eighth.

This theory also helps explain why the Second, Third, and Fifth Doctors don't remember that Rassilon is the villain, even though the First Doctor is there when the villain is revealed; and why the Fourth Doctor doesn't know what's happening to him and take steps to avoid being caught in Borusa's Time Scoop, so that he can join and assist his "other selves" rather than endangering their existence ("The Five Doctors," 1983). Indeed, if all the Doctors are one individual, why doesn't physical contact between them have consequences at least as disastrous as those of the meeting of the 1977 Brigadier and the 1983 Brigadier ("Mawdryn Undead," 1983), or the meeting of baby Rose and teenager Rose ("Father's Day," 2005)? Easy! Later Doctors needn't remember everything that earlier Doctors thought or did, if no occupant of the Doctor role is identical with any other. Time doesn't unravel, and Reapers don't fly, if two *distinct* individuals meet each other.

There's plenty of evidence supporting the other view. When the Second and Third Doctors first meet, they seem clear they're the same Time Lord: "I am he and he is me" ("The Three Doctors); and even in "The Power of the Daleks" (1966)—a major source of skepticism about the orthodox view. In fact, there are plenty of hints that the new Doctor is the same individual as the old: such as when he remembers meeting Marco Polo, and when a revived Dalek, relying perhaps on some alien power of intuition, recognizes the Second Doctor, despite having encountered only the First.

Conclusive proof that the "non-rigid designator" theory is wrong comes when the Fifth and the Tenth Doctors meet. The Tenth Doctor is able to save the day by remembering and doing what the Fifth Doctor saw the Tenth Doctor do to save the day ("Time Crash," 2007). Here, the Tenth Doctor and the Fifth Doctor share the memory of the Tenth Doctor manipulating the TARDIS so as to avert the destruction of the universe, and this couldn't happen unless the Fifth and the Tenth were the same individual, for these "two Doctors" are bound in a loop of time that's impervious to any outside influences that might allow for some alternative explanation.

But if we revert to the standard "rigid designator" view, the original problems resurface. Specifically, if regeneration doesn't mean the literal end of one Doctor, how are we to explain the Doctor's anxiety about the outcome of the process, and the ambiguity of his attitude towards "other Doctors"?

A New Body . . .

Someone might try to answer the first question by returning to the Ninth Doctor's closing thoughts. He muses that he might end up with two heads or with none. Is he seriously worried that his regeneration might result in something non-humanoid? Given that the Doctor has always been humanoid, this would seem baseless and irrational.[2] For more plausible answers, let's inquire into the nature of the individual that might survive regeneration.

According to philosopher John Locke, a material object is a collection of 'atoms', and if even one atom is added or subtracted from the collection, it ceases to be that very body.[3] Strictly, then, since particles are being gained and lost constantly, all bodies have a

---

[2] He might be thinking of the ectoplasmic snake that the Master became in *Doctor Who: The TV Movie* (1996); but that wasn't through regeneration, and the pre-snake Master wasn't even a Time Lord ("The Keeper of Traken," 1981).

[3] *An Essay Concerning Human Understanding.*

very fleeting existence: none of the bodies that were in this room a moment ago now remains. In this strict sense, it isn't even the same room!

Adopting Locke's conception of body, clearly we can't say that the individual picked out by the proper name "the Doctor" is a particular *body*, because there are distinct bodies on either side of regeneration.

Could we regard regeneration as a process during which this individual, whatever it is, survives a *change of bodies?* The Doctor *Who* series certainly encourages this way of looking at it. Before regenerating, the First Doctor announces that his body is wearing a little thin. "So he gets himself a new one?" says an incredulous companion. And surely "changing bodies" is an appropriate description of the Doctor's Third and Fifth regenerations, for if all the particles of the Doctor's body are being destroyed by radiation ("Planet of the Spiders"), or spectrox toxæmia ("The Caves of Androzani"), it's hard to see how his life could be saved just by reorganizing them. And then we have the Tenth Doctor's own words: "I changed my body, every single cell" ("Children in Need" special, 2005).

But if we use Locke's conception of a material body, regeneration doesn't seem as *special* as it should, because Locke's conception implies that *very many* things "change bodies" constantly, as they gain and lose particles, and thus the regenerating Doctor undergoes nothing more than what each of us undergoes from one second to the next. An appropriate contrast is restored, however, by noting that regeneration is a process in which *all* of the cells of the Doctor's body are replaced *instantaneously.* Any connection between the pre- and post-regeneration bodies therefore can't be at a purely physical level.

So the Doctor, the individual that survives the regenerative process, isn't a physical body. Rather, regeneration is, at least partly, a process whereby that individual *changes bodies.* But what *is* that individual?

Absolutely the Same Man

As we've seen, Locke thinks that if a material body gains or loses any particle, it stops existing, and some other body succeeds it. So when we say that this oak tree used to be an acorn, or that this kitten will soon be a cat, we're talking nonsense if we're talking about the same material body. The fact that, when we say things like this, we're *not* talking nonsense, shows that we can't be focusing on material bodies.

So what *are* we focussing on? "An organization of parts in one coherent body, partaking of one common life," Locke says. The word "organism" seems to capture what he has in mind: an individual living animal or plant capable of growth and reproduction. Locke counts a "man"—meaning a human being—as an organism in this sense. So if we say that young and old Timothy Latimer ("The Family of Blood," 2007) are the same human being, we're not talking about the same body, but about the same *organism*.

Despite the obvious fact that the Ninth Doctor has a "new face, new everything," says the Tenth Doctor, and Harriet Jones comes to agree, he's "absolutely the same man" as the Ninth ("The Christmas Invasion"). This fits the account we're now discussing— at least, if we allow that the organism that the word "man" refers to here isn't a human being but a Time Lord. The First Doctor, the Second, and so on, are stages in the history of one particular Time Lord organism, ushered in and out according to processes driven by the "one common life" uniting them all.

Locke's strict conception of a material body implies that regeneration annihilates the Doctor's old body. Thus we might regard its annihilation as fuelling the construction of the Doctor's new body, as a phoenix rises anew from its own ashes. A somewhat less strict conception of material bodies permits us to say that the "one common life" underlying the organism *transforms* the old body by reconfiguring its constituents, as a butterfly emerges from its chrysalis case ("The Power of the Daleks").

The important thing is that *if* we regard "the Doctor" as rigidly designating a particular organism, we shouldn't regard regeneration as involving the *death* of the Doctor in any sense. The organism survives regeneration, necessarily, because the organism *drives* regeneration. True, if regeneration fails, that's the end of the organism. But equally true, if the organism doesn't survive, no regeneration occurs.

So *should* we regard "the Doctor" as referring to a particular organism? If we did, we'd be at a loss to explain the ambiguity of the Doctor's own attitude towards regeneration, and the anxiety he expresses at the prospect. In "The Parting of the Ways," he's not anxious about regeneration *failing*—about the death *of the organism*—but about the outcome of the full, *successful* regeneration process—about whether he'll *survive* it. "The Doctor" doesn't refer to an organism, but to something else.

I Remember! I Am the Doctor!

Having distinguished between a material body and an organism, Locke goes on to distinguish between an organism—in this case, a man—and a *person*. So, is the individual picked out by the proper name "the Doctor" a *person*?

Some fans of *Doctor Who* would say that all the different incarnations of the Doctor are facets or aspects of the *same* person, while other fans—perhaps even the *same* fans at different times—would say that when the Doctor regenerates he becomes a *different* person.

I'll assume that most people who say the second thing are confusing the concept of *person* with the concept of *personality*. Sometimes a change of personality is noted by saying things like "She's a different person," and of course we do use personality as one way of distinguishing between persons. If I sent an email to someone I regarded as very imaginative and gregarious, and received a reply that was very dull and timid, I might wonder whether the person who replied was the person I sent it to. But personality doesn't *constitute* a person, because it makes perfect sense to suppose that a person's personality might change, and change radically. A radical change of personality doesn't mean a literal change of person.

So what *is* a person? Clearly persons aren't the same as organisms as such, since there are plenty of organisms that we wouldn't regard as persons. I wouldn't say that a tree or a cat was a person, for example. But I would say that most human beings are persons.

Is there a rational basis for denying that trees and cats are persons while granting that human beings can be persons? Or is this just "speciesism"—mere prejudice against members of species other than our own?[4] Well, we're perfectly willing to regard the Doctor as a person even though he's not human. But would we regard him as a person if he didn't *look* human? Maybe we're just prejudiced against non-humanoid species.

---

[3] The term 'speciesism' is most associated with Peter Singer. In *Animal Liberation*, Singer argues that our presumption that human preferences take priority over animal preferences is speciesist.

Again, not so. *Doctor Who* features all sorts of radically non-humanoid persons—the Rills and the Monoids ("The Ark," 1965), Alpha Centauri ("The Curse of Peladon," 1973), K9, the list goes on. And of course we needn't tie ourselves to *Doctor Who* or even to the sorts of creatures that could only turn up in science fiction. If one day my cat sat down and told me of her adventures, I think I'd start to regard her as a person, even though she's a cat.

So a person isn't a personality, since a person can change his personality and yet remain the same person, and a person isn't an organism as such, since many organisms—trees, cats, snails—aren't persons. A person isn't a human being as such, because there could in principle be non-human persons, such as the Doctor. (And some human beings might not be persons—though I haven't argued here for that controversial point.) A person isn't a humanoid being as such, because there could in principle be non-humanoid persons.

So what *is* a person? Well, discounting prejudice against non-humans and non-humanoids, *why* don't I regard my cat as a person? What does she lack that persons possess? Many philosophers argue that what's essential for being a person—necessary and sufficient, as they say—is *thinking*. I mean, thinking in the sense of using concepts, and having beliefs and other thoughts.

Locke proposes that a person is "a thinking intelligent being that has reason," and adds that a person must have "reflection," so that he or she "can consider itself, the same thinking thing in different times and places." To be a person, that is, one must be self-reflecting: in having thoughts and experiences, one must be able to regard them as *one's own* thoughts and experiences, and no one else's.

This account gives Locke a criterion for deciding on *personal identity*—that is, whether person B now is the same person as person A at some earlier time. He claims that person B today is the same person as person A in the past if and only if B can remember some thought or experience of A's *as his or her own thought or experience*. If and only if I can remember, as my own, some thought or experience that occurred in 1993, am I the same person as the person who had that thought or experience in 1993. This is the criterion of *psychological continuity*.

It's been much criticized. Firstly, it seems to imply that it's logically impossible for a person to forget anything that they've thought or experienced, because if you don't remember thinking or experiencing something, it wasn't *you* that thought or experienced it. But surely one *can* forget some of one's thoughts and experiences. Secondly, philosopher Thomas Reid accuses Locke's criterion of breaking the laws of logic. Imagine that Sarah Jane Smith in 2006 remembers writing a certain article in 1996, and that Sarah Jane Smith in 1996 remembers meeting four Doctors in 1983 ("The Five Doctors"). According to Locke's criterion, 2006 Sarah Jane is the same person as 1996 Sarah Jane, and 1996 Sarah Jane is the same person as 1983 Sarah Jane. But if 2006 Sarah Jane doesn't remember meeting four Doctors in 1983 ("School Reunion," 2006), then 2006 Sarah Jane isn't the same person as 1983 Sarah Jane, *even though 2006 Sarah Jane is the same person as 1996 Sarah Jane and 1996 Sarah Jane is the same person as 1983 Sarah Jane!* Thus Locke's criterion violates the logical principle of the transitivity of identity, which says that if C is B and B is A, C must be A.

Philosopher Derek Parfit attempts to amend Locke's theory to avoid such problems.[4] Perhaps psychological connectedness is *sufficient* for personal identity—if C remembers as his own some thought or experience that B regarded as his own, then C is the same person as B. But the *necessity* of psychological connectedness for personal identity must be understood differently from the way Locke understands it.

An analogy: in a chain, the connection is between one link and at most two others, not between one link and *every* other. So the latest link in a chain is not connected to the first—it doesn't have direct contact with it. But it *is* connected to a link that's connected to a link, and so on, all the way back to the first link. Thus we can say that they're parts of the same chain. Analogously, a person's current psychological states needn't be connected with some specific earlier psychological state in order for that earlier psychological state to belong to the same person. As long as a person's current psychological states are connected to psychological states that are connected to psychological states, and so on, back to the specific psychological state in question, there's sufficient *psychological connectedness* for personal identity.

Thus 2006 Sarah Jane *is* the same person as 1983 Sarah Jane because, even though 2006 Sarah Jane doesn't remember, as her own, certain of 1983 Sarah Jane's experiences, 2006 Sarah Jane *does*

---

[4] Derek Parfit, *Reasons and Persons.*

remember, as her own, certain of 1996 Sarah Jane's experiences, and 1996 Sarah Jane *did* remember 1983 Sarah Jane's experiences as her own. The memories *overlap*, in other words.

The Doctor *after* regeneration can remember *as his own* certain of the thoughts and experiences of the Doctor *before* regeneration. This goes for every regeneration so far. He forgets certain things, as do we all. But there's sufficient psychological continuity for psychological connectedness and thus for personal identity, even across the nine-hundred-year life of the underlying organism. All of the Doctors are one and the same *person*.

Time Will Tell

When the Doctor regenerates, the *organism*—the *animal*—survives regeneration; for the organism drives the regenerative process which replaces one *body* with another, all at once. Regardless of physical and personality changes, the Doctor is the same *person* post-regeneration as pre-regeneration, if and only if there's sufficient psychological continuity for connectedness with some pre-regeneration Doctor.

Crucially, *the organism and the person might part company*. The same organism underlies, drives and survives regeneration, but if the regenerative process shook things up to such an extent that there was insufficient psychological continuity or connectedness— if, for example, the post-regenerative person never remembered as his own *any* of the thoughts and experiences of the pre-regenerative person—that *would* be the death of the person picked out by the designator "the Doctor."

Doctor Who provides evidence that regeneration carries this awful possibility of personal annihilation. Quite often, the "new Doctor" suffers a spell of amnesia. This is usually partial ("The Power of the Daleks"; "Castrovalva," 1982; "The Twin Dilemma," 1984; "Time and the Rani"), but can be almost total ("Doctor Who: The TV Movie"). And the amnesia has so far been temporary. But who's to say that after some future regeneration it won't be total and permanent?

Perhaps that's what happened—or has yet to happen—in the case of the Valeyard, a future "evil" version of the Doctor, existing "somewhere between his twelfth and final incarnations" ("Trial of a Time Lord," 1986). Given his exchanges with the Doctor, it seems unlikely that the Valeyard recalls any of the Doctor's thoughts and experiences as his own. By our neo-Lockean criterion, then, the Doctor and the Valeyard are different persons, although the same organism. And this is borne out if we consider that the Valeyard's plan, to possess all of the Doctor's remaining incarnations, would be pointless otherwise. For if the Valeyard is the same person as the Doctor, the Doctor's remaining incarnations are *already* his.

All of this indicates that the Doctor can never be sure that any of the thoughts and experiences he now regards as his own, or has ever regarded as his own, will be regarded in the same way by the consciousness emerging on the other side of the process. Psychological continuity and connectedness might fail. Thus it might strike him as a real possibility that the *person* he is will be extinguished along with his current body, even though the underlying *organism*—the animal—survives.

This helps explain the Doctor's uncertainty and anxiety about the outcome of regeneration, and the consequent ambiguity of his statements about the process. It helps explain, for example, how the Ninth Doctor in his final moments can regard regeneration *both* as a "way of cheating death" *and* as an occasion for sad goodbyes: the *organism* will survive, but the *person* might not. A parting of the ways in quite another sense.

It also helps explain the oddness and inconsistency of the Doctor's interactions with later incarnations. Initially, the First Doctor isn't *absolutely* sure that the Third and Second Doctors are the same person as he is, because he isn't sure that the thoughts of the dandy and the clown are psychologically continuous, or even that they're psychologically connected, with his own. They might indeed be different persons, even though they're all the same Time Lord.

Love and Doctors

The theory just outlined might've proved helpful in resolving a difficulty with the pivotal episode "Journey's End" (2008). Zapped by a Dalek, the Doctor begins to regenerate, but stops the process by siphoning off the regenerative "energy" into the hand that was severed in a swordfight ("The Christmas Invasion"). Later, this energized hand "grows" a new body which outwardly resembles the Doctor's in every detail, although inwardly having only one heart. This "new Doctor," who we'll call "Doctor Two," shares all of the Doctor's thoughts and memories, up to the point of the aborted regeneration.

Now, the series had made clear Rose Tyler's deep, romantic love for the Doctor. The Doctor had seemed to be in love with Rose too, despite regarding his Time Lord longevity as an insurmountable barrier to their relationship ("School Reunion"). Stranded in Pete's World ("Doomsday"), Rose has moved heaven and earth to get back to the person she loves.

At the end of "Journey's End," the Doctor returns Rose to Pete's World. He tells her that she's to stay there with Doctor Two, as he has committed genocide, and so is "too dangerous" to be left alone. Rose is to civilize him as she civilized the Doctor during their time together. While swayed somewhat by the fact that Doctor Two is able, as the Doctor wasn't, to tell her that he loves her, and also by the fact that, since he has one heart and will age as she ages, he can commit himself to spending the rest of his life with her, Rose seems unconvinced.

She's right! The situation seems false and wrong. The episode's writer, Russell T Davies, has acknowledged as much.[5] Concerned that Rose is acting either out of character—she wouldn't allow anyone to come between her and "her" Doctor—or stupidly, in not realizing what's going on, Davies opted to re-write the scene so that, in his eyes at least, Rose actively chooses Doctor Two out of the kind of lust that the Doctor has shown himself unwilling or unable to satisfy.

But surely if Rose chooses Doctor Two over the Doctor, and especially out of lust rather than love, we must conclude that she never loved the Doctor in the first place. Her upset in "Doomsday," and subsequent attempts to get back to the Doctor, now appear as symptomatic of an immature infatuation, satisfiable by hooking up with a mere lookalike.

So let's turn to the amended Lockean theory of personal identity, and see how "Journey's End" might have turned out. Doctor Two clearly has a different *body* from the Doctor's. It's a distinct parcel of matter. And the organism that sprouts from the severed hand is clearly a different organism, since it isn't even a Time Lord organism. So, the Doctor and Doctor Two are two different *men* (if, indeed, we can use the term "man" of a Time Lord and a Time Lord-human hybrid). But we oughtn't to infer from this that Doctor Two is a different *person* from Rose's Doctor.

---

[5] See the final chapter of Davies's and Benjamin Cook's *Doctor Who: The Writer's Tale*.

Doctor Two shares all of the Doctor's thoughts and experiences, up to the moment when he aborts his regeneration. He remembers these thoughts and experiences as his own. There's very strong psychological continuity, in other words. If the original Doctor had died at or before the moment of Doctor Two's creation, both Locke and Parfit would say that the Doctor, that very person, lives on, the same consciousness now associated with a newly created organism. As it is, the Doctor and Doctor Two exist simultaneously. Given this, and given in any case that there was a gap between the aborted regeneration and Doctor Two's "birth," there's what Parfit calls "branching." That is, Doctor Two's thoughts and experiences branch off from the Doctor's. There is *fission*, and a divergence. The Doctor and Doctor Two are two different persons.

But, crucially, Doctor Two remembers, as his own (for they *are* his own), all of the Doctor's thoughts about Rose, all of the experiences they had together, and all of the feelings that he has for her, up to the moment of that aborted regeneration. Then neither the Doctor nor Doctor Two has a better claim to be the same person, the very same Doctor, whom Rose knew and loved. Doctor Two *is* the person she met in the Henrick's basement ("Rose"), and was cruelly separated from, and has been trying to get back to.

This philosophical revelation yields a more subtle and satisfying denouement. Firstly, Rose is neither shallow nor stupid. She *doesn't* settle for second best. She gets the person she fell in love with. And, as a bonus, he's now able to spend the rest of his life with her, as she with him. Secondly, *the very same person* who experienced the heartbreak of losing Rose for the first time now experiences joy at the prospect of a lifetime in her company. In this *full* sense, the Doctor who lost, finally wins.

Of course "our" Doctor—the consciousness associated with the Time Lord organism—loses Rose all over again. His sadness and sense of isolation continue for a little while longer.

21

What the World Needs Is . . . a Doctor

RUTH DELLER

I'm the Doctor. I'm a Time Lord. I'm from the planet Gallifrey in the constellation of Kasterborous. I'm 903 years old and I'm the man who's gonna save your lives and all six billion of the people on the planet below. You got a problem with that?

—THE TENTH DOCTOR ("Voyage of the Damned," 2007)

Imagine a lonely god, the only one of his kind, who travels the world saving souls and bringing redemption. In his mission, he's accompanied by a loyal band of followers, whose lives are so transformed from meeting him that they go on to do even greater things. Through him the whole universe is transformed . . . but is he Jesus Christ, the New Testament Messiah, or the Doctor, a traveling television Time Lord?

It's easy to see parallels between Jesus Christ and the Doctor. Right-wing Christian lobby group *Christian Voice* certainly thought so when they protested against the scene in "Voyage of the Damned" where the Doctor ascended, flanked by robot angels on either side, claiming it portrayed him as a Messiah. Showrunner Russell T Davies has even stated that "The Doctor is a proper savior. He saves the world through the power of his mind and his passion."[1]

So what's this savior Doctor like, and what do the apparent parallels with Christ reveal about him? The nineteenth-century philosopher Ludwig Andres Feuerbach[2] claimed that mankind projected onto Jesus Christ the ideals it sought for itself. Thus

---

[1] Adam Sherwin, "Christians Protest as Doctor Who Is Portrayed as 'Messiah'."

[2] Ludwig Feuerbach, *The Essence of Christianity*.

Christ becomes the idealized human, the person we wish we could be. If we apply this notion to the Doctor, what ideals are projected onto him? Is he an idealized Christ figure, or something else? What can looking at the interactions between the Doctor, his companions, and his enemies reveal about human nature and the potential we have to become something better—or worse—than we are?

That's What You Do. You're the Doctor. You Save People.

Like the Biblical Jesus Christ, the Doctor is a savior. He saves individuals and worlds from peril, and often from their own 'sins' or misguided doctrines and actions. For example, in "Voyage of the Damned" he declares himself the one who will save all of the people in peril. Through the 'prayer' of millions chanting his name in "The Last of the Time Lords" (2007), he saves the world from the threat of the Master, and in "The Doctor's Daughter" (2008), he urges the people of Messaline to form a new society and found it in his image.

Like Jesus, the Doctor is also a 'redeemer'. He makes people and worlds 'better'. The testimony of his companions (or 'disciples') is that their lives are changed by meeting him. In "The Parting of the Ways" (2005), Rose tells Mickey that "it was a better life. And I—I don't mean all the travelling and . . . seeing aliens and spaceships and things—that don't matter. The Doctor showed me a better way of living your life." For Donna's Granddad, Wilf, the tragedy of her mind being 'wiped' in "Journey's End" (2008) was that she'd revert to being the person she was before meeting the Doctor, crying as he says, "but she was better with you."

It's not just his allies who are 'redeemed' through their encounter with the Doctor. He also offers a second chance to his enemies, much as the Biblical Christ offers redemption for sinners. He allows Margaret, the Slitheen, to be reborn ("Boom Town," 2005), tries to negotiate peace deals with the Sycorax ("The Christmas Invasion," 2006) and Sontarans ("The Poison Sky," 2008), and offers both the Master ("The Last of The Time Lords") and Davros ("Journey's End") chances to come with him instead of perishing.

As Jesus Christ offered "life in all its fullness" (John 10:10), the Doctor also offers a life of new possibilities. In "The Girl in the

Fireplace" (2006), Reinette says, "I have seen the world inside your head, and know that all things are possible," an echo of Christ's words that with God "all things are possible" (Matthew 19: 26 and Mark 10: 27). River Song is so aware of the possibilities offered by life with the Doctor that she sacrifices herself in "Forest of the Dead" (2008), in order that the Doctor doesn't die and therefore the wonderful times that her past self and his future self enjoyed together will still occur.

Those who spend time with the Doctor are often changed so much by the experience and the new opportunities it's given them that they carry on the work after these encounters, much as Jesus's disciples and followers continued his work. We see the 'mission' carrying on through Sarah Jane with her child helpers in *The Sarah Jane Adventures*, Captain Jack and his *Torchwood* team, Martha and UNIT, Mickey and Rose in the parallel universe Torchwood, and even the likes of Mr. Cropper and Harriet Jones, who contribute to the Subwave Network used in "The Stolen Earth" (2008) to unite the Doctor and his companions.

The Doctor's allies also spread his 'gospel', or story, to those they meet, most notably in "Planet of the Ood" (2008), where the Ood sing songs of their liberator(s), Doctor-Donna, "The Fires of Pompeii" (2008) where the Doctor and Donna are worshipped as household gods, and "The Last of the Time Lords" (2007), when Martha spends a year traveling the world telling the story of the Doctor and urging people to believe: "But if Martha Jones became a legend, then that's wrong because my name isn't important. There's someone else. The man who sent me out there. The man who told me to walk the Earth. His name is the Doctor. He has saved your lives so many times, and you never even knew he was there. He never stops. He never stays. He never asks to be thanked. But I've seen him. I know him. I love him. And I know what he can do."

However, unlike the Biblical Jesus, the Doctor is by no means flawless. If we take Feuerbach's notion of people projecting what they want to see onto God, we see that atheist showrunner Russell T Davies has projected onto the Doctor not only the power and majesty of a god, but the problems that come with such status. Nicola Shindler, who worked with Davies on many of his earlier television projects, claimed that "Russell's ideology" is that "the root of all evil is religion and gods, and that the world would be a better place without them."[3] There are certainly aspects of this ideology present throughout the series. It's demonstrated in the villains who display god-like tendencies, such as the Master and his plan to rule the Earth ("The Sound of Drums," 2007), Davros and his creation of a new race of Daleks from his own flesh ("The Stolen Earth"), Cassandra and her desire to be immortal ("End of the World," 2005), and the Emperor Dalek and his worshippers ("Parting of the Ways"). However, it's not just in the villains that the problem of 'gods' and power is revealed, but in the Doctor himself.

There are many references to the Doctor as an 'angel' or a 'lonely god' throughout the series, yet he himself decries the idea that he might be seen as a deity: "Don't worship me—I'd make a very bad God" ("Boom Town"). The fact that he's like a god is also sometimes seen as a negative, as when Margaret chides him in "Boom Town": "From what I've seen, your happy-go-lucky little life leaves devastation in its wake. Always moving on 'cos you dare not look back. Playing with so many people's lives—you might as well be a god."

In "Dalek" (2005), the angry Doctor vows to exercise his power to "wipe every last stinking Dalek out of the sky" and in "The Runaway Bride," he kills all the Empress of the Racnoss's children, despite Donna's pleas not to. In "The Fires of Pompeii" he tells Donna he can't save people because it'll damage the timeline of history, before coming to the dreadful realization that it was actually his presence that caused the eruption of Vesuvius. Likewise, in "The Family of Blood" (2007), Joan Redfern challenges him: "Answer me this, just one question. That's all. If the Doctor had never visited us, if he'd never chosen this place on a whim . . . would anyone here have died?" The Doctor, guilty, can't answer her, and she dismisses him. Although we've never seen it, we also know that the Doctor killed in the Time War between the Daleks and Time Lords and bears the responsibility of those deaths on his shoulders.

Even his enemies see that, like them, the Doctor has war and anger in his soul, and that his life leads to suffering. In "Journey's End," when Rose, Captain Jack, Martha, Mickey, Sarah Jane, and Jackie are all gleefully discussing how to destroy the Daleks,

---

[3] Aldridge and Murray, *T Is for Television: The Small Screen Adventures of Russell T Davies*, p. 146.

Davros addresses the Doctor and says his soul has been revealed through his 'children': "The man who abhors violence, never carrying a gun. But this is the truth, Doctor: you take ordinary people and you fashion *them* into weapons. Behold your Children of Time transformed into murderers. I made the Daleks, Doctor. You made this."

It's also clear that the weight of being like a 'god', and particularly being the only one, isn't easy for the Doctor to shoulder: "Because that's how I see the universe. Every waking second, I can see what is, what was . . . what could be, what must not. That's the burden of the Time Lord, Donna. I'm the only one left." (The Doctor, "Fires of Pompeii").

I'll Tell You What I Can See. . . . Humans. Brilliant Humans

When Feuerbach saw that humanity projected its ideal self and ideal moral core onto the notion of God, and particularly onto the person of Jesus Christ, he believed this was because we needed something to project our values onto to make us want to be 'moral'. Other philosophers disagreed with this notion and thought that man could be moral without an idea of a god to follow or live up to. Friedrich Nietzsche, for example, believed that people were capable of modifying behavior and attitudes themselves to live up to a moral standard.

Nietzsche argued that if humanity could live morally and, by self-improvement and self-restraint, overcome our baser instincts, we could so better ourselves that our old nature would be surpassed by what he calls the 'Übermensch'. This is translated by some commentators as 'superman' or, more accurately, 'overman', and refers to a moral ideal that humanity should set itself. So, instead of projecting these values onto Christ or a notion of 'God', we should accept that 'God is dead' and attempt to become those who don't overcome our 'sin' or weakness through a belief in a supernatural being (as the New Testament suggests), but who overcome *ourselves* and become something more than we once were.

The idea that people can become moral and can better themselves without a god or religion can also be found within *Doctor Who*. Throughout the series the Doctor emphasizes the importance of ordinary people and their potential to become 'special'. When Professor Lazarus changes his form in "The Lazarus Experiment"

(2007), he says, "I'm more now than I was. More than just an ordinary human," to which the Doctor replies, "There's no such thing as an ordinary human." In "The Satan Pit" (2006), when facing the devil, the Doctor speaks of his belief in humanity, and in his companion Rose, as being superior to any notion of gods or deities: "'Cos I'll tell you what I can see: humans. Brilliant humans. . . . I've seen a lot of this universe. I've seen fake gods and bad gods and demi gods and would-be gods—out of all that—out of that whole pantheon—if I believe in one thing... just one thing . . . I believe in HER."

Sometimes the humans in the series are seen as more morally 'correct' than the Doctor. In "Partners in Crime" (2008), when the Doctor chooses not to kill the Adipose, Donna notices that this makes a change from him killing the Empress of the Racnoss and her children in "The Runaway Bride," their encounter a year earlier. She remarks that time with companion Martha Jones must've done him good, and he agrees. The Doctor's companions act as his moral compasses. This is perhaps most poignant in "The Fires of Pompeii," Donna pleads tearfully with him to save someone (much as Abraham pleads with God for Sodom and Gomorrah in Genesis 18), and he eventually relents and rescues Quintus's family. In "Journey's End," the Doctor leaves the 'New Doctor' with Rose after he commits genocide and wipes out the Daleks. Reminding Rose that in the episode "Dalek" he (the Ninth Doctor) was the one who wanted to destroy the Dalek and she stopped him, he says "That's me. When we first met. And you made me better. And now you can do the same for him."

Throughout the series, it's 'ordinary' men and women (be they human or alien) who help the Doctor to save the worlds, from his longstanding companions and allies who not only assist him, but carry on his mission, to the likes of River Song ("Forest of the Dead"), Jabe ("End of the World"), Luke Rattigan ("The Poison Sky"), Astrid Peth, and Bannakaffalatta (both in "Voyage of the Damned"), who sacrifice their lives for the sake of others. In all of these characters we see something of Nietzsche's 'Übermensch' as they rise above their weaknesses to become something 'better'.

The Doctor's morals and guidance often influence the actions of the people involved, but sometimes they act without, or against, his advice, choosing to opt for the choice anyone would make in their situation, the choice they believe is the 'best', or most 'moral.' Although the Doctor had Prime Minister Harriet

Jones deposed after she ordered the destruction of the Sycorax ship in "The Christmas Invasion" (2005), she explains her actions in "Journey's End": "But I stand by my actions to this day, because I knew—I knew that one day, the Earth would be in danger and the Doctor would fail to appear. I told him so myself, and he didn't listen."

Martha Jones and Sarah Jane Smith threaten the Daleks with the Osterhagen Key and the Warp Star respectively in "Journey's End." Outside of *Doctor Who*'s main series, Captain Jack and Sarah Jane Smith lead their teams according to (most of the time!) their new moral values caused by rising above one's self in *Torchwood* and *The Sarah Jane Adventures,* without recourse to the Doctor. One of the most striking examples of a character rising above human nature to become something of an 'Übermensch' is the Hostess in "Midnight" (2008), who sacrifices herself to remove the alien threat, and also to diffuse the angry, unreasonable, mob mentality of the other passengers.

There's even the suggestion in some episodes that to be human might be preferable, or at least more honorable, to being a Time Lord. For example, in "The Next Doctor" (2008), Jackson Lake was revealed to be even more courageous as himself, a man, than when he was under the impression he was the Doctor. When the Doctor's human guise 'John Smith' chooses to return to his Time Lord self in "The Family of Blood," his former love, Joan, points out: "He was braver than you, in the end. That ordinary man. You chose to change. He chose to die." In "Utopia" (2007), we also see that the human Professor Yana was a far more admirable character in that human guise than in his true form of the Master.

Perhaps the most noble human of all—and given her surname, that's not surprising—is Donna. It's Donna who continually challenges the Doctor's ethics, who's not afraid to tell him he's wrong, and who reminds him and the rest of the universe that humans are just as special as Time Lords:

DONNA: What, and you're in charge?

TENTH DOCTOR: TARDIS, Time Lord . . . yeah.

DONNA: Donna, human . . . no! I don't need your permission. ("The Fires of Pompeii," 2008)

Also:

I'm a Human Being. Maybe not the stuff of legend, but every bit as important as Time Lords, thank you. (Donna to the Shadow Architect, "The Stolen Earth," 2008)

In "Turn Left" (2008), Donna is described by Rose as "the most important woman in all of creation." Even though Donna herself often fails to see that she's special, around the world there are people "singing songs of Donna Noble" ("Journey's End") because of what she's done for them. And though most characters are changed only through meeting the Doctor, in "Turn Left," a version of Donna who's never met him is the one who changes everything and saves the universe.

When Donna and the New Doctor experience a 'biological metacrisis' and each become part-human, part-Time Lord, it's the human aspect Donna brings that helps the Doctor, as the 'threefold man' (Donna, the New Doctor, the Doctor—and there's an obvious allegory here with the Christian Trinity of Father, Son and Holy Spirit!), to save the day:

Because you two were just Time Lords! You dumbos. Lacking that little bit of human, that gut instinct that goes hand-in-hand with planet Earth. I could think of ideas that you two couldn't dream of in a million years! Ah, the universe has been waiting for me! ("Journey's End")

However, humanity in the *Doctor Who* universe is only wonderful if it remains human. Once humans take on characteristics of something 'other' or more powerful, this can't—and doesn't—continue. For example, when Professor Lazarus experiments with changing his biology ("The Lazarus Experiment"), and when Sky Sylvestry ("Midnight"), Korwin ("42," 2007), Gwyneth ("The Unquiet Dead," 2005), and Toby ("The Satan Pit") are possessed by something sinister, it leads to their deaths.

In "The Parting of The Ways," Rose absorbs the 'Time Vortex' from the heart of the TARDIS and begins to see as if she were a god. The power is too much for her and almost kills her. The Doctor saves her by taking the power into his body, which causes his regeneration from the Ninth to the Tenth incarnation. He explains that "No one was ever meant to have that power. If a Time Lord did that, he'd become a god, a vengeful god. But she was human."

Similarly, when Donna becomes part-human, part-Time Lord in "Journey's End," her brain begins to malfunction. She and the

Doctor realize she will die unless he wipes her memory of him and all Time Lord-knowledge. Donna pleads with him to let her die instead of sending her back to her old life, but the Doctor, who knows that all humans have the potential to be amazing, even without knowing him (we see Donna fulfilling this potential in "Turn Left"), chooses to save her life by wiping her mind and restoring her to her human self.

I Thought It Was Just the Doctor that We Needed, but It's Both of You

There's an ambiguity at work in *Doctor Who*. On the one hand, there's the message that ordinary people can become extraordinary and fulfill great potential—much like Nietzsche's concept of the Übermensch. We're shown that 'gods' may be powerful, but that power can easily be abused and also comes at great cost. On the other hand, we're clearly shown that the universe needs the Doctor. The apocalyptic events of "The Last of the Time Lords" and "Turn Left" make it clear that without him, the world would suffer from dictatorships, explosions, terrorism, poverty, alien invasion, and a lot of unnecessary deaths.

Perhaps, then, the way the Doctor is characterized shows us that while the universe needs some kind of a savior, that savior needs to be challenged and questioned. Although some of our ideals are projected onto the Doctor as a savior or redeemer, in much the same way that Feuerbach claimed humanity projected its morals onto the figure of Christ, he's by no means a perfect Messiah. His power, unchallenged, can become dangerous, and he still has many weaknesses of his own to overcome. In the spirit of Nietzsche, he's more often portrayed as a flawed being with the potential to overcome himself. In this sense, perhaps he's morally more of an equal to the 'ordinary' human and alien characters as they try to rise above themselves, too. This 'lonely god' helps people overcome their weaknesses and trials, but likewise, his companions and allies do the same for him. The Doctor and ordinary people seem to have a symbiotic relationship—they need each other. It's only when the Doctor and his allies overcome their weaknesses, together, that the universe is saved.

22
Overcoming Evil, and Spite, and Resentment, and Revenge

ADAM RIGGIO

"Utopia" (2007) began the three-episode story that ended Series Three of *Doctor Who*; in this story the Doctor and his companions find themselves at the end of the universe, trillions of years in the future when the few remaining stars are dying or dead. Looking into the sky from the barren rocks of the near-lifeless planet Malcassario, they see only blackness, but they soon discover one last outpost of life: a scraggly colony of humans led by kindly old Professor Yana, who've cobbled together a rocketship to take them to Utopia, a signal in space that offers their last hope for life. Yet in the last moments of the episode, Yana recovers his lost memory, and is restored to his life as a Time Lord—the Master—whose first act is the terrifying murder of his most faithful companion, Chantho. Stealing the TARDIS, he returns to contemporary Earth, and over the final two episodes of the season lays waste to the planet. The Master has no love for the world, and loves only its destruction.

Time Lord, All-Too-Time Lord

The work of Friedrich Nietzsche calls into question whether there's any value at all to be found in existence itself, and if there's any point to living in a valueless universe, the question at the heart of the battle between the Doctor and the Master.

Nietzsche himself has had almost as many incarnations as the average Time Lord, both during his life and after its end. Early in his career, Nietzsche was a brilliant and promising professor of Greek language and culture, earning his doctorate at age twenty-one.

Chronic illness forced him out of teaching, taking a pension from the university as he traveled throughout Europe growing increasingly reclusive and sick. His writings, which date from this nomadic period of his life, weren't financially successful, but gained Nietzsche fame for pushing German philosophy and the German language itself into creative and strange new directions. In 1889, Nietzsche collapsed on a street in Turin, after running to the defense of a horse that was being mercilessly whipped. He remained conscious, yet vegetative, until his death in 1900. During his last years and after his death, his works were unfaithfully edited by his sister, Elizabeth Förster-Nietzsche, to reflect their nationalist and anti-Semitic political and social views. These versions of his work would later inform the philosophy of the Nazi party. This appropriation would've appalled Nietzsche, given his respect for Jewish culture and his disdain for German nationalism, which is evident from the original versions of his work, as well as his conversations with his few friends when he was functional. Another incarnation of Nietzsche was his inspiration for Martin Heidegger's lifelong project of moving philosophy beyond metaphysics, Heidegger calling him "the last metaphysical thinker." However, later scholars of Nietzsche's work, most notably Walter Kaufmann and Gilles Deleuze, would disagree that Nietzsche could find such an easy slot in Heidegger's project.

Deleuze's Nietzsche, described in incredible detail in his second published book, *Nietzsche and Philosophy*, is most faithful to the German's original intent, and also lets one build a deeper understanding of the Doctor himself in his highest nobility, as he who continually fights the base instincts of life, he who refuses to be dragged into despair, he who can stare into the abyss at the end of everything and overflow with laughter and celebration.

Regarding this aspect of the Doctor, his greatest challenge is the Master as played by John Simm, who is in his element at the end of the universe, a time and place of profound emptiness, the empty sky when all the stars have burned out and blown away into scattered waves of atomic dust. What better place to discover the ends of the universe than at the end of the universe? If there's some higher purpose to life and existence, then surely it must be revealed in its final moments, a grand summation of history itself. Yet it all comes to nothing but the cold, darkness, and emptiness. It's all pretty weighty stuff for a Saturday evening sci-fi adventure show.

Among Nietzsche's central investigations is the nature of our ultimate justifications of existence, to catalogue what kind of answers people typically expect to questions like 'Why are we here?' 'What is the meaning of existence?' and so on. After an analysis of Western culture that included among his research the philosophies of Hebrew priests, Saint Paul, Arthur Schopenhauer, and all of European history up to the 1880s, Nietzsche delcared that most people expect the ultimate meaning of the universe to come from a source outside the universe. He often referred to this transcendent source of meaning as God, but this 'God' encompassed the deities of many religions. All that mattered for Nietzsche's point was that the value of the universe, the justification for existence, the reason anyone has for even being alive, can only come from some source larger than life. No living being had the right to justify itself, because justification could only come from that which is beyond life: the final judgment, the word of God. Nietzsche called this nihilism, because according to nihilist philosophies, life itself is seen as inadequate to give meaning to itself. Not having ultimate power is just as good as having no power at all.[1]

It may seem strange to call Simm's Master a man deeply affected by his need to believe in a god, as he often speaks of his desire to become a god himself. In the second episode of his story, "The Sound of Drums" (2007), the Master, on the phone with the Doctor, asks with a deep envy what it felt like to be responsible for the destruction of two mighty civilizations, the Time Lords' and the Daleks', in the final battle of the Time War, saying that it must've felt like being God. But we can also call the Master a pessimist in a peculiar Nietzschean sense. He's been to the end of the universe and seen it limping to a dark, silent death. The conclusions he draws from the pathetic end of existence are spelled out in the following pieces of dialogue in "The Last of the Time Lords" (2007), spoken by the Master, Lucy Saxon, and a captured Toclafane orb, the psychotic cyborgs who are the last remnants of humanity in the dying days of the universe.

MASTER: I took Lucy to Utopia. A Time Lord and his human companion. I took her to see the stars. Isn't that right, sweetheart?

---

[1] Friedrich Nietzsche, *The Will to Power*, p. 7.

LUCY SAXON: Trillions of years into the future, to the end of the universe. . . . Dying. Everything dying. The whole of creation was falling apart. And I thought; there's no point. No point to anything, ever.

TOCLAFANE: There was no solution, no diamonds. Just the dark and the cold.

MASTER: All the human invention that had carried them across the stars. They turned inward. They cannibalized themselves . . . But it didn't work. The universe was collapsing all around them.

He understands that there's no higher being or purpose for the universe other than the existence and eventual death of the universe itself, and so judges the universe to be empty of any value. If the true value of life must be based in some purpose of life higher than life itself, then the fact that there's no such higher purpose means that any value at all for life disappears entirely. The premise of nihilism is, that to be meaningful, one must be founded in that which is superior to life, beyond the everyday order of the living (Deleuze, p. 147). Life itself ends with the end of the universe, with no higher mission, meaning, or value than that which was in life itself.

The foundation of the Master's pessimism is that he believes the universe can only be ultimately meaningful if there's some value superior to life that grounds our mere existence. In this way, the Master still looks for higher values beyond life, even while he can't find it, and doesn't expect to find it. If the denial of anything superior to life necessarily denies the value of life itself, then at the very core of this philosophy is the depreciation of life itself. All his actions articulate many of the different aspects of the nihilist that Nietzsche describes, all of which flows from the nihilist's depreciation of life as that which can have no value on its own. The Master hates life, because with no higher purpose, it's valueless. He has decided that life is worthless.

Resentment Consumes the Master

Nietzsche himself described several articulations of the nihilist way of thinking, and organized them all on a scale of evolution from the simple strong person through to the Overman, the one who defeats nihilism by overcoming it. A person's simple strength is their ability to create, and affirm that which they created. This is the active force of a living person.

Deleuze quotes from Nietzsche's notebooks: "Every body extends its power as far as it is able," and some bodies are more able than others. Not every body is equal, and in a head-to-head contest, the stronger force will always defeat the weaker. Strength itself won't fail through being conquered by a superior force, because this would only be one person defeated by another, stronger person. For this type of person, the simplest form of self-conscious life, life is a struggle, and the victor in the struggle becomes the Master of those he's conquered through his strength. Nietzsche calls this 'master morality' (not to be confused with the Master's morality), the one who says, "I am good, and you whom I've defeated are not quite as good as me." This is a force that affirms its own active creative power, and all its actions and judgments are based on this initial affirmation.

But this kind of strength is simple, a force that expressed itself honestly and openly. The strong force doesn't even conceive of cunning and guile, because it has no need of them. The strong force flexes its muscles in victory, and smiles the vacant grin of the jock showing off his trophy from the arm wrestling contest. The weak forces are identified by the strong force having defeated them. The weak is the one who develops guile, subterfuge, secrecy, and deceit. It's a testament to Nietzsche's black sense of humor that the weak, slavish forces are actually superior to the strong. With these methods, the weak becomes superior to the strong, and Nietzsche does consider weak forces to be superior to simple strong ones because they can develop talents of manipulation and scheming against which the rippling biceps of simple strength are useless.

After its defeat, the weak force whispers into the ear of the strong, like some priestly Iago, "You have defeated me, which makes you evil. Since evil opposes me, I am good." The weak force is priestly, says Nietzsche, because like a priest, its goal is to convince everyone to whom it speaks that what it says is the absolute, unchanging truth. The strong force is honest, with no conception of lying or scheming, so it believes the accusations of the weak force. The strong are defeated when they blame themselves for their own strength, and once that seed of self-doubt is implanted, it can't be forgotten.

The weak force doesn't affirm itself, but only defines itself in its relation to another, which it denounces and comes to hate. This is the kernel of what Nietzsche calls *ressentiment*, a French word meaning 'resentment' in English, but which Nietzsche, writing in German, chose for the subtleties of the word in the French language. This resentment is the key feature of nihilism: blaming others for your weakness and making the strong understand their strength as wrong, sinful.[2] In Nietzsche's picture of humanity, once resentment evolves, it infests all activity. So while one first resents the force that conquered you, eventually everyone resents everyone else.

The strong force comes to believe that it's wrong to be strong, and surrenders its drive to action, what Nietzsche famously called its will to power. All forces have will to power, because the *will to power* is simply the drive to action, to create the act that has never existed before and to affirm that act by doing it. A strong force fully corrupted by resentment is an entirely reactive force. A reactive force has no confidence in its own capacities to act, because it sees every action as evil and sinful, so does nothing except punish itself. Its resentment reduces a reaction force to mere self-punishment, a kind of masochistic twitching. Simm's Master is definitely no priest, no sinner, and no masochist, but instead considers himself the joyful destroyer of all. The kind of nihilism that fits the Master best is one of the most advanced kinds of nihilist.

The man of resentment is created by reactive forces which break down the capacity to act. Nietzsche describes the most advanced form of nihilism where the nihilist becomes able to act again, where the nihilist's will to power articulates itself as the will to nothingness, the affirmation of negativity. This will to nothingness is the will to universal destruction, which is precisely the Master's mission for his war against the universe, to build a new Time Lord empire based on his own drive for violence and death. And he has a wonderful time doing it. "Last of the Time Lords" opens with a musical number where the Master dances around his flying fortress taunting his prisoners, the Doctor and the Jones family. He plays a Scissor Sisters song, of all things, taunting them with

---

[2] While I would encourage people to read as much of Nietzsche's work as possible, some especially juicy anti-Christian material is in *Beyond Good and Evil*, the second essay of *The Genealogy of Morals*, and the appropriately titled, *The Anti-Christ*.

the lyric, "I can't decide whether you should live or die," laughing hysterically while he humiliates them. The Doctor is kept in a quasi-bird cage; the Joneses are spat-upon indentured servants. Many of his murders in "The Sound of Drums" are carried out with punch-lines: opening the door a crack to see if the reporter being sliced to death in the other room is still screaming, playing with his mask and kidding around with his cabinet ministers moments before he floods the room with deadly nerve gas, taunting and humiliating the American president before having him disintegrated. He's hateful and vengeful, and takes a tremendous joy in it. In a sense, he has overcome ressentiment because he's capable of action. But the Master's motivations are still those of a resentful man: the world is valueless to him, but he is determined to have as much fun setting fire to it all as possible. To quote a figure from another story, "Some men just want to watch the world burn." Alfred Pennyworth uses this phrase to describe The Joker in Christopher Nolan's *The Dark Knight*, but it also applies to John Simm's Master.

The Doctor's Overcoming

One character who has watched worlds burn is the Doctor himself, who, during the Time War, was responsible for the destruction of both the Dalek and Time Lord Civilizations. We learn this in the first season of the revived series, when Christopher Eccleston's Doctor was defined by the motivating forces of *ressentiment*: vengeance and hatred. This is openly directed against the Daleks for their role as antagonists of the Time War and so responsible for the destruction of Gallifrey and the Time Lord race. But a more general desire for vengeance and violence bubbled under the surface of Eccleston's performance early in the season, dispensing little mercy to those whom he saw as causing needless deaths for petty reasons, such as Cassandra in "The End of the World" (2005), and the Slitheen family in "World War Three" (2005).

The Doctor had seen worlds destroyed and the entire universe at stake; yet these puny people were casually planning mass murder for money. In Cassandra's case especially, he casually let her die. In "Dalek" (2005), the Doctor was faced with the possibility of living a nobler kind of life, which Rose showed him in her acts of mercy towards a Dalek, and pointing out the Doctor's own murderous rage that made him virtually unrecognizable: "What about you, Doctor?" she asks, "What are you changing into?"

Overcome by resentment and revenge, he's turning into the Master, the man who takes joy in annihilation, in destruction, in death. When he confronts Rose and the Dalek at the end of "Dalek," he understands precisely what he's letting himself turn into by giving in to his reactive forces, giving in to the desire for revenge. Seeing this, he turns against this transformation of vengefulness, and instead chooses to become something else. In terms of the morality he creates and articulates through his life, the regeneration of the Ninth into the Tenth Doctor begins at this point, when he perceives his desire for revenge for the baseness and venom that it really is, and he begins to live his life in a way that can be described in a phrase from Nietzsche: "Into all abysses I carry my beneficent Yes-saying!"[3]

This saying yes, this affirmation, is the celebration of life itself. It's not the simple pleasure the strong man takes in his own strength, but a far more difficult joy: being oneself overcome by hatred and revenge, but understanding it for the baseness that it is, and through this understanding overcoming hate itself. To overcome hate is Nietzsche's spirit of celebration, and the defining characteristic of the Overman.

In the Doctor's case, this celebration of life results from the overcoming of the need for revenge. When the Dalek Emperor in "The Parting of the Ways" (2005) calls the Doctor "the Great Exterminator," it recalls his actions during the Time War when he destroyed the Dalek fleets and Gallifrey. But when given the opportunity to destroy the Daleks again, he refuses. In this refusal is an affirmation of life, even if it's the life of his enemies. The Tenth Doctor embodies this principle even more fully, only taking life when it's necessary for greater survival, and approaching this choice with a great seriousness. Nietzsche quotes Buddha to explain the approach to one's enemies befitting one who overcomes *ressentiment*: "Not by enmity is enmity ended; by friendliness enmity is ended."[4]

When the Judoon police invade a London hospital in "Smith and Jones" (2007), the Tenth Doctor doesn't destroy the Judoon, as a resentful man would do, but delivers them the criminal they're hunting and lets them go, and they return the hospital to Earth. He

---

[3] *Thus Spake Zarathustra*, p. 114.

[4] Friedrich Nietzsche, *Ecce Homo* in *The Basic Writings of Nietzsche*, p. 686.

doesn't confront the Family of Blood in "Human Nature" (2007) and "The Family of Blood" (2007) until it's absolutely necessary, instead choosing to hide, waiting for them to die of natural causes. This, as Son-of-Mine explains, is an act of kindness. He who has overcome the desire for vengeance is strong enough to treat his enemies with kindness and respect. This is Nietzsche's Overman.

How Can a Degenerate Do All This?

Nowhere is this aspect of the Doctor's character illustrated more clearly than in his confrontation with John Simm's Master. This is a confrontation of enmity, the desire for revenge; with that which defeats enmity, what Nietzsche translated in the quote from Buddha as 'friendliness'. The Master acts in such a way that he draws anger from people, making them crave revenge, tricking them into allowing revenge to consume them. Disguised with their perception filters in "The Sound of Drums," Martha watches the Master taunting her family, his prisoners, on an airport tarmac, and is determined to kill him, determined to revenge. After the Doctor and Captain Jack are captured, and the Jones family forced into servitude, they desire the same.

> **FRANCINE JONES:** One day, if I have to wait a hundred years, I'm going to kill the Master.
>
> **TISH JONES:** I'll get him, even if it kills me . . . I swear to you, he's dead.

Meanwhile, Martha has spent the year between the two episodes gathering the parts for a gun that supposedly can kill a Time Lord stone dead, revenge for the slaughter he led. Yet when she finally confronts the Master, the gun destroyed and herself about to be executed, Martha interrupts his grandstanding speech with laughter. The weapon was a joke played on the Master. "As if I would expect her to kill," says the Doctor from his cage, since that would only replace enmity with enmity, a false victory that would be mere surrender to revenge. Of course, the reason the Master believed the ploy was because he does expect her to kill, to give in to vengeance and resentment, because he always does himself.

The Doctor defeats the Master not with violence, for such violence would only make him another Master. Instead, he takes his enemy in his arms and says, "I forgive you," sincere words that only the strongest of all people can say. This is the defeat of enmity with a gesture of friendship. When the Master is handcuffed and his empire erased from history, Francine still wants revenge, shaking with anger, pointing a gun at him. But the Doctor takes the gun away, saying, "You're better than him." The Doctor, just as his name says, literally makes his companions and friends better, better in Nietzsche's sense. The strength of the Doctor is the strength to let revenge go, to affirm and embrace friendship. He's beyond revenge, having overcome it.

Instead of building a weapon with which to kill in revenge, Martha inspired people all over the world with stories about the Doctor, and instructions to think about those stories at a certain time one year after the conquest of Earth, to turn the Master's telepathic satellite network against him. Martha's storytelling was the creative affirmation of she and the Doctor and everyone else on Earth. The Doctor says at the moment of his triumph, "Tell me the human race is degenerate now, when they can do this," using the satellite network to restore his bodily vitality which the Master had taken away. His words are a counterpoint to the nihilistic, jabbering Toclafane cyborgs, and the mission statement of his beneficient Yes! to life. Just because life is finite, with a slow, quiet endpoint, doesn't mean that life is worthless. The worth of life is in what we can do in the finitude of its existence every single day.

Life: A Celebration

"Man, a little, eccentric species of animal, which—fortunately—has its day; all on earth a mere moment, an incident, an exception without consequences, something of no importance . . . the earth itself, like every star, a hiatus between two nothingnesses . . . Something in us rebels against this view."[5] When this rebellion articulates itself as affirmation of the finite, the mere moment of life, it's at its noblest, its strongest. Man "fortunately has its day," Nietzsche says, glad that humanity is finite and will one day die entirely. An infinite being would require no effort to be strong, only patience, because an infinite number of events may pass over the course of infinite time. Part of the challenge of strength is that we each have only a small amount of time to achieve it. The Doctor himself may

---

[5] Nietzsche, *The Will to Power*, p. 169.

have had a few extra centuries more than his human friends, but his strength to forgive his enemy is no less impressive for his longer lifespan. Overcoming the desire for revenge, the nihilistic spiral of hate and enmity, is the mark of the strongest one, what Nietzsche calls the 'Overman'.

The Doctor is such a figure. He overcomes the forces that would end activity, who overcomes the forces of stability and sterility that embody death, who overcomes the specter of a world without change, a world of emptiness, a world without life. His beneficent affirmation overcomes the end of the universe itself when he shows that even though life is finite, that finitude doesn't equal meaninglessness. He and Martha inspire the people of Earth to affirm their own strength, and overcome their vengeful oppressor. The Doctor has the strength to recognize the finitude of existence and celebrate existence in its infinite potential. Where does Nietzsche's Overman carry his voice which all the time says yes? He carries it into the abyss.

The abyss is emptiness, meaninglessness, oblivion of all existence, which is precisely how the Master understands the universe. The Doctor has chosen the mission which he gave himself, which is to protect the flourishing of life in all its forms. No death is a mercy for the Doctor, because a death is the end of a life.

23

Schopenhauer's Master

KEN CURRY

We're fascinated by the problem of evil in the world. We apprehend the world as a struggle of good against evil. We explore the depths of the struggle in literature such as *Paradise Lost* or *The Divine Comedy*. And we especially enjoy the struggle when rendered in a light mode such as *Doctor Who*.

We know the Doctor is the good guy who will narrowly escape death and save the Earth from doom no matter how grim a situation he faces. We can't always tell immediately if the life forms he meets in his adventures are good guys or bad guys, but they rarely come in intermediate forms and are quickly sorted out. The Master stands above all the Doctor's other adversaries as the quintessential bad guy. The Doctor and the Master are evenly matched opponents. They're both Time Lords, and I shall argue even more closely matched than that. They're good and evil as two sides of the same coin, but since *Doctor Who* episodes are always comedies and not realities, evil will always lose by a thread to good and exit with the grim (actually delightful) promise of returning to entertain us in future episodes.

Arthur Schopenhauer is the quintessential pessimist philosopher. Born in 1788, he published his seminal work, *The World as Will and Representation*, in 1818–1819, at the age of thirty. Before Schopenhauer, Kant had insisted that we perceive the world through our various sense organs and form conceptions of the world through the filter of our mind. We can only know the world through our perception and conception of it and not through any direct access. Perception begins with external stimuli that elicit nerve impulses which the brain filters and renders into impressions. Thus light impinging on our eyes elicits nerve impulses that the brain converts to images which appear before us, even though the actual image is created in the brain. Conception is the more complex task of interpreting our perceptions in context with previous experience.

The realization that we experience the world through perception (physical sense) followed by conception (mental filter) is Kant's world of phenomena—things as they appear to us. Behind that world of phenomena and manifesting itself in our perceptions, was the world of noumena, the world independent of our mind and the world we could never know directly. Kant referred to noumenal objects in this world as things-in-themselves.

Schopenhauer refined Kant's ideas about the phenomenal world, the world of our perceptions and concepts, but his most original philosophical contribution was his interpretation of Kant's thing-in-itself, the noumenal world. Schopenhauer reasoned that the noumenal world was undifferentiated, and hence, he referred to it in the singular as the noumenon. He equated the noumenon with force or energy and called it Will. He equated energy with matter, thereby anticipating Einstein. The Will manifests itself in the phenomenal world of our mind as matter characterized in form and changing in time. The Will is part of each of us; a part we know only indirectly through our physical action and change. The Will is understood by us phenomenally as causality.

For Schopenhauer, the pessimist, the Will was a blind, pointless force, and because of its pointlessness, it was more likely to be harmful than beneficial. This sense of evil is aptly captured in Tennyson's line, "Nature red in tooth and claw." Accepting Schopenhauer's position, the Will is inherently evil. The Will is part of everything in the universe, part of each of us—a side of us we can glimpse through our inner self, but never know directly—a dark side of us. Consider this commentary from a world weary poet, Emily Brontë, a contemporary of Schopenhauer, from "I Am the Only Being" (17th May 1839):

'Twas grief enough to think mankind
All hollow, servile, insincere;
But worse to turn to my own mind,
And find the same corruption there.

Enter the Doctor with his dark side, the Master. The Master is part of the noumenal world of which we can have only a glimpse, but in the *Doctor Who* stories, the Master is the personification of evil, the personification of the Will. We're told repeatedly that the Master bears a special relationship with the Doctor.[1] We shall see just what that relationship is as we explore Schopenhauer's Will. The Master, as a personification of the Will, becomes fully part of our phenomenal world as we observe these light-hearted versions of the struggle between good and evil.

His Mind Is My Mind

Schopenhauer's most original philosophical contribution, a master stroke of philosophical reasoning, is the world as Will. Schopenhauer refers to Will as force manifested as causality in our phenomenal world. He insists that matter and Will are equivalent! Causality is a mode of understanding. Whatever exists in the world beyond our senses, causality is how we understand change in that world as we perceive and conceive it.

What we perceive as material change is no more than the exchange of energy and matter familiar to us from twentieth-century physics. But Schopenhauer expressed the idea clearly and forcefully early in the previous century! His unfortunate use of the word 'Will' instead of 'energy' or 'force' doomed him to be misunderstood. His insistence on the Will as an anthropomorphic will to live exacerbated the misunderstanding. If we understand 'will to live' metaphorically, we see that he meant no more than matter taking form through the exchange of energy and matter. In this way we understand what Schopenhauer meant in applying Will to both animate and inanimate objects. We understand change of any material form in terms of causality. Schopenhauer instructs us that the Will is the objectification of matter as material form to our subjective mind.

Schopenhauer reasoned that our bodies are objects in the phenomenal world, and as such, we could know our physical manifestation just as we know any other phenomenal object. But

---

[1] "Terror of the Autons," "The Mind of Evil," "The Claws of Axos," and "Colony in Space" (all 1971); "The Sea Devils" and "The Time Monster" (both 1972); "Frontier in Space" (1973); "The Deadly Assassin" (1976); "Logopolis" (1981); "Castrovalva" and "Time-Flight" (both 1982); "The King's Demons" (1983); "Planet of Fire" (1984); "Mark of the Rani" (1985); "The Ultimate Foe" (1986); and "Survival," (1989).

significantly, we also have an inner knowledge of ourselves (of our bodies) that we can't have of any other part of the phenomenal world. This inner knowledge, a nonverbal sense of ourselves, is manifested in bodily action, both voluntary and involuntary. Schopenhauer called this inner sense Will. He pointed out, long before Freud's explanations, that we can't find a causal connection between willing something to be so and the actual act of motion. Consider what appears to be your direct, willful act. Just because you say or think that you'll do something doesn't actually make it happen. We can find no direct causal relationship between a will-ful act and the act itself. Likewise with our emotions, we can't pin down a causal relationship between the action accompanying the emotion and the sense of the emotion. For example, if we're sud-denly startled, our pulse quickens, but we've no direct sense of the pulse quickening.

Schopenhauer reasoned that our bodies are objects as any other object that we can know subjectively by the same perception and conception through which we're related to the noumenal world. He went on to reason that we each have an inner knowledge of our bodies that is direct, non-sensory, and non-intellectual. This special and very limited type of knowledge gives us a glimpse of the noumenon that Kant thought was beyond us. The view is largely incomplete, "Consciousness is the mere surface of our mind, and of this, as of the globe, we do not know the interior but only the crust."[2] Thus Schopenhauer showed us how we could access, however superficially, the noumenal world, and the thing-in-itself as Will. Our bodies, like other material objects, are the objectifica-tion of the Will to our subjective selves.

When the Doctor says of the Master, "In many ways we have the same mind" ("Logopolis," 1981), we should take him literally. The Master is just an aspect of the Doctor; he's the Will that exists in all of us. But in the *Doctor Who* story, the Master is personified (made part of the phenomenal world) for our entertainment and ease of understanding the conflict of good and evil. Why's the Will evil? The Will is energy or force. We don't understand any purpose driving it. Our sense of causality is the experience of *what* it does, not *why*. Our "laws of physics" just lay out the patterns of causal-ity with which we're familiar, not the reasons for those patterns.

---

[2] *The World as Will and Representation*, Volume II, p. 136.

No sense of 'why' is apparent outside of theological imaginations. We might ascribe to pessimists this first principle, "The undisciplined use of force is inherently evil." Schopenhauer certainly thought that the pointlessness of the Will was sufficient reason to cast it as evil.

The Master's Will

The Master made his first appearance in "Terror of the Autons," shown in January of 1971. The Doctor was played by Jon Pertwee; the Master by Roger Delgado. This episode best illustrates the various themes that characterize the relationship between the Doctor and the Master, which appear in endless variations throughout the series.

The episode begins with the Master's TARDIS appearing on a carnival lot. An unpleasant carnival person, apparently the owner of the carnival, accosts the Master, rudely asking him who he is and telling him he doesn't need a conjurer, a reference to the abrupt appearance of the TARDIS. The carnival owner identifies himself as Louis de Rossini, but the Master tells him disparagingly he is Hugh Russell.

Recall that Schopenhauer had reasoned that the noumenal world, being largely inaccessible to us, should be considered as one thing, the noumenon. Therefore, the Will is one thing, so while we're identifying the Will as the Master and as a counterpart of the Doctor, we must also realize that the Master exists in each of us, including Hugh Russell. Hugh has assumed a fancy European name, Louis de Rossini, but his inner self, his own Master, knows better. The Master hypnotizes him and tells him that unfortunately he, the Master, needs Hugh. We may have an evil side in the Master, but that evil side is stuck with our good side.

We flash to the Doctor before whom a man in a bowler hat, obviously a Time Lord, appears to inform him that the Time Lord Tribunal has sent him to warn the Doctor that the Master is on earth expressly to kill the Doctor. That information is, of course, for the audience along with the conversation that follows. The Doctor expresses contempt for the Master and refers to him as an "unimaginative plodder." Bowler hat reminds the Doctor that the Master's degree in Cosmic Science was of a higher class than the Doctor's. The Doctor replies that he was a late bloomer. The Doctor is obviously wrestling with his own shortcomings.

The Autons are a race called the Nestene. They need plastic to materialize. When we see them briefly as they really are (the thing-in-itself?), they appear as bright lights—a familiar movie visual cue for a pure energy life form. The Master wants to help the Nestene take over the Earth (after all, they're aspects of the same Will), so he assumes the identity of a military man, a colonel, and enlists Mr. Rex Farrel, owner of a plastics factory that isn't doing well financially. Farrel is hypnotized by what we should understand is now the Master as Farrel's evil counterpart in the hope of reversing the financial state of his family business. The Master has no obvious reason for helping the Nestines or for using the unfortunate Mr. Farrel. The Master is the Will personified, a pointless force more likely to be harmful than beneficial.

Meanwhile, the Doctor is aware of the Nestene invasion and has assumed correctly that the Master will be helping them. He has an assistant, Jo Grant, who serves for conversation to let the audience know what's going on, as well as getting into dangerous situations from which she must be rescued and in turn rescue the Doctor from his own folly. The Doctor tells Jo that vanity is the Master's weakness. Jo goes to the plastics factory ostensibly to look around, but she's captured by the Master. The Master, and now he's the Doctor's counterpart, tells Jo that curiosity is the Doctor's weakness and sends her back to the Doctor, hypnotized to report that she has found nothing suspicious.

Mr. Farrel has a factory manager, Mr. McDermott, who becomes suspicious of the Master's intentions. The Master murders Mr. McDermott in front of the hypnotized Mr. Farrel who expresses no sense of surprise. The Master is Mr. Farrel's dark side eliminating Mr. McDermott who stands in the way of what Farrel thinks will be financial success. The plot thickens as Mr. Farrel Senior appears, having been alerted to funny business by Mr. McDermott before that unfortunate man's demise. We see in Farrel Junior a man who wants desperately to show his father that he can run the family business with the same success as Dad. But he just doesn't have good business sense or force of personality.

He's the archetypical character of tragedy with his fatal flaw. He has now committed murder. We saw the Master actually commit the murder, but with no opposition from Farrel, and we understand that the power of the evil Will is controlling the unfortunate Farrel. The Master confronts Mr. Farrel Senior with an attempt to hypnotize him, but that fails. The Master comments, "Your will is exceptionally strong. One might say dangerously strong." Here we should understand the struggle for good and evil is between Mr. Farrel Senior and his Master. Farrel Senior wins the first round, but the Will is powerful. The Master puts a plastic doll in Farrel Senior's car as he drives off to his home from the plastics factory. The doll is of course a Nestene who kills Farrel at his home.

Back to the Carnival

The Master leads the Doctor to the carnival to destroy him. Rossini captures the Doctor, Jo had followed the Doctor and rescues him, then Jo and the Doctor are captured by Autons (Nestene) disguised as (plastic) police. They are rescued in turn by the Brigadier, a character who serves the plot in a similar manner as Jo Grant, but with military authority to bring brute force to bear where finesse won't work. The Master responds to the Doctor's escape, "He's an interesting adversary. I admire him in many ways." No surprise at this statement of self admiration.

The plot continues with a series of action scenes culminating at a radio tower where the Nestene can apparently come through the tower from outer space, if the Master just turns the correct knob in the tower control room. We see the Master in the control room when the Doctor appears just in time to tell the Master that the Nestene will kill the Master as well as all earthlings. Somehow the Master hadn't considered that possibility before agreeing to help the Nestene. Apparently, being good in Cosmic Science leaves deficiencies elsewhere.

The Doctor and the Master cooperate to close the channel and thwart the Nestene invasion. The cooperation of good and evil is a common theme in *Doctor Who* that aptly reflects instances in our own world. They express the *Angst* we all feel when we're in positions of having to cooperate in a situation devoid of trust. They succeed in closing the channel (of course), and the Master escapes (of course). Mr. Farrel makes his final tragic appearance. No longer needed by the Master, his fate is sealed. He's still under hypnosis, and disguised as the Master, tries to shoot the Doctor, but is killed instead by one of the Brigadier's men. The Doctor reminds Jo that he has the Master's dematerialization circuit, so the Master is trapped on Earth. Jo observes that the Doctor doesn't seem very worried. He replies that he's looking forward to the next encounter. Of course that tells the audience that the Master will return for more adventure, but it also points to our fascination with evil and danger—with our own dark sides, with the Will.

The Master appeared in several episodes in 1971 and returned for two episodes in 1972. One important appearance came in "The Sea Devils," shown in February of 1972 with the same cast as the previous year. The Sea Devils are a life form that evolved on Earth, but chose to live under the sea. The Master is trying to help them take over the planet (what else?). Continuing with our analysis of the Doctor having an evil side that is the Master, we understand the Doctor to be a tormented character with a love-hate relationship with Earth. Happily for us and for the series, his good side keeps winning over his evil side. The victory of good over evil is an important escape for us in a world where evil seems so prevalent.

The story opens with the Master apparently a prisoner of the British military in a castle on an island. The commander is Colonel Trenchard. We learn as the story unfolds that the Master controls the Colonel (through hypnosis) and has convinced him that he and the Master are working to stop enemy agents. Nearby ships are being sunk by prehistoric, intelligent life forms, the Sea Devils. A sea fort is in the middle of the area where the ships are going down. We can guess that it's the Sea Devil hangout. Also nearby is a naval base under the control of Captain Hart. The scene thus set, we see the Doctor and Jo visiting the Master in prison. That's just to let us know where all the characters are at the start and to introduce us to Colonel Trenchard. Here we find a man who advances in the British military because of his of good birth and quite beyond his inherent abilities. He's keenly aware of his shortcomings and will do anything to appear to be a hero, a patriot. He's a tragic figure and the Master is his evil side. We know from the start this man is doomed.

Colonel Trenchard has seen the Sea Devils and now believes he's helping the Master to thwart their invasion. The Master tells Trenchard, "All your troubles will soon be over." We know that the Master has little more use for the Colonel and will dispose of him. The Doctor and Jo get back to Captain Hart and convince him that the Sea Devils are mobilizing to take over the Earth. The Master invents a device for communicating with the Sea Devils and calls them to the castle. Captain Hart sends in the troops and the action, already moving faster than the plot, speeds up. Colonel Trenchard tries to call the Ministry for help, but can't get through. This frustration points out the little esteem in which his superiors hold him and he understands all too well what a failure he's been. But here we see a poignant twist. Mr. Farrel from "Terror of the Autons" is simply killed in the end, a victim of his own desire to show his father that he could be successful in the family business. We feel no more than a modest sympathy for him. At the last minute, Colonel Trenchard understands he's played the fool for his own vanity, his Master. He's well-born and in true British fashion (what the British audience will expect), he turns hero, fighting and dying to defend the castle. The Doctor and Captain Hart find him just after he's killed. The Doctor asks Hart, "What would you say was Trenchard's strongest characteristic?" Hart replied, "Patriotism, I suppose." "Precisely," the Doctor observed, "the Master used that patriotism as a weapon." The Master is the evil aspect in all of us. The Doctor can speak of the Master in Trenchard with as much familiarity as if it were his own evil Master. Indeed, we all see, as Brontë did, the Master in others and occasionally in ourselves. All Masters are aspects of one—the Will.

The Doctor goes diving to the seafloor near the fort and is (of course) captured by the Sea Devils. They're living in a building (the sea fort?) with rooms apparently filled with air, not water—fortunate for the Doctor and the Master who's also present. "The Master is the personification of evil," the Doctor warns the Sea Devils. The Sea Devils must also be subject to the Will, and the Doctor reasonably expects the Sea Devils to sense evil as he does. They're presented to us, not as evil themselves, but as a threat to humans pressing a case for control of an Earth they once ruled. We might, as the Doctor has done, reasonably expect the Sea Devils to have their own Masters. Unfortunately the character of the Sea Devils is never explored. They march the Doctor off to await execution. He escapes and is recaptured. Several scenes later, the Sea Devils put the Master in the same cell as the Doctor. Once again, the Doctor and Master must cooperate to save each other and to save the Earth. They escape and the Sea Devil lair is destroyed. The Master feigns illness, hypnotizes someone and puts a Master mask on them to fool the Doctor (hasn't he seen this trick before?), and escapes, ready to return and delight us again.

Escape to *Doctor Who*

Schopenhauer unfolds for us the World as Will and Representation. The world as we know it with spatial, temporal, and causal relationships is a product of our minds. We're "hard wired" to experience the world in a certain way and we can never know what the world, the noumenon, really is. Whatever it is, it manifests itself through our perceptions and the concepts of our minds to create our representation of the world. Causality is particularly important. It's the way we organize and understand the changes that we perceive in matter.

Schopenhauer's most brilliant piece of philosophy was understanding that we could get an inkling of the noumenon, the Will, through our inner self. This inner self gives us a sense of the Will, the blind force, the energy, that we understand in our phenomenal world causes change in matter. Schopenhauer saw the Will as evil, precisely because it was pointless. Events could unfold phenomenally in any number of ways. Most unfoldings wouldn't be favorable for the subject of those unfoldings. The pointlessness of the universe was terrifying for Schopenhauer, and all share to some degree that terror in the vastness of the universe and the obvious insignificance of our position it in. We frequently feel helpless and at the mercy of the Will, but the Will has no mercy. Schopenhauer writes at length about temporary escape from our plight through art. He assumes an intelligent person who can immerse in art or music and detach from the world.

For the masses, Schopenhauer saw little hope. But now we have television and *Doctor Who*. This is a trivial escape, not at all what Schopenhauer had in mind, but we do use it as an escape. We watch the forces of good and evil, as the Will imposes its cruelty on us, but in a trivial manner that amuses rather than oppresses. We see ourselves in the various characters and project ourselves into the stories. Schopenhauer's philosophy can teach us much about ourselves, whether applied through the light-hearted approach with *Doctor Who* or the more serious study of Schopenhauer's writings themselves. The god Apollo advises us through his oracle at Delphi, "Know thyself." I suggest you use Schopenhauer as a guide to follow this ancient and most excellent advice. Remember Brontë!

24

Sympathy for the Master

PAULA SMITHKA

MASTER: Can't you hear it? Listen—Listen—Listen—Listen! Every minute, every second, every beat of my hearts, there it is, calling to me. Please listen!

DOCTOR: I can't hear it.

MASTER: *Listen*!

DOCTOR: I heard it. . . . What's inside your head?!

—"The End of Time, Part 1" (2009)

The Master is described as the "quintessential villain."[1] But is he, really? It's clear the Master wants to lord over humans and even Time Lords. He demands to be recognized as *the Master*, not merely in name but as a sovereign—the one who holds the power of life and death over all of his subjects.

In "The Sound of Drums" (2007) he, as Harold Saxon, gets elected Prime Minister of Great Britain, brings the Toclafane to help him establish his dominion over Earth, kills the US president, ages the Doctor, and unleashes destruction on the human race. His closing remarks to this episode are:

And so it came to pass that the human race fell, and the Earth was no more. And I looked down upon my new dominion as Master of all; and I thought it good.

In "The Last of the Time Lords" (2007), the TARDIS has been cannibalized and turned into a paradox machine and the aged Doctor,

---

[1] Ken Curry, in Chapter 23 of this volume.

reduced in size, is kept in a bird cage. When the Master is "reconstituted"[2] in "The End of Time, Part 1," we see a Master who gives no thought to those who effected his reconstitution. Lucy Saxon, the Master's "Earth-girl" wife, begs him, "You're killing them!" The Master's response is, "Oh, let them die; they're just the first." His reconstituted body is "so very" hungry.[3] He devours any food he can get his hands on, including whole human beings. No, there's not much to like about the Master. We think him cruel, immoral, and evil. Yet, the Master may simply be a paradigmatic "world historical individual," characterized by Georg Wilhelm Friedrich Hegel in *Reason in History*.

My Lord, Master . . .

Human beings are social creatures. We need other people to acknowledge our existence; we need to see ourselves through the eyes of others. Others are mirrors for us. Hegel argues that without others, we only have self-certainty; that is, we're only aware of our own existence, desires, and our place in the world of things, but we lack the *truth of certainty of self*.[4]

For example, you're planning to attend some special social event—a New Year's Eve party, a Mardi Gras Ball, a prom—you get all dressed up in your gown or tux, accoutrements all in place. What's your question to your significant other (party, ball), or your parents and siblings (prom) when you emerge from your dressing room? It's: "How do I look?" But, why would you ask this question? You know you look good, but that's just not enough. You want recognition from others—you want them to *confirm* that you look great. In Hegel's terms, you had certainty of self when you emerged from your dressing room (you know you look good), now have *truth of certainty of self* because others acknowledge you as gorgeous. You've seen yourself "mirrored" in their eyes.[5] This is an

---

[2] I use 'reconstituted' because 'resurrected' isn't quite accurate since it's not the whole of the Master's body which returns.

[3] We see this in Matt Smith's Eleventh Doctor in Episode 1, "The Eleventh Hour" (2010).

[4] Hegel, *Phenomenology of Spirit*, especially Section IV: "The Truth of Self-Certainty."

[5] This is not a subtle borrowing, though one has to be a fan of the film *Manhunter* (1986), based on Thomas Harris's novel, *Red Dragon*, where Hannibal Lecter makes his debut in the form of Brian Cox.

oversimplified version of the process of recognition, but it's something to which we all can relate.

The Master, like us, craves recognition from others. He needs to be acknowledged as "the Master," in the eyes of his subjects. But to be a 'master', one needs a slave to acknowledge a master as master. Hegel, in his famous section of the *Phenomenology of Spirit*, "Independence and Dependence of Self-Consciousness: Lordship and Bondage," commonly referred to as "the Master-Slave Dialectic" by philosophers, details the struggle for recognition between two self-consciousnesses. In other words, two people who are each aware of him- or herself, each have certainty of self, and come to "blows" when each runs into a consciousness like itself. Since "self-consciousness is Desire,"[6] the first thing a single self-consciousness tries to do is to preserve itself against other things—against an "other."

Hegel says, "[self-consciousness] preserves itself by separating itself from this its inorganic nature, and by consuming it."[7] Thus, an "other" is merely an object for the self-consciousness's desire—"one being only *recognized*, the other only *recognizing*."[8] In order for a living being to survive, nutrition is necessary; thus, food is an object for the living being which consumes it. We see this exemplified in the Master, newly reconstituted in "The End of Time, Part 1." He devours food with a voraciousness we find surprising, and perhaps unbefitting of a Time Lord or even a human being. What we find frightening and most disturbing, as does Ginger and his companion, is the skeletal remains of the workers in the sandwich truck. We realize that the Master has devoured them! "Dinner time!" yells the Master and we understand that Ginger and the companion are next. Why we are so disturbed by the thought of the Master consuming whole human beings is our realization that they, like the Master, are self-conscious beings. They deserve to be recognized, and not treated as mere objects—like a sandwich. Yet, the Master only sees them as objects of his desire.

Seeing other self-consciousness beings as mere objects fails to bring the desired recognition a particular self-consciousness wants. That's the catch. According to Hegel, the recognition ultimately sought must come from an equal and independent consciousness,

---

[6] Hegel, *Phenomenology of Spirit*, paragraph 174, p. 109.

[7] Paragraph 171, p. 107.

[8] Paragraph 186, p. 113.

not from a "lesser" and dependent consciousness. In other words, genuine recognition can only happen *between equals*—there must be a mutual recognizing of each other; a kind of mutual respect. For example, take two people in a crowded pub. A man spies an interesting woman. After some moments, the woman realizes that she's being ogled. She's the object of his gaze. Similarly, he becomes the object of her gaze. Each now sees the other as an object of desire. If the "process of recognition" stops here, then each is nothing more than a piece of meat for the other (though not in the reconstituted Master's sense). The term 'sex object' is apt here. But no one (well, most people) don't want to be seen simply as "a piece of meat." Hegel says:

> Self-consciousness is, to begin with, simple being-for-self, self equal through the exclusion from itself of everything else. For it, its essence and absolute object is 'I'; and in this immediacy, or in this [mere] being, of its being-for-self, it is an *individual*. What is 'other' for it is an unessential, negatively characterized object. But the 'other' is also a self-consciousness; one individual confronted by another individual. Appearing thus immediately on the scene, they are for one another like ordinary objects, *independent* shapes, individuals submerged in the being [or immediacy] of *Life*— . . . Each is indeed certain of its own self, but not of the other, and therefore its own self-certainty still has no truth.[9]

Instead, we want to be recognized as an equal and respected, and not be a mere thing to be used by another. So, if the recognition process continues, the two people will meet, dialogue, and get to know one another; they form a bond as human being to human being, self-consciousness to self-consciousness. According to Hegel:

> They *recognize* themselves as *mutually recognizing* one another. . . . But according to the Notion of recognition this is possible only when each is for the other what the other is for it, only when each in its own self through its own action, and again through the action of the other, achieves this pure abstraction of being-for-self.[10]

The Master, however, seems to look for genuine recognition in all the wrong places. He thinks that by lording over members of other

---

[9] Paragraph 186, p. 113.
[10] Paragraph 184, p. 112 and paragraph 186, p. 113.

species (such as humans and the Toclafane) he'll achieve the recognition he desires. But, according to Hegel, this is a myth, since a master needs a slave to be acknowledged as 'master' or 'lord'—it's inherently an unequal relationship. Ironically, the Master actually has the desired recognition from an equal but he can't see it. He can't see it because he's really an instrument of history; a world-historical individual whose life is to fulfill a destiny, as we'll see.

The Struggle unto Death, and Its Irony

The process of recognition and the attainment of "truth of certainty of self" requires the staking of one's life, according to Hegel. Recall, self-consciousness is desire. Thus, when two people, each a particular self-consciousness, meet, each seeks to consume the other. They are at first a mere object for the other. There's risk involved in the sense that one may not "win" the appropriate recognition desired. One could be dismissed as insignificant, unimportant, not a *person*, and remain a *thing* for the other. Hegel states:

> Thus the relation of the two self-conscious individuals is such that they prove themselves and each other through a life-and-death struggle. They must engage in this struggle, for they must raise their certainty of being *for themselves* to truth, both in the case of the other and in their own case. And it is only through staking one's life that freedom is won.[11]

Consider a boxing match. Each contender wants to win the match and gain recognition as "the Champ" from the opponent as well as the fans. They're "objects" for each other to be "boxed" until the match ends or one can't continue the match. Thus, each contender stakes his own life because one could be seriously injured and possibly killed, and certainly stakes his reputation on the match. Neither wants the recognition of being the 'loser', so they battle each other in the ring. The struggle of one contender against the other continues until "time" is called and there's a 'winner'. The winner has achieved the recognition of fans, the opponent, the media, and himself as champion—he's the *master*, or "*lord* of the ring." The loser has demonstrated that he's an inferior boxer; he's the *slave*, or "*bondsman* of the ring." Of the outcome of the struggle of the two self-consciousnesses, Hegel says:

---

[11] Paragraph 187, p. 114.

> Since to begin with they are unequal and opposed, and their reflection into a unity has not yet been achieved, they exist as two opposed shapes of consciousness; one is the independent consciousness whose essential nature is to be for itself, the other is the dependent consciousness whose essential nature simply to live or to be for another. The former is lord, the other is bondsman.[12]

"This trial by death, however, does away with the truth which was supposed to issue from it, and so, too, with the certainty of self generally,"[13] Hegel claims. In other words, the champion was supposed to attain truth of certainty of self. He was supposed to gain the recognition of equals. Yet, who gives the champ his recognition? The opponent, but he was defeated; he's not an equal. The fans, but they're not boxers, or if they are, they're "wanna-be-boxers." In either case, neither are equals of the champ, he alone is *the* champion and can remain so only as long as he remains undefeated in the ring. If he's defeated, he's lost his "lord of the ring" status and become the "slave of the ring" and the new champion has become lord.

The truth that results from the struggle, according to Hegel, is that even though the master or lord *thinks* he's an independent consciousness, needing no one because he's "top of the heap," he's really a dependent consciousness. He's a dependent consciousness because he needs others to retain his status as *the champion* and recognized as such. Without others, he's no *champion* at all. The defeated boxer, on the other hand, realizes that he's lost a match and returns to training just as he did before. The fans, either elated or disappointed about the outcome of the match, leave the arena without need for the contenders, until the next time. The "lord of the ring" alone is the one left needing the others. How ironic.

My Name Is 'the Master'

Having successfully repaired the Gate, which is a medical device that transmits a template for a medical remedy across an entire planet, that's in the possession of Joshua Naismith and his daughter, Abigail, "Harold Saxon" is praised for his excellent work. "My name is the Master," the Master sneers. Despite having been con-

---

[12] Paragraph 189, p. 115.
[13] Paragraph 188, p. 114.

fined to a straight jacket by Naismith's security guards—Naismith is right to be cautious of the Master—the Master is poised to effect his plan to lord over the human race and Earth. No mere straight jacket, a collar, and a leash can restrict the power of the Master, however. He dramatically breaks free and jumps into the Gate, turning the human race into himself; well, except for Wilfred and Donna—Donna doesn't change because she's been the Doctor-Donna and exposed to the Time Vortex; but why not Wilfred? That's a good question, and one that remains unanswered—I suspect because he's got to be the one to knock four times to fulfill the prophecy of the Doctor's "death." Of course the Doctor doesn't change, because he's not human and neither do the Cactuses ('Cacti' is racist, after all!) because they're not human either, and the Master set the template to human.

"Hopeless was I, destitute and dying! Look at me now!" the Master exclaims to the Doctor and the others present, as each human begins to change into himself. Now that he's "upgraded" the humans, albeit not in Cyberman fashion, he can control the planet, providing himself with the "proper" recognition that he seeks and deserves; or so he thinks. There's something paradoxical, however, about being both the Master and the Slave of yourself, or rather yourselves, in this case. One would think that if each new individual Master really was *the Master*, then they'd all simultaneously have the same thoughts, something more along the lines of *Star Trek*'s Borg. Instead, the "real" Master governs the other Masters, albeit with no dissent. All the Masters of the world are in *Gleichschaltung*; the regime is accomplished: the Master race achieved.[14]

The Master as a World-Historical Individual

The Master has trampled on the values most humans hold sacred: individuality, autonomy, respect. He invaded human's dreams, disrupting what's to be a time of rejuvenation; he kills (and sometimes cannibalizes) them; and he's taken away their individuality and autonomy, and made them himself, without their consent. We don't like the Master, but he's a world-historical individual, in Hegel's

---

[14] *Gleichschaltung* is a term used in Nazi Germany to "bring into line" or "co-ordinate" aspects of German life, such as business, commerce, and social attitudes, under totalitarian control.

sense. He's driven by passion and self-aggrandizement to accomplish what he thinks are his own goals of mastery and domination, even though they're part of a larger, more universal, plan. As Hegel puts it:

> A world-historical individual is not so sober as to adjust his ambition to circumstances; nor is he very considerate. He is devoted, come what may, to one purpose. Therefore such men may treat other great and even sacred interests inconsiderately—a conduct which indeed subjects them to moral reprehension. But so mighty a figure must trample down many an innocent flower, crush to pieces many things in its path.[15]

The Master is good at destroying things and people; that's why he's the "quintessential villain."

He can't help but be on a "Quest for Mastery"; his passions drive him. Robert Tucker explains that when Hegel uses the term 'passions', he "has in mind the range of emotions which center in the will to be great; pride, ambition, the love of fame, the craving for power, the urge to conquer."[16] This, indeed, describes the Master. "Mastery is self-seeking in that it gives the world-historical individual affirmation of his proud self-image." Recall, however, that the desired recognition must come from an equal; the master-slave relationship is unequal and it's the master-consciousness that's held in bondage, dependent on others for their recognition. The Master has the recognition of an equal from the Doctor but he can't acknowledge it, because he's entirely too consumed with his own self-aggrandizement. According to Tucker:

> Hegel clearly conceives the passion for self-aggrandizement as a kind of fanaticism, a condition in which the individual is driven compulsively by forces within over which he has no control and can exercise no constraint. (p. 270)

In "The End of Time, Part 2" (2010) there's an emotionally moving scene between the Doctor and the Master after the Master has turned all of the humans into himself. The Doctor is restrained in a chair and the Master is interrogating him regarding the location of the TARDIS.

---

[15] Hegel, *Reason in History*, p. 43.
[16] "The Cunning of Reason in Hegel and Marx," p. 270.

DOCTOR: You could be so wonderful. You're a genius; you're stone-cold brilliant, you are! I swear, you really are. But you can be so much more. You could be beautiful—a mind like that! We could travel the stars together. It would be my *honor*. 'Cause you don't need to own the universe; just see it. Having the privilege to see the whole of time and space, that's ownership enough.

MASTER: Would it stop then? The noise in my head?

DOCTOR: I can help.

MASTER: Don't know what I'd be without that noise . . .

DOCTOR: Don't know what I'd be without you.

MASTER: (*emotionally and tearing up*) . . . yeah.

Wilfred then interrupts asking about the noise and we hear the story of the Master's childhood experience looking into the untempered schism; into the Time Vortex itself.

In true world-historical individual fashion, the moment of sincerity and mutual recognition between the two Time Lords can't last long. The Master, compulsively driven by his passions, reflects on the source of the signal, the constant four drum beats in his head; the Doctor offers to find the signal together. The Master then surmises that it's coming "from so far way . . . from the end of time." In true Master form, he declares that the prophecy shown to the Doctor, that "something's returning," is "me!" He then realizes that the noise in his head is now manifested in six billion other heads. If they were all triangulated, they'd find the source of the signal. The Master re-emerges . . .

Along with the passions and drive of the world historical individual comes a price, however. A world-historical individual will pursue the quest for mastery to the injury of his own health, and perhaps even his own life. The drive consumes his whole life; all energy is devoted to accomplishing the goal that must be achieved, "the founding of an empire, the conquest of a foreign nation, or the establishment of a new order of civilization." Tucker states of the world historical individual's quest for mastery: "it is self-destructive in that it takes a tragic toll of his life-energies and happiness. He sacrifices to it his health, his calm and enjoyment, and even his life itself" (p. 70).

The Master is shot by his earth-wife Lucy Saxon in the "Last of the Time Lords." He refuses to regenerate, despite the pleas from the Doctor to do so. In "The End of Time," Parts 1 and 2, we see the life-energy of the reconstituted Master being used up; his appearance altering into skeletal form then back to his Time Lord form. "The Gate wasn't enough," the Doctor says, to heal the Master's body. "This body was born from death. All it can do is die," says the Master, but even still he strives to conquer.

The Master: The Slave of the Time-Lord Cunning of Reason

Hegel portrays world-historical individuals as the means by which history, or World Spirit, must unfold. The great, strong individuals of history who have made significant contributions, such as Abraham Lincoln, Martin Luther King, Jr., John F. Kennedy, Gandhi, Queen Victoria, Wagner, Julius Caesar, or Napoleon, whether we judge their contributions to be positive or negative, they are, according to Hegel, the tools of the Cunning of Reason. As individuals they have passion out of which they act, but their passion is in service of history's progress. According to Hegel:

> The particular has its own role to play in world history; it is finite and must, as such, perish. It is the particular that exhausts itself in the struggle, and part of which is destroyed. . . . It is not the general idea that involves itself in opposition and combat exposes itself to danger; it remains in the background, untouched and uninjured. This may be called the *cunning of Reason*—that it sets the passions to work for itself, while that through which it develops itself pays the penalty and suffers the loss. (*Reason in History*, pp. 43–44)

The Master is the tool by which the Time Lords make their return and the attempt to restore Gallifrey. He's their pawn.

We learn from the Master the origin of the noise in his head—the constant four drum beats—in a story that he tells Wilfred in "The End of Time, Part 2" just after the emotional dialogue between the Doctor and the Master, where each recognized the other as equal, even if only for a short time. The Master tells us that, as a child of eight, he was taken for initiation. Such initiations require the young Time Lords to stare into the untempered schism, a gap in reality that allows one to see into the Time Vortex itself, as we're informed by the Doctor. And, the Doctor says, "It hurts." the

Master's initiation was done at night—a scary thing even for a young Time Lord. "I heard it calling to me—the drums. The never-ending drums," says the Master.

The drums remained a part of the Master's consciousness since that time—we might assume something along nine hundred plus years, because the Master reminisces with the Doctor in the waste-land scene of "The End of Time, Part 1" about them running through the red grass fields of his father's estate on Gallifrey. The Doctor and other Time Lords thought the Master was insane, and it's even recorded that way in Time-Lord history. The drums were thought to be a symptom of that insanity, but not so. The drums beating in a rhythm of four is the heart-beat of a Time Lord. The Master is the connection required to free the remaining Time Lords in the time lock and to restore Gallifrey. Driven by his passions, the Master succeeds in opening the time lock and the Time Lords return. Also in the self-aggrandizing spirit of a world-historical individual, he initially taunts them with his success at turning the human race into the Master race and suggests he'll do that for the Time Lords as well. Lord President, Rassilon, reverses the Master's success and restores each human to his or her original form—not because he's kind and wants to help humans—the restoration of Gallifrey entails the destruction of Earth and all its inhabitants—but merely to demonstrate to the Master that he can. The Master isn't getting the recognition he desires from the Time Lords—he's been their tool all along. Rassilon tells him, "You were diseased, albeit diseased of our own making." Realizing he's not getting that desired recognition, he asks the Time Lords to allow him to ascend with them in their becoming beings of pure consciousness. He's rejected. He's still their slave.

The Doctor, meanwhile, deals with his own dilemma: whether to kill Rassilon or the Master. The Master, after all, was the link used by the Time Lords to free them from the time lock that promises the end of time itself. Rassilon seeks to restore Gallifrey at the expense of Earth and time. The Doctor destroys the controls to the Gate which was a means for the Time Lords' return, but in this struggle, the Master recognizes his own dependent consciousness—the need for recognition as 'Master' from others. He finally becomes an independent consciousness when he stands up to the Time Lords, killing Rassilon. Hegel says:

> Let us now cast a look at the fate of these world-historical individuals. . . . they were not what is commonly called happy . . . they achieved

[their aim] through toil and labor. . . . Thus, they attained no calm enjoyment. Once their objective is attained, they fall off like empty hulls from the kernel. They die early like Alexander, they are murdered like Caesar, transported to Saint Helena like Napoleon. (p. 41)

Though the fate of the Master is unclear at the end of the episode, he's no longer a dependent master-consciousness, but attains the freedom that, according to Hegel, is inherent in slave-consciousness. He no longer needs or desires the recognition of others and, he's free from the bondage of the Time-Lord Cunning of Reason; well, at least for now.[17]

---

[17] This chapter's title is not so subtly borrowed from The Rolling Stones, "Sympathy for the Devil," *Beggars Banquet* (Decca, 1968).

25

Is the Doctor the Destroyer of Worlds?

ROMAN ALTSHULER

"**I** name you forever: You are the destroyer of worlds!" With this pronouncement, Davros concludes his role in "Journey's End" (2008). It's a role in which he oversees both the revelation and the explosive fulfillment of a prophecy made by Dalek Caan: that the Doctor's soul will be revealed. At a pivotal moment, when both Martha and Jack threaten mass destruction if their Doctor (and the Earth) isn't released, the Doctor seems to recognize that the prophecy is coming true. Davros helpfully explains:

> The man who abhors violence, never carrying a gun. But this is the truth, Doctor: you take ordinary people and you fashion them into weapons. Behold your children of time transformed into murderers. I made the Daleks, Doctor. You made this.

> Already I have seen them sacrifice today for their beloved Doctor... How many more? Just think, how many have died in your name?

> The Doctor, the man who keeps running, never looking back because he dare not out of shame. This is my final victory, Doctor. I have shown you yourself.

No doubt the Doctor has flaws, but is he really a destroyer? Is his alleged "transformation" of his companions morally on a par, even remotely, with the creation of the Daleks, a species bent on extermination? And, in any case, how can the actions of the companions, the children of time, reveal the Doctor's soul rather than just their own choices and actions?

Yet there's something biting, too, to Davros's last point: the Doctor *is* loath to look back. But why should he be? Davros's other points, too, aren't entirely new to the show: upon meeting Martha, Donna asks the Doctor, "Is that what you did to her? Turned her into a soldier?" ("The Sontaran Strategem," 2008) Similar issues can easily be raised with regard to Jack's involvement with Torchwood, or Harriet Jones's trigger-happy use of that institute. But even if we accept that these companions have undertaken morally problematic actions, sometimes bordering on evil, why should the Doctor be held responsible for their deeds? Is Davros worth engaging with, or is his "final victory" mere posturing?

Here's a more plausible moral criticism. Having defeated the Family of Blood, the Doctor attempts to convince Joan Redfern to come with him. She responds with a pointed question: "If the Doctor had never visited us, had never chosen this place on a whim, would anyone here have died?" ("The Family of Blood," 2007) This criticism seems far stronger than the previous ones, both because it's made by a more sympathetic (and less morally suspect) judge of character, and because it reflects directly on the Doctor's actions without the intermediary of others acting "in his name." And it rings true, to boot: had the Doctor chosen to fight the Family of Blood instead of hiding, he would've spared their victims.

The Doctor's ostensibly flawed decision in this case shows a clear pattern of behavior. By attempting to reason with the Nestene Consciousness rather than using his anti-plastic, the Doctor allowed Autons to kill innocents while he struggled to free himself. By choosing to surrender rather than destroy the Daleks, he placed the entire universe at risk, an act he seemed ready to repeat in "Journey's End." By giving the Sontarans a choice, the Doctor risked the possibility that they might somehow prevail and destroy the Earth. And by rejecting Jack's plan to kill the Master, he allowed the Earth's population to be enslaved and "decimated" (something he couldn't have been certain was reversible) and Martha's family to be tortured. So, it isn't just once that the Doctor has placed the lives of others at risk, sometimes resulting in many deaths, in order to avoid seemingly inevitable violence.

Is the Doctor wrong to risk the deaths of innocent people, sometimes with devastating consequences, and if so, what could justify such apparent disregard for life? Also, how can the Doctor's connection to his companions reveal his soul, and why should this revelation show him to be a destroyer?

I Used to Have So Much Mercy

We might go about offering a response to these questions in different ways, but the best place to start is to examine the Doctor's character: his reasons for acting, his characteristic approach to conflict, and his relations with his companions. The traditional ethical approach best suited for an examination of character is the virtue ethics tradition descended to us from Aristotle. Virtue ethics approaches moral questions primarily by asking not about the principles agents ought to follow or the consequences that actions might bring about, but rather about the sort of character that the agent has, what kinds of virtues or vices he exemplifies in his actions.[1] A brief excursion into the Doctor's virtues can help us to "see the heart of him," fulfilling Dalek Caan's prophecy.

The traditional list of virtues includes such traits of character as courage, moderation, justice, generosity, practical wisdom, truthfulness, and compassion. Most standard views, in addition, hold that no one can have the virtues in isolation: one can't be truly wise without acting on that wisdom, for example; nor can one always be truthful without a certain amount of courage. And indeed we find that the Doctor exhibits most of the virtues (though he's a bit sloppy on truthfulness). The Doctor also seems to exhibit a singleness of vision and a distinctive way of dealing with conflicts; he isn't simply an all-around good guy, but displays a particular approach that guides him through many of his interactions with hostile life forms. This approach is what unifies the Doctor's many admirable qualities; it's a chief virtue that gives unity to his character. But what is this virtue?

The most obvious answer that comes to mind from the traditional list is compassion. Compassion is generally understood as a feeling involved in recognizing the suffering of another person and wanting to end or alleviate it through a concern for the other's good. The Doctor's compassion for humans ("Utopia," 2007), subjects of medical experiments ("New Earth," 2006), and other sentient species is a common element of the show. After being inhabited and almost killed by a living sun in "42" (2007), the Doctor still insists, "That sun needs care and protection just like any other living thing." He also seems to be the only one concerned about his failure to save the Ood at the conclusion of "The Satan

---

[1] An excellent outline of this approach can be found in Chapter 1 of Rosalind Hursthouse, *On Virtue Ethics*.

Pit" (2006), and feels that he owes them as a result ("Planet of the Ood," 2008). He even explicitly offers to show compassion to the last Dalek ("Evolution of the Daleks," 2007). Does the Doctor's compassion, then, provide an answer to our first question? Is it out of compassion (or mercy, as suggested in "The Family of Blood") that he attempts to save all sentient beings, even those bent on destroying others?

This answer isn't wholly satisfactory. For one thing, compassion seems to be something the Doctor learns or relearns, at least partly, from his companions. For example, the Doctor shows no compassion for Cassandra, the "last human," in "End of the World" (2005), despite Rose's pleading for him to help.[2] But the Doctor's refusal to destroy a sentient being out of hand, knowing full well the risk this refusal poses to others, is already evident in his earlier dealings with the Nestene Consciousness. So it seems that something other than compassion is behind his action. He doesn't feel sorry for the Nestene Consciousness; he doesn't seek its good. Rather, he wants to allow it to seek its own good without endangering others. And here's the key: throughout the show, whenever any creature threatens the well-being of others, the Doctor offers it a choice (see: "The Next Doctor," 2008; "World War Three," 2005; and "School Reunion," 2006).

To some extent compassion lies in the background of the choices the Doctor offers, which almost inevitably take the same form: back off and let me help you without harming anyone, or I'll stop you. He's loath to take action against any aggressor until the latter has *chosen* to escalate the confrontation, and he's prepared to work out a peaceful solution that will allow the aggressor to thrive on his own terms—provided, of course, that he ceases his aggression. So compassion does go a long way toward providing an ethical justification for the Doctor's risking so many innocents to protect a being that aims to destroy them. But to really understand the Doctor's motives, we must look at his emphasis on choice.

I Am Giving You a Choice

Choice figures prominently in the metaphysics of the Whoniverse. We might say that it's a fundamental building block of reality. For

---

[2] He shows a great deal of compassion next time he meets Cassandra, but only once she accepts her death.

instance, there're several creatures on the show that feed specifically on the products of choice, the "potential energy" of choices that could've been made but weren't due to some temporal meddling: Weeping Angels ("Blink," 2007) and the Time Beetle ("Turn Left," 2008). The Doctor frequently implies that ordinary people are important ("Father's Day," 2005), presumably because their choices shape the universe. And he even suggests that every time someone makes a choice, a parallel world comes into being ("Doomsday," 2006). This is a bit metaphysically suspect (some might call it a "plot hole"), since in "Turn Left" the Doctor claims that the universe usually compensates for small changes in choices, and creates a new world only in extreme cases, like the choice that kept Donna from their fateful encounter. Whatever the difficulties, however, choice plays a major role in the constitution of the Whoniverse.

Aware of this value of choice, the Doctor seeks to make the universe better not at the expense of choice, as would occur if he simply took choice out of the hands of all aggressors, but rather on the basis of the choices they make. What happens to them as a result of their disregard for others must be their own doing, and they must always have the possibility to make a choice for the better. This is why the Doctor normally takes care not merely to issue a "cease and desist" order to his adversaries, but to offer them an alternative that'll be for their own good. This attempt to allow others to make their own choices, to seek their own good or destruction, thus seems to be the Doctor's most characteristic virtue.

Following the philosopher Martin Heidegger, we might call this virtue "concern," or more specifically, "*authentic* concern."[3] Heidegger distinguishes between two kinds of concern that characterize our relations to others. First, we might attempt to resolve others' problems for them, making decisions for their own good. Treating a person in this inauthentic way compromises her role in shaping her own existence, her ability to choose the sort of being she is, and her responsibility for her life. Instead, *we* shape her existence, or "leap in" for her, and drop her back into her life unchanged. Authentic concern, on the other hand, gives the other person a role in the way she relates to and cares about the world, others, and most importantly, herself. It allows "the other to

---

[3] Martin Heidegger, *Being and Time*.

become transparent to himself *in* his care and *free for* it" (p. 115). In other words, we can choose to treat others as objects in ways we see fit for their own good, or we can treat them as persons capable of shaping and taking responsibility for their own lives. The latter way helps others recognize that they *are* free to choose the ways in which they care about others and themselves, and to take responsibility for that freedom.

This notion of authentic concern, in various forms, has permeated much of existentialist literature.[4] Even if we incorporate it into an account of the Doctor's portrayal of virtue ethics, it's still not clear that having the virtue of concern justifies the Doctor's actions. In order to attempt to match our moral intuitions with the Doctor's, it'll be helpful to reformulate our initial question: "Is the Doctor justified in risking the lives of innocents in order to promote an aggressor's freedom of choice?"

Imagine a being having godlike knowledge and skills with a TARDIS. Such a being has great potential to do good, but also great potential for evil. Should such a being attack other living beings unprovoked, it'd clearly be an evil act. However, if he attacked beings that clearly meant harm to others, but did not provoke him, that might still be evil—but it might be the lesser evil, and thus might be the right thing to do. So, how do we distinguish between beings that may, and those that may not, rightly be harmed? The answer might seem obvious: any serious intent to harm another sentient being makes one deserving of harm. But this is much less obvious than it seems, as we can easily illustrate with an example.

Suppose you're quietly studying in your den when the buzzing of a fly disturbs you. Absent-mindedly and wishing only to get back to work, you grab a fly swatter. The fly is within reach and you're about to swing when, suddenly, an alien entity appears with a warning: "If you wish to continue quietly studying, I can help move you to a room without flies or I can take this fly outside where it will no longer distract you. But this fly is a living thing with interests of its own, and if you attempt to kill it, I will be forced to stop you." You can still choose to swing at the fly, but now something has changed. Earlier, when you first intended your swing, you were doing it without thinking, almost instinctively. The interests of the

---

[4] See Jean-Paul Sartre's *Being and Nothingness* or his "Existentialism Is a Humanism."

fly never occurred to you. And now, perhaps, they still don't; after all, it's only a fly. But if you continue swinging at the fly after this warning, after having been forced to consider the consequences of your action, and consciously weigh your values (Is killing the fly really *that* important to you?), you've become genuinely responsible for your action in a way you weren't before.

The many hostile species the Doctor encounters are, often, much like you; and their intended victims are much like the fly. These hostile beings frequently act on instinct, as the Daleks do, or out of a sense of honor, like the Sontarans, or simply out of greed, like the Sycorax. Regardless of their motives, they probably haven't considered that humans[5] (or whoever their victims are) have interests worthy of consideration. Their plans seemed to need no revision. They, like you and the fly, weren't genuinely responsible for the harm their actions would cause, because they weren't forced to reflect on them. Punishing these hostile beings without first making them aware there's a choice to be made, and asking them to make a choice, would be as wrong as, say, decimating the human population for its unkind treatment of flies.[6] Concern—a virtue focusing on giving another a choice, or an opportunity to take genuine responsibility—may not always have the best consequences. But an immensely powerful being acting without concern might quickly pave the road to hell with his good intentions. The Doctor's genuine concern for the responsibility and choice of every entity, no matter its nature or history, is what makes him a morally sympathetic hero rather than a violent destroyer like the Master.

The Doctor's long history with some species may raise special problems. For example, he has good reasons, solidly grounded in past experience, to believe that neither the Sontarans nor the Daleks will change their course of action despite his strong warning and their belief that he will succeed in stopping them. To date, only a couple of species over the course of the new series have agreed to back off after a warning from the Doctor: the Vashta Nerada in "Forest of the Dead" (2008) and the Atraxi in "The Eleventh Hour" (2010). But if the Doctor has good reason to

---

[5] A nice reversal of this trend occurs in "Planet of the Ood," where we discover greedy humans mutilating and enslaving another species for profit.

[6] Even if they *had* already considered the possible wrongness of their actions but failed to take it seriously, it may be wrong to punish them without first offering them a chance to examine their values.

believe that his adversary won't cease hostilities, and knows that offering a choice may lead to the deaths of innocents, is he still right *not* to "shoot first"? The Doctor could be justified in acting without first offering the adversary a choice only if he knew for *certain* that, despite the choice, his adversary will still make the wrong one. But even a Time Lord doesn't know the future with such certainty. Some events are in flux, and the Doctor can see the different possibilities without knowing which one will occur, as he tells Donna in "Fires of Pompeii" (2008). Given the metaphysical importance of choice in the Whoniverse, the future choices of free beings are probably beyond the Doctor's knowledge.

She's My Plus One

Returning to Davros's original accusation, is the Doctor responsible for the actions of his companions? To answer Davros, let's look at why the Doctor has companions in the first place. Sometimes the Doctor simply needs help because he can't succeed alone: "I am sorry," he tells Martha in "Evolution of the Daleks," "but you have to fight." And, as we're frequently reminded, he's lonely. But let's look at the deeper reasons.

Aristotle lists a number of reasons why a virtuous person needs friends. Here are two: First, remaining virtuous is hard work. Having virtuous friends can help the virtuous person to practice his own virtue.[7] Compassion isn't the Doctor's strongest virtue, and at times he seems to slip. His companions, filled with human compassion, can help keep him on the right track. Rose may fail to convince the Doctor to save Cassandra in "End of the World," but she succeeds a few episodes later in "Dalek" (2005). Similarly, even Donna appears horrified by the grief of the Empress of the Racnoss, while the Doctor seems unmoved. By "Fires of Pompeii," Donna is ready to insist that the Doctor show compassion, compelling him to rescue a family from the volcano. The Doctor, on the other hand, allows his companions to recognize their own potential for virtue and heroism. As Rose tells Donna in "Turn Left," "You needed him to show you that you're brilliant. He does that to everyone he touches."

In addition, the virtuous person must seek to better understand himself, and since observing others is easier than observing one-

---

[7] See Aristotle, *Nicomachean Ethics*, Chapter 9.

self, the virtuous person can study himself by studying his friends, "since a friend is another himself," as Aristotle tells us. The virtuous person sees himself reflected in his friends, because he chooses friends who are like him. And this is precisely why the Doctor *is* responsible for what his companions do. When the Doctor's clone briefly becomes his companion, this point is driven home. Not only are his companions frequently in a position to cause great harm and destruction thanks to him, but they're also friends he's chosen, lived with, and who reflect his own self back to him. Their actions are more than simply actions that he enabled; they are, in a sense, his own actions.

We shouldn't, perhaps, be too troubled by the tendency of some companions to sacrifice themselves for the Doctor, even though he wouldn't approve. After all, it's good to preserve yourself, and since your friend is another yourself, it's good to preserve a friend. But since a friend isn't literally yourself, and it's even more noble to do things for others than for oneself, it's especially noble to sacrifice oneself for a friend. This is particularly clear if we consider that, usually, the companions don't simply sacrifice themselves for the Doctor: they sacrifice themselves for those lives that only the Doctor can save. On a virtue ethics approach, their self-sacrifice is right when it's based on the right virtues. And we can grasp those virtues when we examine the companions' willingness to kill in the Doctor's name.

I Am the Bad Wolf

Genuine friendship requires equality between the friends: should two friends become unequal, their friendship may still survive, but, as Aristotle warns, "when one side is removed at a great distance—as a god is—then it is no longer possible." The actions of the Doctor's companions may be his own, since he's opened their eyes to their abilities and virtues, and since he's chosen them as his friends. But his actions can't be theirs because they're too far removed from him. No matter how close their friendship, he sees the world in a radically different way than their limited human perspective allows. Any human who acquires the Doctor's knowledge will die unless that knowledge is removed, as we discover with Donna and Rose. The companions have their eyes opened to the great crises of interspecies relations, but lack the outlook and wisdom to act with the concern that governs the Doctor.

What do they lack? First, they lack knowledge of which events are fixed and which may be changed. The Doctor, for example, can't return to the Time War to save his people, and he's hinted that this isn't simply because it was time locked: it's a fixed event. "Fixed" events are not events that can't be changed, but are events that ought not to be changed. Those who don't have a Time Lord's knowledge of the universe are likely to make mistakes. Donna wants to warn the people of Pompeii; Rose attempts to save her father, and she brings Jack back to life. In the first case, her attempt clearly had disastrous consequences, but it's not clear (to us) that bringing Jack back was wrong—though it had a consequence Rose hadn't anticipated. "You can't control life and death," the Doctor tells her; but because neither she nor we can know why, Rose replies aptly: "But I can." The Doctor is, perhaps, a good judge of wrong in such circumstances, but we aren't.

So is there a moral failing on the part of the companions that *we* mere humans can recognize? Let me briefly return to the Doctor's own virtue. Concern—allowing each being to have a choice and making this choice the condition of whether or not it may rightly be punished—must be impartial. In my analogy, it requires seeing that both the interests of the human with the swatter and those of the fly are valuable. This is why the fly needs to be protected, but also why the human must be given a choice. Fully recognizing the importance of choice in the Whoniverse might require knowing the potentials that hang on each choice. But as Aristotle stressed, practical wisdom—knowledge of what things are valuable—isn't enough for good action. One must also have virtue, or a disposition to *act* in ways that promote what is valuable. The Doctor's human companions aren't guided by concern; they're guided by compassion, and compassion and concern can come into conflict. Concern requires impartiality; compassion doesn't. Someone may be fully compassionate, yet show compassion only to certain individuals and not others. Compassion alone isn't sufficient for either good moral action or sound judgment because compassion blinds impartiality.

Compassion shouldn't be the *only* virtue that guides action (nor should it be dominant), as the Doctor illustrates, because acting out of concern helps one avoid the pitfalls of compassion by taking the freedom of both sides into account. His companions, on the other hand, sometimes allow their compassion to cloud their moral judgment: Martha's threat to use the Osterhagen key to destroy the

Earth—to end the suffering of the human race; Jack's threat to destroy the crucible—killing everyone on board; and Harriet Jones's decision to destroy a retreating ship all involve crucial oversights because of their human limitations.

Thus the problem, which I christen the "Bad Wolf Syndrome." As the Bad Wolf, Rose is only an example—though a particularly outstanding one—of a more general failing. The companions travel with the Doctor and learn from him, but their humanity keeps them from having the knowledge and, more importantly (since they can acquire the knowledge at least briefly), the correct moral disposition,[8] to adjudicate conflicts in a way that recognizes each party's ability to make choices regarding their futures and to take responsibility for those choices and actions. In fact, compassion will necessarily be skewed in this way, because it's primarily directed at those who are suffering through no real fault of their own. So, unless it's guided by a proper respect for choice, compassion will inevitably overlook the aggressor entirely in favor of the victim and this, as I've been arguing, is a moral error. If the Doctor's companions are inevitably moved by compassion rather than concern because of their humanity, then the Bad Wolf Syndrome is inevitable: the Doctor won't be able to train his companions to apply the virtue of concern properly.

And now we can see why the Doctor is always running, as Davros asserted. His past is filled with choices, many of them terrible, and many of them shared with his companions.[9] It's bad enough that the Doctor must live with the knowledge of the suffering he has caused, but he must also know that those who've shared his choices shared them for the wrong reasons. He acts out of concern; they act out of compassion. Their judgment and their virtue are systematically distorted. Their actions are—because they are friends—his own actions. But they're also not his actions, because their foundation is morally misguided. Their heart is in the right place ("They're only trying to help"), but their reasons aren't.

---

[8] I've already hinted at the possibility that knowledge plays a crucial role in concern. Maintaining concern as a virtue might only be possible for someone who, like a Time Lord, literally sees the outcomes brought about by virtuous choices. This is why compassion can't blind him to the value of choice.

[9] He and Donna explicitly share responsibility for the destruction of Pompeii, but normally this sharing of responsibility is more implicit, which doesn't make it any less significant.

The Doctor abandons his companions and runs from them for the same reason he runs from his past—because their actions are his own and yet not his own. When he looks back—at Rose committing genocide, at Martha dressed as a soldier with a key to destroy the Earth, at Jack holding a warp star—he sees what he fears himself to be: a destroyer of worlds.

Brilliant! Fantastic! Molto Bene!

Aesthetics in Doctor Who

26

The Horror of the Weeping Angels

MICHELLE SAINT AND PETER A. FRENCH

Don't blink. Blink and you're dead. Don't turn your back. Don't look away, and *don't blink*.

—TENTH DOCTOR ("Blink," 2007)

You don't think of angels as scary do you? But these ones will send you behind the sofa in fear.

—Gbjazz1, IMDB.com forums

. . . the brilliance of this episode was the way it upped the psychological terror. Your survival is entirely in your hands; all you have to do is *not blink*. And, eventually, everyone blinks.

—MARCIA, "5 Creepiest, Scariest TV Monsters," Popvultures.com

"Blink" (2007) won the Hugo award for Best Dramatic Presentation, Short Form, and was nominated for the Nebula Award for Best Script. Its writer, Steven Moffat, won the British Academy of Film and Television Arts Craft and Cymru awards for best writer. It regularly sits atop the lists fans compile of both the most horrifying and the best episodes of the entire *Doctor Who* series.

Anyone new to the show will undoubtedly be besieged: "You *must* watch the one with the statues, 'Blink'—you simply must!" With such accolades from critics, fans, and even those otherwise unfamiliar with the *Doctor Who* universe, there can be no doubt— Episode 10 of Series 3, the episode entitled "Blink", is a masterpiece. One of the major reasons "Blink" receives such praise is what it successfully does to the viewer: it's horrifying.

The story centers on the exploits of Sally Sparrow, a young woman who has never met the Doctor and only interacts with him for a few brief moments. She's a photographer, and we first meet her as she's breaking into an old, abandoned house. As her attention is drawn to a wall with words barely visible behind peeling wallpaper, we notice, through a window behind her, a beautiful statue of a crying angel. Sally peels off the wallpaper in time to see that the words behind it are a message *to her*, telling her to duck. She does so, just in time to avoid being hit with a rock flying through the window—and just in time for us to notice that the beautiful statue has moved.

The statue is one of the Weeping Angels. Any time one is seen, a Weeping Angel will appear as just a stone figure, carved into the shape of an angel, usually with its dainty hands covering its eyes as if it were weeping. When observed, they're peaceful and lovely. But the Weeping Angels aren't ordinary statues. Though they're stone whenever observed, they're capable of extremely quick movements whenever *not* observed. If you blink, a Weeping Angel will have silently come up beside you. All it takes is one blink for the Weeping Angels to touch you, no matter how far away they were. One touch from a Weeping Angel and you're gone—in more ways than one.

The Doctor explains that the Weeping Angels thrive by consuming all of the energy from the future lives of their victims. They then deposit their victims in a past time, not a time through which they've already lived. Their victims feel no pain and the rest of their lives are theirs to live as they're able in their new temporal and spatial locations. The Doctor describes them as "the only psychopaths in the universe to kill you nicely."[1] Upon being touched by an angel, Sally's friend, Kathy Nightingale, is transported to Hull of the 1920s, where she married, became a mother, and died peacefully. Billy, whom Sally meets but a few minutes before he's a victim of the angels, is sent to 1969 London where he became a video producer, lives a normal lifespan, and then dies later the same day he meets Sally, whom he originally met before being touched by an angel.

Reportedly, a large number of *Doctor Who* fans claim that "Blink" is horrifying to them and that the Weeping Angels are terrifying monsters. Why? The Weeping Angels are the sort of objects that might ornament a formal garden or be on display in a

---

[1] In one way, they don't kill you, given that your physical body is left unharmed, but in another sense, they do.

museum. They're smooth stone, with (usually) tranquil expressions and lovely appearances—a far cry from disturbing or distressing objects. Unlike the Daleks, whose bodies result from grotesque genetic mutation and whose minds have been warped to hate, or the Cybermen that once were human beings but have been carved up to fit a metallic form, the Weeping Angels convey the impression of serenity, shyness, and beauty. Whereas the Daleks are constantly planning and scheming to destroy the human race, methodically hunting us down and exterminating us, and the Cybermen ceaselessly desire to force us into their half-dead conformity, the Weeping Angels aren't a serious threat to depopulate the world of humans or even, it seems, to destroy their victims in the sense of physically mutilating and killing them.[2]

Kathy Nightingale reveals in her letter to Sally that her fate in Hull was not an unhappy one, she managed to live a fulfilling life from 1918 on. Billy, when reunited with Sally after his life since the late 1960s is at peace with the direction his life took. Victims of the Weeping Angels suffer nothing like the torturous murders that both the Daleks and the Cybermen instigate. Why are these statues that don't physically harm their victims considered to be among the most horrifying monsters encountered in *Doctor Who*? [3]

The attempt to answer that question calls for a foray into the nature of horror and the concept of a monster. A leading authority on issues relating to horror is Noël Carroll. His theory of the horrific will be the touchstone of our attempt to account for the horror and monstrosity of "Blink."

Carroll and Horror

In *The Philosophy of Horror*, Carroll distinguishes between what he calls "natural horror" and "art-horror."[4] Natural horror is the emotion to which one refers by uttering a sentence such as, "The

---

[2] EDITORS' NOTE: The Weeping Angels do kill people in Series 5, Episode 5, "Flesh and Stone" (2010), written by Steven Moffat. We found this a bit puzzling, but the dire need of the Angels to survive and their need to communicate (through the soldier Bob) seem to be the motives.

[3] Often, those who claim the Weeping Angels aren't the most frightening will cite the Vashta Nerada from "The Silence in the Library" (2008). Very, very rarely, does one see the suggestion that the Daleks or Cybermen should claim the title of Most Frightening Monster over the Weeping Angels.

[4] *The Philosophy of Horror or Paradoxes of the Heart*, p. 12.

prospect of nuclear war is horrifying." That's a different kind of horror than experienced while watching a "slasher" movie of the *Halloween* sort. Carroll proposes we call the latter sort "art-horror." As Carroll explains, art-horror is "the sense of the term 'horror' that occurs when, for example, in answer to the question 'What kind of book is *The Shining?*' we say a horror story" (p. 12).

Even though the term, "art-horror," may be unfamiliar, the concept it's meant to capture is firmly embedded in our ordinary discourse. We recognize a distinction between that very grave emotion the prospect of nuclear war can cause and the spine-chilling feeling experienced when watching *Frankenstein* or *Nightmare on Elm Street*. We use the term "horror" in what follows, but we're referring only to Carroll's art-horror when doing so.

According to Carroll, horror is an emotional response to a monster, where a monster is an entity that's inexplicable by our current scientific knowledge, threatening, and impure. Monsters "are unnatural relative to a culture's conceptual scheme of nature. They don't fit the scheme; they violate it" (p. 34). They're creatures from other planets or dark, secret and nasty places. They're mysteries, menaces outside of the natural order of things. But, as Carroll notes, superheroes like Superman are unnatural and scientifically inexplicable; there's more to a monster than the transgressing of scientific laws.

What matters for horror, Carroll maintains, is that the unnatural entity in the story elicits a distinct emotional response, a mixture of both fear and disgust in the viewer (or reader). Horrific monsters are threatening, whether physically, "psychologically, morally, or socially" (p. 43). They're destroyers, frightening in their capacity to harm. But even more than frightening on Carroll's account, they must be disgusting. A horrific monster is something with which we humans don't want to come in contact with—we recoil from them, feel nauseated by them, and want to avoid them even when the threat of harm from them is removed. Carroll notes, "Monsters are identified as impure and unclean. . . . They're not only quite dangerous but they also make one's skin creep" (p. 23). So, a horrific monster, as opposed to just a dangerous character, must provoke disgust in the viewer.

Monsters typically are bastardizations, belonging in more than one category of things; they straddle two categories, being wholly neither one nor the other, like the zombie who's both living and dead, or the werewolf who's both human and wild animal. Or the impurity of the monster may be revealed by the difficulty of categorization, it's neither this nor that but something without firm definition. Its impurity might also be shown through the association with indisputably impure objects, such as a beautiful woman who lives with rotting corpses. What all horrific fictions have in common, according to Carroll, is the presence of some sort of monstrous being, which "is essentially a compound of danger and disgust" (p. 52). If "Blink" is horrifying, then, according to Carroll, it should be because the episode contains monsters that make us both frightened and disgusted. But do the monsters in "Blink" meet those criteria?

Fearing Angels

Are the Weeping Angels frightening? Going on Carroll's theory, the Daleks should be frightening because Daleks threaten not only our lives but also our entire civilization. Similarly, the Cybermen should be frightening because they threaten to destroy our bodies with the worst perversions of surgical equipment in order to convert us into unthinking automatons. Thus, Carroll's theory persuasively explains why viewers might be frightened by both types of monsters. But can we explain fear of the Weeping Angels in the same way? What feelings do they conjure up once we grasp what their touch does to humans?

Victims of the Weeping Angels have their lives up to the point of contact and their planned-for futures stolen from them. They're transported to another time and place where they have to start anew. They also report experiencing a bit of nausea when being transported into the past—certainly unpleasant. However, being transported back in time is a far cry from being torn to pieces or having one's brain stuffed into a metallic shell. Being forced, against one's will, to begin life anew in a different time and place is nothing at all like having alien enemies overtake your planet, exterminating everyone in their way, and performing experiments on the rest. Compared to the threat of either the Cybermen or the Daleks, the Weeping Angels seem tame, almost benign. While we can't imagine anyone actively wishing for the fate the Cybermen[5] and Daleks provide, it's possible to imagine some people thinking

---

[5] For an argument why one might actively wish for the fate the Cybermen promise, see Chapter 18 in this volume.

the fate inflicted by the Weeping Angels is desirable and exciting, a welcome change. When compared to the other *Doctor Who* monsters, what they do seems relatively unthreatening.

But while they may not threaten our bodies or our civilization, they threaten us in another sense: as particular persons. It is the threat to us as particular persons that the Doctor warns us about.

There's more to a person than just a physical body that can be annihilated or mutilated. What it means to be a person has much to do with how one thinks, feels, plans, and lives, and where and when one does all of that. It matters, in other words, that a person cares. Persons care about other persons and things surrounding them and ideas and plans they have, and that distinguish them from other persons. To make this point, we help ourselves to a well-known position of Harry Frankfurt.[6] You only care, in the sense of "give a damn about," what's important to you, and for something to be important to you, you must give a damn about it. If you "really give a damn"—really care—about something, then it's very important to you. It's an element in defining the specific person you are. If it weren't, you wouldn't care so much about it. Such cares are irreducible, thick cognitive and non-cognitive complex states that constitute what's important to persons and central to their identities. Care, used this way, is a scalar concept. A person may care about something a great deal, a bit, somewhat, or hardly at all. The amount of care tracks the amount of importance the object of care has for the person doing the caring. Caring is trying to guide your actions in a certain way, along a specific course, intentionally avoiding other courses. Frankfurt writes, "A person who cares about something is, as it were, invested in it. He identifies himself with what he cares about in a sense that he makes himself vulnerable to loses and susceptible to benefits depending upon whether what he cares about is diminished or enhanced" (p. 83). Really caring about something involves structuring your life in a certain way and that, in large measure, makes you the person you are.

Your cares have "inherent persistence" (p. 84). To care about something, you must conceive of yourself as a being that casts itself into a future—not just any future, but one in which you further what you care about in the present. Bernard Williams argues that an

---

[6] *The Importance of What We Care About.*

important aspect of our moral lives is the value each of us places on our personal projects and commitments.[7] What makes the premature termination of personal projects morally significant, even frightening, is the fact that people identify themselves through the aims and means of projects they find ultimately worthy of fulfillment.

Frankfurt argues that "caring, insofar as it consists in guiding oneself along a distinctive course or in a particular manner, presupposes both agency and self-consciousness" (Frankfurt, p. 83). Peter French and Mitchell Haney write:

> Insofar as agents have cares, they have choices to make and reflection on the options become necessary. An agent without cares would be no agent at all. Such a person would have no choices to make and nothing worthy of reflection. . . . Insofar as people care about the fruition or continuation of a project, they will personally identify with the objects and activities of that project, and they will be personally harmed or benefited by the fates of their objects of care. ("Changes in Latitudes, Changes in Attitudes," pp. 127–28)

Frankfurt maintains: "the outlook of a person who cares about something is inherently prospective, that is, he necessarily considers himself as having a future."[8] A person's objects of care, to a significant degree, determine which features are relevant both for interpolating a person's foreseeable future and interpreting a person's actual past. Alasdair MacIntyre offers a related view when he maintains that persons construct their identities via coherent narratives. People, MacIntyre claims, integrate the various facts and roles of their lives together into meaningful, continuous timelines by filtering relevant from irrelevant features followed by foregrounding the most relevant elements and allowing the rest to fade into the background. This means that a person is a "story-telling animal," whose ability to understand herself depends on her ability to understand what narratives are available through her life.[9] Our personal identities depend, at least in part, on there being a comprehensive thread of narrative in our lives, but such "lived narratives" require "a certain teleological character. We live out our lives, both individually and in our relationships with each other, in the light of

---

[7] "Persons, Character. and Morality," p. 209.

[8] Frankfurt, p. 83.

[9] *After Virtue*, p. 201.

certain conceptions of a possible shared future, a future in which certain possibilities beckon us forward and others repel us." In effect, we create the particular persons we are from and by what we care about.

When the Weeping Angels rip Kathy out of her location in space and time, depositing her in another point in time, they're tearing Kathy away from everything she cares about. Her family, friends, livelihood, plans for the future, and hobbies are suddenly, irrevocably lost to her future. She finds herself, instantly, in a land as foreign to her as another country, without any access to those things she cared about, that were important to her. If, as we maintain, our personal identities are composed of, probably in large part, what we care about, then, by ripping her away from all those things that mattered to her, the Weeping Angels have demolished a significant part of Kathy's identity. She no longer can be who she used to be, because she no longer has the capacity to live her life and plan her future, focused on those things that were important to her. Though she continues to be alive, and though her physical body and mental capacities are mostly unchanged, there's an important sense in which Kathy is no longer herself. By removing Kathy from her own place and time, and therefore from the things that held importance for her in her life, the Weeping Angels remove Kathy *from herself*. Their actions force her to build a new life in which the memories and plans of her previous life will become incoherent, disjointed, and conceptually unintelligible.

The Weeping Angels do significant harm to their victims insofar as their victims are time- and place-bound persons. They rob their victims of their sense of who they are.[10] One might call this fate a form of "death," as the Doctor does, albeit one that allows for a kind of "rebirth," because most victims will begin caring for aspects of their new surroundings. Persons care, only wantons do not. When Sally receives the letter Kathy has written, she asks confusedly, "Kathy? *My* Kathy?" In one sense, the letter's author is indeed

---

[10] Suppose a historian who dedicated his entire life to the study of a particular era in the past were to become a victim of the Weeping Angels, discovering himself transported to that same era he studies. It's at least possible that this historian wouldn't suffer the same loss of self that any other victim would, given that all that he cares about is contained in that era. It's possible. What matters, for our purposes, is that this historian likely wouldn't see the Weeping Angels as threatening and frightening as the rest of us, with more current interests, do.

her Kathy, in that the same physical body wrote it. In another sense, however—and this is the sense in which the Weeping Angels causes viewers to fear them—she's wrong; her Kathy was replaced with a different Kathy, one that had to build anew an identity, beginning in 1918 and ending before Sally was born.

Adopting what we believe is a credible theory of a significant constituent of personal identity, what we care most about, reveals why the Weeping Angels are terrifying monsters. On a conception of personal identity that, in large measure, reflects Frankfurt's cares and MacIntyre's narratives, one that maintains that a person's identity is, in part, shaped by plans for the future, projects, and cares, contemplating what the Weeping Angels do to their victims can be really terrifying for viewers. Being involuntarily transported to another time and place, on such an account, threatens the dissolution of one's personal identity. If, as we believe, a person's identity isn't just that of a persistent physical body or a particular mind, but also consists in projects with trajectories into the future that the person cares about and around which the person has built a sense of self, the fate inflicted on their victims by the Weeping Angels is a reasonable cause for fear. Death, of course, terminates all cares and most plans, and short-circuits narratives. But there may be a sense that most of us ascertain that experiencing the same sort of termination but living on and having to find new cares and make new plans while haunted by the remnants of the old memories is a fate worse than death. In the strange world into which one is thrown by the Weeping Angels, one is also a stranger to oneself, a person with an incoherent past in search of an identity.

We've suggested an explanation for why the Weeping Angels, who don't physically harm their victims, are frightening. Carroll doesn't explicitly mention the sort of threat the Weeping Angels pose, but it fits comfortably within his broad account of what it means for a monster's abilities to provoke fear in the viewer. We turn to the emotion that is the second half of Carroll's formula for horror: disgust.

Disgust and Blinking

Disgust is a visceral response to something gross, icky, abhorrent, repugnant, nauseating. The Daleks or the Cybermen are disgusting in the visual sense and in what they do to their victims. The Daleks, for instance, look like octopuses when removed from their metallic casings—they're wrinkly, blubbery, and the color of unhealthy flesh. The Cybermen are the brains and tissues of humans, butchered and contorted into a robotic shell. The sight of an unmasked Dalek is repugnant. Just the sound of the tools used to make people into Cybermen can be nauseating.

What about the Weeping Angels? Are they disgusting? They're transcategory monsters in a number of ways. They're both living and inanimate, human-looking and stone. They also reside in an old, dilapidated, decaying, and overgrown house at the edge of town. On Carroll's account we should expect the Weeping Angels to disgust us. However, they're not disgusting, *per se.* They have nothing like the distasteful appearance of zombies. Maybe the viewers of *Doctor Who* are wrong; maybe "Blink" isn't horror after all.

When we first notice a Weeping Angel, it appears to be nothing more than a beautiful statue. After Sally has learned of Kathy's disappearance and faces several Weeping Angels, we fear for her as she moves closer to them, and we may even describe ourselves as uneasy or uncomfortable, but not because they disgust us. It's precisely because they're *not* disgusting that the episode "works" as a horror story. It's a natural thing for a person to run her hands over a statue, feeling its texture, the contours of the stone. It's a typical tactile aesthetic experience. The experience wouldn't be like confronting a zombie. No matter how many categories they cross, no matter how many features they have that should arouse disgust, the appearance of a Weeping Angel simply isn't disgusting; they're attractive, pleasing to the eye. There's no reason to turn one's eyes away from them in disgust. They can't be horrific monsters on Carroll's theory.

Yet, given what we learn about what they do, and especially how it's done, the Weeping Angels *are* horrific monsters and it's no wonder so many viewers report feeling horror in response to them. Something's got to give: either we (and the viewers themselves) are mislabeling viewers' emotional reactions to "Blink" or Carroll's theory needs revision. Carroll claims that his theory is based on observations of what is generally accepted to be horrific, and that the way to test his conditions of fear and disgust is "to see if they apply to the reactions we find to the monsters indigenous to works of horror." "Blink" is our test case. We don't propose to toss it out of the category of horror just to preserve Carroll's theory. We propose an emendation to that theory to accommodate it and, we believe, to include a fairly large number of other monster tales in film, television programs, and fictional literature in the horror genre.

At the beginning of "Blink," the viewer doesn't know what the statues are. She may be curious about them, but certainly not horrified. As more of the pieces of the plot fall into place—as Kathy disappears and the Doctor's message is discovered—the viewer may begin to feel frightened for Sally, but not horrified. The horror creeps into the viewer rather late into the episode. It's provoked once the Doctor explains the importance of not blinking. The horror sneaks up on viewers, culminating when Larry is left alone with a Weeping Angel directly in front of him, his eyes forced as wide as possible, his head starting to shake, his brow starting to sweat, as he tries, as hard as he can, to complete that impossible task, to *not blink*.

The fact that the monsters work their evil by using that natural process, blinking, in order to attack humans makes the Weeping Angels horrific and not just frightening. If it weren't blinking but, say, the intended victim merely turning her head in another direction, the episode wouldn't be horrific. It's not blinking, specifically, that makes the viewer's skin crawl, as opposed to the appearance or even the thought of the Weeping Angels; what leaves the viewer disquieted is the task that burdens their potential victims if they're to save themselves. There's nothing particularly disgusting about being required to not blink, but there's something very unsettling in contemplating having to do so for an interminable period of time to save your identity. To understand how "Blink" is horrific, reflect on enduring the rising discomfort, while watching Larry's eyelids as he struggles not to blink. Blinking is controllable (at least for a certain period of time), but eventually everyone, (except zombies), blinks. We've no real hope of preventing ourselves from doing it over an extended period of time. Against our own blinking, we're ultimately powerless, impotent.

Learning that our survival as the persons we are and hope to be when confronted by a Weeping Angel depends on not blinking is tantamount to learning that we can be saved only by performing an impossible, unnatural task. "Blink" reminds viewers of the anxiety most humans feel about controlling their bodily functions and extends it unnaturally over something we know we never can wholly control.

The entire plot of the episode turns from merely frightening to downright horrific because of how important it is to not blink and how devastating the consequences are when one fails at this impossible task. One's identity lost in a blink of an eye, but not with the relief of total amnesia! Alice's perplexing question in Wonderland, "Was I the same when I got up this morning?" has only an ambiguous answer in "Blink," as it does in Wonderland. But in "Blink," as opposed to Wonderland, one doesn't have the luxury of a slow decent into confusion and a strange world. Blinking, so slight we often don't even notice it, is all it takes: one moment we're comfortable in a familiar place; the next, without witnessing the scenery change, we're somewhere far away and incomprehensible.

A fragment of a second is all it takes for Kathy to be deposited where the identity she has constructed of, and for herself, can't survive. That bodily movement that most of the time we barely even register performing, is all that separates her past life, where she understood who she was and how her actions fit into a longer narrative, and her strange new circumstances, where ultimately her memories of her old identity must be suppressed if she's to rebuild a coherent sense of self. It's not the thought of losing one's identity alone that's horrific; it's the way the episode forces the viewer to conceive of losing it: by the victim failing to perform an impossible task, exposing our impotence vis-à-vis the monsters.

There's little dispute in the philosophical and psychological literature about the crucial importance the sense of control is to a person's conception of themselves and their identity. Frankfurt, for example, argues persuasively that loss of second-order volitions is equivalent to loss of personhood.[11] Losing control of one's identity because one hasn't the ability to make one's desires effectual, is a form of torture.[12] Many argue that what makes rape horrible isn't just unwanted sexual contact but losing autonomy over one's own body and sexuality. The feeling of powerlessness, helplessness, gives rise to resentment, shame, loss of a sense of dignity and self-esteem, and panic.

The feeling of impotence, powerlessness, to prevent what the monsters do, is distinct from fear. It augments the fear. "Blink" is horrific because it causes viewers to feel both fear and impotency. In contrast to Carroll's fear and disgust account of the horrific, we

---

[11] See Harry Frankfurt, "Freedom of the Will and the Concept of a Person," in *The Importance of What We Care About*, Chapter 2.

[12] See Peter A. French, *War and Moral Dissonance*, Chapter 7.

maintain that the recipe for horror is a monster we should fear and the exposure of our powerlessness to defeat the monster. Our account of horror, we believe, has more explanatory power than the one offered by Carroll.

Consider the first criterion Carroll lists for the creation of a monster: it must be something that transcends our knowledge of the world. Carroll's account never fully explains the need for this criterion. Why is it so important for a monster to be something scientifically inexplicable? There're real creatures that are both frightening and disgusting—why aren't they monsters, except, perhaps metaphorically? On our account of horror, that old saw, 'knowledge is power', provides an answer. If one can understand the nature of a thing in the usual investigative way, then one is closer to being able to control and overpower it. That's a plot turning point in many of the horror and science-fiction films of the Cold War period and especially in the 1950s.

A creature that can't be understood within the framework of science, however—something that obeys no known physical laws—is something against which we are likely to be powerless. Bullets can't stop a zombie, nuclear attacks only empower Godzilla. How can we defeat the Blob? Monsters in horror fiction are impenetrable by our scientific understanding and methods. That's no minor matter, as Carroll's account might suggest. It's at the core of our feeling of impotence when entertaining the thought of them. This also explains the prevalence of disgust in the examples of horror that Carroll provides. Disgust is a response to something impure, and Carroll provides a possible explanation for what makes something impure. But what's the emotional importance of impurity? An answer emerges when considering what happens, psychologically, when one feels disgust, and that answer ultimately bolsters our account of horror as fear and impotency.

In "Disgust: The Body and Soul Emotion," Paul Rozin, Jonathan Haidt, and Clark R. McCauley argue that disgust began as a response to poor food, and the core notion of disgust "can be thought of as a gatekeeper for the mouth, guarding against oral incorporation of improper substances." When we eat something, it becomes a part of us, and our capacity to experience disgust is derived from the important task of keeping things rotten or toxic from becoming part of ourselves. Central to the notion of disgust is the idea of contagion, that we can become harmed in some way through contact with a disgusting thing. As humans evolved, however, disgust, "a mechanism for avoiding harm to the body became a mechanism for avoiding harm to the soul."[13]

As Haidt explains, the experience of disgust correlates with a particular "dimension of social space": the "purity versus pollution" dimension.[14] How this dimension of social space is understood is "somewhat similar across widely disparate cultures, religions, and eras. The basic logic seems to be that people vary in their level of spiritual purity as a trait . . . and as a state. Purity and pollution practices seem designed to insure that people interact with each other, and with sacred objects and spaces, in ways that keep the impure (low) from contaminating the pure (high)" (p. 3). This dimension of social space is most obvious in cultures like that of Hindu India and is almost invisible in the United States—we operate often along this dimension, but we're less likely to recognize it (p. 4).

Central to this idea of pollution is that a thing already polluted is capable of polluting whatever comes into contact with it, whether through digestion or other forms of contact. Zombies, being far more polluted or impure than the rest of us, can contaminate us, making us less pure, less human, and disgust is the reactive attitude to such contamination. Nothing can wash away the disgusting touch of a zombie: "once in contact, always in contact."[15] But, while physical contact with a disgusting thing yields a strong disgust response, that same response is there even when simply seeing or smelling a disgusting thing. We're left feeling contaminated, polluted, or impure when we physically touch a disgusting thing, and we're left feeling the same way if the impure image of the thing enters us through our eyes or its scent through our nostrils. Any contact, not just tactile, but also visual, aural, or olfactory, leaves one feeling disgust—that sense of having been polluted.

It's clear why disgust figures so often in horror stories, as Carroll notes: disgust is a basic human emotion, with strong affect, that's felt in response to having been contaminated in some way, and contamination is something very hard to control. Once you've spotted the zombie, his vile stench and rotting visage is with you, polluting you—you can't scour that image from your mind. Once the

---

[13] Rozin, Haidt, and McCauley, "Disgust," p. 650.

[14] Haidt, "Elevation and The Positive Psychology of Morality," p. 2.

[15] Rozin, Haidt, and McCauley, "Disgust," p. 641.

zombies have surrounded you, there's nothing that can be done to stop them from touching you, polluting you further. Impurity is contagious, and out of the infected's control. The cases in which disgust figures centrally in a horror story's plot are cases in which the heroes are incapable of avoiding the disgusting monster, impotent to keep themselves from becoming impure through association with it. And we, the audience, through having seen those images on the screen, or read the description on the page, have also experienced the disgust, the pollution that comes from viewing a disgusting thing, and thus share the sense of impotency to avoid the impurity. If we're correct that the feeling of horror is a mixture of fear and impotency, then an obvious way to ramp up the feeling of impotency is to make the monster something that's disgusting, something humans are powerless to stop from affecting them negatively, from polluting them, turning them into zombies or vampires or werewolves.

It's easy to produce a feeling of horror through the use of disgust, but "Blink" doesn't take the easy, tried and true, route. We don't feel disgust, but the writers of "Blink" found a different way to produce the feeling of powerlessness in the viewer, one that's interwoven into the very essence of the plot. The feeling of impotence is inherent in the way the Weeping Angels succeed in claiming their victims.

"Blink" surely isn't the only case where Carroll's disgust requirement isn't met by monsters in what's generally seen as a work of horror. Another example may be Hitchcock's *The Birds*, in which flocks of birds terrorize the inhabitants of a small town. No single bird in the movie is particularly disgusting, and the flocks are no more disgusting than their members. It can't even be said that the size of the flocks is disgusting, given that flocks of such size are unlikely to provoke disgust in real life. Such a sizable flock, however, means that we can't keep track of all its members, can't protect ourselves from them. Without any explanation for how the birds could have developed such murderous intent or keen intelligence, we're incapable of gauging which birds will attack, when, or how—we're powerless against them. The birds are horrifying, because we've no means to stopping their attacks.

We agree with Carroll that horror requires a threatening monster that defies, contradicts, or crosses what we take to be natural categories. We disagree that feeling horror in response to the monster implies we must feel disgust. We maintain instead that the required emotional reactive response is, for want of a better term, the feeling of impotence in a deadly threatening situation, and that feeling can be activated by the thought of what monsters do and how they do it. The disgust that Carroll recognizes in many horror films is a means of activating the sense of impotence or power-lessness. But, monsters that turn the vulnerabilities and inadequacies of their victims against themselves, making their survival depend on their accomplishing an impossible task, directly linking the sense of impotency to the monster's ability to harm, are truly horrific. The Weeping Angels clearly belong in that class.

One More Thing, Don't Blink!

The Weeping Angels threaten personhood, not bodies or minds. The fate the Weeping Angels inflict may keep their victims physically and mentally unchanged while shattering their identity as the persons they were, their sense of self that is spatially- and temporally-indexed. After all, virtually no one's identity-defining cares are ahistorical. We invest ourselves contextually, and the Weeping Angels have the power to pluck us from our contexts and deposit us elsewhere where we're out of context, where we have no footing, where we have to begin again to create our personal identities, to "write" our personal narratives. Some people may welcome that; most will find it terrifying.

It's horrific that the only way we can protect our personal identity from the Weeping Angels is unnatural, unpleasant, and ultimately impossible. Should we find ourselves in the presence of a Weeping Angel, if we do what we physiologically can't prevent ourselves from doing for more than mere seconds, namely, blink, everything we care about that's related to who we are in a certain time and place will be lost to us. We'll not continue to be the persons we were, and we have no capacity to save ourselves from this fate. Thinking about that prospect, for most people, is horror.

27

Beauty Is Not in the Eye-Stalk of the Beholder

CLIVE CAZEAUX

The Daleks are beautiful, aren't they? Their casings, I mean. Not the squid-like creatures inside. It's their shape, their combination of forms: lines, curves, domes, the semi-spherical head, and the way they glide. And the sound of the voice: while I wouldn't go so far as to call it "beautiful," it nevertheless has a beauty to it. It is striking; it embodies their character, and does the job perfectly of telling us "here is an alien life form." But isn't beauty applicable only to a narrow range of things: people, animals, landscapes, and certain works of art? Can it be applied to a monster from a science-fiction television series: an over-sized, elaborate pepper-pot, with a few grills, slats, and semi-spheres?

Beauty—that delight or pleasure we experience when looking at an artwork or a person or listening to a piece of music—is a complex phenomenon. It's occupied philosophy since Pythagoras and the pre-Socratic philosophers. Because perceptual delight stands out against the routine flow of experience, it poses a challenge to theories of experience. A phrase which frequently comes to mind when talking of beauty is that it lies "in the eye of the beholder," which is taken to mean that beauty is subjective; what one person finds pleasing, another may not.

If we take this approach, then I'm on safe ground: I can call the Daleks beautiful because what I find pleasing is determined by me. But this is just one particular historical understanding of beauty from the eighteenth century when taste, as something which discerning people might possess, comes into being as a concept. If we return to the time of Pythagoras though, beauty isn't a subjective idea but a facet of the numerical structure of the universe. If we

313

move towards the present day, the question of whether beauty is subjective or objective is in fact part of a revolution in eighteenth-century philosophy, initiated by Immanuel Kant. Kant's philosophy requires us to consider that mind and reality are linked in a fundamental way, with beauty being one of the experiences where this link is evident.

Part of this debate includes the idea that any judgment of beauty has both a subjective and an objective component. In calling something "beautiful," I'm not just expressing an opinion, not just making a casual remark which I'm happy for my friend to disregard. Calling something "beautiful" is an expression of passion, and I want my claim to hold for everyone. I find the Daleks beautiful, and I want the rest of the world to agree with me.

My interest is in the philosophical issues surrounding the idea that the Daleks are beautiful. Philosophy can help us understand the ideas responsible for a conceptual problem. It also has a history of theories regarding the nature of beauty. The two combined will take the seemingly odd notion of the beauty of the Daleks and show that it draws on and implies some of philosophy's central ideas, ideas that aren't just to do with beauty but with the nature of reality itself. From the complex and contested nature of beauty, the idea of the beautiful Dalek forces us to examine the definition of beauty, and the place beauty occupies in the history of Western metaphysics (theories of the nature of reality)—a territory where the Daleks and *Doctor Who* are very much at home.

Earth Versus Skaro

If we're to get to grips (or should that be "suckers") with the beauty of the Daleks, then we need to address the fact that they occupy two worlds: the *Doctor Who* universe and our world. Why? Because it affects how we assess their alleged beauty. In the *Doctor Who* universe, the Daleks took refuge in 1930s New York, fought (each other) for the Hand of Omega in London in 1963, and attempted to invade Earth in the year 2150. For the beings who share this universe and know the Daleks, or know of them, they're afraid. Cross a Dalek and you'll die.

Why am I pointing this out? Because in the *Who* universe, the Daleks aren't creatures of beauty. Even on the two occasions when a Dalek becomes an exhibit—in "The Space Museum" (1965) and in "Dalek" (2005)—it's because of its scientific curiosity-value and not for its appearance. When van Statten introduces the Ninth Doctor to the "Metaltron," as he's named the Dalek, at no point does he describe it as beautiful. He's more interested in it as a creature, as something with which he might communicate.

When I call the Daleks "beautiful," I'm not speaking from the perspective of the *Doctor Who* universe; I'm not regarding them as real creatures. I'm viewing them from the point of view of the everyday world in which *Doctor Who* is a television program and the Daleks are a race of fictional beings created as enemies for the Doctor by Terry Nation and Raymond Cusick in 1963. They're only real to the extent that they appear on television screens, photographs, posters, pencil cases, or duvets. There's a genuine philosophical reason for making the point.

A key distinction in modern aesthetics is between beauty in art and beauty in nature. There's a big difference between seeing beauty in a human-made object, such as a painting, and seeing it in the natural world, as in the case of an animal or a range of mountains. In our terms, this is the difference between seeing the Dalek as a "work of art" by Nation and Cusick (in our world) and seeing it as a part of Skaro's natural environment (in the *Who* universe). The difference is due to the fact that modern aesthetics explains beauty in terms of the relationship between the human mind and the world. Immanuel Kant, the founder of modern aesthetics, argues that the perception of beauty in nature is higher than the perception of beauty in art because beauty, as he understands it, is about our becoming aware of the fit between the human mind and reality. But with beauty in art, our experience of it is indirect, due to the fact that what we perceive has been mediated by human design; that's to say, it hasn't come directly from nature.

Georg Hegel, Kant's critic, has an entirely different world-view, and one which leads him to argue the opposite. Hegel asserts that mind and reality aren't just interconnected but actually one and the same thing. Life is the process whereby we come to realize this. Beauty, for Hegel, is our becoming aware of this oneness through the recognition of thought in matter.[1] On this basis, beauty in art is higher than beauty in nature because art involves perceiving ideas

---

[1] *Aesthetics: Lectures in Fine Art.*

through sensory form, for example, through clay, paint, or sound, whereas nature simply involves the perception of matter.

The Embodiment of Evil

What this disagreement shows is that competing theories and values are at stake when assessing natural and human-made objects of beauty. Because beauty is seen as something involving the relation between mind and world, it becomes significant whether or not an object of beauty is natural or something which is the product of a mind. I'm looking at the Dalek primarily as a human artifact, a "work of art." If I were to conduct this study from the point of view of a member of the *Doctor Who* universe, I would be talking about natural beauty, the beauty of another creature, and a specific set of questions would arise.

Although Kant places nature higher than art, he also warns against "dependent" beauty, where something is admired for being a perfect example of a particular form. So I might be sitting having a coffee with a friend, and we see a Dalek glide by. I might exclaim "Wow, that's one good-looking Dalek," if I thought it was a particularly fine specimen. This would be a limited form of beauty for Kant, since beauty which is dependent on a template, on a concept of *what something should look like*, isn't free to experience the purposive fit between the human mind and reality. The same point covers the fact that the Daleks are in Davros-designed casings. I might say to the Dalek (at my peril), "Nice bumps! Where'd you get them?" But as far as Kant is concerned, this beauty is limited, is "dependent," because the Daleks' casings have been designed with a purpose: to make the creatures inside the supreme beings in terms of survival and power over others.

Hegel's take on the situation would be somewhat muted. Following his claim that beauty is the perception of thought manifest in matter, comes the idea that the perfect form for thought is the human body. As he argues, the human body is the form it is because it has evolved "as the one and only sensuous appearance appropriate to spirit" (p. 86). This is part of his account of the ancient Greek and Renaissance interest in the human form: classical art is beautiful because it displays the harmony between our inner, mental being and our outer, physical appearance. Strictly speaking, while the human body is the appropriate form for thought, it's only at its most beautiful when it's celebrated in sculpture. (In this regard, the Weeping Angels from "Blink" (2007) are an interesting creation. With their basis in classical sculpture, they aren't so much a case of the *beauty of monsters*, but more a matter of being *monsters of beauty*.)

So Hegel can't help us, as occupants of the *Doctor Who* universe, in appreciating the "natural beauty" of the Daleks. However, we can question him as to whether or not the human body is "the one and only sensuous appearance appropriate" to thought. Hegel's history of beauty is based on the varying degrees to which matter is appropriate to thought, with the classical human form as a point of harmony at which mind and matter are balanced. But this account leaves room for the possibility that there may be different modes of consciousness, different ways of thinking which manifest themselves perfectly in different forms. From the Daleks' point of view, who's to say that their modified, squid-like nature, housed in an individual tank, isn't the perfect expression of their mental life of hatred and universe-domination? Although the Daleks are living creatures and not works of art in the *Doctor Who* universe, if someone were to produce a sculpture of a Dalek, perhaps the sculptor on Necros who made that very good likeness of the Sixth Doctor in "Revelation of the Daleks" (1985), then we might have a Dalek sculpture that would be judged "beautiful."

Katy Manning and a Discreetly-Placed Sink Plunger

Let's turn to consider the beauty of the Daleks in this world. Talk of the beauty of the Daleks is odd because beauty and monstrosity are assumed to be opposites. But is this the case?

Beauty itself isn't a straightforward term. As Anne Sheppard observes, "beautiful" in the English language has a narrow usage. "In English," she maintains:

> Landscapes, women, horses, and flowers may be beautiful but men are described as "handsome" and cows or wine as "fine" rather than "beautiful." Aesthetic appreciation would have a very narrow range of objects if it were confined to those objects to which "beautiful" happens to be applicable in English.[2]

---

[2] *Aesthetics: An Introduction to the Philosophy of Art*, p. 56.

The situation, Sheppard goes on, doesn't just affect the English language. While the French "*beau*" and German "*schön*" have wider application than "beautiful," nevertheless there are occasions when these languages require alternative terms of aesthetic appreciation, such as "*joli*" and "*hübsch*." Here, then, is one reason why my notion of the beauty of the Daleks is odd: I'm applying a word which has a very narrow range in an unusual context. But this still leaves the wider field of what Sheppard calls "aesthetic appreciation": the enjoyment we get from perceiving art, design, and nature at large. Other words are often used to acknowledge this wider sense of aesthetics, for example, "fine," "elegant," "handsome," and "graceful." Even if I give up the notion of the "beauty" of the Daleks and talk in terms of their "aesthetics," this still leaves *the aesthetics of the Daleks* to be explained.

But I don't think I should give up referring to "beauty." As we've seen from Sheppard, beauty shades into these other aspects, meaning there's no definite point at which "beauty" is swapped for an alternative word. More importantly, there's the view that we should actively encourage the broadening of our concept of beauty. Alexander Nehamas declares that the commonly-held notion of beauty described by Sheppard is, in fact, the narrowing of a much more worldly and passionate understanding of beauty entertained by the ancient Greeks.[3] Looking on something as beautiful for Plato, Nehamas asserts, was the beginning of the desire of wanting to become engaged with and care for that particular person or thing. In the *Phaedrus*, Plato describes a man who sees a beautiful boy for the first time. The man at first "shudders in cold fear" but then "his trembling gives way to a strange feverish sweat, stoked by the stream of beauty pouring into him through his eyes and feeding the growth of his soul's wings" to the point where he feels that losing everything "would make no difference to him if only it were for the boy's sake."[4]

Does this mean I am moving towards saying "I love the Daleks"? Perhaps that's what Katy Manning was declaring when she did her nude photo-shoot with a Dalek in 1978. Yes, I suppose I'm saying "I love the Daleks," except I'm taking "love" not in the "sexual relationship" sense, but in the Platonic sense of being drawn in by

---

[3] *Only a Promise of Happiness.*
[4] *Phaedrus,* lines 251a–252a.

something, being made to care for something, becoming attentive to the needs of another. Underlying all of Plato's philosophy is a commitment to the Forms. Existing in a higher, metaphysical realm, the Forms are singular, perfect versions of each and every thing that exists in our world, and act as templates for our world. Love is the process whereby each person tries to make the world and others around them better, so each one moves towards becoming her or his perfect version.

To find the Daleks beautiful in the Platonic sense then is to be fascinated by them as things (not creatures—we aren't in the *Doctor Who* universe) to be engaged with. They're things that we want to treat as creatures. Isn't this where the design of the Dalek succeeds so well: as the portrayal of an alien race, something that's distinctly different from us, something with which we have to engage? Whereas most science-fiction aliens end up being a person painted an unusual color with some additional knobbly bits on their face, the Dalek bears no resemblance to human form. They're wholly other. They're beautiful—the design works—because we see in them the possibility of another form of life, something that could move around and manipulate the world in a way that's wholly different from our own.

Inferno

Beauty then can have different meanings, narrow and wide. So far, Plato has been the most helpful. The Daleks are beautiful in a Platonic sense because their design gives them the appearance of a way of life, a set of capacities, that's other than our own. But this still leaves us with the fact that we're finding beauty in something that's designed to be a monster. Notice I say "designed to be a monster." It could be argued that, in our world, the Dalek isn't a real monster, isn't an evil thing, but merely something designed to be monstrous. But the very fact that a thing which has been designed to look monstrous nonetheless appears beautiful means that the beauty–monster contrast still stands.

The problem is that beauty and monstrosity are taken as opposites. Is this necessarily the case? Conflicting accounts can be found in history. As Umberto Eco points out, beauty and monstrosity are opposites in ancient Greece. He notes that a variety of creatures in Greek mythology, such as fauns, Cyclops, chimaeras, and minotaurs "are considered monstrous and extraneous to the canons of beauty as expressed in the statuary of Policlitus or Praxiteles."[5] This confirms my problem. Yet, in the thirteenth century, in the *Summa*, attributed to Alexander of Hales, monstrosity is seen as a necessary condition of beauty. This is on the understanding that the universe has been created as a whole, and that the presence of monstrosity is needed to balance the presence of beauty. The words of Alexander of Hales from the *Summa* will in fact be echoed by the Fourth Doctor at the end of "Genesis of the Daleks" (1975):

> Evil as such is misshapen. . . . Nevertheless, since from evil comes good, it is therefore well said that it contributes to good and hence it is said to be beautiful within the order [of things]. Thus it is not called beautiful in an absolute sense, but beautiful within the order; in fact, it would be preferable to say: "the order itself is beautiful."[6]

So it's the overall order of things—to which evil contributes—that's beautiful, not the individual evil act or thing. But this doesn't help the beauty of the Daleks, since it's the Daleks themselves which I think are beautiful, not the universe of which they're a part. Although this universe isn't bad, it's a lot better now that *Doctor Who* is back.

Beauty and monstrosity (or ugliness) are given another relationship in Karl Rosenkranz's "aesthetic inferno" from his *Aesthetics of Ugliness*, published in 1852. For Rosenkranz, there's an intimate connection between the beautiful and the ugly in as much as ugliness only exists as the negation of beauty. Drawing on Dante, Rosenkranz presents the universe as an inferno in which beauty is "the original divine idea," and ugliness is the negation of beauty. Because of its primary status, beauty is a necessary condition for ugliness in the sense that it brings ugliness into being as its own negation. Yet the same "beautiful" force negates ugliness and returns it to its original state. Beauty, Rosenkranz writes, "reveals itself as the force that brings the rebellion of ugliness back under its control and dominion."[7]

The idea here is that ugliness contains a component of the force of beauty. So when I look at a Dalek, although it's been designed as a monster, its appearance is never wholly buried in monstrosity

---

[5] *On Beauty*, pp. 131–33.

[6] Alexander of Hales, *Summa Halesiana*, quoted in Eco, *On Beauty*, p. 149.

[7] Quoted in Eco, *On Beauty*, p. 136.

but rather contains a seed of beauty in as much as beauty is the governing principle of the aesthetic inferno. There's some similarity with Alexander of Hales in that the possibility of beauty is claimed to reside not in the ugly thing itself but in a larger process. However, Rosenkranz offers us a slight advantage. Whereas Alexander of Hales can only apply beauty to the entire order of things, Rosenkranz allows talk of individual ugly things becoming beautiful as part of the transition from beauty to ugliness and back again.

What's attractive about Rosenkranz's aesthetic inferno as far as the alleged beauty of the Daleks is concerned is that it represents perception as a dynamic process. In looking at a Dalek, we don't see one thing or the other—beauty or monstrosity—but a transition in which the two are moving between one another. If we adopted this line of argument, its strength would depend in turn on just how convincing we found Rosenkranz's inferno theory. Rosenkranz was a follower of Hegel. We can see this in Rosenkranz's idea that ugliness contains a seed of the beautiful.

The notion that an idea or an object includes its opposite is the engine of Hegel's thesis that life is the process whereby thought and reality become one. The principle of finding a notion within its opposite is one of the most potent forms of expression in the arts, and continues to be the subject of philosophical study, for example, the tension between presence and absence in art and literature examined philosophically by Jean-Paul Sartre and Jacques Derrida. *Doctor Who* has itself played with beauty and monstrosity as interconnected opposites. Typically, this has taken the form of the monsters turning out to be the good guys, as in "Galaxy 4" (1965), "The Curse of Peladon" (1972), and "The Impossible Planet" (2006).

Daleks in Moscow

One final possibility remains. Although the Daleks are presented as monsters, their monstrosity is arguably not to be found in their casings. Instead, it lies in their actions, the roles they're assigned within a story. This means we can talk about the beauty of the Daleks as objects, as casings alone, without having to consider them as monsters. In aesthetics, this position is called "formalism": finding beauty in purely the formal, material aspects of objects, their line, shape, form, and color, irrespective of what the objects are or what the objects themselves might signify. According to Clive

Bell, one of the formalist movement's principal voices: "to appreciate a work of art we need bring with us nothing from life, no knowledge of its ideas and affairs, no familiarity with its emotions . . . we need bring with us nothing but a sense of form and colour and a knowledge of three-dimensional space."[8]

Formalism can be traced back to Kant's preference for finding beauty in objects which serve no purpose or which aren't exemplars of a particular kind. The play of forms—lines, grills, slats, spheres—in the Dalek design, considered independently of any function the forms might have, means the casing could easily occupy a plinth in a Bauhaus or Constructivist exhibition. As Adrian Wiltshire observes in his letter in *Doctor Who Magazine* 371 (19th July 2006), there's a strong similarity between the Dalek casing and the *Flying City* or "*ville volante*" design from 1928 by the Russian Constructivist Georgii Krutikov. Although upside-down as far as a Dalek is concerned, and looking more like a shuttlecock, the design nevertheless possesses a head semi-sphere, head rings, and discs which closely resemble skirt bumps.

Whether Cusick was inspired by Krutikov's design isn't the point. Rather, the 1928 work cements the notion that the beauty of the Daleks can reside in an appreciation of their form alone, as something abstract, removed from any connection it might have with its worldly values of evil or monstrosity. But this option means that our response to the problem of the beauty of the Daleks is to deny it: to talk about the beauty of the Daleks *as objects* is to lose the Daleks, to lose them as *Doctor Who* monsters. We would instead be dealing with an object, a sculpture almost, which happens to bear a strong similarity to a certain early twentieth-century Russian architectural design. I don't think we want to lose the Daleks.

A Beautiful Destiny

I haven't reached a definite conclusion with regard to the beauty of the Daleks. That's sometimes the way with philosophy. The value of the subject lies in its drawing attention to the ideas that are at work in a situation. The question of the beauty of the

---

[8] "The Aesthetic Hypothesis," p. 115.

[9] Krutikov's *ville volante* design can be found at <www.villes-en-france .org/utopies/utopied20.htm>

Daleks has a puzzle at its heart: how can something monstrous be beautiful?

As we've seen, beauty is a complex idea. Far from being in the eye of the beholder, it's a state of pleasure which has been understood in terms of some of the deepest ideas in the history of philosophy: Plato's realm of the Forms, Alexander of Hales's universal order, Kant's intersection of mind and reality, and Hegel's union of mind and reality. While we may still dispute whether or not the Daleks are beautiful, we at least know now that the dispute, rather than just being a conflict between personal opinions, is something which requires us to consider the nature of the universe and our place in it.

If the Doctor must continue his annoying habit of thwarting every attempt the Daleks make at universe-domination, then maybe they might achieve it indirectly, by another means, namely, by their crushing good looks.

28

Monadology of the Time Lords

GREGORY KALYNIUK

If you consider the conceptual premises used to philosophically ground the science-fiction realities of *Doctor Who*, you'll find many having a great deal in common with the thought of the great early modern rationalist philosopher, Gottfried Leibniz. From the monadic character of the dimensionally transcendental TARDIS to the pre-established harmony overseen by the Time Lords, Leibnizian motifs recur throughout the long history of *Doctor Who*—though the manner in which they're evoked, more often than not, proves to be fragmentary, just as Leibniz's philosophy (called "monadology") was.

Some of Leibniz's ideas truly seem to be the stuff of science fiction, and it's hardly surprising that contemporary readers use science fiction to help make sense of them. In fact, *Doctor Who* and the epic 1986 serial "The Trial of a Time Lord" are uniquely useful in helping us to understand of some of Leibniz's key ideas.

What Makes the Doctor "the Doctor"?

When a Time Lord's body is approaching death a process of regeneration is triggered which produces a new body from out of the old one. With each succeeding incarnation, the Doctor assumes a new physical form. What qualifies these physically different incarnations of the Doctor as the same person? For the Doctor at least, it's never as simple as a mere body switch. Regeneration seems to affect his whole personality, and his companions often can't believe that he's still the same person without some convincing. Not only does his body change, but his mind also changes as a result of these transformations. What, then, makes the Doctor "the Doctor"?

Leibniz believes that everything which can be analyzed to be true about a subject, meaning all the relations which it forms and all the events which it can undergo, are already contained within the individual concept of that subject. This individual concept belongs to a point of view upon the world occupied by what Leibniz calls a *monad*, or simple spiritual substance. According to Leibniz's "principle of sufficient reason," each monad has an individual concept that contains all of its relations and events as a subject contains its predicates. We might picture, for instance, a monad which contains the Doctor's individual concept as a point of view upon the universe, with his changing bodies, his relations with other individuals, and relations with things in the universe, all of which are predicates of his individuality.

Sufficient reason helps illustrate what makes the Doctor singularly "the Doctor" distinctly from the events in which he participates. Leibniz distinguishes necessary predicates, inherent to the singular individual, from contingent predicates which arise through substantial relations with other monads, or *appurtenances*. The Doctor's contingent predicates are incarnated through relations of appurtenance between the thinking monad which defines him as a singular individual and the simple monads that belong to the parts of his body, which become instantaneously renewed in their totality each time he regenerates.

The Doctor nonetheless remains identical to himself between incarnations because a thinking monad, which contains his individual concept, endures while the appurtenant monads fall away and are replaced. While the Doctor may contain certain predicates within himself necessarily, it's through his actions in the world that his individual concept acquires contingent predicates, which impact who he becomes and the worlds to which his various incarnations belong. Whether necessary or contingent, all predicates must have a sufficient reason for belonging to a particular subject. This sufficient reason is expressed through their individual concept, which can only be completely known by God, since attaining such knowledge would require an infinite analysis. As we'll see, Time Lords have quite a bit in common with Leibniz's God.

But this still leaves us at a loss to explain how the necessary predicates which make the Doctor "the Doctor" are different from his contingent predicates. In "Inferno" (1970), the TARDIS console transports the Doctor "sideways through time" into a parallel universe, where he encounters Liz Shaw's double in a fascistic version of contemporary England. While Section Leader Elizabeth Shaw never becomes a scientist in this parallel universe, she still has many of the same characteristics as the version of Liz in the Doctor's universe, so much so that the Doctor is able to use his familiarity with these common characteristics to gain her trust.

This scenario demonstrates how an individual concept could possess necessary predicates which would remain the same across parallel universes, such as Elizabeth Shaw's ambition to become a scientist, realized in one universe and abandoned in another. Leibniz would say that the two Lizes are *incompossible* with one another.

The Laws of Time and the Best of All Possible Worlds

The Time Lords oversee that the Laws of Time aren't broken and the primary timelines of the cosmos aren't disturbed. On several occasions, they enlist the Doctor's help to restore order to Time when some event skewed the proper course of things. Like Leibniz's God, the Time Lords apparently know the sufficient reason for the proper course of things

Leibniz famously styled himself as God's attorney, justifying why there should still be evil in the best possible world. Because each monad reflects the whole world from within itself, while not allowing anything to come in or go out, they're "windowless." Since monads have no windows and are isolated from one another, their ability to have a point of view upon themselves and the world depends upon God's point of view. God pre-establishes a harmony between the monads that guarantees the greatest diversity of elements in the combinations that make up their world, leaving evil as the unavoidable consequence of this diversity. In the best possible world, there's only a minimum amount of evil, but evil nonetheless.

What makes Leibniz so sure that God's choice of the actual world is really the best possible? The Doctor has often criticized the Time Lords for their lack of interest in creating more justice in the universe, and for only showing concern when their own interests are at stake. The Doctor's attitude is in this sense similar to the skeptical reader of Leibniz who doubts how God could've wilfully chosen a world full of evils as the best possible. The Time Lords only interfere when the conditions ensuring harmony and diversity in the cosmos are threatened, and excuse the lesser evils for being necessary in this grander scheme. Coincidentally it's the Doctor who accepts the necessity of evil, rather than the Time Lords, in the "Genesis of the Daleks" (1975), when, against the instructions of the Time Lords, he refuses to prevent the Daleks from coming into being. Clearly, the role of the Time Lords is analogous to Leibniz's God in the respect of allowing evil in the universe.

For Leibniz, God can read everything that has been or will be done by passing into the monads as into the pages of a book to determine their sufficient reason. Similarly, as beings standing outside of Time, the Time Lords are able to observe events from across the whole space-time continuum using their space-time visualizers. The Time Lords can also travel forward or backward to any point in space-time in their TARDISes, which aren't only like windows that can assume any point of view, but also doors that can materialize at any of these points at any time, allowing for the world to be acted upon directly. But wouldn't this mean that any such action upon the pre-established world would break the Laws of Time?

Dimensional Transcendentalism and the Principle of Indiscernibles

The TARDIS is a time-machine/spaceship bigger on the inside and smaller on the outside, or *dimensionally transcendental*, as the Doctor puts it. Dimensional transcendentalism seems to be compatible with Leibniz's principle of indiscernibles, according to which there can be no purely external features of things, because things can't differ from one another by place and time alone.[1] Thus, Leibniz thinks it necessary that some internal difference account for their discernibility. Since any one region of space is indiscernible from any other region, space can't properly exist on its own, so the dimensionally transcendental space in the TARDIS couldn't exist

---

[1] Gottfried Leibniz, *Philosophical Writings*, pp. 133–35. Leibniz may have had a difficult time explaining this to Scaroth in "City of Death" (1979), whose identity was splintered across time, dividing him into twelve selves according to purely external features.

apart from the Doctor and its other occupants. The relations of quantity and position between the Doctor and his companions inside the TARDIS would be derivable from their innate qualities, even though they appear to be produced by motion. Like time, space is an ideal, innate, and accidental feature of monads, without having any absolute reality in the external world. The Doctor frequently implies that dimensional transcendentalism simply produces an illusory representation of greater space within the TARDIS—Leibniz would go a step further and assert that according to the principle of indiscernibles, this sort of dimensional transcendentalism applies to all forms of perceptual experience.

While the Doctor often refers to the TARDIS as a machine, he sometimes speaks of it as though it were a living thing. Accordingly, the dimensionally transcendental space in the TARDIS could be derived from its own individual concept. The Doctor refers to the TARDIS as a "she" on many different occasions. It's as though he were like an embryo inside a womb which could travel through time and space. Is the TARDIS the Doctor's appurtenance, or is the Doctor an appurtenance of the TARDIS? Since they share a symbiotic relationship, it would seem to be both. Strangely enough, one of Leibniz's original inspirations for the monad came to him when he was looking through one of the first microscopes at an amoeba. He imagined a monadic vinculum mediating relations of appurtenance with other monads like a cellular membrane mediating the passage of nourishment. The inside of the TARDIS could be understood as the dimensionally transcendental interior of such a monadic vinculum, which would mediate an exchange of information with the space-time continuum.

The Matrix, Perception, and Pre-Established Harmony

As part of the Amplified Panatropic Computer Network, the Matrix contains the bio-data extracts of all Time Lords both living and dead, storing their memories and knowledge in an extra-dimensional framework while also receiving input from sensors in all of the TARDISes, such as the Doctor's. The TARDIS is symbiotically linked to the Doctor, thereby sending the Matrix a continuous stream of information from his experiences. In addition to being a record of the past, or afterlife of deceased Time Lords, it also predicts the future using all of its combined knowledge. It's a machine which works out the pre-established harmony of the cosmos from the amalgamations of data received from all Time Lords, analogous to Leibniz's God. However, within the Matrix only confused perceptions and nightmarish hallucinations exist.

When the Doctor goes inside the Matrix in "The Deadly Assassin" (1976), the hallucinations the Master conjures against him can only be overcome by denying their reality. The Master is like the evil demon of early modern rationalist philosopher René Descartes, challenging the Doctor to suspend his belief in a hallucinatory reality. For Descartes, the possibility of a hallucinatory reality is the ultimate hypothesis guiding his method of doubt, which aims to identify beliefs whose truth can be known for certain. For Leibniz on the other hand, this hallucinatory "reality" is the background of confused perceptions before consciousness is able to form clear perceptions.

As a monad, the Doctor undergoes a natural series of changes involving a plurality of affections and relations which become differentiated by degrees, confusedly represented by perception. Desire, or what Leibniz calls appetition, produces the change or passage from one perception to another. For something to be rendered discernible, attention towards it must first be desired. It's only through the force of his appetition that the Doctor is able to deny the hallucinations of the Matrix. Apperception is only given to the Doctor when he becomes conscious of the perceptions his appetition produces a change in, or when he's conscious of where desire focuses his attention. The Matrix denies him such reflective knowledge of apperception in both "The Deadly Assassin" and "The Invasion of Time," though under different circumstances. In the former, it results from the evil demon's temptations; in the latter, it results from a sort of divine fury.

All Engin can observe through the Matrix while the Doctor is connected to it is the workings of the machine from the outside, and not the Doctor's actual hallucinatory perceptions ("The Deadly Assassin"). According to Leibniz, observing the Doctor's hallucinatory perceptions would be impossible, since they're contained within his thinking monad and the monads are windowless. Leibniz uses the example of a machine similar to the Matrix to show how the variety of our perceptions is something which is produced from within ourselves:

Suppose that there were a machine so constructed as to produce thought, feeling, and perception, we could imagine it increased in size while retaining the same proportions, so that one might enter as one might a mill. On going inside we should only see the parts impinging upon one another; we should not see anything which would explain a perception. The explanation of perception must therefore be sought in a simple substance, and not in a compound or a machine. (p. 181)

Rather than discovering sufficient reason from the godly point of view internal to the Matrix, the Time Lords regress to a state of confused perception when exposed to the Matrix. There's nothing in the framework of the Matrix itself which explains their confused perceptions—the explanation for the perceptions can only come from the monads experiencing them. Each Time Lord's perceptions are fused into the Matrix and generate its own internal perceptions, but there's no pre-established harmony between their perceptions. This doesn't stop the Matrix from calculating the pre-established harmony of the cosmos, however.

The Incompossible Valeyard

The Doctor we're familiar with is good, though we are confronted with an evil Doctor in "The Trial of a Time Lord." This appears to be a contradictory state of affairs, however, if we consider the worlds in which these Doctors act, we find that the good Doctor and the evil Doctor aren't merely contradictory, but *incompossible* (self-contradictory concepts incapable of being formed at the same time).

In "The Trial of a Time Lord," the Doctor attempts to convince the High Council of Time Lords that the evidence being presented against him, *via* the Matrix, doesn't match the events as he remembers them. The Valeyard, or learned court prosecutor and presenter of the evidence, complicates the problem even further when it's revealed that he's himself a future incarnation of the Doctor, or amalgamation of the darker sides of his nature, somewhere between his Twelfth and final incarnations. The evidence extracted from the Matrix is incompossible with the Doctor, but perhaps compossible with the Valeyard. The Valeyard's timeline could have diverged from the Doctor's right before the events which are presented as evidence for the trial, leaving him prosecuting the Doctor for the crimes done by his own past self.

According to sufficient reason, if each individual concept contains all of the events which that individual will undergo as its predicates, then how could the Doctor and the Valeyard both have the same individual concept? The singularity of their individual concept would have to be cut from its prolongation in the events which distinguish them.[2] To make sense of this, we'd need to speak generally of *a* Doctor, instead of the particular Doctor who does good or evil. The Doctor in general wouldn't yet belong to any definite world. Through the prolongation of his singularities into events, and the convergence of its series with those of other monads, a world which includes them all is rendered compossible. Worlds become incompossible when series of events diverge, as the series of events converging on the Valeyard's world might have in relation to the series of events converging on the Doctor's world.

According to the principle of indiscernibles, neither time nor space can be taken to be constitutive of innate qualities any more than they can be taken to be purely external features of the world. Rather, they're contingent derivations of innate qualities, like the singularities which prolong themselves in events. When the Master describes the Valeyard as an amalgamation of the darker sides of the Doctor's nature, we still don't know if the Valeyard is any particular future incarnation of the Doctor. He's a future Doctor in general while his historical continuity with the Doctor remains indefinite, but also, perhaps, an evil Doctor in particular for acting treacherously against the Doctor at his trial. The Valeyard is promised by the High Council of Time Lords the remainder of the Doctor's regenerations, in exchange for finding him guilty, which would paradoxically cancel him from existence before allowing him to relive more than half of his regeneration cycle. These "darker sides" of the Doctor's nature could be interpreted as being not only evil in particular, but also obscure in general.

The last adventure to be shown as evidence at the Doctor's trial is actually one which hasn't yet taken place from the Doctor's point of view. If the Doctor were found guilty, then this adventure would become incompossible with his timeline and would not take place, leaving him convicted for things which he never had a chance to do (but which the Valeyard perhaps had already done). But if he

---

[2] This comes from contemporary French philosopher Gilles Deleuze's interpretation of Leibniz in *The Fold: Leibniz and the Baroque*, pp. 63–64.

wasn't found guilty, this would leave the Doctor with foreknowledge of his own future. Assuming this isn't normal, even for Time Lords, wouldn't it create a paradox? How could the events play themselves out as the Matrix had predicted?

An important section at the end of Leibniz's *Theodicy* quotes a long passage from medieval Italian humanist Laurentius Valla's *Dialogue on Free Will,* in which Sextus Tarquinius visits Apollo, seeking divine foreknowledge of his life, only to hear that he'll be a traitor to his country. Leibniz continues the story with Sextus visiting Jupiter to complain about his fate, only to be told not to return to Rome and to renounce any hope of attaining its crown.[3] He refuses to leave. Meanwhile, Jupiter instructs Theodorus, a High Priest curious about Sextus' fate, to visit his daughter Pallas. Pallas shows Theodorus an immense pyramid with an apex but no base, made up of infinite halls, each containing a possible world in which Sextus' life plays itself out differently.

Leibniz uses Theodorus in place of Sextus to get around the problem which the Doctor is faced with after seeing his possible future adventure with the Vervoids. Some of the lower halls in the pyramid portray a happy and noble Sextus, while the most beautiful hall at the apex portrays the Sextus who rapes Lucretia, deemed the best possible world because it brings about the beginning of the Roman Republic. The base of this dimensionally transcendental pyramid descends infinitely and is paradoxically bottomless, since there can be no worst possible world, though Leibniz's goal is to show the infinite possibilities of human freedom. Did the Doctor's adventure with the Vervoids come from the most beautiful hall or from one of these lower halls?

Considering the inconsistency of the Matrix with the Doctor's timeline in the adventures presented as evidence in the trial against the Doctor, one's future may not be as deterministic as the Time Lords believe; it shows alternate events are possible. In a similar vein, Leibniz disagreed with Valla's attempt to show how divine foreknowledge of beings in existence could not impair freedom. Instead of associating Jupiter with an even more deterministic divine providence as Valla had, Leibniz associates Jupiter's daughter Pallas with knowledge of simple intelligence, which embraces all of the possible.

---

[3] *Theodicy,* pp. 365–373.

While Leibniz doesn't deny divine foreknowledge and God's choosing of the best possible world, he nonetheless emphasizes the importance of knowledge of simple intelligence and possibility as that which grounds human freedom. Sextus could have left Rome, but his ambition prevented him from making this sacrifice. Likewise, the Doctor could've let the Vervoids live to reach Earth, but he defends his future decision to kill them off—as the best possible, albeit with an anthropocentric bias. Whether the events play themselves out as envisioned by the Matrix is not explored, though it would have presented some interesting problems for the question of free will had it been.

By the end of "The Trial of a Time Lord," it's revealed that secret knowledge was being exported from the Matrix to outside civilizations all along, and that the tampering suspected by the Doctor had been done to cover up the details of this smuggling, which actually figured in the first of the adventures presented as evidence. Perhaps the evidence wasn't tampered with at all, but was the mysterious fate of the extracted knowledge which caused the ripples in the space-time continuum, simultaneously giving existence to the Valeyard and creating a compossible world in which the Doctor was implicated in smuggling. If so, then the Matrix would cease to carry out its godly role in determining the future by choosing the best possible world to actualize, as Leibniz claimed his God did. Instead, it allowed for many incompossible worlds to exist at the same time, just as the Chinese philosopher-architect Ts'ui Pên claims in Jorge Luis Borges's short story, "The Garden of Forking Paths":

> He believed in an infinite series of times, in a dizzily growing, ever spreading network of diverging, converging, and parallel times. This web of time—the strands of which approach one another, bifurcate, intersect or ignore each other through the centuries—embraces *every* possibility. We do not exist in most of them. In some you exist and not I, while in others I do, and you do not, and in others yet both of us exist. In this one, in which chance has favored me, you have come to my gate. In another, you, crossing the garden, have found me dead. In yet another, I say these very same words, but am an error, a phantom. [4]

Was the Valeyard such an error or phantom, or was the intersection of his strand with the Doctor's actually a matter of the calculated

---

[4] Jorge Luis Borges, *Ficciones*, p. 100.

purpose? Ts'ui Pên's garden admittedly has more in common with the Matrix than does Leibniz's bottomless pyramid of infinite halls, since the conditions of paradox are internal to its very working. The Valeyard would never appear in a world of pre-established harmony, but in a world of forking paths where incompossibles paradoxically communicate through the Matrix; he's right at home.

The Odd Thought of *Doctor Who*

Leibniz was interested in science fiction. In one of his most curious texts, *An Odd Thought Concerning a New Sort of Exhibition*, Leibniz envisions an Academy of games to which people would flock to experience an exotic variety of educational wonders and amusements.[5] Among the exhibits, there would be such things as games of cards and dice, magic lanterns, detachable moving pictures of very unusual and grotesque objects, representations of charity and cruelty, friendly disputes, simulated war games, experiments on water, air, and vacuum, exotic animals, instruments that play themselves, comedies of all nations and trades, ridiculous styles, speaking trumpets, adding machines, magnets, and all sorts of other things. In other words, Leibniz's Academy would include some of the most characteristic features of *Doctor Who*.

Leibniz's expectation that such an Academy would promote the advancement of knowledge and morality is echoed in the very notion of *Doctor Who* as an educational program. While Leibniz may have sought to uncover reason and order behind everything, he also valued experiences of wonder and dizzying confusion enough to imagine an institution for creative learning founded upon such principles. His "odd thought" is indeed the very substance of *Doctor Who*.

---

[5] Leibniz, *Selections*, pp. 585–594.

EPISODE 6

Lots of Planets
Have a North!

*Human and Time Lord
Culture*

29

The *Evil* of the Daleks

ROBIN BUNCE

TEMMOSUS: I believe the Daleks hold the key to our future.

From the very beginning, the Daleks were a triumph. The design, the voices, and the scripts all contributed to the genesis of an iconic villain. The Daleks are undoubtedly the most alien and most menacing alien menace ever to have invaded the small screen.

Doctor Who fans owe the Daleks a great deal. The Daleks transformed *Doctor Who* into a national phenomenon. In fact, Dalekmania, as it was called, was bigger from 1963 to 1966 than the Power Rangers at the height of their success in the 1990s. The Daleks gave the Doctor an arch-enemy, and the show a super-villain that boosted the ratings and ensured *Doctor Who*'s survival.

The Daleks may be one of science fiction's best known villains but what is it that makes them villainous? Certainly, the voice is chilling and the shape is strange. But beyond this, and perhaps more importantly, there's a moral dimension to the Daleks that's recognizably bad or, to use a stronger term, evil. Evidently, evil comes in different flavors. Catwoman, for example, is bad, but in a very different way to Ming the Merciless, Darth Vader, the Mekon, or for that matter, the Daleks. Why then do we recognize the Daleks as evil? What's it about them that's morally repugnant? And how did Terry Nation go about creating a creature with a moral dimension?

First, what *is* evil? The magnitude of this problem can hardly be overstated. Philosophers have wrangled over this issue for millennia, and will doubtless continue to do so. Secondly, how's it possible to understand the meaning of a complex text such as *Doctor Who*? This question may seem a little easier. Even so, it's still a tricky one, after all the Daleks have made numerous television appearances, featured in two films, and a host of books and comic strips not to mention fan fiction. It'd be foolish to assume that the Daleks are always the same. How should a philosopher proceed in the face of two such intractable problems?

Looking at the script of "The Daleks" (1963), focusing on the author's intentions and situating them in their historical context, should give us a consistent account of the Daleks as Nation originally conceived them. In this way we can recover the Daleks as their original audience saw them. In writing "The Daleks" Nation tried to create a story that would be intelligible to the audience of the early 1960s, and therefore, he uses language, imagery, and ideas that meant something to the audience of the time. Nation appeals to cultural knowledge, such as the smell of dodgem cars, which originated outside *Doctor Who* and outside "The Daleks."[1] With this in mind, we can see what Nation was trying to do when he originally created the Daleks, and we see that the *evil* of the Daleks is bound up with what it means to be human.

Evil, Rationality, and Dehumanization

Nation presents the Daleks as evil by emphasizing their lack of humanity. This general approach is far from new. The renowned philosopher Richard Rorty argues that, traditionally, there've been three strategies by which we turn others into enemies. First, we choose to think of others as animals rather than human. Secondly, we describe others as childlike and therefore, assume that they're incapable of governing themselves and suppress any attempt they make to assert their independence. Finally, we feminize our opponents; we equate humanity with masculinity and refuse to recognize the humanity of those we deem to be effeminate.[2]

Each of these strategies is a strategy of dehumanization. Significantly, each strategy equates humanity with rationality. Animals aren't rational; women and children (according to traditional prejudices) aren't fully rational—consequently, they aren't fully human. Moreover, rationality is the key to moral action, since

---

[1] Terry Nation, *Doctor Who, the Scripts: The Daleks*, p. 81.
[2] *Truth and Progress: Philosophical Papers*, Volume 3, p. 169.

only rational people can understand moral truth and discipline themselves to act ethically. Therefore, our irrational enemies are both less than human and evil.

Nation, too, made the Daleks villains and enemies by dehumanizing them. But Nation's specific strategy is novel because his understanding of what it means to be human is unconventional. The Daleks aren't enemies because they're animals who are less rational than us; they're enemies because they're *more* rational. This is obvious even before we properly meet the Daleks. From the very beginning, the Doctor is clear: the unknown creators of the dead city are "intelligent, very intelligent . . . What these instruments tell us is that we're in the midst of a—a very, very advanced, civilized society."[3] The Daleks have become inhuman and immoral because their emotions have withered. They feel no pang of remorse when plotting to annihilate the Thals, no compassion for the suffering of the Doctor and his companions, and they're apparently indifferent to the fate of the Daleks who are perishing due to the effects of the Thals' drugs.

Nation's insight is counter to the dominant tradition of western philosophy—the tradition that extends from Socrates to Kant, which argues that rationality is at the heart of what it means to be human. Nation appeals to a new set of metaphors for dehumanization which emerged in the twentieth century. The first is the metaphor of human as a robot or computer. The second is the human who has become a product of a mechanized process. This second metaphor is best-known from novels such as Aldous Huxley's *Brave New World* (1932) or Yevgeny Zamyatin's *We* (1921) in which humans become dehumanized as the result of a scientifically ordered society.

These metaphors are rooted in a new philosophical understanding of reason. In both cases, rationality is considered a danger to authentic humanity rather than the part of our nature that makes us human. This twentieth-century view of humanity suggests that being human is about feeling rather than thinking. As Rorty puts it, we're different from other animals because, "we can feel *for each other* to a much greater extent than they [other animals] can."[4] According to Rorty, it's our emotions and our imagination that makes us human and ground our potential to be good. This idea is

---

[3] Nation, p. 48.
[4] Rorty, p. 176.

bound up with the notion that humans are individuals. Reason, at least in theory, leads all rational people to the same conclusions. What reasonable individual could doubt that two plus two equals four? Feelings, on the other hand, don't conform to logic. Consequently, there's a much greater scope for individuality in a moral philosophy rooted in emotions. The rational Daleks have lost any sense of individuality. Nation makes this plain in a conversation between Susan and a Dalek about a letter she has written:

DALEK ONE: What is the last word here?

SUSAN: The last word?

DALEK ONE: Sew-san? (*Susan giggles, which alarms the Daleks.*)

DALEK ONE: Stop that noise!

SUSAN: Well, it's . . . it's . . . it's what I'm called. It's my name. (p. 77)

Through this exchange Nation underlines the alienness of the Daleks. The Daleks have no conception of an individual name. It's also significant that they don't understand laughter. The Daleks can understand the Doctor's rational desire to survive and get the Thals' drugs, but they can't comprehend the irrational, emotional, human aspects of their captives. "The Daleks" shows Nation's villains at their least individual. Later stories introduce clearly individuated Daleks such as the Black Dalek, the Dalek Emperor, and the Dalek Supreme. There are no such distinctions in the dead city of "The Daleks."

The Daleks are morally repugnant because they've lost the ability to feel as we feel. They've lost the sense of themselves as individuals and due to this, have ceased to be human. This is why they're horrifying: we know that once they were better, and we dread becoming like them!

The War, the Bomb, and the Survivors

The Daleks are the product of their environment, which, in turn, is the product of an apocalyptic war. We discover this through a fictional history, in fact, three fictional histories: an oral history which the Daleks reveal to the Doctor, a written history which the Thals possess, and a natural history which the Doctor and his companions piece together from observations of the dead planet. Central to each of these histories is a war and a bomb:

> Ov-er five hun-dred years a-go there were two ra-ces on this pla-net. We, the Da-leks, and the Thals. Af-ter the Neu-tronic war, our Da-lek fore-fath-ers re-tired in-to the city, pro-tect-ed by our ma-chines. (p. 77)

The consequences of the nuclear war dominate "The Daleks." Indeed, with the exception of the scene around the TARDIS's food machine the Doctor and his companions talk about little else for the first two and a half episodes.

Nation constructs the Dalek's moral character by appealing to the audience's knowledge and fear of nuclear war. "The Daleks" was written at a time of intense nuclear hysteria. The Cuban Missile Crisis has brought the world to the brink of nuclear holocaust just a year before "The Dead Planet" (1963) was shown. The crisis in Cuba was the third time in five years that the world had faced nuclear oblivion. Between 1958 and 1961 there was a tense stand-off over West Berlin; and prior to this, the USA and USSR deployed nuclear weapons to support their allies on either side of the Taiwan Strait. President John F. Kennedy stoked public apprehension of all-out nuclear war during the Berlin crisis by publically committing $207 million to the construction of fallout shelters.[5] Kennedy described the period from 1958 to 1962 as the years of "maximum danger" (p. 79). Bomb "biographer" Gerard J. DeGroot concurs, arguing that the late 1950s and early 1960s was a uniquely perilous phase of the Cold War.[6] This period of maximum nuclear danger is the immediate context for "The Daleks" and is essential to an understanding of Nation's villains.

Nation's description of Skaro clearly appeals to popular knowledge regarding the effects of nuclear war. "The Dead Planet" is laced with clues about the nuclear horror that the planet has witnessed. The soil has been scorched by "indescribable" heat and the Doctor and his companions soon feel dizzy and weak—showing symptoms of radiation sickness.[7] These aspects of nuclear war were well-known in the early 1960s. Less than two years before "The

---

[5] R.J. McMahon, *The Cold War: A Very Short Introduction*, p. 84.

[6] G.J. DeGroot, *The Bomb: A Life*, p. ix.

[7] Nation, pp. 22, 42.

Daleks" went into production, the Soviet hydrogen bomb 'Tsar Bomba' created the biggest artificial explosion in history, resulting in a fireball almost five kilometers in diameter. Radiation sickness had also come to the public's attention in during a 1958 US bomb test over the Bikini islands. The Japanese boat, *Lucky Dragon*, which had been fishing ninety miles from the test sight, was showered with radioactive ash. As a result, the fishermen developed radiation sickness. Those who survived were hospitalized for more than six months. Western newspapers covered the story, horrifying the public with details of an invisible radioactive killer.[8]

Public knowledge of nuclear warfare was also based on the science fiction of the 1950s and 1960s. Indeed, the grotesque effects of nuclear war proved fertile ground for science fiction. Nuclear weapons and atomic war were consistent themes in films such as *X The Unknown* (1956), *On the Beach* (1959), *The Time Machine* (1960), *The Day the Earth Caught Fire* (1961), and *Doctor No* (1962); in books like Wyndham's *The Chrysalids* (1955), Peter George's *Red Alert (Two Hours to Doom)* (1958), and Miller's *A Canticle for Leibowitz* (1960); and in pulp sci-fi magazines such as *Amazing Science Fiction* and *If*.

Nonetheless, "The Daleks" contains an unusual element that clearly locates the story in the world of the early 1960s. Skaro had been devastated by a "neutron war."[9] The bombs used were not the atomic bombs, in the conventional sense; Skaro was destroyed by a neutron bomb. This reference may be lost on the modern audience and therefore the nature of the device and the public's knowledge of it in the early sixties needs to be considered carefully. The phrase 'neutron bomb' seems to have come into popular usage in 1959.[10] The nature of the bomb was discussed in the British and American press fairly extensively between 1960 and 1963. For example, the May 1960 edition of *US News and World Report* carried the following description: "The weapon—in one possibility being discussed—could be built as a 'light-weight' device able to send out streams of poison radiation greater than those produced by today's big 'conventional' nuclear bombs."[11] Similarly, the US

---

[8] P.D. Smith, *Doomsday Men*, pp. 366–67.
[9] *Nation*, p. 111.
[10] I.W. Russell, "Among the New Words," p. 146.
[11] *US News and World Report* (May 1960), p. 34.

periodical *News* from November 2nd, 1962, described them thus: "'death ray' bombs-which would kill without leaving wide destruction."[12] In Britain, *The Times* tackled neutron bombs on a number of occasions in the early 1960s. *The Times's* correspondent in Washington described the neutron bomb as "a devastating weapon which would destroy life but would not destroy matter."[13]

The neutron bomb creates much less blast and heat than a uranium, plutonium, or hydrogen bomb. However, it emits a much more powerful dose of radiation. Consequently, within days of a detonation all life in the effected area is destroyed, but buildings, remain undamaged. Nation's script contains a great deal of evidence that Skaro had been ravaged by a neutron bomb. The trees in the forest are "brittle," they've been turned to stone.[14] Clearly, Nation imagined that the neutron radiation had knocked out all of the tree's living cells, but left the solid parts of the organism intact. The Dalek city, too, is dead but unscathed. The Doctor describes the effects of the neutron bomb in terms immediately recognizable from the 1960s debate: ". . . neutron bomb. Yes, it destroys all human tissues, but leaves the buildings and machinery intact" (p. 49).

The link between the Daleks and the bomb is central to their nature. Their bodies have mutated due to the bomb's radiation. What's more, they're physically dependent on the bomb as without its radiation they can no longer survive. Most importantly of all, the Daleks are evil because they're the embodiment of the bomb. The Daleks have internalized the unfeeling reason that led to the creation and use of the bomb. The neutron bomb after all was the product of brilliant minds, but minds that were devoted to the remorseless extermination of entire nations. This inhuman reason has become the Dalek's defining moral characteristic.

The Mutants: Possible Futures: Evolution and Degeneration

The moral character of the Daleks is bound up with the future. One way in which we think about morality is in terms of the consequences of our actions. If our actions create a better future we consider them morally good; whereas if they make the future worse

---

[12] *News* (November 2nd, 1962), p. 1.

[13] *The Times*, (June 26th, 1961), p 8.

[14] Nation, p. 22.

we think of them as bad. Nation makes the Daleks bad by linking them to popular fears about the future. "The Dead Planet" followed "100,000 B.C." Consequently, many of the original audience assumed that while the first story was about the origins of humanity, the second story was about humanity's fate. They assumed that "The Dead Planet" was a vision of the Earth following a nuclear war. Nation played on this perception repeatedly in the script. The ambiguity of the location is reinforced by Ian's skepticism regarding the Doctor's claim that they've landed on another planet (p. 26). Immediately, then, Nation pushes us in the direction of considering ourselves and our own future.

The Daleks as we encounter them in the story are the products of an evolutionary process. They weren't always soulless creatures who lurked in metal shells. They were once much like us (p. 74). However, the neutron bomb changed them, turning the humanoid Dals into mutant Daleks. "The Daleks" leaves the appearance of the mutant creature unclear. Nonetheless, Nation's vision of the creature is embodied in a production sketch of the Dalek creature that dates from 1963. Essentially, the Dalek mutant is like an octopus. Its body comprises a large brain and tentacles.

The mutant nature of the Daleks played on popular fears of a post-holocaust future. Moreover, they also appealed to popular understandings of evolution. "The Daleks" is part of a science fiction tradition, extending back to Victorian times, which plays on the fear that evolution might turn human beings into monsters. Nation's conception of evolution and the nature of the mutant creature owes much to H.G. Wells. *The Time Machine* (1895) is Wells's best-known tale of human evolution gone wrong. Wells paints the unsettling picture of humanity evolving into two separate species the Eloi and the Morlocks. There are undeniable similarities between the Eloi and the Thals on the one hand, and the Morlocks and the Daleks on the other. This resemblance is widely acknowledged.[15] Nonetheless, the philosophical similarities between *The Time Machine* and "The Daleks" have been ignored.

In general terms, Nation follows *The Time Machine*'s characterization of evil. Wells's novel explicitly argues that both the Eloi and the Morlocks have evolved into something that is inferior to

---

[15] Howe, Stammers, and Walker, *Doctor Who: The Sixties*, p. 31; J.K. Muir, *A Critical History of Doctor Who on Television*, p. 80; Bignell and O'Day, *Terry Nation*, p. 71.

humanity. The Eloi have lost their knowledge of science and technology, their inquisitive spirit and their initiative. The Morlocks, on the other hand, retain their ability to use technology and still display curiosity but they've become cannibals. Yet, Wells's sympathies lie with the Eloi. In the final analysis the Eloi have retained their ability to feel love and sympathy for one another and consequently, Wells argues, they're more human than the ingenious but unfeeling Morlocks.[16]

The two debates, the nuclear debate and the Victorian debate about evolution, are linked by the film *The Time Machine*, which Nation saw in 1960. The film mixes Wells's story of evolution gone wrong with a nuclear war. In so doing, it explains Wells's bleak vision of the future with popular concerns about the possibility of a nuclear war. Nation takes this a step further by mixing Wells's vision of evolution with more contemporary science fiction, such as Wyndham's *The Chrysalids*, which explores mutation following a nuclear war. In this sense, "The Daleks," like *The Time Machine*, is a vision of our future.

"The Daleks" also owes a massive debt to Wells's *The War of the Worlds* (1899). This novel, too, contains a description of human evolution. In fact, Wells's Martians, the villains of *The War of the Worlds*, bear an uncanny resemblance to "The Man of the Year Million," an essay on human evolution which Wells published in 1893. By the Year Million, Wells suggests, human beings will have evolved in such a way that their bodies will have shrivelled and all that will be left is tentacle like "hands" attached to a massive brain. The Martians, too, have huge brains and enfeebled bodies largely made up of tentacles.[17] What's more, Wells's Martians sit inside metal war machines armed with ray-guns. This could easily be a description of the Daleks. Evidently, Wells's Martians are the Daleks' closest fictional relative. Moreover, the Daleks, like Wells's monsters, have become evil through a process of evolution.[18] Their brains have expanded as their bodies have shriveled. Their physical appearance perfectly matches their moral character. The growth of the brain emphasizes the dominance of reason, and the withering of the body parallels the fading of their emotions.

---

[16] H.G. Wells, *The Time Machine and Other Stories*, p. 71.
[17] H.G. Wells, *The War of the Worlds*, pp. 12–15.
[18] Nation, p. 124.

The Daleks are evil because we recognize they were once better; they're evil because they're the future we dread. They were once capable of genuine emotion and real moral good. However, five hundred years after the bomb was dropped, they've ceased to be human. They're what we might be like on the other side of Armageddon. Like the Morlocks, they've become trapped underground surrounded by machines. They've evolved or mutated into soulless brains who, for all their intellectual brilliance, are evil because they can no longer feel for their fellow creatures.

Bunker Mentality or Love?

The Doctor's companion Ian sums up why the Daleks are evil: "They obviously think and act and feel in an entirely different way. They just aren't human" (p. 109). The Daleks were once great and noble. They were once human, but the neutron bomb has remade the Daleks in its own image. The idea of the neutron bomb caused moral outrage in the early 1960s because of its appalling inhumanity. All nuclear weapons are horrifying, but there was something peculiarly callous about a bomb that targets people and not things. In this sense, the neutron bomb represented the triumph of technology and science over humanity.[19] It's this triumph that the Daleks embody, and it's this that makes them evil.

Nation's view of evil is peculiarly apt for the nuclear age. The philosophical debate over why humans are good and evil can be traced back to ancient times. Rorty says that Socrates and Jesus, the two great ancient moralists, left us with two different answers. For Socrates, reason and knowledge make humans good. Jesus on the other hand preached love.[20] Nation, like the atheist Rorty, sides with Jesus. The neutron bomb provides the final proof that reason and knowledge don't necessarily lead to moral progress. The neutron bomb didn't emerge from the sleep of reason, it was the product of some of the world's finest minds. The Daleks, as I have argued, embody the bomb. They're dominated by a bunker mentality: safe in their underground city they create a new neutron weapon and plot the total extermination of the Thals. The Daleks'

---

[19] G. Rogoff, "The Juggernaut of Production," p. 132; B.B. Seligman, "On Work, Alienation, and Leisure," p. 353.

[20] Rorty, p. 176.

physical appearance sums this up. Each Dalek is a rational brain inside its own heavily armed bunker.

The Daleks are also evil because they represent a nightmare human future. The Daleks are what we might become after the bombs fall. They're the mutant survivors of an apocalyptic war who have been locked in a nuclear bunker for five hundred years. They're sexless, heartless brains, shut up in machines incapable of intimacy; they've forgotten what it means to laugh and no longer think of themselves as individuals. We recognize them as evil because the Daleks have lost all that we hold most dear.

But Nation also offers us a positive moral message. The Doctor and his companions remind us and the Thals of what it means to be good. Indeed, Ian presents us with a lesson on how to be a moral philosopher. Initially, the Thals are unwilling to stand up to the Daleks. But Ian teaches them a moral lesson. His appeal to reason fails. As a last resort he threatens to take one of the Thals to the Dalek city and exchange her for the TARDIS's fluid link. Immediately, the Thals see that their friend's life is more important than a piece of technology. They realize that there's something special about the life of a friend. Ian's appeal to their emotions works and the Thals learn that evil must be resisted. Again, this moral message chimes with Rorty's philosophy. Moral progress, according to Rorty, is achieved through enlarging the moral imagination, not by increasing our stock of knowledge or by becoming ever more rational. Empathy is the key. We're more likely to act well when we imagine what the world feels like from our enemy's point of view; if we remember that our enemy, however different from us they may seem, is part of a community who'll grieve if they're harmed (p. 185). The Doctor makes a similar point. In response to his companion's endless ethical debates he retorts, "[t]his is no time for morals. This is time for action!" [21] The Doctor understands that doing the right thing is always more important than abstract moralizing. The Thals are good because they love each other. The Daleks don't, and that's why they're evil. [22]

---

[21] Nation, p. 117.

[22] Many thanks to the following *Doctor Who* fans: Roger Bunce (pictured below), my Dad, who worked as a cameraman on many of the *Doctor Who* stories of the 1960s, 1970s, and 1980s; Mark Anstead, Nick Potamis, Jamie Hailstone, and Andy Diamond; and my daughter India who's living proof that the Daleks are still terrifying. I must also thank Dr. Peggy Watson of Homerton College, Cambridge,

Roger Bunce at BBC Television Centre some time in the 1970s

for inviting me to present the essay which became this chapter to the College's students, and the undergraduates who came, for their stimulating questions. Finally, thank you to Barry Hart for commenting on a draft of this chapter.

30

The Decline and Fall of the British Empire, Sponsored by TARDIS

DEBORAH PLESS

Man is, and always has been, a maker of gods. It has been the most serious and significant occupation of his sojourn in the world.

—JOHN BURROUGHS, American essayist

It may not be a popular topic, but man has been creating god for himself since before he could talk. We create gods to fill some inner lack and to give ourselves something or someone to emulate. Even more than this, though, is the human creation of heroes, mystical people slightly better than the rest of us, who can serve as intermediaries between our ideals and us, and in so doing, show us how to really live. This tradition may be thousands of years old, but never has it flourished so fantastically as in the twentieth and early twenty-first centuries, as television and movies gave culture the opportunity to create heroes on a massive scale.

Given this new stage for heroics, once relegated to oral traditions and epic poetry, one would think that the world would become less unified, as everyone became free to choose their own hero. Yet this hasn't happened. As time has progressed, we've seen several heroes become symbols for their nations, inspiring the people onward as the world grows darker. In America, this trend can be tracked by the popularity of different superheroes through the years. In Britain, though, the national hero has most decidedly been the Doctor, from *Doctor Who*.

A Romantic Wanderer

This is, of course, in direct conflict with the fact that the Doctor is an alien. John Fiske reconciles this fact by considering the Doctor as a character more than human, and only slightly less than divine: "The significance of the Doctor lies partly in his structured relationship to gods and man. He is an anomalous creature in that he is neither God (or Time Lord) nor man, but occupies a mediating category between the two. He has a nonhuman origin and many nonhuman abilities, yet a human form and many human characteristics."[1] In other words, the Doctor is a compromise between the strength and power of a god and the ingenuity of man. It's this balance itself that makes him the ideal.

Tom Baker, the Fourth Doctor, and the one that best exemplified this ideal of the Doctor as Britain's hero, refused to play the Doctor as some sort of silly man always flitting about, but rather insisted that he portray him as the "romantic wanderer." Dressed in a large fedora, long coat, and trailing, rainbow scarf, Tom Baker simultaneously elevated the Doctor and also made him relatable. He became like a favorite uncle, the type of person one would like to be when one grew up. As June Hudson, who worked on the show during that time said, "The Doctor had always been the still center in a spinning world of aliens and monsters."[2] More than that, however, the Doctor was conceived from the start as an unconventional, non-patriarchal figure, a plan only marred slightly by time. Verity Lambert, *Doctor Who*'s first producer, always intended the Doctor to come off as utterly anti-establishment, like a child pointing out the ridiculous in the society.

The History of Ordinary Events

"After the travails of the immediate post-war years, British leaders had expected that the end of the decade would find them in calmer waters. . . . Hopes such as these were doomed. The new decade brought no relief and revival, but a further round of crises."[3] On first glance, post-World War II Britain doesn't seem the most likely

---

[1] John Fiske, "Popularity and Ideology: A Structuralist Reading of 'Dr. Who'," p. 180.

[2] Piers D.G. Britton, "Dress and the Fabric of the Television Series," p. 353.

[3] John Darwin, *Britain and Decolonisation: The Retreat from Empire in the Post-War World*, p. 163.

candidate for an upsurge in hope. In the years immediately following the war, Britain was faced with crises in its many colonies,
leading in most cases to decolonialization, an unrestricted immigration policy, only rescinded when it became clear that the nation
was practically bursting at the seams, and a dispute over the meaning of British citizenship itself, the foundation of the Empire. It was
in these conditions that Britain began to dream of a better future.

Immediately following the World War II, Britain gave India its
independence, and split it from Pakistan, removing itself entirely
from that section of the world. Though this was a blow to the
Empire, Britain at this time still ruled numerous countries in Africa
and Asia. The majority of these territories became independent
over the course of seven years, from 1957 to 1964, sometimes
referred to as "Readjustment." The Empire's goal wasn't so much to
set the nations free, possibly out of a belated sense of duty or
pride, as some have suggested, but generally for far more mundane
concerns. As the years progressed, it became increasingly difficult
for Britain, weakened by Germany's sustained attacks during World
War II, to maintain political control of its colonies. Most were
released simply because they'd become too expensive to keep.
Between 1960 and 1964 alone, seventeen of Britain's colonies in
Africa became independent, including most of the modern African
powers. This rush for independence left Britain feeling gun-shy and
weak; it was cut off from the resources it had been able to rely on
for, in some cases, the past three-hundred years.

The relationship between decolonization and Britain's general
decline in international prominence was not direct and uncomplicated. Both events, Britain's loss of its colonies and its decline in
the international sphere, were signs of a new era in British politics.
Instead of being able to continue to rely on overwhelming power,
both military and financial, Britain would have to act much more
diplomatically for the foreseeable future.

In the midst of the sudden rush of decolonization, Britain
enacted a surprising piece of legislation that allowed unlimited
immigration from its colonies. The purpose of the act was to
encourage migration from the older colonies, such as Canada and
Australia, but the effect was that for the fourteen years that this law
remained in effect, citizens of the empire, primarily from Africa or
Asian citizens living in Africa, poured into Britain. Begun in 1948,
the law stayed on the books until 1962, when Parliament decided
that it couldn't handle any further immigration. Following this

reversal, British immigration laws became overwhelmingly restrictive, and remain so to this day, only lightening slightly in the 1970s during the droughts and famines in Africa, to provide some relief to their former subjects.

What's remarkable in all of this, then, is the single piece of legislation that put it all into action: simply put, in 1948 Parliament declared that any citizen of the British Empire, was an equal citizen, whether one lived in London or Kenya. All people are one people. Though this law was later repealed, it left a lasting impression on the culture, evidenced by the relative harmony of multiculturalism in modern Britain. It also laid the foundation for a later citizenship law, one that would yet again make all citizens of Britain equal under the law.

Preparing Britain and the World for *Doctor Who*

All of these crises set the stage for 1963. They generated the cultural climate that created *Doctor Who*. Every question that these political events dealt with was later rehashed thematically on a science-fiction show, designed to exhibit the best of the British spirit. The frustrations of decolonization became the Doctor's policy never to stick around and interfere after he was done saving a planet. The Doctor is a weary man, from a race of beings who were known for their wisdom, but who had created an empire too large for itself. The Doctor is strongly anti-imperial. Yet, while he's rejecting his people's empire, he can't help but cling to his identity as one of them. The Doctor is continually identified as a Time Lord, forever branded as one of his race even as he rejected them. The Doctor represents what Britain hopes it can be: proudly British, while rejecting Britain's exploitative past.

Further developing Britain's desire to see in the Doctor a resurrection of their old glory reformed for the new world, the Doctor became a diplomat. In "Creature from the Pit" (1979), the Doctor acts as an intermediary force between two cultures, not personally invested in the outcomes of his mediation, but morally obligated to help guide them to the light. One can easily see in this the beliefs of a Britain burned by direct involvement in international affairs, but still anxious that the world run as it should. Yet, inherent in this view of the Doctor as self, is a sort of denial of reality.

The Britain of the mid-1970s and early 1980s wasn't a world power any longer, though still a prominent nation. This disconnect is more aptly recognized in "The Sun-Makers" (1977) wherein the Doctor criticizes, and ultimately vanquishes, a Big Brother-like government, dominated by cameras. This fact stands in stark contrast to the simple truth that Britain has for many years had the most sophisticated CCTV system in the world. They employ more cameras to watch more areas of the nation than any other, with the intent to cut down on crime. This innocent hypocrisy seems only to reinforce the fact that the Doctor represents the nation that Britain wants to be, not the nation that it actually is.

Despite all of this, though, the Doctor remains a true populist hero, as he was always intended to be. "Dr. Who *[sic]* wins his struggles not by superior technology (which in science fiction generally means superior force—technology is both totalitarian and imperialistic) but by reason, fearlessness, humor, and curiosity" (Fiske, p. 167). Rather than just trying to conquer the universe with his superior technology—and it is most decidedly superior, *Doctor Who* leaves the audience with no doubt that the Doctor could trounce his enemies with no trouble if he were to stop playing fair—the Doctor adheres to a strict moral code, one which always entails him defeating the cold, calculating science with "warm humane science," and perpetuating liberal democracy. Moreover, the Doctor's main function appears to be one of cleansing society of evil, an attribute that John Fiske claims to hint at the Doctor's Christ-likeness, along with several other things:

> The intergalactic timelessness of the Doctor is not unlike the eternal heaven of Christ; his dislike of violence and his sexual abstinence are other shared characteristics, as is the fact that both are leaders. (Fiske, p. 180)

The Doctor's status as a possible Christ figure only serves to enhance his populist appeal.[4] In addition to being a stand-in for the British nation, he's genuinely someone that the British people can understand and desire to emulate.

Appearing in the later years of Tom Baker's time as the Doctor, Romana, played by Lalla Ward, came to signify the vision of the

---

[4] For a further discussion of the Doctor's Christ-likeness, see Chapter 21 in this volume.

ideal British woman. Cheeky, yet refined, Romana was unfettered by the typical gender restraints. She was the Doctor's equal in every way, sparring with him verbally and ideologically when they came to a disagreement. Where the Doctor's companions prior to her had largely been attractive but stupid women, Lalla Ward was determined to make sure that Romana was easily identified as a modern woman. Even her style of dress was emphasized to make her visually recognizable as strong, especially notable in one episode where the Doctor and Romana encounter a Minotaur, Romana dressed elegantly in English hunting pinks: "The conventional relationship between helpless maid and ravening monster was thus inverted, with Romana becoming visually identifiable as a hunter—and a sportsman hunter at that."[5] More than this, though, with the Doctor's quirks and tendencies associated with traditionally feminine roles, Romana was left free to become the more masculine side of the pair, adopting a more brusque attitude and cold, reasoning intelligence. While the Doctor used intuition to guide him, and reaped all the creative benefits of that, Romana used logic.

The Doctor and Romana at all times act in an idealized way: they're the way that the British, at that time, wished they could be. Completely unfettered by the constraints of a normal life, they flit from place to place, always remaining curious, funny, engaging, and spirited. In "City of Death" (1979), they visit Paris, and exhibit what one could easily take to be the ultimate British response to the city:

> **DOCTOR:** It's the only place in the universe where one can relax entirely.
>
> **ROMANA:** That bouquet!
>
> **DOCTOR:** What Paris has, it has an ethos, a life, it has—
>
> **ROMANA:** A bouquet?

Their witty banter masks the fact that they show a surprising level of cultural sensitivity and curiosity. They aren't there only to take a quick glance at Paris and be gone, but to look for a long time, and perhaps solve a mystery as well. Nor do they behave as one might fear that the stereotypically British traveler might, complaining

---

[5] Britton, p. 353.

about the traffic or the rude Parisians or the language. Rather, they revel in the city itself and marvel at its beauty.

The Doctor, Defender of British Dreams

Doctor Who ran continuously for twenty-six years, from 1963 to 1989. It's difficult to stress how influential it was on British culture. Television in and of itself has long been recognized as being a highly effective form of media, efficacy only increased by the length of time that a given show is on air. From a negative perspective, this can lead to violent or immoral shows having an adverse affect on a society. In the case of *Doctor Who*, though, it led to a re-imagining of the British people, in the Doctor's image. The Doctor became the hero of every man, and Romana that of every woman—at least this was the ideal. One must always remember that, to some extent, the Doctor was a character created consciously to bring up the nation. "Every discussion of motion pictures as a propaganda device must include consideration of television because this medium, incorporating cinematography as it does, is the most efficient delivery system for bringing films to the masses of the world's populations."[6]

Though there has been no official social-science study on the subject, there's a clear and established link between portrayals of violence in the media and violence in the culture that consumes that media. Couldn't there also be a link between portrayals of hope and perseverance and those qualities being evinced by the British culture at large? Science fiction, long considered to be a merely an escapist fantasy, has now become recognized as a true form of social commentary, allowing *Doctor Who* to be recognized as a popular work of social criticism. More than that, though, it's popular. The show and its emblems, from Tom Baker's scarf to the not very terrifying Daleks, have become ubiquitous emblems of the British people, recognized around the globe. The popular British sketch comedy show, *Mock the Week*, contained a section during one program entitled "Unlikely Lines to Hear in an Episode of *Dr. Who*" *[sic]*, (2008). The Doctor, in the form of his fourth incarnation, has even graced American televisions in satire, appearing in two episodes of *The Simpsons*, if only for a moment, in the episode "Sideshow Bob's Last Gleaming" (1995) and "Treehouse of Horror X" (1999).

---

[6] Bernard Rubin, "International Film and Television Propaganda," p. 83.

It's also produced two spin-off series, each filling a gap in *Doctor Who*'s overall appeal. *The Sarah Jane Adventures* follows Sarah Jane, a companion of the Fourth Doctor, now in her forties, and the adventures of her son and his friends. Though *Doctor Who* is indisputably a family show, it's not precisely one for children, giving *Sarah Jane Adventures* an area to cover. The violence and more traumatic themes of *Doctor Who* are left out, leaving a simple adventure plot with lots of fun puzzles. This isn't, of course, to suggest that *Sarah Jane Adventures* is trivial. Far from it, in fact. It's a children's show that manages to engage its audience and teach about courage and adventure, without condescending or alienating its audience.

Torchwood, the other spin-off, takes an entirely different route. Given that *Doctor Who* is, in fact, a family show, there's no room in the script for gratuitous violence, any sex, or any swearing. All of that comes out, instead, in *Torchwood*, a grittier story about a companion of the Ninth and Tenth Doctors, Captain Jack Harkness, and his team of alien fighters. While *Torchwood* does on occasion devolve into nothing more than the wish-fulfillment of frustrated *Doctor Who* writers, as in the episode about the sex alien or the fight between the Cyberwoman and the pterodactyl, most of the time it manages to live up to its concept as a darker, more intense outpouring of the same ideals as *Doctor Who*. Where in *Doctor Who* one sees clearly a story about the need for hope, with an uncomplicated happy ending and the restoration of harmony, in *Torchwood* one sees a more complex story with an ambiguous ending, stressing perseverance and skin of their teeth luck.

More than just a television show, *Doctor Who* has become a cultural phenomenon. When it was canceled in 1989, mostly due to BBC budget cuts, not at all due to a lack of public interest, the characters took on lives of their own, living on in book series, fan magazines, comic books, and radio plays. Resurrected in 1996 for a movie, the show was retired again until it was fully revived in 2005 by Russell T Davies and his creative team, who imagined an even deeper, and higher budgeted, *Doctor Who*. When it was off the air, *Doctor Who* began receiving a large amount of belated critical acclaim. In 1996, BBC declared that *Doctor Who* was the best "Popular Drama" they'd ever produced, and in 2000, it was ranked third in a list of the *100 Greatest British Television Programmes* of all time.

But all of this says nothing about what Britain is like today, forty-seven years after the Doctor's debut. On the surface, it doesn't seem that much has changed. The world is still a messy place, and British politicians still strive to make sense of it all, only to find themselves ostracized for their efforts. Yet there's an undercurrent of hope and optimism that was, if not lacking, then at least much harder to see in the early 1960s. Even throughout all of the tribulations of the new millennium, Britain retained that idealized sense of itself as a just, courageous and persevering nation, and one can only think that this ideal has helped it.[7]

While I call this recent time "post-*Doctor Who*," that's actually inaccurate. It's actually more accurate to say that this is the "Second Age of *Doctor Who*," as the show is experiencing a sort of renaissance right now. With the arrival of the new series in 2005, record breaking ratings and some fantastic critical awards, *Doctor Who* seems to have finally broken out of its place as a well-done children's show, and become recognized as a true drama. It's even been exported to the United States, where it enjoys a dedicated and growing audience. It serves as a more perfect mirror for Britain, showing how the nation wishes it were, and how it thinks it ought to be.

All of this is thanks to the character of the Doctor, and the way that he's so entirely a heroic figure. A show about a lesser man, or more accurately, a *man* at all, would've had considerably less cultural impact, and one could say reasonably would've done little to raise the spirits of the British people. The Doctor's status, then, as a being more than human but less than god, allows him to transcend our lives and go off on adventures, while still retaining the authority to tell us how to live. As a hero, that's all that we can ask.

---

[7] A case in point about resilience: the London Underground bombings in 2005 were shocking attacks, killing fifty-two and injuring many more. There were four bombs that were part of a coordinated plot to cripple London. The very next day, people were back riding on the London Underground. Despite being injured, Britain picked itself up and carried on. Britain's predilection towards hope can be seen in the rejection and ousting of Tony Blair, the British Prime Minister who collaborated with the Bush administration and mired the British army in Iraq.

31

Doctor Who as Philosopher and Myth Maker

ALEXANDER BERTLAND

The echoes of myths pervade *Doctor Who*. Myths often serve as models for the narratives of the Doctor's adventures. The Fourth Doctor serial "Underworld" (1978), for example, is an imaginative retelling of the story of Jason and the Argonauts. *Doctor Who* also plays with myths by suggesting that they're historically true. In the Fourth Doctor serial "Pyramids of Mars" (1975), the Doctor reveals that Egyptian myths are actually historical records of an alien race called the Osirans.

Myth becomes a philosophical question when we wonder why it has a lasting hold on our culture. People remember the stories of Zeus, Thor, and Isis, even if only through cartoons and comic books. Why are these myths still hanging around? Is it good we remember them? Are they positive institutions that hold our culture together? Or are myths a threat to the advancement of science?

Doctor Who often portrays the conflict between myth and science, between ancient traditions and new scientific technology. What does *Doctor Who* ultimately suggest about resolving this conflict? One would suspect that being science fiction, *Doctor Who* would praise science and deride mythic superstition. Nevertheless, *Doctor Who* presents a deeper point about the relationship of myth to science. It reminds us that while myth may appear primitive and naive, science is also made by humans and it has its limits. Rather than simply rejecting myth, *Doctor Who* suggests we ought to find a balance that respects both ways of understanding the world.

Tigella: Battlefield in the War between Myth and Science

Doctor Who often champions the power of science, and rational investigation in general, to free people from the grip of superstition. This is typified in the Third Doctor serial, "The Daemons" (1971). The Doctor reveals that all the horned creatures portrayed by Earth religions, like the devil in Christianity, are misrepresentations of an alien race, the Daemons. This serial reduces myth to mere superstition, assuming that myth is nothing more than bad science based on random observations with no methodology. It sees myths as nothing more than attempts of a fortune-teller to predict the future.

However, myths can be thought of more richly as a way of confronting the world. Myths aren't just stories or allegories but ways of constructing reality. One of the first and most important thinkers to see myth this way was the Italian philosopher, Giambattista Vico (1668–1744). Vico suggests myths shouldn't be seen as a bad form of science. He argues philosophers misunderstand myth because they assume that ancient thinkers thought the same way as modern thinkers do. Vico calls this "the conceit of scholars."[1] "The Daemons" assumes that when myths were written, the mythmakers were trying to write actual history and actual science but somehow were too primitive or ignorant to do so. So they misinterpreted the alien race as gods and magic as science. Vico argues this doesn't make sense because the mythmakers wouldn't have history or science as a goal. Instead, they must've wanted to achieve something else.

Vico speculates that the original mythmakers must've thought like children. He means this in a positive way, suggesting that children have an ingenuity that adults lose, and writes, "Children excel in imitation; we observe that they generally amuse themselves by imitating whatever they are able to apprehend."[2] Children don't learn by theorizing about what to do but by imitating the actions of their elders. Children on playgrounds often imitate the actions of sports heroes or television characters. So, Vico speculates, the first people must have used their imaginations to imitate actions rather than to analyze them, and notes that when children learn to speak,

---

[1] *The New Science of Giambattista Vico*, paragraphs 122–24.
[2] Vico, paragraph 215.

they often do so with rhythm and songs that they combine into dances.[3]

Vico surmises that mythical thinkers conceived the entire world through rituals, powerful dances where followers imitated tribal leaders. The rituals held society together by forcing people to control their violent passions. Mythic thinkers, much like children, must've had strong selfish and animalistic urges to eat and roam wherever they wanted. The ritual dances sweep up that energy, forcing the people to stay put and work together. Every activity of these thinkers, whether it be farming, hunting, or socializing, must've had ritualistic dances to channel passionate drives into productive activity.

Vico claims myths weren't originally stories. Rather, these stories are remnants of those dances. Over the centuries the actions of the dancers were turned into fictional tales. Yet, the fundamental purpose of myths is to develop compelling rituals that bind community together. The rituals force primitive people to put aside selfish emotional desire and work for the group. Leela's tribe the Sevateem in "The Face of Evil" (1977) stays together through a ritualistic devotion to the god Xoanon. Their rituals are good because they keep the tribe alive in such harsh conditions. Unfortunately, these rituals also tend to keep primitive people from thinking freely. The members of the Sevateem are so locked into their rituals that they can't easily understand the power of technology.

As society gives rise to science and rational thought, conflict inevitably develops between tradition and technology. In the Fourth Doctor serial, "Meglos" (1980), the inhabitants of the planet Tigella have a mysterious power source called the dodecahedron. The Tigellans are divided into the religious Deons and the scientific Savants. The Deons, led by Lexa, hold the dodecahedron to be a religious artifact and prescribe strict rituals of worship to it. The Savants, on the other hand, use reason to investigate its power. As the serial unfolds, Meglos, the evil alien antagonist, compromises the power of the dodecahedron. Lexa claims that science is blasphemy, refuses to listen to any scientific resolution and tries to sacrifice the Doctor to the gods. This almost destroys the Tigellans.[4]

---

[3] Vico, paragraph 228.

[4] This theme may be found in many other serials. For example, in the Fifth Doctor serial, "Planet of Fire" (1984), a similar conflict occurs as the worshipers of the planet's sun god refuse to accept scientific accounts of the volcanic activity on

This serial reveals myth's dangerous ability to prevent people from thinking freely even to the point of working against a community's self-interest. The Doctor ends up the hero and science prevails over the binding power of myth. However, other serials show a positive side to the power of myth.

Terra Alpha and Varos

Vico argues that the conflict between science and myth can't be resolved. Instead, history travels in an eternal cycle, shifting between the two structures of thought. When civilizations are born, they grow through the power of myth. This growth leads to the rise of science and critical thinking, which breaks the power of myth. This brings technological benefits and political rights to the people. However, the cost is that the rituals keeping society unified break down. The moral codes associated with these rituals weaken. People become greedier as their selfish desires take over. People start caring about their own selfish pleasure instead of working for the community. This creates a state of decay that Vico calls "The Barbarism of Reflection." Since the people of a nation no longer channel their passions into common rituals that unite society, they head off separately to fulfill their own wants. This leads to civil war and the collapse of society.[5] Vico suggests that myth is necessary because it's the basis of morality. Myth will inevitably be outgrown, but this will only call for a return to myth

Sometimes, science creates its own myths to replace superstitious myths. Science hopes to hold society together while eliminating superstition. However, when science tries this, there have been devastating results. The German philosopher Ernst Cassirer (1874–1945) describes how the Nazis created modern scientific myths and rituals to strip the Germans of their freedom.[6] *Doctor Who* often portrays this totalitarian use of myth. In the Seventh Doctor serial "The Happiness Patrol" (1988), the government of Terra Alpha forces citizens to act ritualistically happy. In the Sixth Doctor serial "Vengeance on Varos" (1985), humans must ritualistically vote in elections in a way that keeps them from question-

---

the planet. The Fourth Doctor serial, "The Brain of Morbius" (1976), portrays a conflict between the evil Frankenstein-like scientist Solon and a mystic sisterhood.

[5] Vico, paragraph 1066.

[6] *The Myth of the State*, p. 284.

ing the political system as a whole. In both of these cases, totalitarian regimes combine technology with the ancient power of myth to take control of a society. This is clearly a bad way to combine myth and science. Can we find a deeper mythical wisdom? Is there a way that mythical thought can be portrayed as liberating? What's the true power of mythical thought?

Manussa and the Power of Mythical Thought

Rituals can subdue primitive animalistic passions to get people to work together, but instead of emphasizing ritual, it's also possible to talk about the nature of mythic wisdom. The Fifth Doctor serial "Snakedance" (1983) and its prequel "Kinda" (1982) are extremely rich, relying heavily on Buddhist imagery and ideas of the unconscious. These serials reveal the importance of respecting ancient wisdom.

The Mara is an evil snake-like creature that possesses the minds of its victims. In "Snakedance," the Mara manipulates the Doctor's companion, Tegan, to trick the Doctor into bringing it and her to the planet Manussa. Five hundred years earlier, the Federation had defeated the Mara. The battle in which the Mara was banished back to the unconscious has attained the status of myth and is now recreated in ritual. However, over the five hundred years, the power of the mythical Mara ritual has lost its strength and the people of Manussa seem morally weak. The Director of Historical Research, Ambril, dismisses the importance of the ancient rituals, particularly the value of the ancient Snakedance. He's revealed to be a greedy, selfish researcher who'll do anything to advance his career. The prince of Manussa, Lon, is lazy and decadent. Souvenir sellers and crowds of curious tourists drain the sacred aura from the rituals.

Throughout the story, the Doctor critiques this decadence and shows that the ancients may know more than they're given credit for. In one scene, Ambril mocks the ancient religion because an old headdress, which ostensibly represents the six heads of delusion, only has five heads on it. The Doctor has Ambril wear the headdress, pointing out that when the headdress is worn, the wearer becomes the sixth head of delusion.

The Doctor saves the day by seeking out Dojjen, the former Director of Historical Research who left his position to learn the truth of the ancient customs. Rejecting the decadence of the society around him, he studies the meditative practice of the Snakedance that has the power to resist the Mara. Dojjen teaches the Snakedance to the Doctor, who uses it to destroy the Mara. The Doctor provides something of a scientific account of the ritual. However, it's not really technology that wins the day. The Doctor overcomes the Mara because he has the mental ability, unclouded by moral depravity. The ancient mythical wisdom saves the society from decadence. Myth has the positive force to reject the temptations of selfishness and see the world clearly.

In contrast to "Meglos," mythical thought in "Snakedance" isn't just a binding force. Mythical thought contains a positive wisdom that can maintain the health of a civilization. Further, science can sometimes lead to its own sort of decadence by encouraging greed and the selfish quest for knowledge over social responsibility. This contrast makes one consider whether myth is more or less liberating than science.

The Doctor at the Walls of Troy

The Doctor may be seen as a symbol of science and its limits. Sometimes the Doctor can do whatever he wants, defying what seems consistent with the laws of science, other times he seems bound by them. In the Second Doctor serial, "The Invasion" (1968), the Doctor prevents a Cyberman invasion of contemporary Earth with no concern for the future time stream, thereby defying what might be "the laws of time." Other times, the Doctor struggles to keep history consistent. For example, in the Fifth Doctor serial "The Visitation" (1982), the Doctor lets the great fire of London burn because it's a historical fact. In the Tenth Doctor episode, "The Unicorn and the Wasp" (2007), the Doctor leaves Agatha Christie ignorant of what happened during her time of disappearance because that's historical fact. In these cases, the Doctor seems limited by "the laws of time."

But what is it that limits the Doctor's power? Is it that there are things he simply can't do or things he can't understand? There's good reason to think the latter. In the Ninth Doctor episode "Father's Day" (2005), Rose Tyler changes the course of time by saving her father's life. This rupture in the time continuum causes winged, dragon-like creatures to attack Earth. When asked about the creatures, the Doctor explains that the Time Lords used to prevent these creatures from attacking Earth, but this explanation is incomplete and unsatisfying.[7] It seems that the Doctor's knowledge of science is limited in that he really can't grasp how time may be altered. The Doctor isn't, in fact, all-knowing, and so it seems to be his own incomplete understanding of time that limits his power, rather than the laws of time.

Another example where the Doctor is limited by his lack of scientific knowledge occurs in the First Doctor serial, "The Myth Makers" (1965).[8] The Greeks capture the Doctor and threaten his life, if he doesn't help them infiltrate Troy. His companion, Steven, tells the Doctor the obvious choice is to invent the Trojan Horse. The Doctor refuses because he actually doesn't think it will work. Instead, he introduces a more technologically advanced scheme involving flying machines carrying Greeks over the Trojan Walls. The Doctor's prototype fails; his knowledge of science can't resolve the situation the way he wants. Out of ideas, he must instead go along with the "proper" course of history, and invent the Trojan Horse. The Doctor is unable to change the past simply because he doesn't have the appropriate scientific knowledge to arrive at a different solution.

In "The Waters of Mars" (2009), the Tenth Doctor makes a conscious decision to change a major event in history by trying to save the crew of the first Mars base. He fails, feels defeated, and horribly guilty for his hubris. If the Doctor understood the laws of time fully, he wouldn't have tried to manipulate them. More interestingly, the Doctor doesn't use this as an opportunity for scientifically investigating the laws of time. Rather, he resigns himself to his old, evidently incomplete, paradigm for understanding his own limits for changing time. The Doctor isn't simply defeated by the laws of time; he's defeated by the fact that he can't question his own understanding.

Mythical thought, as we've seen, has its own moral wisdom but is limiting as a world view. But the same is true of science. Scientific thought, like mythical thought, is another way humans describe the world.

---

[7] There are many other weak examples such as the "Blinovitch Limitation Effect" and the Tenth Doctor ignoring Martha Jones's question as to whether she should step on a butterfly in "The Shakespeare Code."

[8] The content of this serial was derived from the CD, *Doctor Who: Adventures in History*, published by BBC Audiobooks Ltd., 2003.

The Mythologizing of Science

To understand how science limits one's world-view like mythical thought can, let's look at the philosophers Max Horkheimer (1895–1973) and Theodor W. Adorno (1903–1969). In their classic work, *Dialectic of Enlightenment*, they argue that the apparent freedom that science gives us is actually an illusion. They suggest that science isn't an accurate description of the world, but an invented construction. Like myth, science can control thought and limit human freedom. In fact, science often uses the same limiting structures that mythical thought uses. Science, of course, is still a very practical way of describing the world because it can develop theories that predict the outcomes of specific events. Yet, there's still a mythical and therefore limiting element to these scientific descriptions.

The hallmark of mythical thinking is ritual. They're projections of ideas and passions in the mythical thinker's mind. The mythmaker's powerful imagination is so rich, many different gods and rituals are projected onto natural objects. There're dances to make it rain, dances to make the crops grow, dances for fishing and so on. These rituals are linked to everything the mythical thinker does, and don't allow for free rational choice on the part of the members of the community.

I mentioned earlier that misguided religious leaders strip the free-will of their followers, often coercing them to act against their own interests. Because the mythic worldview of these misguided leaders is so powerful, as in "Meglos," they can't easily be reasoned with. Even though science frees people from superstition, it replaces that worldview with its own limiting framework.

Science breaks down the mythical worldview by objectifying everything through mathematics.[9] Objects and events are quantified on graphs and tables. Scientists remove the spiritual power of objects by understanding them in terms of numerical form. In science, individual objects don't matter; what matters is the way general laws govern objects.

So, nature loses all spiritual force. Rain is explained by scientific laws, eliminating the need to perform ritual dances. Further, the whole purpose of a scientific experiment is to test a hypothesis in a way that's reproducible. So, if one runs an experiment on a rabbit, the individual rabbit shouldn't matter. Any rabbit should be

---

[9] *Dialectic of Enlightenment*, p. 10.

able to produce the same result. So any value of any specific object is lost. No particular object or icon has any spiritual power. This should be liberating, since now people don't need to perform any rituals or worship any icons. The Doctor appears to employ science to be the freest creature in the universe, using his scientifically created TARDIS to travel through space and time. But does eliminating ritual and icons really make one free? Horkheimer and Adorno suggest it doesn't because science doesn't stress the importance of individuality, it simply diminishes freedom in a different way.

A person is free when she or he can make a choice without the constraints of a particular framework of thought. Science provides distance from the restrictive structure of mythical thought; it replaces rain dances with theories of cause and effect that allow us to better predict future events and respond accordingly. However, the important point is that what science provides isn't Truth but *another conventional framework of thought*, which depends upon assumptions concerning definite, universal laws of cause and effect in the universe. These laws, invented by scientists, are assumed to govern the scientist as much as anything else. Therefore, Horkheimer and Adorno suggest that scientists are forced to believe that they're restricted by the laws they created. So the Doctor, who sometimes laughs at people trapped in a world of superstition, should realize that he himself is trapped in and governed by his own worldview of conventional scientific laws.

The heroes of the Greek myths were dominated by the whims of the gods; all they could do was bemoan their fate. In an analogous way, because scientists have to admit the existence of an apparently necessary and unchanging order, all they can do is bemoan their fate. If the scientist could get out of their world view, maybe they could find a way to stop an on-coming disaster. But as long as they're trapped in their own self-constructed scientific explanations, they're trapped by their own worldview, just as much as the mythmaker.

Both science and myth are stories we create to restrain ourselves. Horkheimer and Adorno write, "The principle of fatal necessity, which brings low the heroes of myth and derives as a logical consequence from the pronouncement of the oracle, does not merely, when refined to the stringency of formal logic, rule in every rationalistic system of Western philosophy, but itself dominates the series of systems which begins with the hierarchy of the gods and, in a permanent twilight of the idols, hands down an identical content: anger against insufficient righteousness" (p. 11). Scientists, like priests, are left to curse the necessity they think is in the world, but is actually in the constructions of their own minds.

Many argue that science can be dangerous because it's dehumanizing. Indeed, this is what happens in "Snakedance." The unique point that Horkheimer and Adorno try to make is that the real danger of science is precisely the fact that science depends upon describing the universe in terms of absolute necessity. They write, "For enlightenment is as totalitarian as any system. Its untruth does not consist in what its romantic enemies have always reproached it for: analytical method, return to elements, dissolution through reflective thought; but instead from the fact that for enlightenment the process is always decided from the start. When in mathematical procedure the unknown becomes the unknown quantity of an equation, this marks it as the well-known even before any value is inserted." For science, there can be no real mystery. Mystery involves not knowing what the future will bring because the future has yet to be determined. In a math problem, however, the problem itself determines the required solution, so there's no actual mystery. They continue, "Mathematical procedure became, so to speak, the ritual of thinking" (pp. 24–25).

Doctor Who illustrates this. The Doctor holds that science dictates there's an element to time he can't change. However, the science that's doing the dictating isn't necessarily the actual laws of time and space, but the Doctor's limited understanding of these laws. What the Doctor thinks is necessity is really an unfounded construct. In the Tenth Doctor episode, "The Fires of Pompeii" (2008), Donna Noble wants to save as many people of Pompeii by getting them in the TARDIS and taking them to safety. The Doctor insists that he can't change history like that. The Doctor, however, can't give a real explanation as to why; he sticks to the framework of his scientific understanding. The fact that Donna convinces the Doctor to save one family indicates the arbitrary nature of the Doctor's worldview. But the Doctor has to hold onto this construction because that's the nature of the scientific paradigm.

The Doctor Dances

One may wonder: if scientific thought can't bring us to freedom, what's the point of looking for meaning? *Doctor Who* presents an interesting ethical and philosophical response to this: mythical thought ought to balance the power of scientific thought.

As I said earlier, mythical thought contains wisdom that helps one keep from being too decadent and greedy. Indeed, science itself in its quest for knowledge can cause one to lose track of moral goodness. The Daleks are a powerful symbol of that. The Doctor could easily fall into this decadence and use his TARDIS for pleasure, and worse, evil rather than good. But the Doctor doesn't. He actually balances his science with a respect for myth. He recognizes on Manussa that mythical thought is needed to defeat the Mara. Rather than using the best technology available to him, he uses a sonic screwdriver instead of a gun; he uses an old Type-40 TARDIS with a broken chameleon circuit rather than a new one. He respects the cultural tradition and myth of civilizations, when he can. This respect for myth keeps his character balanced.

So, in the conflict between myth and science, *Doctor Who* doesn't simply come down on the side of science. Instead, it indicates that we should understand that myth has an important moral power. Rather than simply rejecting all ancient wisdom outright and replacing it with science, *Doctor Who* suggests we should humbly balance the two alternatives to try to live well.

32

Philosophy, *Fantastic!*

COURTLAND LEWIS

One day I shall come back. Until then, there must be no regrets, no tears, no anxiety. Just go forward in all your beliefs, and prove that I am not mistaken in mine.

—First Doctor ("The Dalek Invasion of Earth," 1964)

Just as philosophy is an important component of our culture, *Doctor Who* is too. In fact, when we examine them side-by-side we see several striking similarities.

Philosophers are involved in performing certain specific tasks. These tasks include things like examining human nature and knowledge, beauty, right and wrong, the inner-workings of science, logic, mathematics, personal identity, and among other things, looking at the ways in which people reason. Some goals of these philosophical investigations include teasing out prejudices, presumptions, and general errors in reasoning. Because of its nature, philosophy requires that people reflect on their lives, beliefs, and be aware of the ways in which they act and treat others, and be willing to buck outdated traditions for something new.

It should come as no surprise, then, that each author in this volume shows how *Doctor Who* addresses one or more of the many issues just listed. Like philosophy, *Doctor Who* is involved in many of the same tasks and has similar goals, and as a result, *Doctor Who* challenges people to reflect on deep philosophical issues and grow not only as individuals but also as humans in relation to others and the wider universe. It's this challenge that draws people to *Doctor Who* and to philosophy, and is why we love them both.

For the Love of Philosophy and *Doctor Who*

Just like watching *Doctor Who*, philosophy is a fascinating, exciting, and sometimes spiritual enterprise. Even if readers or viewers haven't previously made the connection between the two, *Doctor Who* contains several important philosophical elements, which show that they're respectively engaged in complementary enterprises.

If you ask a philosopher, "What's philosophy?", you're bound to receive as many different answers as you would if you ask a *Doctor Who* fan, "who's your favorite Doctor?" or "what's your favorite episode?" There's simply no easy, straightforward answer to give that's universally satisfactory. Simply put, philosophy is the love of wisdom, but really, it's much more than this. Socrates (around 469–399 B.C.) said that philosophy is that which aids one's choosing of the good life (*Republic*), the greatest of arts (*Phaedo*), a sense of wonder (*Theaetetus*), and among other things the love of real knowledge (*Republic*). None of these descriptions completely describe what philosophy is. What's needed is to take these descriptions of philosophy and combine them with a discussion of what philosophy is *not*.

Plato's *Gorgias* presents an example of what philosophy is and is *not*, by defining 'rhetoric' (the art of persuasive speaking). Without going into the finer details of the dialogue, Socrates engages in a discussion with Gorgias, a great rhetorical orator, about what sort of profession Gorgias practices. Based on Gorgias's answers, Socrates makes an important distinction between teaching (what philosophy does) and mere persuasion. Persuasion is presented as a power that orators have over others—to make individuals and groups succumb to the orator's will. In other words, a rhetorician uses words to convince interlocutors about what's wrong and what's right, and is dedicated to winning arguments at any cost, whether by lying, deceiving, or obfuscation.

Due to its nature, rhetoric fails to produce any sort of reliable knowledge. The Master serves as an exemplar of a "master" rhetorician, and shows exactly why persuasion only produces unreliable beliefs. Imagine if the Master needed your help to carry out one of his evil plans to destroy the Earth.[1] The Master needs to convince

---

[1] For an alternative view that the Master is a victim, and not evil, see Chapter 24 in this volume.

you that it's in your best interest to help him destroy the Earth (if he doesn't just hypnotize you first), and the most effective way for him to do this is to play off of your fears and emotions, which keep you from critically thinking about what the best course of action actually is. The *belief* that you must help the Master is only as strong as that on which it's based, and even though you trust the Master to tell you the truth, you're mistaken. Your trust in the Master is unreliable because he's unreliable, and if you were someone like the Doctor, or one of his companions, you'd know not to trust him.

Instead of your belief being based on something more certain, like a critically thought-out plan on how to save the Earth, your belief is based on the Master's persuasive abilities. The result of his unreliability is that your beliefs are unreliable too. Yet, people continue to trust him, and this is because he's such a great rhetorician. He's like a chef who's able to make a rotten piece of meat taste like a fine delicacy. The Master knows what your interests and concerns are, and he uses them to persuade you that you should help him further his goals. It's this knack of persuasion, by creating false beliefs in individuals, which allows him to gain control over so many subjects. Even his use of hypnosis is merely a form of subliminal persuasion. Just like rhetoricians who are only concerned with persuasion, you shouldn't trust the Master, for any beliefs produced by him are unreliable and fail to foster any sort of reliable knowledge.

Teaching, on the other hand, has a very different goal than that of rhetoric. Teaching is the attempt to pass knowledge from one individual to another or to help individuals reach some understanding about truth, usually via the method of critical thinking. It's not concerned with "winning" an argument, nor is it concerned with causing interlocutors to conform to the will of the teacher. Teaching is about engaging others in a dialogue about certain topics and getting interlocutors to arrive at *true* beliefs about a particular subject matter. It's concerned with creating justified belief in some idea or subject. The Master doesn't care about truth, certainty, or knowledge, except maybe in "The End of Time, Part 2" (2010); he merely cares about persuading you to help him. The Doctor, who's a teacher, has an overall dedication to telling you the truth (even if he fudges it from time to time!), giving you as much information as possible, and allowing you to make your own decisions about what ought to be done. This doesn't mean that teachers, and the Doctor, never persuade, but it does mean that they're dedicated to something greater than merely persuading: like truth, consistency, and integrity. Teachers, then, are dedicated to making individuals better by helping them find *knowledge* by thinking for themselves and not merely going with the flow.

According to Plato and Socrates, philosophers should be teachers, and if we combine the characteristics of teachers with the characteristics of philosophy mentioned above, then we've a much clearer picture of what philosophy is. Philosophy is a dedication to self-reflection, truth, and consistency, which as Socrates suggests, is necessary for living the good life and having knowledge. Philosophy might deserve the title of "greatest of arts"—it definitely fits Socrates's other descriptions, namely, aiding in one's choosing of the good life, creates a sense of wonder about one's life and how to live it, and among other things, fosters the love of real knowledge—not just beliefs about what might be true.

Philosophy, therefore, is many things to many people: it's a way of life, a tool to achieve consistency and order in one's life, the search for knowledge and wisdom, and a spiritual quest. Philosophy defies easy characterization because it's concerned with wisdom and understanding, and these pursuits require that it be partially engaged with every field of study and every aspect of existence. As a result, philosophy is a little bit of everything to everyone, and that's good.

Doctor Who as Philosophy

Most viewers know that *Doctor Who* began as an educational show, but far fewer realize it's a show dedicated to *teaching* in the philosophical sense discussed earlier, which means it's dedicated to discovering truth, promoting consistency, and fostering integrity. In fact, *Doctor Who* challenges people in three particular ways: to be reflective about one's own life and the ways in which one reasons, to be reflective about how one treats others, and always be willing change one's views in light of new evidence.

From the very beginning, the Doctor took viewers on adventures to historical places like Rome ("The Romans," 1965), the Aztec Empire ("The Aztecs," 1964), and on a journey with Marco Polo ("Marco Polo," 1964). The show wasn't merely concerned with winning over audiences with exciting stories about time travel, which it did, but it was concerned with teaching the audience about strange new places and aliens, and that we should respect their differences and appropriately adjust how we act around them.

This attempt to teach the audience can be seen throughout the series, but most of the lessons are not historical, they're ethical, moral, and spiritual. It presents viewers with ways of understanding complex issues, and gives them the tools to reflect upon and arrive at consistent philosophical conclusions. "The Green Death" (1973) teaches viewers about the importance of environmental stewardship, but it never lays down dictates for exactly how one should treat the environment; episodes like "The Silurans" (1970) teach viewers about coexisting with other species; "The End of the World" (2005) raises questions about justice, death, and self-importance; and throughout every episode, viewers are challenged to respect life in whatever form, do what is right, and to live life to its fullest.

Doctor Who never merely tries to persuade viewers about "truths." Instead, it presents deep philosophical investigations that are designed to teach and challenge viewers to arrive at their own truthful and consistent conclusions. The authors included in this volume do a wonderful job of teasing out the philosophical themes in a variety of episodes, in ways that are easily accessible to readers. More importantly, they illustrate *Doctor Who*'s influence on the way many of us think about life and morality, and how *Doctor Who* challenges us all to consider how we view our own lives, how we treat others, and how we understand what counts as truth.

By watching *Doctor Who* one is forced to deal with Cybermen, Daleks, Sontarans, Ice Warriors, the Master, Zygons, Jagrafess, the surviving brain of the villainous Time Lord Morbius, Absorbaloffs, Sea Devils, Slitheen, Vashta Nerada, and the Weeping Angels, among others. By learning how the Doctor and others deal with such characters, we engage our own beliefs and learn how to deal with people, strangers, and enemies that actually exist here on earth. It's easy to stereotype all "others" as strangers and enemies, but *Doctor Who* shows viewers that we must be willing to engage and learn from the strangest of beings. The Doctor is constantly giving second chances, forgiving, and offering his help to those bent on destroying him, the world, and sometimes the universe. It's this attempt to understand others and their motives that is the mark of philosophy and *Doctor Who*.

Philosophy and *Doctor Who* teach us to be proactive in engaging the unknown, rather than ignoring doubts and concerns until we're forced to blindly react to them like Brigadier Lethbridge Stewart, whose first reaction is always, "Five rounds rapid, Sergeant!" Therefore, if we watch *Doctor Who* and apply its teachings to our own lives, then we must reflect on our own beliefs, we must reflect on how we treat others and respond to those who are good to us, as well as those who harm us, and we must be willing to change the way we think, in order to live a better life. In other words, *Doctor Who* teaches us to live our lives philosophically engaged.

Ah, Doctor. We Know You by Reputation

Doctor Who has built up a considerable reputation over the past forty-seven years, and this reputation will undoubtedly continue to grow. Hopefully, this book will increase not only its reputation, but also enlighten readers to new ways of understanding their favorite Time Lord. It's easy to get caught up in one's own way of seeing things, and to try and force others to see the world exactly the same way. This mind-set is the driving force behind most of the villains on *Doctor Who*: the Daleks think only they should exist, the Cybermen want to upgrade inferior species, and the Master wants the universe to recognize his "greatness."

Doctor Who, like philosophy, teaches us a different ways of thinking. It calls us to engage ourselves and the world around us. It has the potential to change the way we act and the way we treat others. It makes us consider the possibilities of the impossible. And, most of all, it teaches us to strive for something greater: a life lived according to the good.

Doctor Who and philosophy both show us that we, and the world in which we live, is larger on the inside than on the outside, and that it's this Time And Relative Dimension in *all Spaces* that makes the world exciting and worthy of exploration. Enjoy the rest of your journey with the Doctor, but just make sure you take enough *jelly babies*!

Would You Like a Jelly Baby?

WORDS OF WISDOM FROM *DOCTOR WHO*

LITTLE BOY: Are you afraid of monsters?

DOCTOR: No, they're afraid of me.

—ELEVENTH DOCTOR, "The Hungry Earth" (2010)

One day I shall come back. Until then, there must be no regrets, no tears, no anxiety. Just go forward in all your beliefs, and prove that I am not mistaken in mine.

—FIRST DOCTOR, "The Dalek Invasion of Earth" (also found on *The Hartnell Years*)

You know, you are a classic example of the inverse ratio between the size of a mouth and the size of a brain.

—FOURTH DOCTOR to Commander Uvanov, "The Robots of Death"

Two days! I haven't got time to be lying around for two days.

—FOURTH DOCTOR, "The Face of Evil"

I like lots of people, but I can't go carting them around the universe.

—FOURTH DOCTOR, "The Face of Evil"

Progress is a very flexible word, you can make it out to mean just about anything.

—FOURTH DOCTOR, "The Power of Kroll"

It is not the oil, the filth, and the poisonous chemicals that are the real cause of pollution. It is simply greed.

—THIRD DOCTOR, "Invasion of the Dinosaurs"

He looks like a man that can see around a few corners himself.

—Angus talking about the Fourth Doctor, "Terror of the Zygons"

The thing about ideas is they never come to you all at once.

—Fourth Doctor

Why don't you give me the gun, so I can keep an eye on myself?

—Fourth Doctor, "Horns of Nimon"

If we fight we will destroy this planet, we will destroy ourselves. . . .
If we fight like animals, we will die like animals!

—Seventh Doctor, "Survival"

Unless we are prepared to sacrifice our lives for the good of all, then
evil and anarchy will spread like the plague: The rule of law must
prevail.

—Sixth Doctor, "The Trial of a Time Lord"

Don't worry Ace, it's only a trap.

——Seventh Doctor, "Battlefield"

If you sit there wallowing in self-pity, I'll bite your nose off.

—Fourth Doctor, "The Brain of Morbius"

Come here . . . I think you need a Doctor.

—Ninth Doctor, "The Parting of the Ways"

Nice to meet you, Rose. Run for your life!

—Ninth Doctor, "Rose"

It was a better life. And I—I don't mean all the traveling and . . . seeing
aliens and spaceships and things—that don't matter. The Doctor showed
me a better way of living your life.

—Rose Tyler, "The Parting of the Ways"

You know, when you're a kid, they tell you it's all, grow up. Get a job.
Get married. Get a house. Have a kid, and that's it. Ah. But the truth is,
the world is so much stranger than that. It's so much darker. And so
much madder. . . . And so much better.

—Elton Pope, "Love and Monsters"

I'll work with you—gladly—but for the sake of justice, not your own amusement.

—AGATHA CHRISTIE, to the Tenth Doctor, "The Unicorn and the Wasp"

Everybody lives, Rose. Just this once. Everybody lives!

—NINTH DOCTOR, "The Doctor Dances"

Daleks have no concept of elegance!

—The Daleks responding to the Cybermen, "Doomsday"

ROMANA: Where are we going?

DOCTOR: Are you talking philosophically or geographically?

ROMANA: Philosophically.

DOCTOR: Then we're going to lunch!

—FOURTH DOCTOR and ROMANA on a train in Paris, "City of Death"

You know the very powerful and the very stupid have one thing in common. They don't alter their views to fit the facts. They alter the facts to fit their views. Which can be uncomfortable if you happen to be one of the facts that needs altering.

—FOURTH DOCTOR, "The Face of Evil"

Something's interfering with time, Mr. Scarman. And time is my business.

—FOURTH DOCTOR, "The Pyramids of Mars"

Courage isn't just a matter of not being frightened, you know. It's being afraid and doing what you have to do anyway.

—THIRD DOCTOR, "Planet of the Daleks"

You can't kill me. I'm a genius.

—SECOND DOCTOR, "The Seeds of Death"

It looks like not even the Sonic Screwdriver can get me out of this one.

—FOURTH DOCTOR, "The Invasion of Time"

Pull a trigger. End a life. Simple isn't it? Makes sense doesn't it? A life killing life. . . . Why don't you do it then? Look me in the eye. Pull the trigger. End my life.

—SEVENTH DOCTOR, "The Happiness Patrol"

I used my own, special technique . . . keeping my eyes open and my mouth shut.

—Second Doctor, "The Tomb of the Cybermen"

This is my Timey-Wimey Detector. It goes ping when there's stuff.

—Tenth Doctor, "Blink"

Danger Doctor!

—K-9

You can't rewrite history. Not one line!

—First Doctor, "The Aztecs"

It all started out as a mild curiosity in the junkyard, and now it's turned out to be quite a great spirit of adventure.

—First Doctor, "The Sensorites"

That is the dematerializing control. And that, over yonder, is the horizontal hold. Up there is the scanner, those are the doors, that is a chair with a panda on it. Sheer poetry, dear boy! Now please stop bothering me.

—First Doctor, "The Time Meddler"

So you're my replacements—a dandy and a clown!

—First Doctor, to the Second and Third Doctors, "The Three Doctors"

When I say 'run,' run. . . . RUN!

—Second Doctor, (too many episodes to mention)

First things first, but not necessarily in that order.

—Fourth Doctor, "Meglos"

Nothing in the world can stop me now!

—Professor Zaroff, "The Underwater Menace"

So, freewill is not an illusion after all.

—Third Doctor, "Inferno"

Logic, my dear Zoe, merely enables one to be wrong with authority.

—Second Doctor, "The Wheel in Space"

I am not a student of human nature. I am a professor of a far wider academy of which human nature is merely a part.

—SECOND DOCTOR, "The Evil of the Daleks"

There are some corners of the universe which have bred the most terrible things. Things that act against everything we believe in. They must be fought!

—SECOND DOCTOR, "The Moonbase"

You've redecorated in here, haven't you? Hmm. I don't like it.

—SECOND DOCTOR, referring to UNIT headquarters, "The Five Doctors"

You could take the usual precautions . . . sticky tape on the windows, that sort of thing.

—THE MASTER, on how to survive a nuclear blast, "Terror of the Autons"

I reversed the polarity of the neutron flow.

—THIRD DOCTOR, "The Sea Devils"

A straight line may be the shortest distance between two points, but it is by no means the most interesting.

—THIRD DOCTOR, "The Time Warrior"

There's no point being grown-up if you can't be childish sometimes.

—FOURTH DOCTOR, "Robot"

You've no home planet, no influence, nothing! You're just a pathetic bunch of tin soldiers skulking about the galaxy in an ancient spaceship!

—FOURTH DOCTOR, on the Cybermen, "Revenge of the Cybermen"

Evil? Your evil is my good. I am Sutekh the Destroyer. Where I tread, I leave nothing but dust and darkness. . . . I find that good!

—SUTEKH, "Pyramids of Mars"

Vaporization without representation is against the constitution!

—FOURTH DOCTOR, "The Deadly Assassin"

If they should break through, run as if something very nasty were after you, because something very nasty will be after you.

—FOURTH DOCTOR on the Ogri, "The Stones of Blood"

Now drop your weapons, or I'll kill him with this deadly jelly baby!

—FOURTH DOCTOR, "The Face of Evil"

Please do not throw hands at me.

—Robot D-84, on being attacked by robot parts, "The Robots of Death"

Never trust a man with dirty fingernails!

—FOURTH DOCTOR, on Magnus Greel, "The Talons of Weng-Chiang"

Sometimes my brilliance astonishes even me.

—FOURTH DOCTOR, "The Invisible Enemy"

Excuse me, are you sure this planet's meant to be here?

—FOURTH DOCTOR, "The Pirate Planet"

Don't you like it? I think it'll do very nicely. If the arms are a bit long I can always take them in.

—Romana II, on her new body, "Destiny of the Daleks"

I say, what a wonderful butler, he's so violent!

—FOURTH DOCTOR, "City of Death"

A new body, at last!

—THE MASTER, "The Keeper of Traken"

I've just dipped into the future. We must be prepared for the worst.

—FOURTH DOCTOR, "Logopolis"

An apple a day keeps the . . . Ah, never mind.

—FIFTH DOCTOR, "Kinda"

Well, it wouldn't be cricket.

—FIFTH DOCTOR, "Black Orchid"

There should have been another way.

—FIFTH DOCTOR, "Warriors of the Deep"

Build high for happiness!

—THE KANGS, "Paradise Towers"

Oh, marvelous! You're going to kill me. What a finely tuned response to the situation.

—FIFTH DOCTOR, "Frontios"

That could blow a hole in the space-time continuum, the size of . . . well actually, the exact size of Belgium. That's a bit un-dramatic, isn't it? Belgium?

—FIFTH DOCTOR, "Time Crash"

My last incarnation . . . Oh, I was never happy with that one. It had a sort of feckless 'charm' which simply wasn't me!

—SIXTH DOCTOR, "The Twin Dilemma"

What's [the Master] up to now? It'll be something devious and overcomplicated. He'd get dizzy if he tried to walk in a straight line.

—THE RANI, "The Mark of the Rani"

Small though it is, the human brain can be quite effective when used properly.

—SIXTH DOCTOR, "The Two Doctors"

Whereas yours is a simple case of sociopathy, Dibber, my malaise is much more complex. A deep-rooted maladjustment, my psychiatrist said, brought on by an infantile inability to come to terms with the more pertinent, concrete aspects of life.

—SABALOM GLITZ, "The Trial of a Time Lord"

Madam, this revelation should halt this trial immediately. Surely even Gallifreyan Law must acknowledge that the same person cannot be both prosecutor and defendant.

—SIXTH DOCTOR, "The Trial of a Time Lord"

Yes, that's right, you're going. You've been gone for ages. You're already gone. You're still here. You've just arrived. I haven't even met you yet. It all depends on who you are and how you look at it. Strange business, time.

—SEVENTH DOCTOR, "Dragonfire"

I can hear the sound of empires toppling.

—SEVENTH DOCTOR, "The Happiness Patrol"

Anybody remotely interesting is mad in some way.

—SEVENTH DOCTOR, "The Greatest Show in the Galaxy"

Don't worry, Brigadier. People will be shooting at you soon.

—SEVENTH DOCTOR, "Battlefield"

Good afternoon. The universe is ending. Would you like some tea?

—EIGHTH DOCTOR, *Zamper* (novel by Gareth Roberts)

These shoes! They fit perfectly!

—EIGHTH DOCTOR, *Doctor Who: The T.V. Movie*

I love humans, always seeing patterns in things that aren't there.

—EIGHTH DOCTOR, *Doctor Who: The T.V. Movie*

I just don't like nastiness and people getting away with it, that's all.

—EIGHTH DOCTOR, "The Sword of Orion" (audio adventure)

Lots of planets have a North!

—NINTH DOCTOR, "Rose"

I saw the Fall of Troy! World War Five! I was pushing boxes at the Boston Tea Party! Now I'm gonna die in a dungeon . . . in Cardiff!

—NINTH DOCTOR, "The Unquiet Dead"

D'you mind not farting while I'm trying to save the world?

—NINTH DOCTOR, "Aliens of London"

Harriet Jones. MP for Flydale North.

—HARRIET JONES, "Aliens of London"

If someone's collectin' aliens, that makes you Exhibit A.

—ROSE, to the Ninth Doctor, "Dalek"

What're you going to do? Sucker me to death?

—SIMMONS, "Dalek"

The past is another country. 1987's just the Isle of Wight.

—NINTH DOCTOR, "Father's Day"

Are you my mummy?

—The Empty Child, "The Empty Child"

Everywhere we go, two words following us. Bad Wolf.

—NINTH DOCTOR, "Boom Town"

Okay, Defabricator. Does exactly what it says on the tin. Am I naked in front of millions of viewers? Absolutely! Ladies, your viewing figures just went up!

—CAPTAIN JACK HARKNESS and ZU-ZANA, "Bad Wolf"

New teeth. That's weird. So where was I? Oh that's right! Barcelona!

—TENTH DOCTOR, "The Parting of the Ways"

Am I . . . ginger?

—TENTH DOCTOR, "The Christmas Invasion"

But why? Look at these people, these human beings. Consider their potential! From the day they arrive on the planet, blinking, step into the sun, there is more to see than can ever be seen, more to do than—no, hold on. Sorry, that's *The Lion King*. But the point still stands: Leave them alone!

—TENTH DOCTOR, "The Christmas Invasion"

I wanted her to say, 'We are not amused'. Bet you five quid I can make her say it.

—ROSE, on Queen Victoria, "Tooth and Claw"

Have you met the French? Lovely people!

—TENTH DOCTOR, after too many banana daiquiris, "The Girl in the Fireplace"

I like that, 'Allons-y'. I should say allons-y more often. Look sharp Rose Tyler, allons-y! And then it would be really brilliant if I met someone called Alonso, 'cause then I could say 'Allons-y, Alonso, every time.

—TENTH DOCTOR, "Army of Ghosts"

Daleks, be warned. You have declared war upon the Cybermen. —This is not war. This is pest control.

—The CYBER-LEADER and DALEK SEC, "Doomsday"

It was all in the job title: Head of Human Resources. This time, it's Personnel.

—Tenth Doctor and Lance, "The Runaway Bride"

Oooh, fifty-seven academics just punched the air!

—Tenth Doctor, "The Shakespeare Code"

Expelliarmus!

—Martha, "The Shakespeare Code"

This is the way the world ends. Not with a bang, but a whimper.

—Tenth Doctor, on Lazarus, "The Lazarus Experiment"

Which one of them do you want us to kill? Maid, or matron? Your friend, or your lover? Your choice!

—Baines/Son of Mine, "Human Nature"

It is returning, it is returning through the dark. And then Doctor . . . oh, but then . . . he will knock four times.

—Carmen, "Planet of the Dead"

Anyway. Why don't we stop and have a nice little chat while I tell you all my plans and you can work out a way to stop me, I don't think so!

—The Master, "Utopia"

Max Capricorn cruise liners. The fastest. The furthest. The best. And I should know, because my name is Max!

—Max Capricorn, "Voyage of the Damned"

Mr. and Mrs. Spartacus? Oh, no no no no no, we're not married. . . .

—Tenth Doctor to Luciuus Caecilius Iucundus, "The Fires of Pompeii"

He saves planets, rescues civilizations, defeats terrible creatures . . . and runs a lot. Seriously, there is an outrageous amount of running involved.

—Donna, on the Doctor, "The Doctor's Daughter"

Astrid Peth, citizen of Sto. The woman who looked at the stars and dreamed of traveling. Now you can travel forever. You're not falling, Astrid . . . You're flying!

—Tenth Doctor, "Voyage of the Damned"

What's good about sad? Sad is happy for deep people.

—SALLY SPARROW, to Kathy Nightingale, "Blink"

People and planets and stars will become dust. And the dust will become atoms and the atoms will become . . . nothing. And the wavelength will continue, breaking through the rift at the heart of the Medusa Cascade into every dimension, every parallel, every single corner of creation. This is my ultimate victory, Doctor! The destruction of reality itself!

—DAVROS, "Journey's End"

Back of the neck!

—DONNA, "The Sontaran Stratagem" (see *Alan Partridge*)

DOCTOR: You were expecting someone else?

PERI: I— I— I—

DOCTOR: That's three 'I's in one breath—makes you sound rather egotistical, young lady.

—SIXTH DOCTOR, to Peri, "The Caves of Androzani"

JACKIE: I'm in my dressing gown.

DOCTOR: Yes, you are.

JACKIE: There's a strange man in my bedroom.

DOCTOR: Yes, there is.

JACKIE: Anything could happen.

DOCTOR: No.

—NINTH DOCTOR to Jackie, "Rose"

I just want you to know, there are worlds out there, safe in the sky because of her. That there are people living in the light, and singing songs of Donna Noble. A thousand, million light years away. They will never forget her, while she can never remember. But for one moment . . . one shining moment . . . she was the most important woman in the whole wide universe.

—TENTH DOCTOR, "Journey's End"

You humans have got such limited little minds, I don't know why I like you so much.

—FOURTH DOCTOR, "The Masque of Mandragora"

Would you like a jelly baby?

—Fourth Doctor (Too many episodes to mention)

Your mind is beginning to work. It's entirely due to my influence, of course, you must not take any credit.

—Fourth Doctor, "Ark in Space"

Captain Jack: Who looks at a screwdriver and thinks 'Oooh, this could be a little more sonic'?

Doctor: What? You never been bored? Never had a long night? Never had a lot of cabinets to put up?

—Ninth Doctor, "The Doctor Dances"

I am perfectly capable of admitting when I'm wrong! . . . Only this time I wasn't.

—Fourth Doctor, "The Pirate Planet"

There is no indignity in being afraid to die, but there is a terrible shame in being afraid to live.

—Thal leader, "The Daleks"

As we learn about each other, so we learn about ourselves.

—First Doctor, "The Edge of Destruction"

Our lives are important—at least to us.

—First Doctor, "The Reign of Terror"

To the rational mind, nothing is inexplicable, only unexplained.

—Fourth Doctor, "The Robots of Death"

It is the right of every creature across the universe to survive, multiply and perpetuate its species. How else does the predator exist? We are all predators, Doctor. We kill, we devour to live!

—The Nucleus, "The Invisible Enemy"

Have a good life, Rose. That's it. Have a fantastic life.

—Ninth Doctor, "The Parting of the Ways"

He's just a bit more flexible when it comes to dancing.

—Ninth Doctor, "The Doctor Dances"

I'm the Doctor, and you're in the biggest library in the universe. Look me up.

—Tenth Doctor, to Vashta Nerada, "Silence in the Library"

I'm burning up a sun just to say goodbye.

—Tenth Doctor, to Rose, "Doomsday"

They can shoot me dead, but the moral high ground is mine.

—Tenth Doctor, "Army of Ghosts"

I like bananas. Bananas are good!

—Ninth Doctor, "The Doctor Dances"

Geronimo!

—Eleventh Doctor, "The End of Time, Part 2"

There are worlds out there where the sky is burning, and the sea's asleep, and the rivers dream, people made of smoke and cities made of song. Somewhere there's danger, somewhere there's injustice, somewhere else the tea's getting cold. Come on, Ace. We've got work to do.

—Seventh Doctor, "Survival"

The What, When, and Who of *Doctor Who*

DOCTORS, EPISODES, COMPANIONS

FIRST DOCTOR:
**William Hartnell
(1963–1966)**

An Unearthly Child
The Daleks
The Edge of Destruction
Marco Polo
The Keys of Marinus
The Aztecs
The Sensorites
The Reign of Terror
Planet of Giants
The Dalek Invasion of Earth
The Rescue
The Romans
The Web Planet
The Crusade
The Space Museum
The Chase
The Time Meddler
Galaxy Four
Mission to the Unknown
The Myth Makers
The Dalek Masterplan
The Massacre
The Ark
The Celestial Toymaker
The Gunfighters

The Savages
The War Machines
The Smugglers
The Tenth Planet

SECOND DOCTOR:
**Patrick Troughton
(1966–1969)**

The Power of the Daleks
The Highlanders
The Underwater Menace
The Moonbase
The Macra Terror
The Faceless Ones
The Evil of the Daleks
The Tomb of the Cybermen
The Abominable Snowmen
The Ice Warriors
The Enemy of the World
The Web of Fear
Fury from the Deep
The Wheel in Space
The Dominators
The Mind Robber
The Invasion
The Krotons
The Seeds of Death
The Space Pirates
The War Games

THIRD DOCTOR:
Jon Pertwee (1970–1974)

Spearhead from Space
The Silurians
The Ambassadors of Death
Inferno
Terror of the Autons
The Mind of Evil
The Claws of Axos
Colony in Space
The Daemons
The Day of the Daleks
The Curse of Peladon
The Sea Devils
The Mutants
The Time Monster
The Three Doctors
Carnival of Monsters
Frontier in Space
Planet of the Daleks
The Green Death
The Time Warrior
Invasion of the Dinosaurs
Death to the Daleks
Monster of Peladon
Planet of the Spiders

FOURTH DOCTOR:
Tom Baker (1974–1981)

Robot
The Ark in Space
The Sontaran Experiment
Genesis of the Daleks
Revenge of the Cybermen
Terror of the Zygons
Planet of Evil
Pyramids of Mars
The Android Invasion
The Brain of Morbius
The Seeds of Doom
The Masque of Mandragora
The Hand of Fear
The Deadly Assassin

The Face of Evil
The Robots of Death
The Talons of Weng-Chiang
Horror of Fang Rock
The Invisible Enemy
Image of Fendahl
The Sun Makers
Underworld
The Invasion of Time
The Ribos Operation
The Pirate Planet
The Stones of Blood
The Androids of Tara
The Power of Kroll
The Armageddon Factor
Destiny of the Daleks
City of Death
The Creature from the Pit
Nightmare of Eden
Horns of Nimon
Shada
The Leisure Hive
Meglos
Full Circle
State of Decay
Warriors' Gate
The Keeper of Traken
Logopolis

FIFTH DOCTOR:
Peter Davison (1981–1984)

Castrovalva
Four to Doomsday
Kinda
The Visitation
Black Orchid
Earthshock
Time-Flight
Arc of Infinity
Snakedance
Mawdryn Undead
Terminus
Enlightenment
The King's Demons

The Five Doctors
Warriors of the Deep
The Awakening
Frontios
Resurrection of the Daleks
Planet of Fire
The Caves of Androzani

SIXTH DOCTOR:
Colin Baker (1984–1986)

The Twin Dilemma
Attack of the Cybermen
Vengeance on Varos
Mark of the Rani
The Two Doctors
Timelash
Revelation of the Daleks
The Mysterious Planet
Mindwarp
Terror of the Vervoids
The Ultimate Foe

SEVENTH DOCTOR:
Sylvester McCoy (1987–1989, 1996)

Time and the Rani
Paradise Towers
Delta and the Bannermen
Dragonfire
Remembrance of the Daleks
The Happiness Patrol
Silver Nemesis
The Greatest Show in the Galaxy
Battlefield
Ghost Light
The Curse of Fenric
Survival
Doctor Who: The T.V. Movie

EIGHTH DOCTOR:
Paul McGann (1996)

Doctor Who: The T.V. Movie

NINTH DOCTOR:
Christopher Eccleston (2005)

Rose
The End of the World
The Unquiet Dead
Aliens of London
World War Three
Dalek
The Long Game
Father's Day
The Empty Child
The Doctor Dances
Boom Town
Bad Wolf
The Parting of the Ways

TENTH DOCTOR:
David Tennant (2005–2010)

The Christmas Invasion
New Earth
Tooth and Claw
School Reunion
The Girl in the Fireplace
Rise of the Cybermen
The Age of Steel
The Idiot's Lantern
The Impossible Planet
The Satan Pit
Love & Monsters
Fear Her
Army of Ghosts
Doomsday
The Runaway Bride
Smith and Jones
The Shakespeare Code
Gridlock
Daleks in Manhattan
Evolution of the Daleks
The Lazarus Experiment
42
Human Nature
The Family of Blood

Blink
Utopia
The Sound of Drums
Last of the Time Lords
Time Crash
Voyage of the Damned
Partners in Crime
The Fires of Pompeii
Planet of the Ood
The Sontaran Stratagem
The Poison Sky
The Doctor's Daughter
The Unicorn and the Wasp
Silence in the Library
Forest of the Dead
Midnight
Turn Left
The Stolen Earth
Journey's End
The Next Doctor
Planet of the Dead
The Waters of Mars
The End of Time

ELEVENTH DOCTOR:
Matt Smith (2010–?)

The Eleventh Hour
The Beast Below
Victory of the Daleks
The Time of Angels
Flesh and Stone
Vampires in Venice
Amy's Choice
The Hungry Earth
Cold Blood
Vincent and the Doctor
The Lodger
The Pandorica Opens
The Big Bang

THE DOCTOR'S COMPANIONS

FIRST DOCTOR
Susan Foreman (Carole Ann Ford)
Barbara Wright (Jacqueline Hill)
Ian Chesterton (William Russell)
Vicki (Maureen O'Brien)
Steven Taylor (Peter Purves)
Katarina (Adrienne Hill)
Sara Kingdom (Jean Marsh)
Dorothea "Dodo" Caplet (Jackie Lane)
Polly (Anneke Wills)
Ben Jackson (Michael Craze)

SECOND DOCTOR
Polly
Ben Jackson
Jamie McCrimmon (Frazer Hines)
Victoria Waterfield (Deborah Watling)
Brigadier Alistair Gordon Lethbridge-Stewart (Nicholas Courtney)
Zoe Heriot (Wendy Padbury)

THIRD DOCTOR
Dr. Elizabeth "Liz" Shaw (Caroline John)
Josephine "Jo" Grant (Katy Manning)
Sarah Jane Smith (Elisabeth Sladen)

FOURTH DOCTOR
Sarah Jane Smith
Harry Sullivan (Ian Marter)
Leela (Louise Jameson)
K-9 Mark I (voice of John Leeson)
K-9 Mark II (voice of John Leeson)
Romana I (Mary Tamm)
Romana II (Lalla Ward)
Adric (Matthew Waterhouse)

Nyssa (Sara Sutton)
Tegan Jovanka (Janet Fielding)

FIFTH DOCTOR
Adric
Nyssa
Tegan Jovanka
Vislor Turlough (Mark Strickson)
Kamelion (voice of Gerald Flood)
Perpugilliam "Peri" Brown (Nicola
    Bryant)

SIXTH DOCTOR
Perpugilliam "Peri" Brown
Melanie "Mel" Bush (Bonnie
    Langford)

SEVENTH DOCTOR
Melanie "Mel" Bush
Ace (Sophie Aldred)

EIGHTH DOCTOR
Dr. Grace Holloway (Daphne
    Ashbrook)

NINTH DOCTOR
Rose Tyler (Billie Piper)
Adam Mitchell (Bruno Langley)
Captain Jack Harkness (John
    Barrowman)

TENTH DOCTOR
Rose Tyler
Captain Jack Harkness
Mickey Smith (Noel Clarke)
Martha Jones (Freema Agyeman)
Donna Noble (Catherine Tate)
Astrid Peth (Kylie Minogue)
Jackson Lake (David Morrissey)
Rosita Farisi (Velile Tshabalala)
Lady Christina de Souza (Michelle
    Ryan)
Adelaide Brooke (Lindsay Duncan)
Wilfred Mott (Bernard Cribbins)

ELEVENTH DOCTOR
Amy Pond (Karen Gillan)
River Song (Alex Kingston)
Rory Williams (Arthur Darvill)

Court thanks the creators of Bevis and Duncan's *Doctor Who Guide* <www.ee.surrey.ac.uk/Contrib/SciFi/DrWho> whose online episode guide has been his faithful companion for fifteen years.

The High Council
of Gallifrey

LAURA GEUY AKERS has been a fan of the Doctor and his companions since the early 1980s. She especially loved the playful dynamics of the relationship between Fourth Doctor and the second Romana. She owns a vinyl '45' of the Doctor *Who* theme music but seldom gets to hear it. Ms. Akers is a health behavior researcher at Oregon Research Institute, while working to finish her PhD in social and personality psychology at the University of Oregon. Her academic work focuses on the psychology of narratives, worldviews, values, and the imagination. She lives in Eugene, Oregon, with her horticulturist husband, their younger son, an opinionated cat, and a lively golden retriever. Her previous philosophical publication was on empathy and ethics in human-wasp relationships.

ROMAN ALTSHULER's atoms have recently finished a dissertation on moral responsibility at SUNY Stony Brook, a project from which they sought constant diversions. Upon discovering an obscure show titled *Doctor Who* on BBC America, Dr. Altshuler immediately saw the possibilities for procrastination by consuming all four seasons. Having reached some tentative conclusions about the show, he settled on watching the previous twenty-seven seasons as the only reasonable means of confirming them. Apart from being glued to his TARDIS console, Roman spends his time teaching philosophy, looking for free will under rocks, and studying the native fauna of Brooklyn.

NIALL BARR first peeked out from behind the sofa in 1969, at the age of six, to watch "The War Games," Patrick Troughton's last story as the Doctor. From then on he was hooked, and throughout the tenures of the next five Doctors, Niall spent his Sunday afternoons in front of the television, though never far from the safety of the sofa. Inspired by "Time Flight," Niall went on to study Aeronautical Engineering at the University of

Glasgow, but like the Doctor, he likes to cover many areas. On the way to his current post at the Teaching and Learning Centre, he worked in diverse fields including medical instrumentation, arthropod biomechanics, and information technology.

ALEXANDER BERTLAND was forced by his mother to watch "The Pyramids of Mars" while still in middle school. While struggling to fit in at high school, both among the in-crowd and friends who preferred *Star Trek*, his family could only relate to each other through trips to *Doctor Who* conventions in center-city Philadelphia. When it came time to choose a college, Bertland chose the University of Scranton, largely because Scranton's PBS station showed *Doctor Who* most reliably. It was in the pre-Office Scranton where he became interested in the Philosophy of Myth through the work of Giambattista Vico. He has published a number of articles on Vico in *New Vico Studies* and has written the entry on Vico in the Internet Encyclopedia of Philosophy. He has also worked on Business Ethics and Jean-Jacques Rousseau. He's currently the chair of the Philosophy Department of Niagara University, and is jealous of the new generation of people who can download *Doctor Who* from England instantly rather than waiting for years for it to be picked up by public television.

ROBIN BUNCE is Director of Studies for Politics at Homerton College, Cambridge, and a Bye Fellow at St. Edmund's College, also in Cambridge. At the age of five, he met Tom Baker at BBC TV center during the recording of the "Androids of Tara." Following this meeting, which involved an exchange of jelly babies, he went on to gain a twenty-foot long stripy scarf and a PhD, which means he can now legitimately call himself 'Doctor'.

CLIVE CAZEAUX is Reader in the Philosophy of Art at Cardiff School of Art and Design, University of Wales Institute, Cardiff. He is a Pertwee man: a fan of *Doctor Who* ever since the Daleks and the Ogrons materialized in "Day of the Daleks," although he has some recollection of Patrick Troughton being chased by Ice Warriors. He writes on the various ways in which metaphor and imagery inform thought, and is currently working on the philosophy of art-science collaboration. He lives in the hope that Paul McGann might return one day in a "past Doctors" special, and firmly believes that the "Tenth Planet" Cybermen were the best, but that's another story.

KEN CURRY is an associate professor of Biological Sciences at the University of Southern Mississippi. He was trained first as a microbiologist and then as a mycologist and botanist, but practices science on a broad basis, pursuing research in addition to his immediate area of expertise through collaborations in geology, medical research, zoology, biochemistry, and polymer science. Will Durant's "Story of Philosophy" stirred his philosophical interest as a young man. Durant's account of Arthur Schopenhauer gave him a life-long interest in pessimistic philosophy. Ken was drawn into science as a boy reading adventure books about scientists and watching nature and science fiction television shows. Mr. Spock from *Star Trek* was particularly influential, and *Doctor Who* also captured his imagination. Ken identifies most strongly with the Doctor as played by Jon Pertwee. His philosophical interests are complemented by interests in British literature, poetry, and plays written during or before the nineteenth century, and in European history from ancient Greece to the Great War. He enjoys pre-twentieth century concert music and opera, and he is particularly fond of early church music.

PAUL DAWSON stumbled across the threshold, blinded momentarily as his eyes adjusted to the interior lighting. "A thing that looks like a police box, standing in a junkyard," he cried, his senses reeling, "it can go anywhere in time and space?" "Pint of the usual, is it?" said the barman, not looking up from his newspaper. "Who's the nutter?" a drinker asked. "Oh, don't mind him. That's just Paul Dawson—who, by the way, teaches philosophy in London and plays jazz guitar on the side." Time stopped, briefly. "*Doctor Who* fan as well, I s'pose?" Slowly, silently, like a sage, the barman nodded, his weary gaze soaking into the faded pub carpet, its saddest stain.

KEVIN S. DECKER will be teaching normative and applied ethics, American and Continental Philosophy, and philosophy of pop culture at Eastern Washington University. He very soon will have co-edited *Star Wars and Philosophy* (2005, with Jason T. Eberl), *Star Trek and Philosophy* (2008, with Jason T. Eberl), and *Terminator and Philosophy* (2009, with Richard Brown). He will have had work published on philosophical themes in James Bond, *The Colbert Report*, and the films of Stanley Kubrick, and on teaching *Star Trek* as philosophy in *Teaching Philosophy*. He has met/will meet himself in seven of his previous and future incarnations, and as a result has real trouble with tenses.

RUTH DELLER is an associate lecturer and doctoral candidate at Sheffield Hallam University. Her doctoral thesis looks at portrayals of religion and spirituality on British television. Ruth's other fields of expertise include the sociology and philosophy of religion, internet communication and communities, media representation of minorities, and discussing the merits of reality show contestants on Twitter. Because she got into *Doctor Who* in the mid-1980s, her Doctors are Colin Baker and Sylvester McCoy. Some people see this as a reason to pity her, but she quite likes their Technicolor zaniness.

WILLIAM EATON, while making extensive repairs to his own TARDIS, patiently works as the Assistant Professor of Modern Philosophy at Georgia Southern University. He is the author of *Boyle on Fire: The Mechanical Revolution in Scientific Explanation* (2005) and teaches Early Modern Philosophy, Metaphysics, and the History and Philosophy of Science. Although he has saved the Earth from total destruction on several occasions, he is very modest and prefers not to talk about it.

PETER A. FRENCH is the Lincoln Chair in Ethics, Professor of Philosophy, and the Director of the Lincoln Center for Applied Ethics at Arizona State University. He was the Cole Chair in Ethics, Director of the Ethics Center, and Chair of the Department of Philosophy of the University of South Florida. He has a national reputation in ethical and legal theory and in collective and corporate responsibility, as well as in criminal liability. He's the author of nineteen books including *The Virtues of Vengeance*; *Cowboy Metaphysics: Ethics and Death in Westerns*; *Ethics and College Sports*; *Responsibility Matters*. His newest book, *War and Moral Dissonance*, is forthcoming. Dr. French is a senior editor of *Midwest Studies in Philosophy*, and he has published scores of articles in the major philosophical and legal journals. And yes, he's the Time Lord of philosophy.

PHILIP GOFF spent most of his childhood trying to build a time machine. He sadly never succeeded in this, and decided to recuperate losses by becoming a philosopher. After his PhD at the University of Reading, Philip spent four months working as a Visiting Fellow at the Centre for Consciousness at the Australian National University, and then two years lecturing at the University of Birmingham. He's currently engaged in post doctoral research as part of an Arts and Humanities Research Council project on 'Phenomenal Qualities' at the University of Hertfordshire (http://phenomenalqualities.wordpress.com). Philip is mainly interested in the relationship between conscious experience and processes in the brain, arguing that brain science cannot explain conscious thought and feeling. Philip is a panpsychist, which means he thinks that everything, including the book in front of you, has conscious experience. This may sound mad, but if you give Philip an hour or two (and buy him a pint or two of Black Sheep) there is a good chance he can persuade you to become a panpsychist too. Philip's office contains a TARDIS tea caddy and an inflatable Dalek. It also had a 'Police Public Call Box' sticker on the door, but this was removed by the Powers That Be.

BONNIE GREEN is currently completing a PhD in Sociology at the University of Exeter. Prior to this she was a research assistant on the BioethicsBytes project within the GENIE Cetl at the University of Leicester. Within this role she undertook research aimed at drawing out some of the bioethical, social and philosophical issues raised by popular media portrayal of advances in biomedical science and technology. Her background is in the sociology and philosophy of science and technology, and she also possesses an MSc in Social Research Methods and Social Psychology from the London School of Economics and Political Science.

MICHAEL HAND is a philosopher of education at the Institute of Education, University of London. He holds degrees from the Universities of Oxford, Cambridge, and Manchester and is currently a visiting scholar at Stanford. His first behind-the-sofa Dalek encounter occurred in 1974, at the end of the Jon Pertwee era, but it was Tom Baker's Fourth Doctor who really captured his childhood imagination. There ensued a decade of feverish Saturday-night excitement, ardent hero-worship and total immersion in the Whoniverse, until the spell was broken in the late 1980s by the cruel double-whammy of adulthood and Sylvester McCoy. Still a fan of the show but no longer in its thrall, Michael these days spends his free time tinkering with his robotic dog and going on excursions with his three children, Tegan, Nyssa, and Adric.

RICHARD HANLEY is in the Philosophy Department at the University of Delaware. He's written extensively on popular and science fiction, including *Is Data Human? The Metaphysics of Star Trek* (1997) and *South Park and Philosophy: Bigger, Longer and More Penetrating* (2007). He teaches a course on time travel, and it's probably *Doctor Who*'s fault. He writes and records philosophy music as Gourmet Rapport, and that's *not* anybody else's fault.

SIMON HEWITT is a PhD student at Birkbeck College in the University of London. When he isn't busy with LINDA activities, he spends his time working on metaphysics, logic and the philosophy of mathematics. And running. Seriously, there is an outrageous amount of running involved.

SARAH HONEYCHURCH grew up in a small village with no color television. At the age of nine she first saw *Doctor Who* in color and was both horrified and fascinated by the Doctor's involvement with technicolor aliens. How was it, she wondered, that a Time Lord could feel compassion towards such creatures? An interest in questions such as this led to Sarah studying Philosophy at the University of Southampton, graduating with a BA and an MA in Philosophy. She's currently a PhD candidate in the Department of Philosophy at the University of Glasgow, writing a thesis on human rights.

DAVID KYLE JOHNSON is currently an assistant professor of philosophy at King's College in Wilkes-Barre, Pennsylvania. His specializations include philosophy of religion, logic, and metaphysics. He has written extensively on the interaction between philosophy and popular culture, including a book on NBC's *Heroes*, and chapters on *South Park*, *Family Guy*, *The Office*, *Battlestar Galactica*, Quentin Tarantino, Johnny Cash, *Batman*, Stephen Colbert, *The Onion*, and Christmas. He also regularly teaches a philosophy class on Pop Culture (the last one focused on *Star Trek*). Kyle can proudly say that he has watched every episode of *Doctor Who*, including the old black-and-whites (that have not been lost)—although sometimes it wasn't easy. After much consideration, he concluded that he best identifies with the Third Doctor; his love of science and hatred of superstition is needed in this world—although Yana (the Master's human incarnation) and his scatterbrained hopes for a utopia make him a close second.

GREGORY KALYNIUK in part blames classic *Doctor Who* episodes, which obsessed him when he was little, for warping his then impressionable mind enough to later want to take up the higher calling of Philosophy and thinks that the new *Doctor Who* series should go back to that grand old transcendental style so that future generations of young viewers can undergo a similar sort of educational experience. He is, at the present moment, completing his PhD in Cultural Studies at Trent University, but would gladly accept a modest salary from the BBC to work as an Ideas Man for *Doctor Who* in the near future.

COURTLAND LEWIS's earliest memories are of watching *Doctor Who* at his grandfather's house, and of having his brother try to explain regeneration to him after Tom Baker became Peter Davison. Such experiences created a sense of wonder that culminated in a love of philosophy, history, and sci-fi that continues to dominate his life. He is a PhD candidate at the University of Tennessee, where he studies Social and Political philosophy and Ethics. He has contributed essays to *Mr. Monk and Philosophy: The Curious Case of the Defective Detective* (2010) and *Ruminations, Peregrinations, and Regenerations: A Critical Approach to Doctor Who* (2010). Courtland is the president of Rocky Top Doctor Who fan club and a member of KINDA (Knoxville Investigative 'N Detective Agency), with his smashing wife Jenny and friend Dale. And even though he has a deep affinity for the Cybermen, he would like to give special thanks to God, Jenny, his Mom, Paula, friends, family, and all of those involved (past, present, and future) with the *Doctor Who* universe, especially Tom Baker and Peter Davison for infectiously capturing his imagination, and never letting it go!

GREG LITTMANN is a reddish-brown fungus, possibly of extraterrestrial origin, that grows under rocks and inside water pipes. Its main interests are metaphysics, philosophy of logic, philosophy of mind, ethics, and pulsating softly, releasing its spores into the air. For reasons that Earth's scientists have been unable to determine, it has published in the philosophy of logic and has written philosophy and popular culture chapters for *Doctor Who and Philosophy, Dune and Philosophy, Final Fantasy and Philosophy, Terminator and Philosophy,* and *The Onion and Philosophy.* It is employed as an Assistant Professor by Southern Illinois University Edwardsville, where it teaches Metaphysics, Philosophy of Mind, Media Ethics, and Critical Thinking, all in a sibilant whisper. UNIT recommends that if you encounter any Greg Littmann, it should be completely incinerated, but whatever you do, *never look directly at it!*

DEBORAH PLESS recently completed her degree in Social Philosophy at Hamilton College. She is now working towards her Master's degree at New York Film Academy. Every day, she gets better and better at not blinking.

ADAM RIGGIO is a PhD candidate at McMaster University in Canada, writing his dissertation on environmental philosophy and contemporary European thought. He has been watching *Doctor Who* since 1987 at the age of four, and the Doctor himself has been his role model since that time as well. He owns two Tom Baker inspired winter scarves, a Christopher Eccleston leather jacket, has anticipated Matt Smith's hairstyle for the past five years, and on rainy days carries his umbrella like Sylvester McCoy. He actually does need glasses to see, but they also make him look almost as clever as David Tennant and Peter Davison. And for the difficult moral growth this essay describes, the Doctor is a model as well.

MICHELLE SAINT has recently completed her PhD in philosophy at Arizona State University, and currently acting as guest editor for the upcoming volume of *The Midwest Studies in Philosophy* entitled "Film and the Emotions." Her area of specialization is the philosophy of fiction, which means she spends a lot of time thinking about things that don't exist in many fascinating ways. Her dissertation is on the nature of our emotional involvement with fictional characters, specifically how it is possible for us to feel pity, fear, worry, or uplifted from untrue stories about unreal people. Her favorite Doctor is David Tennant, her favorite episode is either "Blink" or "Turn Left," and she is a great fan of The Face of Boe.

DONNA MARIE SMITH works in the next best thing to the TARDIS—a library! Her library card is like the key that opens up the Doctor's "magical time machine," allowing her to travel through space and time via the pages of a book or the bits and bytes of cyberspace. Throughout her time on Earth, she has collected more college degrees than companions: a Bachelor's of Arts degree in English and one in Journalism, as well as a Master's of Library and Information Science from the University of Maryland. She has also dabbled in philosophy, gaining membership in The National

Philosophy Honor Society (*Phi Sigma Tau*) as an undergraduate and has taken a fascinating graduate-level course in the history and philosophy of science and technology. In her spare time, she writes book reviews for *Library Journal*, spends time with her friends and family, and travels to "real" places like Alaska and Historic Route 66. She also has been seen waiting patiently on the beach of Därlig Ulv Stranden, Norway—otherwise known as Bad Wolf Bay—for the Doctor to bring her a David Tennant clone, so she, like Rose, can live happily ever after.

PAULA SMITHKA is an associate professor of philosophy at the University of Southern Mississippi. Her research interests are in philosophy of science, in particular, philosophy of biology, and social and political philosophy. She has her PhD and MA from Tulane University and a BA in philosophy and a BS in biology from the University of North Carolina at Charlotte. Paula's co-edited *Community, Diversity, and Difference* (2002) with Alison Bailey. She's always loved science fiction. Growing up without cable television meant that she was *Doctor Who* deprived during her formative years; however, she did have *Star Trek*. Because she's a relative neophyte with respect to *Doctor Who*, namely via the new series with Christopher Eccleston and David Tennant, she's had much catching up to do. And, since Court owns the majority of the Doctor *Who* series, he aided and abetted the developing *Who*-passion, spurring on her research of the previous Doctors. Now, she *really* envies British children who had a Dalek Halloween costume! Her favorite Doctor is David Tennant; and like all *Doctor Who* fans, she mourns the loss her favorite Doctor, but is impressed by the Eleventh Doctor, Matt Smith.

PATRICK STOKES is currently a Marie Curie Fellow in Philosophy at the University of Hertfordshire, England, and has previously held teaching and research positions in Australia, the US, and Denmark. He's the author of *Kierkegaard's Mirrors* (2010) as well as several journal articles and book chapters, and is interested in philosophical questions about selfhood, moral psychology, mortality and subjectivity. His earliest memory of *Doctor Who* is hiding behind the couch in fear every time the Daleks came on, but eventually he got over that. Well, sort of.

J.J. SYLVIA, IV recently completed his MA in philosophy at the University of Southern Mississippi, where he researched and wrote about the epistemological and ethical issues involved with the medium of television. Many of his students have told him that the constant questioning involved in studying philosophy depresses them, but he simply reassures them that, as Sally Sparrow says, "Sad is happy for deep people."

MARK WARDECKER is a librarian at Dickinson College and an occasional writer of mystery and horror fiction and nonfiction. He has been a fan of

Doctor Who since childhood, when PBS first began airing episodes in the US in the 1970s, and wishes for your sake that he could write half as well as his favorite script editor, Robert Holmes.

ED WEBB teaches Political Science, International Studies, and Middle East Studies at Dickinson College. His particular interests include authoritarianism, the politics of education, and applications of digital technology to teaching and learning. He's also "committed" poetry. The Sea Devils were the first *Doctor Who* monsters to terrify him and they still have a special place in his heart. Like the Fourth Doctor, he owns a very, very long scarf and is fond of jelly babies.

CHRIS WILLMOTT is a Senior Lecturer in the Department of Biochemistry at the University of Leicester, and a National Teaching Fellow. Originally a molecular biologist by training. Chris studied the mode of action of, and bacterial resistance to, the antibiotic "Cipro" for his doctoral thesis. During the past ten years he has been increasingly involved in the teaching of bioethics to undergraduate students. His work in this field has included the establishment of www.bioethicsbytes.wordpress.com, a web-based repository of materials for teaching about the science and ethics of developments in biomedicine, with particular emphasis on the use of multimedia resources and case studies.

PETER WORLEY's earliest memories include running around the playground with a long scarf and a blazer pretending to be a strange hybrid of a Pertwee Doctor and a Baker Doctor and crying for days at the passing of the Baker era. He also considers the *Whoian* maverick virtues of independence and thoughtfulness the starting point for his career as a consultant philosopher working in primary schools in South East London. Peter started teaching philosophy to primary school children in 2001 and after developing his own program of philosophy in schools founded The Philosophy Shop CIC in 2007 in order to bring philosophy more widely into the community. The Philosophy Shop now trains philosophers in how to deliver philosophy in schools, and how to get children philosophizing, as well as running adult philosophy groups and training teachers in developing thinking skills in children. For more information visit <www.thephilosophyshop.co.uk>. Peter has a BA from University College London and an MA from Birkbeck College, and is a trained philosophical counselor. He has a book coming out next year called *The If Machine*, containing philosophical thought experiments for young children which will, hopefully, encourage some more young *Whos* to follow in the Time Lord's footsteps.

The Matrix of Time Lord
Bibliographic Sources

Adams, Douglas. 1995. *The Hitchhiker's Guide to the Galaxy*. New York: Ballantine.

Aldridge, Mark, and Andy Murray. 2008. *T Is for Television: The Small Screen Adventures of Russell T Davies*. Richmond: Reynolds and Hearn.

Alsford, Mike. 2000. *What If? Religious Themes in Science Fiction*. London: Darton, Longman, and Todd.

Arendt, Hannah. 2000 [1963]. Eichmann in Jerusalem. In Arendt 2000.

———. 2000. *The Portable Hannah Arendt*. New York: Penguin.

———. 2005. *The Promise of Politics*. New York: Schocken.

Aristotle. 1998. Nichomachean Ethics. <www.netlibrary.com>.

———. 1999. *Nicomachean Ethics*. Indianapolis: Hackett.

Ashby, Warren. 1997. *A Comprehensive History of Western Ethics*. Amherst: Prometheus.

Arp, Robert, and Kevin S. Decker. 2006. 'That Fatal Kiss': Bond, Ethics, and the Objectification of Women. In *James Bond and Philosophy: Question Are Forever*, edited by James South and Jacob Held (Chicago: Open Court).

Ashby, Warren. 1997. *A Comprehensive History of Western Ethics*. Amherst: Prometheus.

Balaguer, Mark. 2001. *Platonism and Anti-Platonism in Mathematics*. Oxford: Oxford University Press.

Baldwin, James. 1985. *Giovanni's Room*. New York: Laurel.

BBC. 2010. *Doctor Who Companion Compendium: Top Trivia for Time Travellers*. London: BBC.

———. 2010. *Doctor Who: The Secrets of the Tardis*. London: BBC.

BBC News Online. 2000. Fawlty Towers Tops TV Hits. BBC News Online (5th September).

BBC Wales. 2008. End of an Era. Doctor Who Confidential: Cutdown. Narrated by Anthony Head (5th July).

Beauchamp, Tom L., and James F. Childress. 2001. *Principles of Biomedical Ethics*. Fifth edition. New York: Oxford University Press.

Beauvoir, Simone de. 1976. *The Ethics of Ambiguity*. New York: Citadel.

Bell, Clive. 1992 [1914]. The Aesthetic Hypothesis. In *Art in Theory 1900–1990*, edited by Charles Harrison and Paul Wood (Oxford: Blackwell).

Bentham, Jeremy. 1986. *Doctor Who: The Early Years*. London: Allen.

Berkeley, George. 1954 [1713]. *Three Dialogues Between Hylas and Philonous*. New York: Bobs-Merrill.

———. 1957 [1710]. *A Treatise Concerning The Principles of Human Knowledge*. New York: Bobs-Merrill.

Bignell, J., and A. O'Day. 2004. *Terry Nation*. Manchester: Manchester University Press.

Boas, George. 2006. Love. Addendum. *Encyclopedia of Philosophy*, Volume 5. Edited by Donald M. Borchert. Detroit: Thomson/Gale.

Bocock, Robert, and Kenneth Thompson. 1985. *Religion and Ideology: A Reader*. Manchester: Manchester University Press/The Open University.

Borges, Jorge Luis. 1963. *Ficciones*. New York: Grove Press.

Bradbury, Ray. 1952. A Sound of Thunder. *Collier's Weekly*. Springfield: Crowell-Collier.

Britton, Piers D.G. 1999. Dress and the Fabric of the Television Series: The Costume Designer as Author in 'Dr. Who'. *Journal of Design History* 12:4.

Bronowski, Jacob, Adrian Malone, and Dick Gilling (directors). 2007. *The Ascent of Man*. BBC Television Service. Time-Life Films and Ambrose Video.

Brontë, Emily. 1934 [1839]. I Am the Only Being. In *Victorian and Later English Poets*, edited by J. Stephens, E.L. Beck, and R.H. Snow (New York: American Book Company).

Brown, Scott. 2009. Scott Brown on Why America Is Finally Ready for Doctor Who. *Wired* 17:11 (November).

Buber, Martin. 1958. *I and Thou*. Second edition. New York: Scribner's.

Burdge, Anthony S., Jessica Burke, and Kristine Larsen, eds. 2010. *The Mythological Dimensions of Doctor Who*. Crawfordville: Kitsune.

Burgess, Anthony. 1989. The Muse. In *The World Treasury of Science Fiction*, edited by David G. Hartwell (Boston: Little, Brown).

Butler, David. 2008. *Time and Relative Dissertations in Space: Critical Perspectives on Doctor Who*. Manchester: Manchester University Press.

Butler, Lawrence J. 2002. *Britain and Empire: Adjusting to a Post-Imperial World*. London: Tauris.

Campbell, Mark. 2010. *Doctor Who: The Episode Guide*. Fourth revised edition. Pocket Essentials.

Carroll, Noël. 1990. *The Philosophy of Horror or Paradoxes of the Heart*. New York: Routledge.

Carter, Rita. 1999. *Mapping the Mind*. Los Angeles: University of California Press.

Cassirer, Ernst. 1946. *The Myth of the State*. New Haven: Yale University Press.

Chapman, James. 2006. *Inside the TARDIS: The Worlds of Doctor Who*. London: Tauris.

Churchland, Paul. 1998. The Ontological Status of Observables: In Praise of the Superempirical Virtues. In *Science, Reason, and Reality: Issues in the Philosophy of Science*, edited by Daniel Rothbart (Forth Worth: Harcourt Brace).

Colyvann, Mark. 2001. *The Indispensability of Mathematics*. Oxford: Oxford University Press.

Cook, Benjamin. 2008. Russell T Davies on Doctor Who's Companions. <www.radiotimes.com/content/show-features/doctor-who/russell-t-davies-on-companions>.

Culf, Andrew. 1996. Viewers Spurn TV's Golden-Age in Poll of Small Screen Classics as the BBC Fetes Its 60th Birthday. *The Guardian* (11th November).

Dainton, Barry. 2001. *Time and Space*. Chesham: McGill University Press.

Darwin, Charles. 1859. *On the Origin of Species by Means of Natural Selection*. London: John Murray.

Darwin, John. 1988. *Britain and Decolonisation: The Retreat from Empire in the Post-War World*. New York: St. Martin's Press.

Davies, Russell T, and Benjamin Cook. 2008. *The Writer's Tale*. London: BBC Books.

Deacy, Christopher. 2001. *Screen Christologies: Redemption and the Medium of Film*. Cardiff: University of Wales Press.

———. 2005. *Faith in Film: Religious Themes in Contemporary Cinema*. Aldershot: Ashgate.

Deci, E.L., and R.M. Ryan. 2000. The 'What' and 'Why' of Goal Pursuits: Human Needs and the Self-Determination of Behavior. *Psychological Inquiry* 11:4.

DeGroot, G.J. 2005. *The Bomb: A Life*. London: Cape.

Deleuze, Gilles. 1994. *Difference and Repetition*. New York: Columbia University Press.

———. 1993. *The Fold: Leibniz and the Baroque*. Minneapolis: University of Minnesota Press.

———. 1990. *The Logic of Sense*. New York: Columbia University Press.

Dennett, Daniel. 1992. The Self as a Center of Narrative Gravity. In *Self and Consciousness: Multiple Perspectives*, edited by F.S. Kessel, P.M. Cole, and D.L. Johnson (Hillsdale: Erlbaum).

Descartes, René. 1996 [1641]. *Meditations on First Philosophy*. Cambridge: Cambridge University Press.

Doctor Who Wiki. Accessed 2008. Rose Tyler. <http://tardis.wikia.com/wiki/Rose_Tyler>.

Douglas, Mary. 1966. *Purity and Danger: An Analysis of Concepts of Pollution and Taboo*. New York: Praeger.

Dupré, John A. 1994. Species: Theoretical Contexts. In *Keywords in Evolutionary Biology* (Cambridge: Harvard University Press).

————. 2003. On Human Nature, Human Affairs. *Journal of the Slovakian Academy of Sciences* 13.

Du Sautoy, Marcus. 2003. *The Music of the Primes: Searching to Solve the Greatest Mystery in Mathematics*. New York: HarperCollins.

Eco, Umberto. 2004. *On Beauty*. London: Secker and Warburg.

Emerson, Ralph Waldo. 2000. The American Scholar. In *Pragmatism and Classical American Philosophy*. Second edition (New York: Oxford University Press).

Feuerbach, Ludwig. 1989 [1841]. *The Essence of Christianity*. Amherst: Prometheus.

Field, Hartry. 1980. *Science Without Numbers*. Princeton: Princeton University Press.

Fiske, John. 1984. Popularity and Ideology: A Structuralist Reading of 'Dr. Who'. In *Interpreting Television: Current Research Perspectives* (Los Angeles: Sage).

Foucault, Michel. 1977. *Discipline and Punish: The Birth of the Prison*. New York: Pantheon.

Fraassen, Bas van. 1976. To Save the Phenomena. *Journal of Philosophy* 73:18 (October). Reprinted in Rothbart 1998.

————. 1998. Arguments Concerning Scientific Realism. In Rothbart 1998.

Frankfurt, Harry. 1988. *The Importance of What We Care About*. New York: Cambridge University Press.

Fraser, Peter. 1998. *Images of the Passion: The Sacramental Mode in Film*. Westport: Praeger.

French, Peter A. forthcoming. *War and Moral Dissonance*. New York: Cambridge University Press.

French, Peter A., and Mitchell Haney. 2005. Changes in Latitudes, Changes in Attitudes. In *War and Border Crossings: Ethics When Cultures Clash*, edited by Peter A. French and Jason A. Short (Lanham: Rowman and Littlefield).

Geivett, R. Douglas, and James S. Spiegel. 2007. *Faith, Film and Philosophy: Big Ideas on the Big Screen*. Downers Grove: IVP Academic.

Gillatt, Gary. 1998. *Doctor Who from A to Z*. London: BBC Worldwide.

Gilligan, Carol. 1993. *In a Different Voice: Psychological Theory and Women's Development*, sixth edition. Cambridge: Harvard University Press.

Greene, Colin J.D. 2004. *Christology in Cultural Perspective: Marking out the Horizons*. Grand Rapids: Eerdmans.

Haidt, Jonathan. 2003. Elevation and the Positive Psychology of Morality. In *Flourishing: Positive Psychology and the Life Well-Lived*, edited by C.L.M. Keyes and J. Haidt (Washington, DC: American Psychological Association). And at <http://people.virginia.edu/~jdh6n/publications.html>.

Haining, Peter. 1984. *Doctor Who, the Key to Time: A Year-by-Year Record*. London: Allen.

Hansen, Chris, ed. 2010. *Ruminations, Peregrinations, and Regenerations: A Critical Approach to Doctor Who*. Cambridge Scholars.

Hansen, Randall. 2000. *Citizenship and Immigration in Post-War Britain: The Institutional Origins of A Multicultural Nation*. Oxford: Oxford University Press.

Harris, Thomas. 1981. *Red Dragon*. New York: Dell.

Haslam, Nick O. 1998. Natural Kinds, Human Kinds, and Essentialism. *Social Research* 65.

Hegel, Georg W.F. 1975 [1835, 1842]. *Aesthetics: Lectures in Fine Art*. Oxford: Clarendon.

———. 1977 [1807]. *Phenomenology of Spirit*. Oxford: Oxford University Press.

———. 1953 [1837]. *Reason and History*. New York: Liberal Arts Press.

Heidegger, Martin. 1996. *Being and Time*. Albany: SUNY Press.

Hepburn, R.W. 1984. *'Wonder' and Other Essays: Eight Studies in Aesthetics and Neighboring Fields*. Edinburgh: University of Edinburgh Press.

Hills, Matt. 2010. *Triumph of a Time Lord: Regenerating Doctor Who in the Twenty-First Century*. London: Tauris.

Hoagland, Sarah Lucia. 1990. Some Concerns about Nel Noddings' *Caring*. *Hypatia* 5:1.

Hobbes, Thomas. 2009 [1651]. *Leviathan*. Oxford: Oxford University Press.

Horkheimer, Max, and Theodor W. Adorno. 1972 [1944]. *Dialectic of Enlightenment*. New York: Continuum.

Horwich, Paul. 1995. Closed Causal Chains. In Savitt 1995.

Houston, Barbara. 1990. Caring and Exploitation. *Hypatia* 5:1.

Howe, David J., and Stephen James Walker. 2003. *The Television Companion: The Unofficial and Unauthorized Guide to Doctor Who*. Prestatyn: Telos.

Howe, David J., M. Stammers, and Stephen James Walker. 1993. *Doctor Who: The Sixties*. London: Random House UK.

Hume, David. Of the Standard of Taste. 2008. *David Hume: Selected Essays*. Oxford: Oxford University Press.

———. 1998 [1779]. *Dialogues Concerning Natural Religion*. Indianapolis: Hackett.

———. *Enquiry Concerning Human Understanding*. 1974 [1748]. In *The Empiricists* (Garden City: Anchor Books).

———. 2009. *Principal Writings on Religion including Dialogues Concerning Natural Religion and The Natural History of Religion*. Oxford: Oxford World Classics.

————. 2008. *The History of England*. Charleston: Bibliolife.

Hursthouse, Rosalind. 2002. *On Virtue Ethics*. New York: Oxford University Press.

Huxley, Aldous. 2001 [1932]. *Brave New World*. London: Harper Collins.

Inwagen, Peter van. 1978. The Possibility of Resurrection. *International Journal for Philosophy of Religion* 9:2.

Ismael, Jennan. 2003. Closed Causal Loops and the Bilking Argument. *Synthese*, 136:3.

James, William. 1950. *The Principles of Psychology: Volume 1*. New York: Dover.

Janaway, Christopher. 1997. *German Philosophers*. Edited by Keith Thomas. Oxford: Oxford University Press.

Johansson, Jens. 2007. What Is Animalism? *Ratio* 20:2 (June).

Kant, Immanuel. 1929 [1781]. *Critique of Pure Reason*. London: Macmillan.

————. 1964. *Groundwork of the Metaphysic of Morals*. New York: Harper and Row.

————. 1983. *Ethical Philosophy: The Complete Texts of Grounding for the Metaphysics of Morals and Metaphysical Principles of Virtue (Part II of the Metaphysics of Morals)*. Indianapolis: Hackett.

————. 1997. *Critique of Practical Reason*. Cambridge: Cambridge University Press.

————. 2007. *Critique of Judgement*. Oxford: Oxford University Press.

Kitson, Peter J. 1998. Beyond the Enlightenment: The Philosophical, Scientific and Religious Inheritance. In *A Companion to Romanticism*, edited by Duncan Wu (Malden: Blackwell).

Kripke, Saul. 1981. *Naming and Necessity*. Malden: Blackwell.

Leibniz, Gottfried Wilhelm. 1951. *Leibniz: Selections*. New York: Scribner's.

————. 1993. *New Essays on Human Understanding*. Cambridge: Cambridge University Press.

————. 1976. *Philosophical Papers and Letters*. Dordrecht: Reidel.

————. 1973. *Philosophical Writings*. London: Everyman.

————. 1985. *The Leibniz-Arnauld Correspondence*. New York: Garland.

————. 1997. *Theodicy*. La Salle: Open Court.

LePoidevin, Robin. 2003. *Travels in Four Dimensions: The Enigmas of Space and Time*. Oxford: Oxford University Press.

Lewis, David. 1976. Survival and Identity. In *The Identities of Persons*, edited by Amelie Oksenberg Rorty (Berkeley: University of California Press).

————. 1991. Survival and Identity. In *Self and Identity*, edited by Daniel Kolak and Raymond Martin (New York: Macmillan).

————. 1986. *On the Plurality of Worlds*. Malden: Blackwell.

————. 1986. The Paradoxes of Time Travel. *Philosophical Papers*. Volume 2. Oxford: Oxford University Press.

Locke, John. 1959 [1690]. *An Essay Concerning Human Understanding*. New York: Dover.

———. 1975 [1690]. *An Essay Concerning Human Understanding*. Edited by Peter H. Nidditch. Oxford: Clarendon.

Lofficier, Jean-Marc, and Randy Lofficier. 2003. *The Nth Doctor: The Inside Story of the Doctor Who Films that Almost Were*. IUniverse.

Lyden, John. 2003. *Film as Religion: Myths, Morals, and Rituals*. New York: New York University Press.

MacIntyre, Alasdair. 1981. *After Virtue*. Notre Dame: University of Notre Dame Press.

Magee, Bryan. 1983. *The Philosophy of Schopenhauer*. Oxford: Oxford University Press.

Manning, Rita C. 1992. *Speaking from the Heart*. Lanham: Rowman and Littlefield.

Martin, Joel W., and Conrad Eugene Ostwalt. 1995. *Screening the Sacred: Religion, Myth, and Ideology in Popular American Film*. Boulder: Westview Press.

Martin, Raymond, and John Barresi. 2003. Introduction. In *Personal Identity*, edited by Raymond Martin and John Baressi (Malden: Blackwell).

Mayden, Richard L. 1997. A Hierarchy of Species Concepts: The Denouement in the Saga of the Species Problem. In *Species: The Units of Biodiversity*, edited by M.F. Claridge, H.A. Dawah, and M.R. Wilson (London: Chapman and Hall).

McCall, Storrs. 1995. Time Flow, Non-Locality, and Measurement in Quantum Mechanics. In Savitt 1995.

McMahon, R.J. 2003. *The Cold War: A Very Short Introduction*. Oxford: Oxford University Press.

Midgley, Mary. 1981. *Heart and Mind: The Varieties of Moral Experience*. New York: St. Martin's Press.

Miles, Lawrence, and Tat Wood. 2004. *About Time IV: The Unauthorized Guide to Doctor Who 1975 to 1979, Seasons 12 to 17*. Des Moines: Mad Norwegian Press.

———. 2005. *About Time V: The Unauthorized Guide to Doctor Who 1980 to 1984, Seasons 18 to 21*. Des Moines: Mad Norwegian Press.

———. 2006. *About Time II: The Unauthorized Guide to Doctor Who 1966 to 1969, Seasons 4 to 6*. Des Moines: Mad Norwegian Press.

———. 2009. *About Time III: The Unauthorized Guide to Doctor Who 1970 to 1974, Seasons 7 to 11*. Expanded second edition. Des Moines: Mad Norwegian Press.

Mill, John Stuart. 2001. *Utilitarianism*. Indianapolis: Hackett.

———. 2002. *The Basic Writings of John Stuart Mill: On Liberty, The Subjection of Women and Utilitarianism*. New York: Modern Library.

———. 2008 [1859]. *On Liberty*. Radford: Wilder.

Morrison, Grant. 2008. *Doctor Who*, Issue 2. San Diego: IDW.

Muir, J.K. 1999. *A Critical History of* Doctor Who *on Television*. Jefferson: McFarland.

Nation, Terry. 1989. *Doctor Who, The Scripts: The Daleks*. London: Titan.

Nehamas, A. 2007. *Only a Promise of Happiness: The Place of Beauty in a World of Art*. Princeton: Princeton University Press.

Newman, Kim. 2005. *Doctor Who*. London: British Film Institute.

———. 2008. *Doctor Who: A Critical Reading of the Series*. New York: Palgrave Macmillan.

Nietzsche, Friedrich. 1961. *Thus Spoke Zarathustra*. London: Penguin.

Noddings, Nel. 1984. *Caring: A Feminine Approach to Ethics and Moral Education*. Berkeley: University of California Press, 1984.

Nozick, Robert. 1983. *Philosophical Explanations*. Cambridge: Harvard University Press.

Nussbaum, Martha C. 2001. *Upheavals of Thought: The Intelligence of Emotions*. Cambridge: Cambridge University Press.

Paley, William. 1860 [1802] *Natural Theology*. Boston: Gould and Lincoln.

Parfit, Derek. 1984. *Reasons and Persons*. Oxford: Clarendon.

Parkin, Lance. 2007. *Ahistory: An Unauthorized History of the Doctor Who Universe*. Second edition. Des Moines: Mad Norwegian Press.

Parsons, Paul. 2010. *The Science of Doctor Who*. Johns Hopkins University Press.

Perry, John, ed. 1975. *Personal Identity*. Berkeley: University of California Press.

Plato. 2005. *The Collected Dialogues of Plato, Including the Letters*. Edited by Edith Hamilton and Huntington Cairns. Princeton: Princeton University Press.

Pratchett, Terry. 1998. *Hogfather*. New York: Harper Prism.

———. 1991. *Reaper Man*. London: Gollancz.

———. 2001. *Thief of Time: A Novel of Discworld*. New York: Harper Collins.

Radio Times. 2008. Russell T Davies and Billie Piper on Rose Tyler in Doctor Who. <www.radiotimes.com/content/show-features/doctor-who/companion-rose-tyler/>.

Ramachandran, V.S. 1999. *Phantoms in the Brain*. New York: Harper Perennial.

Rayner, Jacqueline, Andrew Darling, Kerrie Dougherty, and David John. 2009. *Doctor Who: The Visual Dictionary*. DK Adult.

Rea, M.C. 2003. Four Dimensionalism. *The Oxford Handbook of Metaphysics*. Oxford: Oxford University Press.

Reid, Thomas. 1994 [1790]. *Essays on the Intellectual Powers of Man* and *Essays on the Active Powers of the Human Mind* in *The Works of Thomas Reid, Volume 1*. Bristol: Thoemmes.

Richards, Justin. 2003. *Doctor Who: The Legend*. Random House UK.

———. 2006. *Doctor Who: Aliens and Enemies*. Random House UK

———. 2009. *Doctor Who: The Ultimate Monster Guide*. Random House UK.

Ricoeur, Paul. 1995. *Oneself as Another*. Translated by Kathleen Blamey. Chicago: University of Chicago Press.

Robb, Brian J. 2010. *Timeless Adventures: How Doctor Who Conquered TV*. Harpenden: Oldcastle.

Roberts, Gareth. 2003. The Brain of Socrates. In *Short Trips: The Muses* (Maidenhead: Big Finish).

Robinson, Walter. 2008. Death and Rebirth of a Vulcan Mind. In *Star Trek and Philosophy: The Wrath of Kant* (Chicago: Open Court).

Rogoff, G. 1963. The Juggernaut of Production. *The Tulane Drama Review* 8:1.

Rorty, Richard. 1998. *Truth and Progress: Philosophical Papers*, Volume 3. Cambridge: Cambridge University Press.

Rosenkranz, Karl. 2007 [1852]. *Ästhetik des Hässlichen (Aesthetics of Ugliness)*. Ditzingen: Reclam.

Rothbart, Daniel, ed. 1998. *Science, Reason, and Reality: Issues in the Philosophy of Science*. Forth Worth: Harcourt Brace.

Rozin, Paul, Jonathan Haidt, and Clark R. McCauley. 1999. Disgust: The Body and Soul Emotion. In *Handbook of Cognition and Emotion*, edited by Tim Dalgleish and Mick J. Power (Chichester: Wiley).

———. 2000. Disgust. In *Handbook of Emotions*, edited by Michael Lewis and Jeannette M. Haviland-Jones. Second edition (New York: Guilford).

Rubin, Bernard. 1971. International Film and Television Propaganda: Campaigns of Assistance. *Annals of the American Academy of Political and Social Science* 398 (November).

Russell, Gary. 2006. *Doctor Who: The Inside Story*. London: Random House UK.

———. 2007. *Doctor Who, The Encyclopedia: A Definitive Guide to Time and Space*. London: Random House UK.

Russell, I.W. 1962. Among the New Words. *American Speech* 37:2.

Ryle, Gilbert. 1954. *Dilemmas*. Cambridge: Cambridge University Press.

Sartre, Jean-Paul. 1947. *Existentialism Is a Humanism*. New York: Philosophical Library.

———. 1993. *Being and Nothingness*. New York: Washington Square Press.

———. 2000. *Existentialism and Human Emotions*. New York: Citadel.

Savitt, Steven F., ed. 1995. *Time's Arrows Today: Recent Physical and Philosophical Work on the Direction of Time*. Cambridge: Cambridge University Press.

Schechtman, Marya. 1996. *The Constitution of Selves*. Ithaca: Cornell University Press, 1996.

Schopenhauer, Arthur. 1958 [1818]. *The World as Will and Representation*. Indian Hills: Falcon's Wing Press.

Scott, James C. 1998. *Seeing Like a State: How Certain Schemes to Improve the Human Condition Have Failed*. New Haven: Yale University Press.

Seligman, B.B. 1965. On Work, Alienation, and Leisure. *American Journal of Economics and Sociology* 24:4.

Shafer, Carolyn M., and Marilyn Frye. 1977. Rape and Respect. In *Feminism and Philosophy*, edited by M. Vetterling-Braggin, F. Elliston, and J. English (Savage: Roman and Littlefield).

Shelley, Percy Bysshe. 1977. *Shelley: Selected Poems*. London: Dent.

Sheppard, Anne. 1987. *Aesthetics: An Introduction to the Philosophy of Art*. Oxford: Oxford University Press.

Sherwin, Adam. 2007. Christians Protest as Doctor Who Is Portrayed as 'Messiah'. *The Times* (21st December).

Singer, Peter. 1975. *Animal Liberation*. New York: Harper Collins.

Skinner, Q. 2003. *Visions of Politics, Volume 1: Regarding Method*. Cambridge: Cambridge University Press.

Slote, Michael. 2007. *The Ethics of Care and Empathy*. London: Routledge.

Smith, P.D. 2007. *Doomsday Men: The Real Dr. Strangelove and the Dream of the Superweapon*. London: Macmillan.

Stanford Encyclopedia of Philosophy. Time. <http://plato.stanford.edu/entries/time>.

Strawson, Galen. 2003. The Self. In *Personal Identity*, edited by Raymond Martin and John Barresi (Malden: Blackwell).

Thomas, Lynne M., and Tara O'Shea. 2010. *Chicks Dig Time Lords: A Celebration of Doctor Who by the Women Who Love It*. Des Moines: Mad Norwegian Press.

Thompson, Mel. 2006. *Teach Yourself Ethics*. Blacklick: McGraw-Hill.

Tribe, Steve. 2009. *Doctor Who: Companions and Allies*. Random House UK.

——. 2010. *Doctor Who: The TARDIS Handbook*. Random House UK.

Tucker, Robert C. 1956. The Cunning of Reason in Hegel and Marx. *The Review of Politics*, 18:3 (July).

Tulloch, John, and Manuel Alvarado. 1984. *Doctor Who: The Unfolding Text*. New York: St. Martin's.

Vico, Giambattista. 1984. *The New Science of Giambattista Vico*. Third edition. Ithaca: Cornell University Press.

Wells, H.G. 1946. *The Time Machine and Other Stories*. New York. Penguin.

——. 2005. *The Island of Doctor Moreau*. London: Penguin.

——. 2005. *The War of the Worlds*. New York. Penguin.

Williams, Bernard. 1970. The Self and the Future. *Philosophical Review* 79. Reprinted in Williams 1973.

——. 1973. *Problems of the Self*. Cambridge: Cambridge University Press.

——. 1976. Persons, Character, and Morality. In *The Identities of Persons*, edited by Amelie O. Rorty (Berkeley: University of California Press).

Wiltshire, A. 2006. Reader's Letter. *Doctor Who Magazine* 371 (19th July).

Wolfe, Tom. 1996. Sorry But Your Soul Just Died. *Forbes* (2nd December).

Wood, Tat. 2007. *About Time VI: The Unauthorized Guide to Doctor Who 1985 to 1989, Seasons 22 to 26, the TV Movie*. Des Moines: Mad Norwegian Press.

Wood, Tat, and Lawrence Miles. 2006. *About Time I: The Unauthorized Guide to Doctor Who 1963 to 1966, Seasons 1 to 3*. Des Moines: Mad Norwegian Press.

Wright, Melanie Jane. 2006. *Religion and Film: An Introduction*. London: Tauris.

Yanal, Robert J. 1999. *Paradoxes of Emotion and Fiction*. University Park: Pennsylvania State University Press.

Zamyatin, E.I. 1972. *We*. Harmondsworth: Penguin.

Logically Organized Index, for the Cyberman and Dalek in All of Us